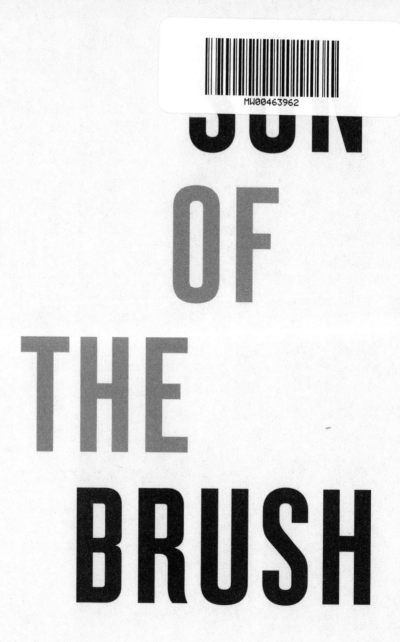

SON
OF
THE
BRUSH

SON OF THE BRUSH

A Memoir

TIM OLSEN

ALLEN&UNWIN

SYDNEY · MELBOURNE · AUCKLAND · LONDON

Allen & Unwin
83 Alexander Street
Crows Nest NSW 2065
Australia
Phone: (61 2) 8425 0100
Email: info@allenandunwin.com
Web: www.allenandunwin.com

A catalogue record for this book is available from the National Library of Australia

ISBN 978 1 74331 805 8

Part Opener design by Kylie Norton
Illustration section design by Kylie Norton
Photographs: p. 111 by Andrew Taylor, *The Sydney Morning Herald*; p. 169 by Monty Coles/*Vogue Entertaining + Travel*; p. 225 by Brett East
Index by Puddingburn
Internal design by Post Pre-press
Set in 12.5/17 pt Adobe Garamond by Post Pre-press, Brisbane
Printed and bound in Australia by Griffin Press, part of Ovato

10 9 8 7 6 5 4 3 2 1

The paper in this book is FSC® certified. FSC® promotes environmentally responsible, socially beneficial and economically viable management of the world's forests.

This book is dedicated to my son James,
in memory of my mother Valerie.

Contents

J.O.'66

Many years ago in my son Tims
green apple time we skipped down to
Camp Cove - Watsons Bay he, on my
shoulders singing "I'm the king of
the castle, & your the dirty rascel —
such joyful innocence — me, his
happy dad.
       Life is a journey & there
fans sunshine & shadows -
  This is his story, beautifully told
of his triumphs & struggles -
insights into that puzzling
jungle known as the art world

PART
ONE

1

THE LONG SHADOW

In the early 1960s, a small tow-haired boy was often left to sit on the steps outside a pub, grasping a huge glass of cold pink lemonade. Inside, the men would be drinking their preferred brew. I would hear a roar and see my father arm in arm with a painter or three, toasting, 'Let's raise our glasses, boys, as we are all Brothers of the Brush!' They were men who stood before blank canvases, clutching the end of hairy, oil-loaded brushes, declaring, 'Take that, you bastard!'

If that rowdy crew were the Brothers, then, without much choice, I was the Son of the Brush. I was the kid on the back steps, an outlying infinitesimal in the shade of a constellation of looming stars, where the centrifugal force was usually my father, the artist John Olsen.

In Australia my father is considered a national treasure, hailed sentimentally as 'Australia's greatest living artist' or, in a throw-away line by many, 'Australia's Picasso'. He is a prolific creative force born from a generation of very industrious artists who lived then in a philistine country. The winner of multiple art prizes, he has been awarded an Order of the British Empire, an Order of

Australia and two honorary doctorates, and he has unequivocally changed the way that the Western world views the Australian landscape.

At the time of my birth, my father was 34 years old, just returned from a three-year sojourn in Europe, the last two in Deià on the island of Mallorca where he had lived in a shack on the edge of the Balearic Sea. There he had painted by day and washed dishes by night when money ran short, relishing and absorbing every aspect of the Mediterranean way of life: the people, their customs, wines, food, cooking, the colours and light. His love affair with cooking and entertaining started here, with the constant stream of visiting artist friends. He began studying Zen Buddhism and befriended the English poet Robert Graves, a man who taught him the value of inner meaning. 'Olsen, you can paint pretty pictures all your life,' Graves told him, 'but without metaphor, you have nothing.'

When Dad returned to Sydney, he was a European fish out of water. In Spain he had evolved into a bon vivant, with an energy and enthusiasm that has never left him. 'What the experience in the Mediterranean did for me was to enlarge my vocabulary,' he remembers. He disembarked from the *Oriana* wearing jumbo cords, a turtleneck and two-tone boots, with gestures that were far more flamboyant than those he had departed with. In a city that still drank milky tea instead of wine, he was celebrated and envied in equal measure, yet swam ever upward.

Soon after, he met my mother, Valerie Strong, a delicate beauty with a heart-shaped face. Dad was instantly attracted to Mum's sensibility, 'so rare and so unique', he says. Their mutual attraction was immediate and explosive. Then an art student studying under John Passmore, she had already heard much about Passmore's favourite protégé, the renowned John Olsen. Passmore had raved about him, as a person and as an artist, and my mother used to say that she had fallen in love with my father even before they had met. Anyone who had lived in Europe was immediately a person of intrigue, and Dad did not disappoint, cutting a romantic figure and kitted out like a debonair poet; with his enormous charm and bravado, he possessed an animal magnetism that attracted everyone in his orbit. Both of my parents were married at the time they met. Dad's first marriage had been over before he had left for Europe, and Mum was married to a doctor, a kind man who simply paled into insignificance in comparison to my father.

For Mum and Dad, this was a meeting of minds—a shared passion for art and for one another. Mum now had found her soulmate, a partner who encouraged and inspired her work. The fact that they were both married was just semantics.

It was the start of an epic love affair that would last more than twenty years.

My earliest concrete memories are of Dad's studio in Watsons Bay, a timber cottage overlooking Sydney Harbour. It was where I spent my first years, dwarfed by canvases that loomed like vast apostles, and it is the place of my happiest recollections. I can still smell the gum turpentine, feel the spent aluminium tubes beneath my bare feet, see the scraped palettes, the oil-stained rags, the uncorked green bottles, a smock hanging in the corner. Always treading carefully around the unfinished paintings leaning in on each other.

Above the fireplace there was so often a glass of red at half-mast, a salute to the night before. To anyone else, the studio may have seemed cluttered or a riotous mess. To me it was home, a place where things were made and invented in the raw, rather than bought new; it was like living inside an early Modernist still life. In the kitchen there was often a fresh fish straight from the sea wrapped in newspaper, ready for the inevitable gathering: a dining table surrounded by loud, opinionated thinkers. Ideas uttered like prophecies, raging opinions and arguments, advice thrown around like sea salt, with dancing, music, laughter and sometimes tears.

It was a childhood of earthy pleasures and eccentric company—Margaret Olley, Russell Drysdale, Donald Friend, Barry Humphries, Sidney Nolan—a dynamic culture unfolding at our kitchen table, one that would be reported on and revered by Australian art critics. The value of painting was a crucible undisputed in our house, making my childhood rich in two assets: art and memory. Dad always talked about art as being the crucible, the melting pot of ideas, the collaboration of nature and the deeper metaphors concerning the experience and feeling of life, acknowledging how an artist is placed amongst art history having incorporated all those concepts. The crucible is the vehicle whereby we come up with something new. It is about art and culture in flux and transition. People did not talk about real estate in the 1960s; they were still struggling with Cubism, the Cold War and free love.

The atmosphere at home was always mercurial. Some days silence prevailed, and on others it was as if the pub had set up shop in the kitchen for lunch. The cast was always changing, with booming overtures followed by melancholic solos for strings. That is what it is like to be the child of an artist: no single day is ever the same. In my case, I was the child of two artists, for Mum was also working on her own canvases.

Mum, of course, worked the triple shift of artist, wife and mother, and her selfless, fragile concentration was so easily broken by the demands of others. While my father was a helio-centric force that always returned to the circle—whether with his famous saffron paella pan surrounded by a swarm of drop-ins, or in the burning ball of cadmium yellow he so often placed in the belly of his paintings—my mother was like a sage. With her own religion, she could speak the wisdom of God. For her, painting was a sanctuary, a place to quietly return to her soul.

My father once told me that I was conceived at the National Art School, at a party held in his honour on his return from Europe. (He now denies this, and my mother did, too.) Yet it is true that I displayed an early flair for art. At the age of three, I crept into my father's studio unseen one morning and 'contrib-uted' to a large painting that he was working on at the time. At breakfast there was an uproar: 'He's buggered the painting!' John thundered. Then, later in the day, in the pre-dusk that he called 'Chardonnay time', mellowed after his second glass of wine, he called out, 'The kid's a bloody genius!'

The painting was *Entrance to the Seaport of Desire*, a work now in the collection of the Art Gallery of New South Wales (AGNSW). It is a painting about entering through the Heads into Sydney Harbour on his return from a cold Europe, sailing through the arms of his 'sun bitch goddess', as he describes Sydney. Creatively it was a milestone, resplendent in colour, a precursor to the series that went on to culminate in the Sydney Opera House mural *Salute to Five Bells*.

As a young man I had the temerity to study to be an artist and the wisdom not to become one, although given the myth of my conception I can say that I am a true product of the National Art School. Seven years of art school taught me something, but watching my parents and living through every artwork on a highly personal level taught me more. Seeing works such as

Sydney Sun is like looking through an old photograph album, with the memories coded in paint.

It is a rare privilege to grow from infancy to maturity within a vast body of work. In many ways, John's paintings have the ability to distort and play with time. The joyful immediacy of his mark conceals the gravitas that forms the bedrock of his six decades of painting.

The line connecting art and life was never broken for my sister and me as we lived through every physical manifestation of the Olsen landscape in the years to follow: Lady Penelope Allen's basement in Notting Hill; a communal village in Mojácar, Spain; a miner's cottage in Hill End; a house without doors in rural Dural; and, still my idyll, the white weatherboard cottage in Watsons Bay.

We were shuffled from one scene to another to vary my father's work, or for the lure of a commission or a new art form, and we did so willingly. History views an artist's progress through bodies of work. My memories are of places. Wherever we were, it was usually a long way from suburbia.

Yet strong sunlight casts a long shadow. I looked up to my father as the King Sun but felt instinctively growing up that I would never glow that warmly, never have that luminescence. It has taken many years for me to own my reserve and my own unique contribution to the art world.

To understand my father's art is to understand his passion and drive, the pivotal elements that so influenced my own life and subsequent career. Through his art, we are intrinsically bound.

With my father's work, it's the flow and the touch, the interplay of space and perspectives, that captivate the viewer. It is the relationship between the positive and negative space, in both his landscapes and interiors. The eye is constantly seduced and moved around the image, between the solace and the descriptive. His work's influences go back to the tradition of ancient Chinese painting and the art of the continuous scroll, where the image is rolled out and portrayed in a continuous simultaneous vision, where we rest at no particular point. The path of the viewer's eye is constantly driven around the space and never ceases moving. We are perpetually travelling and navigating through pictorial space.

Like the concept of the universe, where the image begins and ends is irrelevant. Like the ebb and flow of rivers, or traversing the diversity of the galaxy, we become encapsulated in the descriptive image that is not based in fixed time. Pictorial space with no vanishing point or fixed horizon. Dad's vision is inspired by Cubism, viewing an object from many perspectives at once. Like Braque or Picasso, but without any obvious geometry, from multiple angles in a spontaneous moment yet always mindful of the underlying structure. Some works should be described as Soft Cubism.

His work also reflects the movement of time, expressing passing activity in a still image. There are no parameters limiting the experience of one set scene. Like with great classical music, we are enjoying the movements of a symphony, not knowing how it got us there, or where we are going within the music. It is all in the experience, in capturing the memory and essence of things, where there is more truth than in the art of realism. Like the flow of water from mountain tops into creeks, rivers and then the sea, we are in constant motion through the artwork. Ultimately there are pauses in time and visual space; they, too, become part of this kinetic experience of moving through the landscape or open space. All this in turn becomes a metaphor for the odyssey of our lives. The ability to feel and see your way through a painting becomes a reflection of living and survival. The emptiness is its fullness. It questions our own internal centre.

Conceptual art is often too obsessed with the 'wow and now'. To me, it's the resonance of the image always evolving that is most important, as we, too, emotionally awaken. That is what keeps us coming back to look at things again, and maintains our fascination for great art. The big result from engaging with and loving art is that, in time, we learn to understand ourselves better, and experience the evolution and maturing of our own souls.

2

DADDY'S BOY

I was born in Crown Street Women's Hospital, Surry Hills, just weeks after my parents were married. A month after my father had stood in a family courthouse with my mother as she divorced her first husband. Dad had finalised his own divorce from Mary Flower on his return from Europe.

Raised on the leafy, conservative North Shore of Sydney, my mother, Valerie, turned into a free spirit at art school, and fell madly in love with—and became pregnant to—her erudite art teacher. (John had taken over teaching Passmore's abstract class, and Mum was one of his students.) Mum's parents were not concerned, however, having had constant assurances from Dad that they would be married as soon as they had finalised their respective divorces.

Those were the days when a divorce required fault and blame, and attracted public shame. In the divorce papers, Dad is named co-respondent. My mother's swollen belly would have said it all. In a highly confronting moment, the judge took one glance over his nose at her and inquired, 'Who is responsible for that?'

Valerie pointed to John, clutching his now signature black Basque beret. He nervously replied, 'I am, your honour.'

'Well, sir, then you are now also responsible for the court costs,' the judge declared. He slammed down his gavel and announced, 'Divorce granted.'

Fresh from the hospital, we lived in a small house in Comber Street, Paddington, owned by the portrait painter Bryan Westwood. This suited Dad; it was not far from the National Art School, a converted colonial-era women's prison set among the dissecting energies of historic Taylor Square, with its old sandstone buildings and open streets. It was Sydney's own Piccadilly Circus, with the circumference of a turning bullock team.

It is hard to conceive how shocking it must have been for Valerie, the daughter of a British officer, to be living there, in a raw and ungentrified neighbourhood streaked with cat piss. It was a long way from the conservative picket fences of Pymble, where she had been brought up. Her life had taken a full turn and would become the most colourful and challenging one that she could ever have imagined.

We take bohemian life choices largely for granted now, but in those days it was scandalous to be the first to stray from the flock. Ironically, my mum detested attention or any form of confrontation. If Mum was a black sheep, she was of the petite, refined, cashmere variety.

My parents' somewhat rocky beginning, with Mum standing pregnant in the courthouse, does not tell the story of their true marriage of minds with sufficient dignity. From their first meeting, they had a complicity and an intricate bond that perhaps has been obscured in the more gossipy, sometimes inaccurate accounts of my father's life—a life described in minute detail from before my birth, recorded as Australian art history, in books, magazines, audio recordings and film. Our lives have been public fodder for as long as I can remember.

After a very brief period at Hill End when I was a baby, we moved to the aforementioned harbourside village of Watsons Bay. The gentle atmosphere and its slight detachment from the prying eyes of a small and insulated art world suited Valerie far better. Mum and Dad had bought a freestanding fisherman's cottage; you could see the harbour from their attic bedroom. Although my father was now an acclaimed artist, the purchase emptied the Olsen bank account, though it was replenished with a windfall when John won the inaugural Georges Invitation Art Prize in 1963 with his work *Tree of Life*. After winning the prize, Dad went down to his local to buy everyone a drink. One man asked him, 'Where did you buy the ticket?' Dad had to explain that he had won a different kind of lottery.

Watsons Bay was my little fishing village, our *Under Milk Wood*. Dad later rented another wooden fisherman's cottage, four doors down the road, called Doomee, a play on the Scottish term 'bonnie doon', or a happy home. Dad said it might be a humble abode, but it will 'do me'. This was his studio, and it was here that he created his first acclaimed Sydney Harbour series, and designed all the studies and preliminary drawings for his career-defining Sydney Opera House mural.

Perhaps many people remember their toddler years like dappled light with carefree moments. I was a child of the sun, and these were the happiest days of my early life. Apparently, my favourite attire was complete nudity and a plastic toy helmet until the age of four. My preferred escapade was a swift escape through the back door. I was always missing. One day they found me alone on a stationary mechanical rocking horse on the Watsons Bay wharf, outside the now famous Doyles fish and chip shop. From that day on, the catchphrase became 'Where's Tim?' and still is today.

But in fact my earliest memory was underwater. Literally. Just in time, I was scooped out of a goldfish pond by my father at a family lunch on the North Shore, after wandering off in a nappy, unnoticed. Lily ponds and frogs have been a recurring theme in my life, as they have been in the artwork of my father.

In the year I was born, art dealer Frank McDonald commissioned Dad to paint the ceiling of his sitting room in Woollahra. It was my father's first ceiling work, and the brief was simple: 'to bring the light in' and be 'light, bright and airy'. *Summer in the You Beaut Country* did exactly that. Inspired by the Baroque ceiling paintings in Europe, the idea to create a contemporary version was irresistible to my father, especially with the location: his art would become an integral part of the home. Thinking of the owner possibly moving in the future, Dad used large, easily dismantled hardboard panels installed directly on the ceiling, around a still-hanging chandelier.

He stood on scaffolding, painting directly above by hand while listening to jazz. Without realising how the music was affecting him, Dad painted in direct response to the jazz music of *Chicago* with bold, vibrantly coloured strokes. Noticing what was happening and worried that the work was becoming too heavy, McDonald would change the music to Mozart's horn concertos, the change in tempo resulting in a lighter, more fragmented application, until Dad would call out for the music to be changed back! The concept of painting on the ceiling was an inspired idea that captured the imagination of everyone who saw the finished pieces. More projects followed.[1]

To say I was angry and jealous when my sister Louise was born is an understatement. When Mum came home with a plastic English 'Bob' the policeman toy to placate me, I threw it immediately in the incinerator in protest. When Mum removed me from the breast for Louise, I was put out for a while, being a good drinker.

Dad had been working on another ceiling commission while Mum was pregnant for gallery owner Thelma Clune, in the hallway of her apartment, which was completed shortly after Louise's birth. Dad would paint during the day, then visit Mum in the hospital in the evenings. *Life Burst* reflects Dad's joy at Louise's birth; it was another celebratory work, vibrant and dynamic, almost 6.4 metres in length. This work is now in the Newcastle Art Gallery collection. Both of these early ceiling works introduced a circular mandala shape, a sun, the universal symbol of wholeness, with calligraphic lines flowing out. It is a motif that continued in Dad's work—*Sydney Sun*, *King Sun*, *Seafood Paella*—with the mandala shape morphing from a sun to a rock pool to a paella dish. More ceiling works followed, with the opulent *Sea Sun of 5 Bells* (also in the Newcastle Art Gallery) later in the year, which included a large, menacing bull against the sea.

Dad also painted a distinctly personal work to commemorate Louise's birth as a gift for Mum, *The Mother*, inscribed verso with 'For my darling Valerie, John Olsen '64'. For Mum, this was the ultimate expression of his love for her and our family.

With Mum's attention naturally absorbed by my newborn sister, I had the opportunity to become Daddy's boy. Every morning throughout the year, I would get up with John, climb onto his shoulders, and we would stroll down to the water. This practice would continue for most of my childhood. Around the age of five, after our return from Europe, I would sing 'I'm the

15

king of the castle and you're the dirty rascal!' as we walked, then watch Dad swim his laps of Camp Cove, wanting to join him out there each day, wading a little deeper, wishing to ultimately swim just like him until we swam side by side. Afterwards, we would buy fresh fish from the fishermen, now drinking their profits down at the pub, where Dad, always the village man, would join in for one. Then off to school for me, and for him, the studio for the day—our timeless daily ritual. Once, when we were alone, he said, 'We will always be together', and I believed him.

Our parents were loving, indulgent: 'I enjoyed my family very much,' my father has said. 'Really liked them. Loved them. Liked them naughty, not naughty. It didn't matter.' Like most young children, I idolised my father, emulating him whenever possible, enthralled by his every word, a mini John Olsen sans beret.

Now, with a son of my own, I'm aware of the way so many men look at their sons as extensions of themselves and their egos. Children allow us to revisit our own vulnerability, fragility and lost innocence, and the mistakes we made—and perhaps the opportunities we missed. We want to toughen them up so they do better than us. The anger and frustration many men feel with their sons—on the footy field, academically, in their choice of careers, in whom they choose to love—is an anger and frustration with themselves. It is the time we wish we could have again. In some ways, my father looked at me as a shard of himself. But, looking back, I was never going to be my father, even though I pretended for decades that I was.

A certain naiveté was always important to Dad's work. To be spontaneous and haptic, he would forget he was an adult, reclaiming his lost innocence. He says, 'To think like a child and to keep everything fresh requires the maintenance of a child's mind'. There is no art like children's art. My father was proud of his childlike imagery. His mantra to his students was 'stay with your dream and learn to play'. While some saw it as infantile, my father saw the ability to look at an adult concept through a child's eye as true sophistication. His work was enhanced by having children; all of his observations of Louise and me were carried into the studio.

Idealising these early, carefree years so much probably has not served me well. This perception infected everything that came after, setting the summit of life far too high. Memory is light shot through with shadow.

Our family values were skewed towards a strong sense of honouring and fostering talent—our own, and that of the gifted in our midst. We protected it like a ritual flame that had to be relit each morning. Money might be inherited but I think creativity is sometimes bred, and with it comes an even greater sense of responsibility.

Unknowingly, we kids got an unusual work ethic from watching our parents sticking at their art through feast and famine, and that contributed greatly to Louise's independence and success as a designer with her company Dinosaur Designs, and to my own eventual tenacity as a gallerist. The unspoken credo in our house was that anything was allowed except mediocrity. You can't throw in the brush!

Dad had fought hard to cast off the shackles of an uncreative early upbringing—a childhood with no books or art on the walls, the mundanity of working as a cleaner to survive while studying—before he was able to live from art alone. It was an everyday tightrope act. The concept of my father being born with the gift of a rare, brilliant mind was a psychological hurdle for me. It seemed baffling and unattainable; it made the world seem more complex and intellectual than it really is. Coming to

17

understand the fact that art was really only one way of trying to grapple with and understand the world was liberating. Dad mostly developed his mind through his natural passion for art and literature, but he also had the imagination and dexterity to be a successful artist. It was something of a calling—not just a God-given talent.

Not long out of school, when he decided to give up his first job as a bank clerk, his concerned father approached him and declared that he had three issues with him enrolling in art school: 'Firstly, you'll never make any money. Secondly, the art world is rife with homosexuals. And thirdly, how are we going to explain this to the neighbours?' I think Dad was bemused, not recognising any issue. Educated at a Marist Catholic boarding school, he was the best at drawing women's tits, which led to popularity and appreciation for his natural ability among young men craving some kind of pornography. Perhaps he realised then that art was his true calling.

Dad often refers to Klee's quote about a drawing being 'a line going for a walk'. Often in the evenings I call him and ask, 'How was your day?' And he replies, 'I went into the studio and took the line for a walk.' He makes it sound so romantic.

Our lives were soon to change irreversibly as we followed Dad abroad, meeting him in London—the first of many times we too would follow 'the line'.

3

SPANISH ENCOUNTER

There are still photographs of Louise and me sitting in Hyde Park, aged two and four, respectively. We are looking glum. For all the grandeur of London—particularly memories of watching the Queen's Guard making its way to Buckingham Palace—I was dismayed by our departure from Sydney, leaving the Arcadia of Watsons Bay.

John had outgrown the parochial concerns of the Sydney art scene. London was the great cultural magnet of the decade, so it was inevitable that he, and therefore we, would end up there, at least for a period of time.

Nearly every young Australian artist was making their way to the Northern Hemisphere, specifically London, spearheaded by Sidney Nolan and Russell Drysdale in the 1950s. The 1960 exhibition *Recent Australian Paintings*, curated by Bryan Robertson,[1] had resulted in the purchase of Brett Whiteley's *Untitled Red Painting*,[2] and a Godfrey Miller was acquired by the Tate. By 1963, the number of Australian artists in London was increasing by the day—Arthur Boyd, Len French, Michael Johnson, Charles Blackman—yet their reception by the British press was lukewarm, with a sneering, derogatory note—not so much towards the artists, their nationality or even their art, but towards Australia itself.

My father was a young artist who did not fit into any school of thinking. Miró, Dubuffet and the COBRA (or CoBrA) movement had all influenced him, and yet he was pushing for something more. Something generated utterly by his own hand, in his own language.

The trip was primarily to supervise the weaving of his first tapestry, *Joie de Vivre*, at Portugal's Manufactura de Tapeçarias de Portalegre, and to organise his first solo exhibition in London, with the possibility of another in New York. Inspired by the ceiling painting created for Frank McDonald, he had created his first tapestry design soon after, but this was not to commence production until 1964. Influenced and enriched by the explosive sunburst of *Summer in the You Beaut Country*, it had the same enthusiasm, the vibrant, sunny colours and the wandering lines that would become so intrinsic to his work.

Dad was immensely pleased with the quality of the tapestry, the texture and warmth of the wool adding a new dimension to the imagery, adding to the celebratory mood. The process required a greater degree of definition than the spontaneous brushstrokes he had applied to the ceiling, and the final result was a triumph. Completed in 1964 as an edition of six, the work was 2.38 by 1.78 metres and was catalogue number 1 in Dad's 1965 solo exhibition at Clune Galleries in Sydney, an exhibition described in *The Sydney Morning Herald* as 'the most joyful exhibition to be seen in Sydney in recent memory'. The work editions were acquired by the AGNSW, the National Gallery of Victoria (NGV) and the Harold E. Mertz Collection of Australian Art in the United States.[3]

Dad left for London first. It was a miserable time for him: lonely, missing us all and hating the English cold, even in summer. Communication was only by letters then, and the long periods of silence were cruel for both of them. Dad was determined not to repeat what had happened with his eldest daughter Jane, our half-sister; they had become estranged during his absence on his last trip overseas, which pained him greatly. At the time, though, we were completely unaware of Jane's existence.

Mum and Dad were very much in love then, and it was unthinkable for him to be away from us for an extended length of time. 'My darling, I love you and the children so much and I can't wait until I meet you at the airport,' Dad wrote to Mum. 'My life has been most incomplete, successful, but emotionally empty since I left. All I hope is that I mean as much to you.' Her response, firmly in the affirmative, was never received. Incorrectly addressed, it was returned to sender, arriving back in Australia just as we landed in London.

Our arrival was an emotional reunion for the whole family.

Despite suffering an eye infection and dealing with two small children, Mum was excited at the prospect of her first visit to Europe. 'I've never been abroad before and I feel that I'm more than ready, with all this experience behind me,' she wrote. 'I feel that I'm just the most fortunate person I can imagine.'

Travelling with young children is never easy, and it was a trial for both of our parents. We lived briefly in Pat and Penelope Allen's basement in Holland Park, where Dad had painted a sensational mural for their dining room ceiling, *Summer in the You Beaut Country No. 2* (now in the collection of the Art Gallery of Ballarat, Victoria). But Dad was eager to move on so, renting a car, we travelled across the Channel, then commenced the long drive down through France to Portugal. It was around the same distance as from Sydney to Adelaide, and with a typical Australian disregard for distance, this just seemed like potential for an adventure.

As is well known, our family was involved in a terrible car accident in France. In Dax, close to the Spanish border, Mum tried to correct a tight curve on a wet road and our Austin Tourer hit a tree head-on. The accident meant that we ended up convalescing for several months. Dad had put his arm out to protect Louise, saving her life, snapping his painting arm. He had to have the arm re-broken and re-set, and because there was infection in the wound there was even the unimaginable talk of amputation. Apart from being my father's sole form of expression, his painting was also the lifeblood of the family, the implement of his creativity and vocation, and our only means of income and livelihood.

Sitting in the middle of the car, I had gone through the windscreen into the tree and was in a coma for three days. The near-death-moving-towards-the-light experience is not a cliché: I experienced exactly that. All my life I have had difficulty with auditory processing, and I cannot help but wonder if the head injuries I sustained in the accident contributed to these learning difficulties.

There is a photo of us all in the Clinique Saint Vincent de Paul in Dax, all sharing a room. We were all in traction. Mum had broken all twelve of her ribs, my arm was broken and I had fractured the base of my skull, and Louise had fractured a leg. The story goes that, with Dad completely hamstrung and unable to grasp with his fingers, the French hospital registrar slapped the bill for our treatment onto Dad's fractured chest, adding insult to injury. Dad said in a letter to his dealer Frank McDonald that he had 'glimpsed into the corridors of death'. Neither Mum nor

Dad was able to speak French well, so they struggled to properly understand the details of our injuries. In constant pain and with continual money worries, they found it a terrifying experience. We were all lucky to survive.

Dad and I went back to the mangled car at the wreckers outside Dax. The vehicle resembled a sculpture by American artist John Chamberlain, who constructed his works with smashed metal from used cars. Among this compacted mess, to my surprise, I was able to open the glove box and there was an intact, unbroken bottle of Ribena, the only sweet drink we were allowed to consume as children. I wanted to take it with me, but my father refused to allow me to take anything away from that crushed object of near tragedy.

After we had recovered physically from the accident, we were badly in need of respite, shattered and vulnerable. It was as if a line had been smudged and torn on the map, and we needed to retrace our intended journey. Pat Allen came to the rescue, his cousin offering the use of a house in the south-east of Spain, in a little village called Mojácar. The house had a studio, so Dad would be able to paint and work on the tapestry designs. It is a place I remember fondly, nestled on the Mediterranean in the south of Andalucía, in a Spain simplified by impoverishment: dry, barren, devoid of tourists and the property resorts that would change the landscape irreparably. It was beautiful.

We lived in that tiny village, which circled around a grand cathedral, and slowly returned to normal. Dad and I would visit the market town of Vera together. After the quiet of our village, it was a little overwhelming for me. Dad wrote in his journal: 'Tim holds my hand, quiet and a little frightened, amid the jostling and the noisy voices. I love my children, as much as anything I have ever known in the world.'[4]

I kissed my first girlfriend at the small local school, where I quickly became fluent in Andalucían Spanish. Paradoxically, a week later, she stabbed me under the desk with a compass, which I've come to understand as being very Spanish. To slaughter a bull or to murder your lover was quite the norm!

Art costs time, and time is expensive wherever you are. Although Spain was cheap in comparison, we were constantly struggling to get paid by Frank McDonald. Mum was perpetually distraught, asking, 'Why hasn't Frank wired the money?' My policy on paying people properly and swiftly definitely stems from these memories. It is all too easy to forget how precarious the lives of artists and their families are, living not from pay cheque to pay cheque but from show to show.

Spain served as an extreme, almost gothic contrast to Watsons Bay. We were living opposite a park where a deranged, constantly weeping woman mourned her husband who had been murdered in the civil war. Dad was having his artistic renaissance, but we were living in the Old World. This was post-medieval village life: there was barely a radio and just one solitary television in the village. The gift was that we experienced 'ancient' Europe. There were bullet holes in the walls from fascist executions; women queued up at the local fountain balancing ceramic vessels on their heads to carry water back to their homes. My father paid a man to bring water to the house on a daily basis, one jug saddled either side of his donkey.

I remember aubergines and garlic, cheap cuts of lamb, black olives, puddles of oil on casseroles, broken bread, flagons of wine, an abundance of rosemary—always the Mediterranean feast. Meals were very rustic and cheap. We were poor, but we ate well.

My love of dancing began in Spain; the tempo and syncopation of the flamenco were intoxicating. Every night in the restaurant after dinner, I could not resist moving to the sounds that beat at the very heart of Spanish culture, stomping my feet, probably making a spectacle of myself. But I loved it.

The only television we saw was when we went down to the local tapas bar where the hum of a bullfight seemed to always be on the screen. Mum would implode when she saw the drawn-out torture served up to the bull, but it was the Spanish gladiatorial tradition. It is the sort of violence you can only absorb in retrospect or through philosophy, like Nietzsche understanding the fine line between birth and tragedy.

In retrospect it was wonderful to experience what life could have been like in another era, but living frugally with two kids must have been challenging for Mum and Dad. Desperate to replenish our depleted funds, Dad was determined to win the commission to design a tapestry for Harry Seidler's Australia Square building, then the tallest tower in Sydney. He had Frank McDonald send the plans and photographs in readiness for our arrival so he could start work immediately.

There were more pressing concerns though. While the rest of us had fully recovered physically, Dad was still experiencing pain in his arm and discovered it was infected. We travelled to Madrid to see a specialist about it, and he was told the fracture was so bad it would take four years to fully recover. He would need another operation.

While we were there, we were introduced to a very elegant woman at a function, and I proudly greeted her in my Andalucían Spanish.

'Your son speaks Spanish like a peasant,' the woman said to Mum.

To which my darling, timid mother, who had the heart of a lion where her children were concerned, replied, 'Much like your English.'

We rushed back to London for the operation as soon as we could afford to. To our palpable relief, it proved a success. This was a crisis point for Dad, with the operation and with his work, and his 'attempt to develop a richer mode of expression'. Nevertheless, Frank McDonald had no qualms pushing him to start work immediately after the operation.

We stayed in shared rooms near Regent's Park, in a large apartment at Hanover Gate Mansions, where Louise and I quickly wore down the patience of the other childless adults. Mum and Dad found the situation very stressful, and it was clear we had to move on. We were to learn later that the rooms we took over belonged to Diana Stearn, who had been Dad's girlfriend before he met our mother.

We left for Portugal, travelling to Castelo de Vide in the Alto Alentejo region, near the Spanish border and close to the tapestry workshop in Portalegre where *Joie de Vivre* had been woven. To both of my parents' relief, Dad had won the Harry Seidler submission and work had already commenced on this important new tapestry.

Most of the works my father made during this time were tapestries, with three more in 1966, each woven on a momentous scale suited to public buildings: *Nude with Clock*, *Yellow Summer* (also known as *Abstract*) and *Verdure* (now in the Westpac Banking Corporation collection). His passion after creating *Joie de Vivre* prompted him to call for the establishment of a tapestry workshop in Australia. The Victorian Tapestry Workshop—now the Australian Tapestry Workshop—was established in 1976 and has produced numerous designs for him since. This was, in part, promoted by his discovery in Portugal that only Australian wool was used in the tapestries in Portalegre, being the only wool to have the 'required elasticity'.[5]

While my father's work was being thrust into the epicentre of Sydney Modernism, our life was as strangely archaic as a Piranesi etching. The village we lived in was perched on a hill surrounded by olive groves. All my memories of this time are sensory: the smell of crushed olives; smoky cafes smelling of roasted quails; and that sense of being perched and enclosed, still very much within a fortification, on the edge of the Basque country. Hemingway did not exaggerate. There were soldiers and guards hanging out at the local cafes, and one man who had had his tongue cut out. My father would often go to this man, as he was the eyes and ears of the village, in regard to my whereabouts when I had once again run away. 'Onde está o Tim?' he would ask. The man would respond in sign language to my father that he had seen me, or he would just try to chase me in vain as I disappeared into the olive groves. I can still smell the oil when I close my eyes.

We lived in a hotel at Castelo de Vide. I still remember the sound of the Fado they played in the restaurant every night and my surprise at seeing people cry. It was very disconcerting to see adults, men and women alike, with tears running down their cheeks. I remember madeira, morbid folk music with the rhythmic flamenco, and the Fado constantly in the background. My lasting memories from Portugal are of people crying. The country seemed cemented in profound melancholy.

The language barrier does not matter much to children and I rapidly learned Portuguese, though it was never as fluent as my Andalucían. The local boys took great delight in teaching me swear words, encouraging me to use them in the wrong context, much to their amusement. As the only foreigners in the village, we were outsiders, and the boys would tease me mercilessly—to the fury of Dad when he caught them at it. Being so young, I was oblivious.[6]

Soon after, in 1967, we made our way to Lisbon, where we boarded the *Oriana* back to Australia. I almost jumped ship: after slipping between the rim of the vessel and the gangplank, I was rescued by a fellow passenger by a whisker. It would have been an absurdist tragedy if I had died then, considering what the family had been through. Drama has its limits.

In that strange window of time, it was very easy to forget the promise of the 1960s, yet those experiences in Europe inspired years of my father's painting. The rest of us were filled with relief at leaving. After this major European encounter, we were finally heading home.

After the strange uncertainty of our European travels, Watsons Bay quickly became our Eden again. For two magical years it was idyllic, the time forever etched in my memory.

We quickly settled back into home and school, and Dad prepared for his grand relaunch into the Sydney art scene with his new works. Our time abroad, the accident, and Louise and I getting older had drawn us into a close family unit.

The Bay was my personal playground and, now old enough to roam free, I spent my days swimming, exploring the rock pools, and playing cricket and football with the local kids. By then I could swim properly, and I have retained the ritual of those early-morning swims all my life. A few shark sightings took me out of the ocean, into the netted pool, but otherwise our lives were the same, the days drifting into one another. It was a truly magical period.

Although I had considered my pre-accident years as the

ultimate haven after the trauma of France, this really was idyllic—and Dad was the pinnacle. These days were filled with wonder and fun as we saw the world through his eyes, through long walks along the coast where he would point out elements of the landscape. His enthusiasm for everything around him was infectious and exhilarating. He would reel us both in, enchanting us with his work, his knowledge and his sheer zest for life. Our home was filled with laughter, songs, poetry and, of course, art everywhere.

Having grown up seeing the creation of his huge paintings of the harbour and the ceiling works, I now discovered his animals as he brought the rock pools alive, with drawings and paintings of squid, fish, birds, insects and all the surrounding flora and fauna.

We were now aware of Dad's naughty side, his mischievousness. He delighted in surprising and entertaining us. One afternoon, returning from school, we found the kitchen completely transformed since the morning: every paintable surface, from the stove and cupboard, to the refrigerator and our toys, had been painted in the vibrant colours of the flowers he loved so much. Even my wooden pushbike had had a makeover. The whole place looked like an installation. It was a joyous expression of love.

And the food. Dad ruled in the kitchen, and it was sensational. Whatever Dad and Mum were eating, we ate, too, every morsel rich with flavour. We soon realised that we ate differently to our friends. The Mediterranean diet, pungent with garlic and spices, was miles away from the standard meat-and-three-veg meals our friends sat down to. The appreciation of food and drink was instilled in us from as soon as we could eat solid food. There was no fussy eating in the Olsen house. You ate, savoured and relished whatever was put in front of you. Mum, relegated to washing-up duties, was relieved in a way. The competition was too great; Dad could always cook so much better.

Dad shared everything with me in those days, no matter how much garlic, or how much wine was added to my water. What he consumed, I did. Believing in the European practice of introducing children to wine with their food, he did not ever imagine this might influence a propensity for drinking that, later in my life, would raise its ugly head.

Although everything seemed perfect, there were dark times, too, yet we never felt our family was in jeopardy. My first doubts came as I sensed the fragility of my parents' marriage in the times when Dad was away painting, teaching and carousing, and Mum was left alone to raise us.

I remember my mother crying in the kitchen and only realised later, in retrospect and amid rumour and gossip, that my father had been living the life of a free-loving Pre-Raphaelite. With Mum's help, Dad had started his own art school, The Bakery in Paddington, and it was the place to be. Long days of nude life drawing interspersed with flagons of wine and paella cooked in the old ovens set the tone. A rescued wild parrot would fly around the high ceilings of the studio, adding to the colour and chaos. Mum taught a children's class on Saturday mornings, and there was a constant stream of visiting well-known artists: Russell Drysdale, Fred Williams, Len French, Donald Friend and Judy Cassab.

Dad's alcoholic, often homeless father Harry was the caretaker at the school for a while, but Dad tired of the vagrant women he would bring home. There was no option for him but life on the streets again, and this scarred Dad for life. He would worry about his father at night, living rough, being homeless, drifting into an underclass where people can be terribly cruel to each other.

Dad was a revolutionary teacher, enlightening countless students about art and life within a society that was often drab. Many a housewife was corrupted, with one husband, a judge, complaining that since his wife had been attending the school, she had become rebellious and feral. My father responded by asking, 'Are you sure you wouldn't like to join us?' When he ran the nude life-drawing classes, he would advise students to 'bring charcoal, gouache watercolours, good paper and be prepared for anything!'

His interest in nurturing emerging artists began in his teaching days. Later in life he would go out into the bush with a group of younger artists (who affectionately referred to Dad as 'Olly Paint'), staying out for a few days and painting en plein air. Dad loved those trips—the camaraderie, and the living, thinking and dreaming art. I have seen how beneficial these interactions with my father have been for younger artists; the opportunity to work with him and learn from him is an invaluable experience.

The Bakery ran for just three years, but it left an indelible mark. Juliet Schlunke was a student at The Bakery and one of Dad's old flames; almost 50 years later, she wrote the book *Buns in the Oven: John Olsen's Bakery Art School* about her experiences and Dad's teaching methods.[7] He was very much the darling of the Sydney art scene then, with his awards and countless exhibitions and his reputation as a groundbreaking artist and larger-than-life persona.

My mother was stoic and hid her hurt; their bond was stronger than my father's misadventures. A very private woman whom I hardly ever saw nude, she was genteel and elegant, and almost

Victorian in her ability to contain her emotions. That she loved us all immensely was so evident. For a time I felt that perhaps she had not hugged me as much as a child as I would have liked, but she was possibly restrained by the innate refinement that Dad admired so much in her. She really had a lot of 'Eastern' sensibilities: her self-contained smile, the secrets left unspoken. Without knowing it at the time, her delicate strength was one of the pillars that held up the sheltering sky above our heads. It was a loving support that we never imagined losing.

The iconic *Spanish Encounter* was painted in a frenzied five hours the night before Dad's exhibition at Terry Clune Galleries opened, shortly after his return from Europe. The monumental, groundbreaking work rocked the Sydney art scene. The triptych encapsulated 'a vitality stemming from Olsen's experience of Spain combined with the pulsating activity of Sydney's inner-city life', as described by the AGNSW, where it now resides as a highlight of their collection. It is known for its exuberance and vitality, a work of sheer emotion.[8]

It has been written that the genesis behind the work was a 'lovers' tiff', reducing the painting to 'a landscape of desire, sex and frustrated love'.[9] When asked recently, Dad was adamant that this was not the case and stands by the statement he wrote to the AGNSW in 1960.

4

UTOPIA DOES NOT EXIST

In 1969, on the cusp of the new decade, Mum was restless and yearning for a peaceful bush haven, and Dad had reached the milestone of turning 40. 'I feel at a crisis time in my career, I feel the work I have been doing in my thirties has come to an end and I will now have to renew myself,' he wrote in his journal.

You never know the exact moment you are leaving your childhood behind, but that is how it went with our exodus from Watsons Bay to rural Victoria. My memories of peaceful respite were shattered like shards of glass. The shape of our life as a young family followed the knotted upheaval of the times. We never seemed to settle anywhere for long before the gypsy caravan was moving once again.

Our new home was at Dunmoochin, an artists' community on the bush property owned by painter Clifton Pugh, some 30 kilometres out of Melbourne at Cottles Bridge. Here, the liberation of the 1960s was in full swing, and the look was long scrawny tresses, knobbly beanies, woolly jumpers and awkward-fitting denim. I grew my hair—everyone grew their hair. The houses were mudbrick with corrugated iron roofs, stained glass windows, tacked-on homemade verandahs, and outhouse toilets that were lime pits. Materials were salvaged and recycled, and had to be suitably aged to harmonise with the surroundings. It was spartan. Without our pot-belly stove, we probably would have frozen. Louise and I remember drawing in front of the stove on rainy days, as Mahler's *Songs of a Wayfarer* was played repeatedly in the background.

Cottles Bridge had a completely different landscape to Sydney: dry, rolling hills, dusty paddocks, dams surrounded by eucalyptus trees. The most significant change for me was the colour: fawns, creamy ochres, chocolate, honey, all the shades of brown; the straw colour of parched grass; the bright yellow of wattle. Fred Williams, Clifton Pugh and Dad worked nearly every day, side by side, in their 'open studio' around Dunmoochin, or travelled to the Wimmera to paint. Mum joined them, when she was able. Dad searched for the 'feeling of the landscape, its unimaginable details', his canvas tied to a tree or flat on the ground. Now he was intent on capturing the 'life force' of his environment, the 'essential rhythms'. He would return home covered in paint, exhilarated. Fred Williams was a prolific worker with an accurate eye for reducing the landscape to pure, well-observed marks. He was always so well organised, his paper pre-mounted and its grid drawn, that Dad would joke that by the time he had strapped his huge canvas to a tree to stop it from blowing away, Fred had already painted two gouaches. The three of them were truly 'Brothers of the Landscape'.

We would sometimes join their excursions. The mood was one of camaraderie and enthusiasm; there was a great rapport between the artists. We noticed how differently each artist would view the landscape, how their styles and insights differed. They would work, stop for a billy tea break mid-morning, start again, and then picnic, for lunch, before working again. It was mesmerising.

Louise and I attended the local one-teacher school at Arthurs Creek, encircled by fields of cows and horses. Some kids would ride their own horses to the school each day. Our teacher was Alan 'Froggy' Thomson, an Australian Test cricket fast bowler. If he was angry, he would pelt us with a tennis ball at high speed and could inflict a bruising punishment that he would probably be punished for today. Small as the school was, it was gravely lacking in resources—so much so that Dad organised an exhibition to raise money, drawing work from friends and the resident artists who had been inspired by the landscape. With the works valued at over $60,000, including works by Mum, a Clifton Pugh, two landscapes by Dad and an Albert Tucker, the locals organised a vigilante committee to sleep in the hall with their rabbit guns to safeguard the paintings.

Attracting crowds from Melbourne, the exhibition raised enough money to buy the badly needed equipment, even a television set. Dad wrote in his journal: 'It was the best opening I have attended.' Unfortunately, this did not compensate for the standard of education we were receiving. Having just one teacher for a class of mixed-age children, and no discernible curriculum, meant that Louise and I fell sorely behind academically. Shuffling between countries and schools also contributed to my struggles in primary education, especially when coupled with my own anxieties to 'fit in' with everyone and everything.

The Dunmoochin community revolved around the turbulent home of Clifton Pugh, his wife Marlene and their two boys, Shane and Dailan. Clif set the tone, running an anything-goes cult of free love. Ever the naturist, his usual mode of dress was complete nudity. It was quite common to find him naked

35

with a young muse in a Manet pose, a *demoiselle de jardin* à la Dunmoochin, outside his house. Adult nudity was so normalised that it was like living in a Bruegel painting. Clif had built his own pub on the other side of the hill, and frolicking naked bodies would often spill out from the bar, like a debauched medieval bacchanal. Dunmoochin was rustic yet worldly. When we moved in, its artistic residents included Frank Hodgkinson, Frank Werther and Peter Laycock. Albert Tucker was down the road at Hurstbridge, and Barry Humphries, the soon to be prime minister Gough Whitlam, and actor Patrick Macnee from the UK drama series *The Avengers* all passed through.

It was known as a 'bohemian village', the atmosphere of the place creative yet decadent. Everyone skinny-dipped in the dam (except my mother, who refused to get among the yabbies, let alone be publicly naked), long lunches turned into early mornings, and everyone was an artist (or a potter, weaver or writer). Dunmoochin has been called Australia's first artists' 'commune', but to me it was a benign and natural environment, albeit seething with human follies. Imagine a painting by Frederick McCubbin scripted by David Williamson, with a touch of Dante, all marinated in red wine.

No one at Dunmoochin had any boundaries; the only fences in the whole village were to keep the emus in. Clif Pugh had a sanctuary where emus, kangaroos and wombats, wounded or injured, were taken in and rehabilitated. The animals would roam freely through the houses; an emu would put its head through the kitchen window, wombats would appear in the lounge. He even had a lizard atrium built off the lounge room.

One day Clif took me with him to the vet after he had rescued a kangaroo with a broken leg. A normal farmer would have just shot it—a quick, cheap bullet—but he wanted it euthanised humanely, despite having his own firearms, which were lying carelessly around in the house.

There was always a gun beside his bed, not locked away as the law now demands. Once, bored and tired during one of the many late-night dinner parties at the Pughs', I was told to go and join Louise, asleep in Clif's bed, until everyone was ready to leave. Spying the gun, I found it impossible to stop myself picking it up and waving it around, aiming at imaginary targets in the dimly lit room. My mother suddenly appeared in the doorway to check on us, just as I levelled the gun directly at her—fully primed and loaded, as we were later to discover. She screamed and ran out to berate Clif for leaving his loaded gun around her children. The punishing lecture I received from Dad for nearly accidentally shooting my mother filled me with shame.

By anyone's standards, 1969 was a wild year. One of my toughest experiences was when Mum went back to Sydney with Louise to visit her parents in Cremorne and left me alone with Dad. We went to the Pughs' for dinner and, after feeding the wombats in Clif's sanctuary, I was put to bed early. Later, wandering half dazed out of my room, I witnessed a ménage à trois in full swing on Clif's sofa: Clif, Dad, and the wife or girlfriend of one of the other artists. On her return, I told Mum about it. Dad later castigated me: 'You and I are men, and there are some things men, as a code, keep secret.' I was seven years old.

It is a wry truth that I saw things that a child really should not see, and by then I had recognised that unconditional love does not always guarantee fidelity. Witnessing this confusing '60s love-in certainly muddled my seven-year-old mind with regard to the fragile institution of family, and the concept of what a loving parental bond should look like. It was the day I learned about secret men's business, and it set the scene for what would happen years later.

The only religion at Dunmoochin was sensory and visual gratification—at any cost. Unfortunately, the free love of the time took its toll on many of Dunmoochin's occupants as they were caught up in the quagmire of philandering. By the darkest stroke of irony, my mother had gone to the commune for peace, quiet and a stable family life. She had found more time to paint, enchanted by the bush flowers, and I can remember the camaraderie of her and Dad as they mixed paints together, painting side by side. Yet despite this, Mum felt that we didn't belong and was becoming increasingly eager to leave, recognising that my father had discovered his own kind of primal sexual energy. She lived in a constant state of concern: there were so many distractions and temptations, and Dad had been in part corrupted by Clif, whose own moral compass swung so widely. It is hard to imagine the freedom they experienced then, but even Eden has a tendency to go to seed.

Mum did write, much later in her life, that 'My ideal environment is something like Dunmoochin was, with lots of interesting people in the landscape, and John'. The fact that my mother continued to include Dad in her 'ideal' world—that she continued to be my father's greatest advocate, friend and supporter—is testament to her character, her ability to love and to forgive. The underlying love and respect that still seemed apparent between Mum and Dad, long after their later separation, dismisses the notion that we were a 'broken' family.

Socially I searched for my place at the table and struggled. Shy and withdrawn, I found school in particular difficult, and it seemed at the time that no one noticed. In hindsight, they must have. 'I must try to be more of a sheet anchor for Tim, to help him through his crisis of school and his uncertainty with friends,' Dad wrote in his journal. 'I feel I should do more things with him, talk to him, take him to the theatre, become a friend to him, not just a father.'[1] It is a sentiment that I now try to uphold with my own son.

At that point, it seemed my life would always be seen in the context of my father—until I made it my own.

It was at Dunmoochin that I first came to understand not only the sexual debauchery of this artists' society but also its petty jealousies. The art scene generally is a very judgemental, tribal community, and Dad has always said that the envious bile generally comes from artists of limited talent.

In 1969, he had made the outstanding painting *The Chasing Bird Landscape*, showing the area he knew as (John) 'Perceval's Hill'. The work had been started en plein air on a memorable Melbourne Cup Day, with Dad working alongside Clifton Pugh. It went on to win the Wynne Prize in 1969, and critic James Gleeson would call it a 'masterpiece'. (Gleeson thought up the idea of the Sydney Opera House mural, suggesting it to the Dobell Foundation.) As Laurie Thomas wrote in *The Australian*, 'It is a work of simple majesty that lifts it right out of the class of landscape reporting and makes it into a work of art, imaginatively and visually exciting in its own right. It recreates the landscape in a way unknown in the Wynne Prize for years.'[2]

John was suddenly the landscape hero. He had elevated himself to stand with Fred Williams, Sidney Nolan and Arthur Boyd. Given the favourable press Dad's win gave to Dunmoochin, we assumed that it would be cause for celebration among our neighbours. But, inexplicably, the attitude towards the Olsens changed. Behind closed doors in the village, the envy had started to develop, and children could hear their parents talking about 'those bloody Olsens' being upstarts.

One afternoon, walking home from school alone towards our house, I was suddenly ambushed by about eight kids. Many voices in unison said: 'You and your dad are fucking arseholes.' They held me down and, one by one, took turns pissing on my face. I remember the urine burning my eyes and the stench of ammonia. Even a girl lifted her skirt and squatted over my mouth. It was like something out of *Village of the Damned*.

The denigration I felt after this assault is hard to explain. It was such a deeply personal violation and humiliation, fuelled by so much unexpected vitriol. While feeling that I had copped a punishment for my father's success, I also knew it was an offence directed towards the whole family. Dad mentioned only recently how much this incident affected me—that I became withdrawn and nervous among gatherings of people, something I still fear. It has left me with an indelible lack of trust, even of close mates, as I had considered some of those children my friends.

Dad drove over to see Don Laycock, the potter, who was the father of the ringleader. Don promised, 'No, John, I'll punish him.' Not much else was done. Perhaps the men, for all their new-age bluster, were still stuck in the 1940s in terms of their fathering, and I was expected to take it 'like a man'. For weeks afterwards I was deeply traumatised, and its lasting effects came out later in my behaviour. Dad noted in his diaries my frustration and angry outbursts: 'When Tim starts shouting it is perhaps an expression of his not being listened to sympathetically. One should always give him the impression of being reasonable and not lose one's temper with him.'[3]

Dad must have sympathised, though, as he had had a similar experience as a child. Proudly decked out in an outfit made by his mother to have his photograph taken, he was complimented by three local boys, who then gave him a 'swift kick up the arse', saying, 'Take that you pretty little shit' and laughing as they ran away. He wrote that he had felt cheated and violated, something he has never forgotten: 'this outfit was responsible for my first awareness that mankind was not to be trusted'.[4] Children can be undeniably cruel.

Dad has a childhood scar on his back that looks like a stab wound. As a small boy, I asked him what had happened; he would reply, 'It's an injury from the art war.' Thinking he had been stabbed by a palette knife or the end of a paintbrush, I believed him just like I believed in Santa Claus until I was about eight.

In the two years we spent at Dunmoochin, Dad was incredibly productive: many major paintings, numerous works on paper, tapestries with the Brudea Tapestry Studio, a large ceramic mural at The University of Melbourne, and highly successful exhibitions. Here, too, he discovered his passion for handpainting ceramics. Dad would visit potter Robert Mair, often taking Louise with him; she would make clay animals while they talked and worked together, Mair throwing and Dad hand-decorating the pieces. Their collaboration would produce a unique body of work that resides in collections across Australia.

Dad and Robert shared an instant rapport. Mair shared his books on Japanese ceramics, and the images of the Oriental calligraphic designs were inspiring. It was a stimulating but frustrating time, with the unpredictability of the firing process and Dad's often unconventional approach. While they started off working on just a few small pieces, they were soon given a commission from private collector Terry Whelan to produce an entire dinner service. They became almost obsessive over the project, which grew exponentially until it was a dinner setting for sixteen, encompassing over 160 pieces, including tea and coffee pots, even a candelabra, all decorated in blue and white glazes to have 'something of a Grecian and Mediterranean feeling'—a region Whelan loved to be in. The whole dinner set was laid out in its splendour at Dad's retrospective in Melbourne in 2017.

Some years before, Dad had become friends with art dealer Rudy Komon, and by 1969 he had been persuaded to become part of Rudy's stable, joining Fred Williams and Clif Pugh. The works Dad created at Dunmoochin were exhibited in his first show with Rudy that year, titled *The Donemoochin* [*sic*] *Summer*. The reviews were ecstatic: 'The resulting landscapes must be ranked among the most beautiful ever painted in this country,' wrote James Gleeson. Dad eventually lost patience with the 'old fox' and moved on some years later. Especially since the day after the last exhibition he held that Rudy had opened, Rudy had jumped on a plane to Europe, leaving the show unattended.

The scope and range of the work my father has produced in his career is staggering. His work ethic is ingrained, the need for discipline and a routine essential. Paradoxically, Dad often spoke of the distractions of living at Dunmoochin: the social gatherings, his domestic responsibilities, his own gregarious nature in such an indulgent setting. He was continually conscious of his alcohol consumption, afterwards writing: 'I am rather pleased with myself for I have not been drinking, and I have concentrated on practical matters . . . I feel I have been very successful and creative.'

A standout work from this time by Dad was *Love in the Kitchen*, inspired by the tempestuous, disintegrating relationship between Clif Pugh and his wife Marlene, with their sons struggling to cope with the hostility surrounding them. Marlene was loud, boisterous and a terrible swearer. Louise and I were scared of her; she seemed to be the polar opposite of our mother. The Pughs' fights were legendary screaming matches where they threw things at one another, regardless of anyone around them.

The work was the antithesis of Dad's usual kitchen paintings: the room was chaotic, misshapen, with everything broken or in the midst of shattering. Dad had painted the words 'Oops . . . falling in . . .' on one side, and on the opposite side an outline of a heart indicating love. But what captured my attention was the lone figure drawn in black in the foreground: Dailan, the Pughs' son.

Dailan was living at Dunmoochin when we were there, an irascible teenager who bullied me relentlessly. I found him terrifying, especially after the pissing assault (although Dailan was not party to that, being a lot older than those kids). Mum and Dad had watched from the sidelines as the Pughs' marriage disintegrated completely and Marlene walked out, exasperated by Clif's endless infidelity, leaving Dailan with his father. Marlene was quickly replaced with another woman, and then another. Clif, too, had his priorities: art, then women, and then his son, way down the list. Dad saw Dailan's abject misery and loneliness. Even though living under the same roof as his father, he had been completely abandoned.

When looking at *Love in the Kitchen* not long after, when Dad had left our family, I empathised with that lone figure so much more. It could have been me. Yet, even though Dad had done essentially the same thing as Marlene, my life was very different to Dailan's. Our parents loved each other and our home life was

43

harmonious. We felt cherished and loved. The only reason Dad left was that he met Noela.

Clif Pugh went on to win the Archibald Prize three times. Ironically, considering how he and Marlene had fought so violently, he was a lifelong pacifist and anti-war activist. Part of his legacy was to establish the Dunmoochin Foundation, which provides residencies for emerging and established artists, and to which he donated his Dunmoochin landholdings and art collection. Dailan became an artist, potter, writer, illustrator and conservationist. Our paths have not crossed again.

It has been written that our move to Dunmoochin was in response not only to Dad's need to renew himself but due to his new relationship with a student at The Bakery, an affair so intense that it was threatening my parents' marriage. Dad does not deny the affair, but he does dispute that it was the reason for our move. Yet another affair, however, was instrumental in our return to Sydney (sometimes I wonder where he found the time). Mum was right: Dunmoochin was not a place to bring up children. It had been an amazing experience: I remember seeing the moon landing on a little black-and-white television, catching yabbies in the brown-water dam and roaming the hills that became part of Dad's paintings. But it had revealed many flaws in the 'bohemian community' ideal, and it had brought out many demons. Eventually the artists' utopia had turned into a living hell for me.

Dad had also fulfilled his sabbatical as a Victorian artist; he often spoke of the importance of being in Melbourne for his work, that the 'psyche' of Australian art was there. He felt that he needed the acceptance and acknowledgement of the Victorians, saying, 'You haven't made it in Australia until you've made it in Melbourne.' It is a sentiment some people still feel today.

However, the time came to leave, and Sydney was about to offer him his greatest challenge—something Melbourne could not better. John Olsen was now well and truly an Australian artist, not just a Sydney one. So we set off again. Through all our constant vagabonding, it was always the work that motivated him.

When we left Dunmoochin, Louise and Mum flew back to Sydney, and Dad and I drove back, the car full of our possessions, dropping into a country pub halfway that night. While waiting for our steak, I went to the outhouse toilet and, as I stood at the urinal, a man who had been watching me came in. He asked me if I had heard of sex and if I wanted twenty cents to go into the toilet cubicle with him, and he threatened to kill me if I told anyone. Terrified, I turned and ran. It was my first encounter— but not my last—with a paedophile.

Louise often says we were free-range kids, but by then our innocence had been lost.

5

BOHEMIAN ROYALTY

As a family, we went from tree change to sea change: from Dunmoochin back to Camp Cove, next to Watsons Bay. In another seismic change, I went from a one-room, one-teacher school to Cranbrook, an elite private boys' school nestled above the harbour in the exclusive suburb of Bellevue Hill—a school Dad could afford thanks to the Sydney Opera House mural commission.[1] It was a turning point for us financially as a family, and one of the most prestigious commissions ever granted to an Australian artist.

Cranbrook was a huge contrast to the tiny country school in Arthurs Creek. I was badly behind in any form of curriculum, and after one year the school recommended that I repeat Year 4. Mum refused to accept this, shepherding me off to an IQ test where my intellect was verified; within two years I was receiving school awards for effort, and gaining distinctions for English and History. At Cranbrook I took naturally to rugby, finding a welcome form of structure, my strong legs and bullock-like frame at last proving their worth. On the rugby field for the first time I was part of a team, no longer an outsider, and on graduating I won the school's rugby award as the team's most promising forward. Rugby changed me, and the way the world responded to me changed accordingly.

At this time my father was painting the Sydney Opera House mural, nine panels of marine ply bent into a curve, so large (21 by 23 metres) that it had to be painted off site and installed panel by panel. 'I have to say it's not a job for boys,' he said. With Dad away for long hours at a studio in an old warehouse in The Rocks, the camaraderie of our morning swims was disrupted, but I found other activities, too. Both of my parents had instilled in Louise and me an amazing work ethic. My first job was working at the Camp Cove Milk Bar, aged eight, then delivering the *Wentworth Courier*. Being financially independent was essential. I was always looking for a job and have never stopped working since.

The Sydney Opera House commission was Dad's most ambitious yet. In his diary, he wrote that the work was 'my finest work—it has a power about it, perhaps, for some—that Sydney Harbour will never be looked at the same way again'.[2] *Salute to Five Bells* was a vast and delicate mission, a nocturnal submersion based on a poem by Kenneth Slessor about his friend, the cartoonist Joe Lynch, who accidentally drowned in Sydney Harbour. Lynch had fallen off a ferry on his way to a party, weighed down by beer bottles in his trenchcoat pockets. 'A true Australian death,' says Dad.[3]

Now one of Australia's greatest monuments, at the time the Sydney Opera House was a statement of modernity. Some were angry that Jørn Utzon, a Dane, had designed their Opera House: people were unsure if the tiled peaks even resembled sails, and were upset over the cost, which represented money being siphoned into the arts rather than into schools and hospitals.

By the time Dad had won the commission, Utzon had walked off the job, disgusted at the lack of support and non-payment.

Dad wrote to Utzon regardless before commencing, to ask his opinion. Utzon replied, 'Thinking about its position, make it move from east to west and become a part of the Harbour.' The work hangs outside the Sydney Opera House concert hall today where it follows Utzon's suggestion, facing the water that inspired its narrative. In keeping with Slessor's poem it is set in moonlight, an iridescent purple indigo with evocative creatures jiggling around in an oceanic firmament that echoes the vastness of the harbour.

At the opening, in front of a media throng that Dad described as 'so large Australia could have been declaring war', Mum accompanied Queen Elizabeth, and Dad escorted an absent-minded Prince Philip alongside the mural. Mum had been nervous about what to wear to meet the Queen. Realising the etiquette of wearing a hat, she wrapped a silk ribbon around the top of her gardening hat from the shed, pressing it with steam on a block, drawing upon her training and skills as a milliner. They discussed abstract art as they strolled the length of the mural.

Her Majesty the Queen did not catch the metaphor at first. Dad then pointed out the various aspects of the mural to the Queen and told her about the poem. Her expression transformed into a smile as she started to recognise the fish and sea creatures. She expressed how much she liked the work, saying, 'Frankly, I find it most enjoyable.'[4]

The Duke of Edinburgh seemed more interested in looking at the bright purple carpet beneath his feet. 'What's this all about?' the Prince asked.

'Sydney Harbour,' replied Dad.

'Where's Luna Park?' the Prince responded.

Prince Philip seemed so disinterested that my father renamed him 'Prince Philistine'. On another occasion, he suggested to my father, 'I think that Picasso fellow is rather overrated.'

Dad replied: 'Your Highness, artists, art critics and much of the cultured public would disagree.'

Whereupon the Prince's protective official factotum quietly whispered, 'Mr Olsen, it is poor protocol to contradict the Royal Family.' There was to be a follow-up royal dinner on the *QEII*, but my parents never heard another word about it.

When finally installing the mural in the large, light-filled room of the Sydney Opera House's front foyer, Dad had to deal with tradesmen heckling him, saying things like 'My five-year-old child could do better than that'. Another attacked it with a chisel after Dad had left the site. Others played a game of noughts and crosses on one panel, which is still faintly visible. An envious fellow artist even told a Dobell committee member who commissioned the work that they had made a grave and silly mistake.

The mural changed the tide of Dad's career and, unwittingly, the public perception of our family. At assembly the following Monday morning, Mark Bishop, Cranbrook's headmaster, announced how proud the school was that the Olsen family had attended the opening with *the Queen*. It was the sort of embarrassing moment when everyone turns and looks at you, but I'd had nothing to do with the event. From then on, my nickname at school was 'Prince Tim' and I've never lived it down.

Art was an extraordinary agent of social mobility and ascension. It was shocking how fast things moved and changed, and it seemed absurd to think how much had evolved in a two-year period. We still live in a village—the art world is its own village. It is capricious and impossible to be everybody's cup of tea.

Australia is particularly guilty of punishing its most successful sons and daughters with a very subtle aura of retribution. There is no such thing as uncontested success here, unless it involves a bat or a ball. The worst crime in our culture at the time was to be conspicuous, even worse while wearing a jaunty black beret.

People need to bear this uncomfortable truth in mind when walking through any retrospective of a great artist: the pinnacles they reach attract as much suspicion and avarice as admiration. Dad never let the bastards get him down; he always dusted himself off and got back into the studio. A place of ceasefire, neutral and immune to any outside criticism. His favourite quote was always 'There are lovers and others, and you know what you can do with the others'. Long live the lovers. Paul Keating quoted the same, and attributed it to Dad in federal parliament in describing the attitude of the opposition party when prime minister.

In this light, John's beret is not just a nostalgic stroke of eccentricity, an artistic statement or dandyism; it is his celebration of being a little bit different, his way of bringing the Mediterranean to Australia—and on a practical note, protection from our blazing sun!

When I was about five or six, Mum told us we had a half-sister called Jane. Louise and I found this very strange: we had another sister, but she was not in our lives. Our invisible sister. Dad had never once mentioned her, which made it even stranger as we were so close a family. It was a wonderful gift to discover there was another important part of the family. She nurtured Louise and me: bathed us, played dress-ups with Louise, teased us about drinking the bath water.

Mary Flower, Jane's mother, came from an artistic family. Her great-uncle Cedric Flower had been a very famous Australian artist, so living with an artist was not foreign territory to her. Marrying one, though, was another situation altogether, especially one who was an art student for a decade, working as a cleaner at night to pay the bills. Money was a constant issue, and the strain upon their relationship eventually proved insurmountable. Dad loved his daughter, but after trying to make the relationship with Mary work for so many years, the marriage had simply become untenable. Dad has often been demonised for his failed relationships, but others played their part. When Dad and Mary moved to Melbourne, it was Mary who decided to stay there when Dad returned to Sydney.

When Dad was given the once-in-a-lifetime chance as a young artist to go to Europe, under the patronage of Robert Shaw and Paul Haefliger, it was unthinkable that he would not go. By then the marriage was well and truly over. Dad has spoken of waving goodbye to Sydney on the boat, ecstatic at the possibilities and the adventures to come. He wrote in his journal that Mary wasn't there to wave him off as the *Orion* slipped out through the Heads, but Jane can remember waving goodbye and Mary recalls Dad's mother, my grandmother, looking 'sad and somewhat worried'. There is no doubt that Dad missed Jane, but he felt that the opportunity was too good to miss. Dad has simply said, 'It could be interpreted as ruthlessness, but the fact of the matter is that I had primary needs to deal with which in the end more than justified itself.' I would have done the same thing, given the opportunity, at his age and stage of his career.

Now we were settled and so happy to be back at Watsons Bay (again) after Dunmoochin, Dad and Mum had managed, with difficulty, to track Jane down, and invited her to come and live with us. Mum open-heartedly welcomed her into the family, turning her studio into a bedroom, pleased to just have Jane as part of our family. Mum had no concerns about Jane 'usurping' us, emotionally or financially. For Mum, Jane was John's blood, our half-sister, and that was all that mattered.

Dad has reiterated that never, at any time, was Jane discarded or excluded from our family by choice. He had found it difficult with Mary, who was still bitter at the dissolution of their marriage, constantly trying to drive a wedge between them, and it made Jane feel guilty about being with her father. Building a relationship with Jane was further impeded by the time we had spent abroad, or elsewhere. The reality was that, since the age of four, she had barely seen him.

Jane lived with us for some months. She was very shy, introverted, a teenager. Louise remembers her as being very beautiful. Despite the welcome, it was hard for her to feel part of our family and she soon moved out to live with friends. Sleepy Watsons Bay must have seemed a million miles away from everything after the excitement of living near the city, and, being a teenager, she naturally missed her friends. Regretfully Dad acknowledged that the 'early separation was perhaps too long, at too crucial a time' for them both.[5]

Mum and Dad really did try with Jane, though. Having finished secondary school, Jane went on to attend Desiderius Orban's art school, where Dad had also studied, and the St Albans School of Art. She became a life model at the Julian Ashton Art School for a period, having modelled as a child. Years later, my friend Paul Delprat (who now runs the Julian Ashton Art School) gave me a little painting he had done of her at the time, which I still have and cherish.

Jane soon wanted more independence, so Dad got her a job working at Eric Porter's animation studio in North Sydney. She was later employed by Hanna-Barbera, working on classics such as *Blinky Bill* and *Dot and the Kangaroo* with Yoram Gross Films.

At eighteen, Jane, living in her first share house, had invited us all to a pre-Christmas lunch, but a simple miscommunication meant that we did not attend and Jane, deeply hurt again, disappeared from our lives. Dad did not even know where she was living. Jane moved on with her life, became a teacher, married and had her own family. Life went on. Nearly twenty years would pass before we would see her again.

When I look at *Salute to Five Bells* now, I see it as a work commissioned for its time, and of that time, in fact, a painting before its time. It is nocturnal Sydney mythology played out in a harbour setting, its scenery surrounded by buildings and people, all competing for a view as if they are in a Greek amphitheatre. I cannot imagine a painting replacing it. Dad himself thinks it has well and truly stood the test of time, saying in 2015, after the launch of his book *My Salute to Five Bells*: 'I think the mural is looking *better*. In point of fact, I'm looking at it with experienced eyes. All your children—and I'm talking about paintings—as time wears on them, some don't look so good. But I'm looking at this with, I think, dispassionate eyes and I think it's looking damn good!'

Of course, Dad's work being considered 'before its time' is nothing new. At one of his early shows in the 1950s, Dad says Laurie Thomas got up and said, 'This art is a shock to Australia, before its time. Who is this art sorcerer? Too orphic and sophisticated for an audience that is still grappling with the concept of Spaghetti Bolognese.'

Dad does think the purple carpet in front of the mural is

still 'fucking dreadful' though.[6] Luciano Pavarotti felt the same way in 1983 when he was brought in to perform and to attend a large reception held in his honour. Starting down the stairs, he noticed the colour of the carpet and refused to enter, believing that purple brings bad luck.

The Greeks and their amphitheatres showed the world the meaning of entertainment. Sydney Harbour does the same. Our Opera House is our pantheon, built on a sacred Aboriginal site, reflecting the highs and lows of our history. The Sydney Opera House stands alone as a symbolic object that applies the essential constructs of nature: the cone, cube and sphere (despite the fact that Clive James described it as looking like six nuns in a rugby scrum). It embraces the way that art plays out in music and in theatre, with all the lows, joys and tragedies of human existence.

In the early 1990s, the Sydney Opera House Trust was 'dead keen' to replace Dad's mural with a ceramic version. The artwork had been damaged, and was originally thought to be beyond restoration, due to exposure to UV rays, and fluctuations in room temperature and humidity. Dad's response in a radio interview was that he was prepared to produce a 'dazzling' new version in ceramic, at cost. Instead, the Trust commissioned conservator and sculptor Stephen Coburn of Coburn Fine Art Conservation (and son of artist John Coburn) to restore the work, along with David Stein. Initially Stephen had thought about adding state-of-the-art film to the glass to protect the work from UV damage, but the sheer expanse of glass was too extensive to contemplate. Instead, he realised that the main cause of the deterioration was simply due to the curtains not being drawn by staff after tour groups had moved through—the curtains would be opened to show the hall in all its splendour. Dad had visited with Stephen and a journalist one day and they caught the staff out: they had left the curtains open, even though they had sworn they were closed unless absolutely necessary. The next day an article appeared on the front page of *The Sydney Morning Herald*, citing the damage as simple neglect by the Opera House staff. The curtains have been closed religiously ever since. Louise Herron, the Sydney Opera House's current CEO, is particularly vigilant and concerned about the ongoing conservation of all the artworks. Their value and longevity are considered paramount.

The restoration took over a month, each hardwood panel treated individually. There were areas where the panels had started to delaminate; these were repaired, minimal paint touch-ups completed, and a layer of wax applied. Stephen recalls discovering the area where the workmen had played noughts and crosses. The conservators made it less distinct but felt it should remain as part of the history of the work. After conserving several of Dad's works, Stephen has found that many people find the works enticing and have a childlike tendency to try to contribute to them, making their own marks. The option of replacing the mural with a more durable work, such as a ceramic, is still being tabled, and was raised again in 2017.

Stephen's father, John Coburn, had his own Sydney Opera House dramas when he designed the stunning theatre curtains in 1969, at the same time as Dad was creating the mural. The monumental, vibrant curtains with their bold abstract imagery were an undeniable focus of attention, too much so for some directors and set designers, who felt that they overwhelmed their own set designs. John Coburn said he never received any payment for the curtains, the monies going in full to his agent, but he 'got the glory'.[7] Years later it transpired that the payment had gone to Lucien Dray, Australian agent for the Aubusson Tapestry Workshop in France, who had disappeared without a trace, still owing Coburn and the Workshop to this day. Coburn and his wife, Barbara, attended the opening with Mum and Dad, but they got to join the Queen and Prince Philip on the royal launch afterwards, unlike my parents. After Dad was interviewed by Michael Parkinson on the BBC, we heard that it had got back to Prince Philip that Dad had referred to him as 'Prince Philistine', and they were both barred.

6

INTO THE VALLEY

When my father finished the Sydney Opera House mural, he felt that he had covered all the poetic, romantic and colourful metaphors of a hauntingly beautiful harbour city, as well as the tidal shifts of sea-life aesthetics, with all the concepts of a Mediterranean village applied. Camp Cove and Lady Jane Beach, which would be declared Sydney's first legal nudist beach in 1976, had become popular destinations; parking in the street became impossible in summer, and there was a constant stream of foot traffic passing by, with transistor radios blaring. Dad was unable to work in the studio with the distraction.

Watsons Bay changed when Lady Jane Beach became sexy. For all its intentions of being a place for innocent, sun-seeking naturists, it was quickly ruined by a haunting of peeping Toms. Soon the amount of unsavoury people outnumbered those who just wanted a daylight skinny dip. The perversity of Sydney had descended to our backyard. Going there on a few occasions out of curiosity, it was not uncommon to stumble across some creep masturbating behind a rock. There was a paedophile who used to stalk me at Camp Cove and kept asking me to go on walks.

I relented one day and as soon as I walked out of the sight of others, he started trying to pull down my trunks and my only escape route was to dive into the harbour and swim as if a shark was chasing me. Once again, I kept this to myself, somehow feeling that it was my fault.

I had already had a more distressing experience of this kind, aged nine, at a Crusader Christian camp. One of the camp leaders was a children's television producer and, after I had done a casting for the film *Storm Boy*, the camp leader had told my parents that I could be an actor and convinced them to allow me to go to the camp in Kangaroo Valley to do some casting over a long weekend. One late afternoon he took me down to the river, a small film camera in his hand, and said that he needed to get a shot from high up in a tree. 'I need you to climb,' he said. 'Let me see if you are strong enough.' He bent over me at the base of the trunk and pressed his hard penis against my back. When I felt it, survival instinct propelled me to run, scrambling up a cliff, my face pelted with leaves. Suddenly a huge kangaroo, at least twice my height, rose up above me, ghostly among the ashy leaves. I barely registered the danger, so strong was my need to flee and just get home again. I was traumatised, too scared to say anything as he had threatened to kill me if I told anyone what had happened.

This incident damaged me profoundly. I have carried a deep sense of shame and lack of worth for most of my life, something that is commonly recognised in victims of abuse. Later in life, this emotional pain may have enhanced my desire to medicate and imbibe, to subdue and anaesthetise my own feelings.

My story is all too common and could have been so much worse. The irony is that, when I was tossed into the time warp of an all boys' boarding school with old traditions—an environment not without its dangers of abuse—I was at least shielded

from the decadence and the loose boundaries of the art world
that my parents inhabited.

Around the time that Watsons Bay lost its innocence as a family
destination for daytrippers and became the subject of public
notoriety, my parents decided to leave Sydney.

The bush also beckoned. Having befriended documentary
filmmakers Bob Raymond, Charles (Ken) Taylor and Vincent
Serventy, Dad had embarked on desert art, science and natural-
history expeditions. Perhaps Mum, too, needed the reflected
solitude of tall trees. We gave up Watsons Bay around 1973, selling
the house for $40,000. In 2018, renovated by John Normyle,
it was touted as the creative birthplace of some of Australia's
major masterpieces and sold for more than $4.5 million, with
no car space.[1] To us, as a young and initially struggling family,
the cottage at 12 Cliff Street had represented a thrifty fisherman's
paradise, an artist's retreat. Now it is prime real estate.

On leaving Watsons Bay, my parents bought a five-acre block
of land in a bush valley in Dural. It was 45 minutes out of Sydney,
but it could just as well have been a decade away. Ku-ring-gai
Chase National Park may have been a great place for Skippy, but
after my previous city beach life, it was no playground or adventure land for me. There, my parents struggled to find the right
architect to build their home. Mum and Dad had differences: a
whitewashed Pettit+Sevitt modernist display home could not be
agreed upon. Finally, Richard Leplastrier, then a young architecture maverick, signed on, but halfway through the build he
disappeared to India, leaving us with one large room and three
bedrooms separated by sliding doors—my mother's vision to
keep the house Zen and Japanese. It was an art ashram with a

central fireplace and an old, long table to entertain, but a disaster for any married couple wanting to maintain their intimacy with children sleeping on the other side of wafer-thin rice-paper walls. It was always an unfinished home, not a private environment where adults could be adults.

My mother developed a morning ritual of nude yoga on the verandah overlooking the sanctuary of the valley and its intimate bushland. She was completely holistic about this activity, not sexual. Once I overheard my father discussing how provocative he found this. 'In the end she was rarely in the mood for sensual intimacy,' he said, perhaps justifying seeking intimacy elsewhere. Yet this was not a way of punishing my father; it was a survival mechanism, shutting down that chakra within herself in self-protection and preservation. For years Mum had ignored Dad's indiscretions, and ultimately it had affected their relationship, the loss of trust and the hurt making her withdraw, internalising her emotions.

The breakdown of trust is always the catalyst for the end. I have come to learn this from my own experiences, and to realise just how much everything we say and do resonates. All words and actions have consequences.

The house had its mixed blessings being in a valley. Great to make art in, but lousy to make love and bring up teenage kids. Louise found it disturbing, a place unforgiving of human tres- pass. We had a stalker once who prank-called to say he could see Louise naked through the bathroom window that looked up to the hill above. Dad and I for a while would walk up that hill at dusk, tomahawk in hand, but never caught the phantom stalker. I still suspect it was just one of my school mates prank-calling.

In the 1970s, many people went 'back to nature', and a lot of them found it hard—even a tiny bit boring. There was the physical isolation of living in a bush house. Dural was down a steep driveway that in bad weather became inaccessible. Often after a big rain we would find ourselves trapped by a slide of mud sucked down into the valley. The atmosphere could be ominous. There were caves close by with Aboriginal carvings; a skeleton was found under a nearby cliff on the adjacent property; there were spirits in that valley that seemed to be there with us. There was one particular old angophora tree, with a smooth pink bark rather like a Francis Bacon painting, and twisting boughs like append-ages. The area's folklore told of the local Indigenous people once burying their dead around that tree as they believed the forms of the tree were reincarnations of the dead. We had one such 'Grandfather Tree' off Mum's studio that had survived the ravages of countless bushfire seasons; we buried our pets there, and the ashes of two of my grandparents, believing that the tree had incarnate virtues. It was the tallest, oldest tree in the valley.

Flower-market poachers would invade the valley come spring, stealing all the magnificent, newly bloomed red waratah flowers—a terrible personal violation for my mother, as bad as if someone had broken into the house and stolen our art. She would not let the fire brigade burn back the scrub in winter; the untouched bush was perfect in her eyes. The risk of fire, of even losing the house, was less important to her than keeping the native flowers that grew around her studio. She believed that burning back at a different time to when the traditional Aboriginal people would have burned the bush was too disruptive. She particularly loved the native flannel flowers, wattles and grevilleas that blossomed each season.

We had an outdoor kitchen with a woodfired oven in which Dad would roast chickens or stew paellas. Bob Raymond, Vincent Serventy and Don Dunstan all trouped through. One day Alan Davie, the acclaimed Scottish painter, turned up. Dad showed him around and, in the midst of the grand tour, a small picture of my mother's caught his eye. 'Excuse me, John, but who painted that?' he asked. 'I did,' Mum said softly. He roared, in his rich accent, 'Oh, Valerie, you have such a rare sensibility.' Dad coughed, then hurried him onto the next grand Olsen landscape.

At dusk, the valley had the melancholy of a Frederick McCubbin bushscape. I felt trapped there, isolated. Used to running around the seaside, the sun carnival, now I was stuck in a lonely valley in the midst of puberty with nothing to do and no friends in sight. Coming to the end of an experimental decade for my father, this was a time of tumult and restlessness for him and for me. The landlocked melancholy of Dural was not suited to two innately restless beings.

Yet the valley was intimate enough for my mother's introspective, sensitive understanding of nature and her love of haiku. She loved the quality of being lost in time, but it was an impossible place to keep a virile painter like my father and a pubescent boy who had grown up by the sea. Ultimately, with no splayed landscape to view, and far from any pub with a few artists at the end of the day, it proved too tucked away and too lugubrious for my celebratory father. After his outback trips, his new work had taken on a new aerial perspective of landscape, a perspective not explored by any non-Indigenous artist at the time.

During my childhood, the thing that had always made me feel safest was waking up in the dark hours of the night and hearing my parents in loving conversation, either from the kitchen or the bedroom. Throughout their relationship, the intellectual connection they shared was very strong. During dinner conversations, discussing art exhibitions or poetry, there was never a sense of strained competition—even if someone like Patrick White was at the table. Mum's style was never boastful or domineering, and her pride in Dad was on a more spiritual level. Never competitive, she considered his success to be her success. She was also a deep thinker and ardent listener, with seasoned experience with the orators of her age.

Yet always there were undercurrents, subtexts we young adults were too inexperienced to grasp. There were times when my mother was unsettled, and I would assume it was because of one of Dad's fleeting indiscretions. It was these undercurrents of tension and vulnerability that made me more conscious of the fact that how you feel about yourself is more important than what society feels about you. What kept Mum composed was her dignity in the midst of the embarrassment of the blatant betrayal. Mum always said that dignity will be rewarded within yourself. Mum lived for many years thinking that my father would return. In the end, she found companionship with other men who treated her with more respect. Dad often criticised Mum's esoteric approach to her art and perhaps underestimated the power of their conversations, which affected the content and direction of much of his own art. During the years of his relationship my mother, his work evolved in leaps and bounds—more than in any other period.

Dural is the house where the dream ended and my father left. Three months before the fall, I recall him holding Mum, saying: 'Not only is your mother my great love, but she is also my best friend.' This made the whole event so much more confusing.

I had boarded at Cranbrook for a year after we had moved to Dural, but my parents were missing me and, when I was twelve, they decided to take me out of Cranbrook to be a day boy at The King's School in North Parramatta, about 15 kilometres south of Dural. In addition, they were concerned that there was an epidemic of heroin coming through Sydney's Eastern Suburbs. Up at Kings Cross, Sydney's red-light district, unemployed Vietnam War vets had begun dealing drugs to wealthy kids. At a privileged school in an atmosphere of rebellion and experimentation—the young heir James McGrath would die of an overdose in 1977— my parents did not want me to fall into that kind of crowd.

At the age of fourteen, I told my father to fuck off for the first time and he chased me out of the house with a wine bottle. He threw it at me, making sure not to hit me, but having an object thrown at me symbolised that I had actually gone too far.

Puberty is always a turning point. From boyhood coming into manhood, rugby and rowing saved me. That, and a rough-necked bunch of country boys who couldn't give a rat's arse about art.

Goodbye bohemia, hello King's School.

7

OF CABBAGES AND KINGS

Admittance into one of Sydney's 'Great Public Schools' (GPS) in the 1970s (and even now) was not just a matter of paying the fees. The process—application, exam, interview—was abetted by generational attendance and intellectual, physical or financial assets. Mum's cousins had gone to The King's School, so there was the lineage, and my prowess on the rugby field, having played for Cranbrook's Firsts, was a fast track.

Dad, in an uncustomary use of few words, said to the school bursar in my pre-entry interview, 'He's in the A team', but this was still a slog for our family, and Dad stuck his neck out to get me in. They still had to have references, and those came from Rudy Komon, Dad's dealer at the time, and the Hon. John Holt, then a member of the New South Wales Legislative Council and the husband of one of Dad's former students from The Bakery. Holt's son, Henry, had also gone to Cranbrook with me and then on to King's, later becoming an artist and potter, working with Bruce Arthur on Dad's tapestries at Arthur's Dunk Island Tapestry Atelier.

No one was making money from art in Australia then, and Dad still jokes that he paid my school fees from the proceeds of frogs, because for years in a tough art market, as he puts it, 'They were the only damn things that would sell.' Today, still, everyone loves and wants an 'Olsen frog'.

King's was very much a bush-cocky, country-hick school, full of big, lumbering country boys who were good at football and rowing. Australia's oldest independent school, it was founded in 1831 with the blessing of King William IV of England to educate the sons of British officials and officers, and to build the next generation of leaders. With a massive 148-hectare campus with its own postcode, King's was the first school to play rugby, and possibly cricket, in Australia. The inaugural rugby game was played against Newington. When I arrived, the school uniform had hardly changed in 150 years: a military *Sgt. Pepper's*–like uniform with bright lapels and dark pants, with a red stripe that ran down the outside of each leg, topped off with an olive-green slouch hat with a red band. Looking back, it was such an incongruous uniform in a modern society, more eccentric than anything an artist would wear in the creative world. Regardless of any physical discipline that was dished out, wearing that uniform was more character building than attending the school itself. It was a school with a limited cultural history, but the uniform did have a certain style.

Ultimately my father got sick of driving me to King's when I slept in and missed the bus, and it became obvious that the only way he could get a solid day in the studio—and for me to be a real part of that predominantly bush boys' school—was for me to become a boarder. The 'salt of the earth' country boys I befriended as a boarder either had a very deep sensibility, or a barbaric understanding of Australia. But they were all great characters who taught me more about honesty and mateship than any tricky city kid.

My first years at King's were quite brutal, and a bit bloodstained. Having become a boarder, it seemed that the day boys felt I had abandoned the pack. One student, a bully, decided to king-hit me from behind. In a moment of pure self-defence, in a fight-or-flight reaction, I swung around in response with a punch that split his eye open. My punishment was cursory at best. The head-master implied that I had performed something of a service in putting down the school bully, and I was suddenly a 'made man'. Yet violence is not an inevitable rite of passage or initiation in young manhood, or ever appropriate in life. In recent times there have been tragic repercussions from single-punch assaults. I have never hit a person since.

King's tested me in ways that were beyond emotional and physical. It was a stark contrast to a childhood in which Louise and I had sat silent and dumbfounded by the loudest voices and longest stories at the table. Boarding was a survivalist environ-ment where you lived on instinct as well as the loyalty of friends. Going out into the bush with my new schoolmates was a great adventure: rounding up cattle, being rouseabouts in the shearing shed, helping dip sheep. The food consisted of meat and maybe three veg, with large glasses of orange-flavoured water. When these boys went on holidays, they worked. From an early age they each developed a strong work ethic and a character that did not always carry into the classroom. Once a sign went up on the large school noticeboard announcing, 'Fencing classes this Friday night'. A gathering of bush boys turned up, hoping to eventually impress their fathers by learning the finer art of keeping cattle and sheep in, and dingos out, only to discover a Frenchman dressed in white canvas tights and a protective mask, wielding a sword.

In my early years there, King's was a highly challenging school, distinctly establishment, militant in leaning and rough as guts. It was at King's where I first met people who detested Aboriginal Australians, describing them in racist terms as 'coons' or 'boongs', which I have always found highly offensive. It was hard to grasp the hate and the sheer prejudice for its own sake. King's educated land boys, and those who excelled academically found that to return to the family property was not as intellectually stimulating as working in city jobs. Many city private schools could be held responsible for this kind of brain drain in the bush, though after years of corporate life, many did return to the farms for a more honest, hardworking existence.

Dad would often come to watch me play rugby. He would make a grand entrance in his mustard-coloured Land Cruiser, driving onto the field, when all the other parents left their cars in the car park. He would jump out wearing jumbo cords, a red scarf and a beret. We were out in the rugby field packing into a scrum when some wag said, 'Look at Olsen's old man, he must be a poofter.' I was elated to see after the match John at one end of the field charming the country wives, with every yummy mummy around him eating out of his hand, engrossed in his stories and witticisms. While all the fathers were in a collective male herd, knotted together in their Akubra hats, moleskins and tweed jackets, chatting fertiliser. I announced to my teammates, 'Well look over there now fellas, you tell me, whose father is the poofter?' My father's European flair and charisma could work its charm on any sector of Australian society.

At King's I carved out achievements that were really mine alone, albeit in sports: as stroke of the Junior Rowing Eight, captain of the 14As rugby team, and a school swimming champion— in which, on reflection, I had a clear advantage, having spent years living at the beach. Sporting achievements in this environment were more important than creative or intellectual ones, but sport taught me what it meant to excel. It was sport, not art, that defined my popularity.

When I became captain of the 14As rugby team, we weren't a particularly good team, but played against Sydney Boys High down at the oval in Centennial Park on a regular basis. It was a real arm wrestle. One day, as a courtesy to the opposing team's captain, I went to shake hands after the match. He obviously felt that we had stolen the game from them, even though it was a draw, because as I extended my hand, the only hand that came forward was a solid punch in the face. Our coach immediately rushed in and got hit by the captain as well, and then suddenly there was a flurry of fists as everyone else dived in—parents, teachers, everyone on the teams. It became a huge free-for-all.

After leaving school, I went on to play rugby for the Mosman Whales in the northern suburbs of Sydney, near my grand-mother's house. One of my teammates was Todd Hogan, son of comedian Paul 'Crocodile Dundee' Hogan. One might have expected him to be one of those vocal parents spurring on their sons to run harder, or yelling out that the referee was a cheat. But Hogan was a quiet, loving father who never drew attention to himself, melting into the crowd of onlookers. He would watch the game, and then he and Todd would just head off home. The legendary celebrity truly was just a normal man.

My time at King's was not without mentors and role models. One teacher told me repeatedly that I would never amount to much, but there were others who were encouraging and supportive. We had an art teacher called Tony Bourke, though we called him Bushy Bourke as he wore a toupée. He was a marvellously articu-late man who could talk about art extremely well. Having got a teaching degree myself, I realise, in hindsight, he was not really cut out to be a teacher and was unfairly ridiculed and teased by the boys. When Bushy's back was turned, there would be wet clay and paint tossed around the room as if we were a collective Jackson Pollock. Art was not considered a serious subject despite the fact that artists such as painter John Firth-Smith were alumni of King's, and the great surrealist artist Jeffrey Smart and British modern master David Hockney had both spent time at the school, Smart as an art teacher in the 1950s and Hockney as a visiting artist. They were close friends. In my day, there was one art teacher for 1500 boys—a disgrace, now that I look back on it.

My father, being on the Board of Trustees at the AGNSW, arranged a tour of the gallery for King's art students. On arrival, Dad told us to roam the various rooms by ourselves while he and Bushy went straight upstairs to the restaurant—hardly the guided tour we expected. After a few hours, we all boarded the bus out the front at the required time and waited until Dad and Bushy reappeared. There had been men out the front of the gallery all day repaving the front path, and when Dad and Bushy (both clearly full of chardonnay) stepped off the stairs they went straight into the wet concrete up to their ankles. It was hysterical. Dad caught a taxi home, while Bushy slept all the way back to school and never lived it down.

Another good teacher was my flamboyant English teacher Peter Fay, a truly cultured man who the boys nicknamed 'Gay Fay' and who looked like Tom Baker in *Doctor Who*, with his foppish hair and long scarves. His classroom pinboard was full of cut-outs of important artworks from various books, including, I was proud to see, an image of my father's tapestry *Joie de Vivre*.

When I left King's, it never occurred to me that one day I would contribute to the school's major acquisitional art prize for professional artists, co-founded with Sue Hewitt (former director of Christie's). The school now has an impressive collection. Over the last 25 years, The King's School Art Prize has been awarded to some of Australia's leading contemporary artists, among them Nicholas Harding, Rodney Pople, Geoffrey de Groen, Gloria Petyarre, Aida Tomescu and Jacqui Stockdale.[1] This was my attempt to change the reputation of the school as a culture-less institution.

Unlike some of my fellow students, I look back at my experience at King's fondly. At the time I did not particularly enjoy boarding school, but it was easier than living around Dad's overt personality, despite our love for each other. At school I liked being different but regret that I often played the fool in an attempt to win friends, a behaviour I took into my adult life for too long. This was a story and an act that did not serve me well, and ultimately needed to be supported by drink.

Show me your friends and I will show you your future. At King's I met lifelong loyal friends, including Ari Droga, Ian Jedlin, Martin Upton and his younger brother Andrew, the playwright. They are the type of friends you can always rely on. People say that you are lucky if you can count your true friends on one hand; with mine, I feel truly blessed.

Ari Droga was a superb skier. He grew up at Thredbo, where his father ran the ski fields at Kerry Packer's resorts, and is one of the few Australians to ever represent Cambridge in the intervarsity skiing race—the oldest team ski race in history—where he won a Blue. I used to love staying with Ari in the lodge in Perisher as it was full of art; there were works by Brett Whiteley, Fred Williams and Roger Kemp everywhere. It was like being in an art museum in the snow. Ari is my son's godfather, and I am godfather to his son, Emile.

While a founding principal and partner of one of the world's largest privately managed infrastructure investment funds, Ari is equally passionate about the visual arts; he has sat on the board of the Biennale of Sydney, and is currently the chair of the MCA Foundation. Ari's brother David is an award-winning advertising guru who founded his own firm, Droga5, after a successful career with Saatchi & Saatchi worldwide for many years. Droga5 refers to his position as the youngest of the five Droga children. One of Ari's other brothers, Bo, who lives in Miami, is a sculptor and has shown with me in the New York gallery. Martin Upton is another dear friend and we have travelled together. Likewise, I am godfather to Martin's son Tibbo, a promising filmmaker.

There are also those boys from the bush. When the Royal Easter Show is on in Sydney, they come to town and ring me to catch up for a beer. I love that they still call me 'Olly', and I cherish their sentiment and their ability as solid characters to never change—other than the weathering of their faces from the blazing sun, like corrugated iron on a woolshed. At our 40-year King's School reunion, one of my old country mates said, 'Hey Olly, is your father still painting? The way he's going he'll be painting the inside of his coffin at his own funeral.'

Some people look at the institutional side of a strict private school as a spiritual downfall, a form of socially acceptable incarceration. King's was certainly a mixed blessing. It implemented discipline and structure, instead of allowing me a life of roaming around free. You could not find a more different environment to that of the hippie commune of Dunmoochin, attending heady but riveting artists' dinners. My background made me a little different, yet it ultimately made me feel free to be myself.

Going to King's enabled me to see the world in a different way. As I came to understand and combine my upbringing and my education, I was to learn my own voice. It took years, though, to make sense of it all, oscillating between these two worlds, seeking authenticity.

My first trip overseas without my parents was eventful. I had been raised in a gypsy caravan, always rolling, hardly questioning the discomforts and oddities of a life on the move. But to travel out of the shadow of my father—his tastes, his terms, his tattered and legend-soaked map—was liberating.

It was 1977. Dad picked me up from school at the end of term and said: 'I have organised a little trip for you. You are about to get inoculated because you are taking a flight to China; you are going on a trip with Eugenie McGrath and fourteen Ascham girls.' (Eugenie was the daughter of art critic Sandra McGrath. She attended Ascham, where Mum had taught.) This was way back before communism in China loosened to commerce; we were some of the first Australian tourists to enter what was still called 'Red' China. I was fifteen.

China was astonishing, eye opening. It was before the country had really opened up: few cars, mainly bicycles, masses of people. Everyone was in grey or dark blue uniforms, wearing caps with red stars. We were chased around by an old man who had lived through the Boxer Rebellion. The frail man with a wooden stick looked like a line drawing by Hergé. Some called us *gweilos*— white devils—many of the people having never seen Westerners before. Early one evening, I slipped out alone to wander the streets as the sun set. Outside each of the small houses, people of all ages were cooking over fires on the streets. There was a man playing guitar from a songbook on one street corner; spotting a rare foreigner, he started playing 'Waltzing Matilda'—long before Qantas pulled the heartstrings of every overseas Australian with Peter Allen's 'I Still Call Australia Home'.

There was hardly a car to be seen day or night, and the streets were extraordinarily primitive, lined with open spittoons, swollen with thousands of bikes, so all you could hear were bells. The markets were full of vegetables, poultry, live snakes, live frogs plus roasted ducks suspended from hooks. Every morning there were people doing tai chi in the parks, the moving masses dressed in Maoist blue cotton, all unified by a blanket of humid smog. I bought badges and a cap. We visited Mao Tse-tung (Chairman Mao, Mao Zedong) lying in state; saw the newly discovered Terracotta Army, still half buried; and walked the Great Wall. To have experienced China at this time, at this age, was a true privilege.

The Chinese made sure we had a heroic impression of Mao Tse-tung, and while it was evident how communism had formed a structure whereby the population was clothed and fed, and poverty alleviated to a degree, it is inconceivable for me to revere a man who saw religion as the enemy of humanity and a form of rebellion. For me, communism represented political power over creativity, spirituality and the freedom of the individual. Napoleon was right when he said: 'China is a sleeping lion. Let her sleep, for when she wakes she will shake the world.' While not being an advocate for its regime, in China there was a loving accord between the people, a communal spirit of cooperation, that was clearly evident. I came from the dog-eat-dog environment of Australia with its tall poppy conundrum, and China taught me about collective consciousness.

I nearly had to share a room with Mrs Danziger, the

headmistress of Ascham, because they had overbooked the hotel. With Mrs Danziger being such an authority figure, the girls at the time thought this was hilarious. Despite travelling with a gaggle of schoolgirls at fifteen, there was no frisson with anyone. The Ascham girls were rather condescending to the token male. Maybe it was just our age.

I struggled with my major work for my HSC matriculation. My series of Henry Moore–inspired sculptures had exploded in the kiln. In the end, Dad and I collaborated on my major work and we made a portfolio of still-life drawings in homage to and inspired by the master Italian artist Giorgio Morandi. Despite his help, I still didn't get a great mark. My father takes great delight in knowing he failed the HSC. I wish I could find those drawings for sentimental reasons alone.

Dad was working with poet Jennifer Rankin and her then husband David Rankin, an artist and printmaker, on a book of poems and drawings called *Earth Hold*. David Rankin's arrival at Dural had been a lifesaver for Dad; he was depressed and frustrated, caught up in the nightmare of the house build and Mum's indecision, isolated in what had become an oppressive environment. He was spending more and more time back in the city, leaving Mum and Louise alone. After boarding at King's, I soon moved out of home.

Dad's relationship with Noela Hjorth developed quickly. Noela used to ring the house constantly, and often Mum would answer the phone. Mum would ask her the nature of her inquiry; Noela would reply that she was a finalist in an art prize and needed to speak to John to enlighten him about elements of her work before the final judging.

After Noela finally spoke with Dad, they planned to meet in Melbourne, got together and that was that. Mum thought it would just blow over, but it did not. Dad moved out. Mum was completely shattered, broken; Dad is a hard act to follow. It took her a long time to get over him, but she did.

In October 1980, Dad wrote in his journal: 'Valerie is completely bewildered by my leaving her, mortified and crushed. Louise is also in a state of shock. I feel absolutely terrible about it.'[2]

Like Mum and Louise, I, too, was devastated.

8

PEARLY: ALMOST PARADISE

In art history, no matter how detailed, some places get lost. If two generations of American artists, from Jackson Pollock to Peter Beard, had the Hamptons as their oceanic idyll, a small group of Sydney painters had theirs: Pearl Beach.

Pearl Beach, or 'Pearly' as we called it, is nestled into a hamlet just north of Sydney where the bush meets the sea, and its atmosphere of 1960s idealism and a natural aesthetic lasted into the late 1980s. When we bought our two-bedroom weatherboard, Bower Bird Cottage, the houses were unpretentious shacks and the landscape was an intimate terrarium: a microclimate of primeval ferns and tall, swaying angophora trees and gums that nursed a creek running down to the beach from the waterfall above.

The beach itself was pristine and glowed like the string of pearls it was named after. With its sanctuary of native birds, sociable goannas and bush turkeys, it really was a jewel, nearly every street appropriately named after a gemstone: we lived on Tourmaline Avenue, intersected by Diamond Road, leading to Opal Close. We held on to the house at Pearly for 30 years, a respite from the heat and enclosure of rural Dural, and a reminder of the idyll of Watsons Bay. We had bought at the suggestion of Vincent and Carol Serventy, for whom Pearly was home. Soon after, artist Michael Johnson and his wife Margot moved there, too, and his close friend Brett Whiteley would visit, but presiding over the different generations and disparate art styles was the soft-spoken John Coburn, accompanied by his wife Barbara and their children, Kristen, Stephen and Daniel.

We would all picnic together on Goanna Rock, a cliff over-looking the Hawkesbury. It was weekender distance from Sydney, so there were frequent visitors: Bob Raymond, filmmaker and founding producer of ABC's *Four Corners*, visited often; the novelist and Booker prize winner Peter Carey turned up one year. Playwright David Williamson and his journalist wife Kristin bought into the village, and they invited theatre director John Bell and actor Anna Volska along.

In between the beach picnics, we would splash around, play pétanque, scramble along bush tracks to visit the caves nearby with the Aboriginal rock art and engravings of the Guringai people,[1] and talk, sing and read poetry late into the night. We used to sing, 'Pearly, Pearly / Go to bed late, get up early.'

I became a summertime bush romantic, losing my virginity listening to Fleetwood Mac and Boz Scaggs, and for the first time tried smoking pot. Most of my friends were the other artists' kids, the second generation of dreamers, given a place to hide thanks to the utopian dreams of the elders.

The history of Australian art hinges on depictions of the landscape, and it was fascinating to see the way everyone took different yields from the same crop. Dad described Pearl Beach as a 'Secret Garden'. He loved the simplicity and privacy of the horseshoe-shaped bay, the way it was sheltered from the wind and the wagging tongues of Sydneysiders.

Vincent Serventy—often known as the 'father of conservationism in Australia'—and his wife Carol were the pioneers of passionate conservation in the area. Their advocacy and documentary work hinged on the intimacy they cultivated within their surrounds. 'Vincent was green before greenery became fashionable,' Tony Stephens wrote in his obituary for Vincent in 2007.[2] As conservationists, the Serventys had fought successfully against mining in the Dryandra Woodland in Western Australia,[3] prevented oil leases on the Great Barrier Reef and campaigned for greater public access to the Sydney Harbour foreshores. Vincent also wrote numerous books on nature and the environment, and it was through him that I was first made aware of global warming: at a picnic at Goanna Rock in the 1970s, he made a speech about the 'frog in hot water' fable. A frog will immediately jump out of hot water, so the story goes, but will boil to death if the water is heated slowly.

John Coburn was kind and genteel. As an artist, he taught me that one does not have to communicate complex themes to be successful, and I have drawn on that advice as a gallerist. His paintings stick by an aesthetic formula, a purity, yet despite their simplicity his work has always maintained its interest and authenticity. It had its decorative virtues but also an intellectual rigour. Like Dad, John was a tapestry artist, and I once heard him say that he used the echo of the sea at Pearly as a mantra for his works. He was also an advocate for the Catholic Church, and a lot of his work is now found in religious settings.[4]

Then there was Michael Johnson, the celebrated abstractionist, known for his interest in the diversity of the environment and nature, especially the ocean. One of his most significant quotes is about the waters around Pearl Beach: 'Probably the strongest influence that brought about the metaphor of water, darkness and skies was the mystery of fishing at Lobster Beach at Broken Bay.'

His daughter Anna and I are still great friends. A few years younger than me, she was very confident and colourful. I remember her as not being much of a beach girl, preferring to read under a tree by the creek. It was all so relaxed that everyone could do what they pleased, coming together at the end of the day 'en famille' to eat. Anna was the designated salad maker. Another child of an artist, third generation in fact, Anna has paved her own artistic way as an art writer and artist in her own right, often speaking of her father's work and reflections on growing up in an 'art' family. Anna helped me start to bring this book into being, especially with her understanding of our unique upbringing.

In all, Pearly was a subtropical bush scene that functioned as an intellectual salon and playground at the same time; a resting place for artists, actors and writers who valued cerebral company and understood the therapeutic and creative draw of the land-scape. Most flamboyant were the playwrights and actors. When John Bell and David Williamson turned up, it represented a rare meeting between thespians and painters—creatures with an ego of a very different stripe. It was an exciting mix, and a privilege to be present.

It was also a calm setting for some violent upheavals, offering an inherent support network when needed. The Coburn kids lost their mum when Barbara got cancer, and then, in turn, they were supportive of Mum when my father left. John Coburn, his new wife Doreen and their children were very kind to Mum. Collectively they understood the grief that comes with change. It was tragic how much loss was sustained by a handful of close-knit families in the span of ten years.

Naturally, over 30 years, there were moral and physical lessons to be learned from the landscape, too. We nearly lost Louise at Pearl Beach on Boxing Day 1980, when there was a huge swell off Sydney. Louise was walking along the beach with a couple of friends, including Matthew Serventy, when a long wave swept them into the water. Matthew had enough survival knowledge to swim sideways across the current to reach the shore, but Louise tried to swim straight in and was dragged out, her tiny pale face bobbing out in the water. I jumped on my surfboard and paddled out in an attempt to reach her. Eventually, a rescue helicopter came and tried to catch her with a harness, but a huge wave dragged her under. After several attempts, she managed to grab the harness and was landed back on the beach, fragile, cold and in shock.

When she disappeared under the wave, it took me straight back to a day when I had been very small and had pretended to drown her in the bathtub. The sickening reality of my actions became so real that I was flooded with shame and futile remorse for my petty childhood jealousy of Louise. I realised then how much I loved my sister and how profoundly we would all miss her if we lost her. It was a turning point for me and our relationship. We are now devoted to one another and talk almost every day.

It seems that artist communities often turn against themselves. Gradually Pearl Beach became a place of artist politics and, when Dad left with Noela, Mum rented out the house as a form of small income. We slowly stopped going there. After we patched a verandah around the house, it was sold and Mum bought a house in Bronte a few years later. Yet Pearl Beach remains an escape from the city, for artists and creatives, in direct contrast to the glamour of nearby Palm Beach.

Shortly after Dad left Mum, he had a lunch with dealer David Reid and artists Tim Storrier and John Firth-Smith. A few months later he decided to move on from Rudy Komon, joining David and his picture-framer father, Steven, at the new David Reid Gallery space at Mary Place. The Reids had rented three floors in the Paddington building from owner-architect Julius Bokor, who had envisaged the premises as an architectural studio and gallery; dealers Gallery A and Barry Stern were participating when David Reid joined them. Having Dad in the Reid stable was a real feather in their cap, and a series of high-profile artists soon joined him, including Coburn, Robert Jacks, Suzanne Archer and Liz Coats. In 1980, there was also a joint exhibition of Brett Whiteley's works at Mary Place, organised by Robin Gibson, which set the Sydney art scene alight with excitement.

The gallery was being run in style, with lavish entertaining and glamorous openings. It was a heady time, with hit show following hit show, and their success seemed guaranteed. Unfortunately, while the champagne was flowing, the rent and bills remained unpaid, including payments to the artists. This was not a Rudy Komon set-up: with the Reids, the artists were only to be paid when work sold, and even then the payments did not eventuate. The trust Dad and the other artists had placed in Reid was completely broken; not only did Reid refuse to pay them but he also refused to return any of their works.

In desperation, Bokor had no choice but to lock the Reids out and, on one dramatic day in March 1982, organised for all of the works to be picked up. David was seen grappling with the shippers at the door. None of the artists ever received the money they were owed—which, in some cases, was a considerable sum, especially for Dad. Left stranded and without payment for several years, this was a difficult time for the artists involved. They all moved on, and the Reids quietly retreated. Years later, a member of the Reid family circulated a rumour that the gallery had failed because Dad and the other artists had somehow ripped off David and Steven, bankrupting them. (It's funny how history can be rewritten at will, especially since I knew that the only person my father would bankrupt would be himself.) But the art world knew the truth, and never forgot. It became a cautionary tale: 'Beware of the art dealer.'

It was at the Mary Place gallery that Dad and I saw each other again, six months after he had left, when we ran into each other on a staircase. Looking him straight in the eye, I asked, 'Why did you leave Mum?'

He looked at me coldly and said, 'Well, you left first.'

'But I wasn't married to her!' I burst out.

He replied, almost absent-mindedly, 'Well, so be it', and continued his descent. All that could be heard was the echo of his footsteps in the empty stairwell. Like my father, I, too, have a tendency to avoid confrontation.

Dad joined Barry Stern after the debacle with David Reid, holding his first exhibition with Barry in 1981. Barry had courted Dad with beautiful raw-silk vests and cravats—he knew how to schmooze Dad with flamboyance. Overtly homosexual, he was a complete charmer, and knew how to turn a quid. Dad would call him 'Sir Basil', and whenever he did it to his face, Barry would say, 'Stop it, stop it, John! You know how much I would love a knighthood!'

Another legendary host and lover of entertaining, Barry once held a luncheon party for the Maharaja of Baroda for 200 people, which Dad wryly noted in his journal as an example of the extravagance of dealers while delaying payments to their artists.

Barry had offered me a job in my art apprentice days, but Mum and Dad were concerned about me being a 'pretty boy'. Rex Irwin was alright, they thought, but they drew the line at Barry. Barry told me once, 'In our business you must remember, there is someone to love every picture, you just have to find them. Rather like us.' It was a prudent statement and a lovely sentiment. He also said to Dad, 'Art is like little jars of tea on a shelf. Some stand out more than others.'

Dad replied, 'I've never thought about art like that.'

Dad and Barry used to have enormous laughs together but by 1986 their relationship was a little fraught. Musing in his journal on the 'shotgun marriage between artists and dealers' being always difficult, Dad noted his disappointment at what he saw as Barry's arrogance, his attitude of 'tough luck' at the creators' plight—that plight being the disparity between the artist's return and the dealer's. Dad was disgusted at the 40 per cent commission dealers would routinely command for offering 'practically nothing in service'.

Barry was completely compulsive and obsessive. If his current obsession wasn't an artist, it was clothing, shoes or objets d'art. On one memorable overseas trip, he saw a pair of zebra-skin shoes and had to have them, buying 100 pairs. When he sold his home before moving overseas, the purchasers commented on how beautifully the property had been left by Barry, spotless and intact: every loo had a roll of paper, nothing was broken or damaged, and there were nearly a hundred pairs of zebra-skin shoes under the house. He was a gentleman to the end, the Liberace of the Sydney art scene.

Dad was a guest on Michael Parkinson's talk show on the BBC in 1980, joined by performer Julie Anthony and Alan Bond. Dad had Parkinson in hysterics describing the Royal Family's struggle with abstract art at the Sydney Opera House opening. Julie did her best gracious impersonation of Mary Poppins, while Alan Bond only talked about money. Alan Bond was hailed as an Australian hero for funding Australian challenges for the America's Cup yacht race (which one of his syndicates would go on to win in 1983), but Dad was definitely the more interesting and entertaining guest. They were both visionaries—although one thing Bond excelled in was borrowing money. When Parkinson inquired about Dad's time spent with Prince Philip, Dad referred to him again as 'Prince Philistine', which brought a huge laugh from the audience.

9

VALERIE

Valerie Strong was a great painter, and an inspiring mother to Louise and me. Louise and Mum shared a close, special bond. If my father was the ragged map for the adventures of my childhood and young manhood, my mother was the compass: the levelling influence and guiding star in a life of confusing changes and rapid relocations. A portrait of our family cannot be created without painting her first. A shy artist. A person of fine mind. Through no fault of her own, she became, for a time, the woman in the background, the muse, the artist's wife. And God help the artist's wife—especially if she is an artist herself.

That said, our mother just happened to be married to another painter, in a highly connective meeting of the minds. It was a passionate and, yes, destructive relationship at times, and it caused her the heartache as well as the ultimate heights of love, but this is about Mum, not Dad, however hard it is for me to separate them.

Mum was born in Australia, leaving for New Guinea as a two-month-old where she spent the next eight years, growing up on a coffee plantation in the hills above Wau with her brother

Jim. This was a different era in an exotic yet primitive environment, their home deep in the jungle, which honed her young eyes and instilled in my mother a lifelong fascination for nature; the full richness of the growth and colour was inspiring. As she got older, she remembers the local people splitting coconuts, mumbling in pidgin English that the coconut was the head of the boss (her father) when the blade hit. She found this deeply disturbing and realised that she was in an environment of resentment, which made her very uncomfortable. Grandad wasn't a cruel man, just an authoritarian, and they resented that.

As long as Mum could remember, she was always drawing and painting. Even as a child she found creating art an outlet, with her other passion being music. Like everyone, the Strongs' lives were disrupted by World War II and they left for Sydney before the Japanese invasion, her father returning almost immediately to defend their adopted home country.

When her family moved to the Lower North Shore of Sydney, Mum attended Pymble Ladies College, becoming a proper young lady. Mum was a stunner, appearing on the cover of *The Australian Women's Weekly* (25 July 1951), aged eighteen, as an 'undiscovered beauty', a trained milliner and an accomplished water-ballet champion.[1]

Her parents, particularly her mother, disapproved of her desire to devote her life to art, refusing to fund her study at art school initially. Without any other real direction other than to be creative, to work with her hands and to express herself, she decided to study millinery design, learning about form and colour. Yet her intense desire to paint never left her and, determined, she saved for years to pay for her own studies until her mother relented and she started a five-year diploma at East Sydney Technical College. She has said it was like the beginning of her life; for the first time she found people she could relate to, something she had been searching for forever.

As a student of John Passmore and Godfrey Miller, at college she painted intimate, considered, tonal and intricate works: landscapes, street scenes, interiors. Passmore, Dad's 'art father' and mentor, was inspirational, she said—'the greatest teacher Australia has had'.[2] Her other great mentor was a young John Olsen, who taught Passmore's abstract class after Passmore left for Europe on a Helena Rubinstein Travelling Art Scholarship.

Charisma and celebrity were not new to Valerie. Mum, as a young woman, had dated the actor John Meillon, famous as the voice of the early Victoria Bitter beer commercials, and later for his film work and cameos on *Crocodile Dundee* and *Skippy*. She told me that he was just mad about her, but her parents thought he was not marriage material. By 27, she was married to a conservative young doctor, a match encouraged by both sets of parents. Eric Frogatt was classically handsome, intelligent, kind and charming. But Valerie had discovered art and it was obvious they were completely different people, their incompatibility becoming glaringly obvious. The National Art School had opened up a new world to her and a whole part of herself that she had not known existed. And meeting John was like discovering an entirely different kind of man.

Dad's wit and personality charmed both of Mum's parents and, despite Mum's pregnancy, my grandparents saw the deep, true love between them and knew my conception was purely out of love. But it was my parents' shared obsession with art that united them and remained with them all their lives. For Mum, painting was intrinsic to her being.

When Dad was teaching Mum, he immediately recognised her talent and skill. 'I can always remember my first painting, just using lines and form, one mass against another,' Mum recalled. 'I remember Olsen coming along and saying, "I should have done that. I wish I'd done that line."'

I like to remember her artistic individuality. Mum had a much more feminine, immersive approach to landscape, looking at it intimately. She taught me the difference between subtlety and gesture. Her artistic vision was never the sweeping grand panorama, rather the detail of the source. Mum would pause, reflect and deeply consider each mark before she made it. I think Fred Williams' work has a lot of feminine qualities to it and shares something of her sensibility. Fred always loved Mum's work and wanted to swap paintings with her.

Music was inherent to Mum, too. In a painter's work, she said, 'you can always see this musical feeling, or feeling for music'. Mum would carry her gramophone with her everywhere, even when we were travelling overseas. Music was a constant in our lives growing up; every home was filled with music and beauty. She had an eclectic vision and would create still lifes from a handful of natural objects or items: a collection of antique keys arranged with a single shell; a scattering of feathers or flowers. Our homes had an ethereal beauty to them.

Mum starting teaching at Ascham School straight out of art school, then at The Bakery, and she continued to teach throughout her life: teaching painting and drawing at Hornsby TAFE for over twenty years, Seaforth TAFE, and later at Ku-ring-gai Community College. She was instrumental in the set-up of The Bakery art school with Dad, her input not as obvious but a vital cog in the wheel. Becoming a teacher was a very noble thing for her to do. A former student who studied painting and life drawing with her said that she was a wonderful teacher, extremely insightful and knowledgeable. Her expertise in art history and her own skill as a painter were an invaluable contribution. Her references to modern art and painting, particularly the early twentieth century with Cézanne and other post-impressionists, and how the artists constructed their art were highly informative and interesting. She often spoke of her life as a painter and her relationship with Dad to the class, many of whom were mature-age students.

Always an avid reader, she would take books that had inspired her into the classroom. Artist Ben Quilty's mother was taught by Mum for many years and purchased several of the books that she recommended. It was those volumes, still so relevant and inspirational today, that Ben has said he referred to when he was completing his own studies.

Mum's students found her absolutely delightful. She was universally liked and respected.

The reflection, discussion and research that have gone into this book have been almost cathartic. As a family, we have talked about issues previously avoided, revisited some old grievances (yet again) but with a far more positive approach than ever before. One of the key aspects for Louise and me was discovering a recording of an interview that our mother did with Hazel de Berg in 1965.[3] This was part of a series of interviews that Hazel conducted with poets, artists, writers, composers, actors, academics, publishers, librarians, scientists, anthropologists, public servants and some politicians, now part of the National Library of Australia collection. We knew about Dad's interviews but not about Mum's. This was a revelation. There was a transcript as well as the audio recording. It took several weeks for Louise and me to be able to listen to her voice. We both had to steel ourselves; the thought of hearing her voice was so painful even after all these years. I am so pleased we have this wonderful, irreplaceable insight into our mother as an artist, with her reflections on art and on life.

Dad was pleased, too. The recording had a 'purity and singularity', he said, reflecting 'the sensibility of her, her focus on what she liked to do, her belief and integrity of her work. She had no offence to anyone, respect for the past. What happens so much these days, the young artists are more concerned with their CVs, the accumulation of that. Valerie simply had a purity of vision.'

Dad was continually frustrated at Mum's slow, methodical painting technique and that she was not spontaneous or productive enough. In a letter from one of his trips to the Northern Territory in 1972, he wrote: 'I hope to come back and see lots of work done—the bush, nature. Call it what you will, it is the only thing.' At the time she had two young children, and Dad was away for months at a time. She barely had time for herself, let alone to work. He acknowledges her sensibility, which is very beautiful, but also her lack of drive: her work was 'charming', he said recently, but you cannot 'produce an Opera House mural, working like that!'[4] Mum wrote in her journal at the time about a conversation they shared about painting. John bemoaned, 'I hate the feeling of agony of starting a painting.'

She replied, 'Before it begins to talk to you.'

He said, 'Yes.'

After Dad left, work became Mum's lifeblood. For a time, she could only find her identity through her work, describing her painting as an endless conversation: 'Painting misses me.' Her notes and journals reveal an individual focused on self-improvement, with constant references to her current reading matter, full of meaningful quotes. I see elements of my own lack of confidence and periods of depression in her as she strove to be more outgoing, struggling with the demands of her work, to be more integrative, even more 'interesting' socially.

It was her fascination with the natural world around her that kept her in balance, the 'whole of life, of plants, of humanity, and the birth of time'. While it is Dad who has always been known for his dexterity in his use of language, my mother was the same. Her thoughts on creativity, the processes, are sublime. For her, creating art, the merge of colour, light and texture, was almost a spiritual process. In the same interview she said:

> I think an artist has to seek pure creation, and this only comes out of that moment. This creation leads you into the timeless world which is the only world to really be in. In this world one recognises themselves, a constant seeking and discovering one's marks on the canvas, finding what are the significant forms, finding colours one has never found before, what one colour is asking you to marry it to, the feel of the paint, keeping its lightness, being aware of its featheriness, as well as the rich juicy quality it can have, the cool dank darks or the warm clinging darks or the light transparent thinness of paint, one layer over another, watching the transition; one slowly grows through all this experience and one then discovers what comes out through the unconscious, and this is the only way to really work for me, I feel. I feel that the external figurative world has been taken as far as it can be taken. I feel that the subconscious world has not been plundered as it will be from now on. This has been a marvellous creative development in painting, one that I don't see an end to in resources of people, and a terrific richness of experience has unfolded for the painter.

Mum gained all her organic mystical understandings through looking and developing an affinity with her natural environment. My mother had a spiritual connection to nature. She was a bush mystic. She was concerned that as a society we need to embrace that we are all a part and a cog of nature, otherwise we will destroy it, and ultimately ourselves. When Western and European thinking interpreted the Australian landscape as seeming untidy, Mum looked at the bush as being a place that represented an order greater than the mess of urban society.

As in true Zen Buddhist philosophy, Valerie saw imperfection as beauty. Her work strived to emulate the delicate and intricate aspects of nature, with the mindful wisdom that no human can perfect it. There was nothing ostentatious about Mum; materiality did not interest her. Money only provided the freedom for her to work and support her family.

I remember asking Mum, 'How come it takes you so long to paint a picture?', to which she replied: 'I like to feel the brushstroke and the mark before I make it.' This was the reason she was not prolific: with no commercial concerns, her aim was merely to create work that pleased her.

For Mum, painting heightened her entire life experience. With those she loved, she said that she felt exhilarated by our presence; it was a type of rebirth. She was a feminist, and believed that creating art was both a feminine and masculine process, that a painter needs to draw upon both aspects in their being: 'To create fullness in one's statement,' she said, 'one has to be aware of the primitive, masculine and barbaric, as well as a lyrical, soft and gentle poetry which I suppose is feminine and which a painter must have both of to the extreme.'

She instilled in both Louise and me her love of nature, of all forms of our native life. She was Australian 'to the core'.

Like that of Margaret Preston, her work was imbued with this passion. Transfixed by native flora, she said: 'The plants we have, especially in Western Australia, have this wonderful, barbaric, archaic quality, as well as the lightness of a French tapestry in our little boronias and the Geraldton wax.' She would spend hours in the garden, her metaphorical garden of life. Her work was a constant process of experimentation and inner reflection. Mum would take a magnifying glass to look at plants in the garden or the surrounding bush at Dural, inspecting each petal and their formation. She felt that most people did not appreciate the delicacy of our native flora, the kangaroo paws and catspaws, all the small native shrubs so often overlooked then. Ever protective, she would place small stones in a circle around her favourite bush orchids to stop people accidently stepping on them.

Like Dad, Mum had a great appreciation for poetry. Her most loved poet was Judith Wright, in particular her poem 'The Cicadas':

> On yellow days in summer when the early heat
> presses like hands hardening the sown earth
> into stillness, when after sunrise birds fall quiet
> and streams sink in their beds and in silence meet,
> then underground the blind nymphs waken and move.
> They must begin at last to struggle towards love.[5]

Mum needed solitude to paint, peace and quiet. 'This is the only way I can reach myself and delve into what I call the garden of my mind,' she said. 'I feel that this is a secretive world, and so if anyone else is with me I can't reach it, as I'm half in their world.'

Dad has spoken so frequently about the painters who inspired him, but for Mum they were different. For her it was Arshile

Gorky who was the 'true painter of modern art', rather than Pollock:

> For me, Gorky, with his constant study and search into painting outside himself, not just tapping himself but always external-ising and going back in again into the unconscious, delving, has really shown a path far beyond anyone else. He gets so close to the primitive roots of humanity flowing through all the little sources and inlets, finally to wonderful flowing and flowering; most exotic fruits of experience are there, very deep inner experience, which I find a great inspiration to me.

Her words made me realise the importance of her work, how hard it must have been for her to juggle raising us with her art, and the sacrifices she had to make for us and for Dad to be able to devote himself so completely to his own career.

Mum exhibited her work regularly, first in an early, rare all-female group exhibition in 1963 at Clune Galleries, which was opened by Dad. One review noted that three of the five artists exhibiting were married to 'men artistic by profession'.[6] She exhibited her paintings, drawings and prints at various group exhibitions and at Galaxy Gallery (like Louise and me), with her last exhibition at my gallery in 1998. Having caught the travelling bug with Dad, Mum continued to explore the world throughout her life, working and studying in Africa, Europe, New York and around Australia.

Mum finally sold the Dural house to one of her students, someone who appreciated the design and feeling of sanctuary of the home. She thought her own work could thrive in a haven of creativity that had once been owned by John and Valerie Olsen. She and her husband still live there today and have expressed their ongoing delight in the property.

With that and the sale of Pearl Beach combined, Mum was able to buy a beautiful semidetached house in Bronte unencumbered. Mum was happy there, with her children and, eventually, her grandchildren nearby. She spent her days painting and reading, along with her ritualistic early-morning swims throughout the year at her beloved Bronte Bogey Hole ocean pool.

Mum always appreciated and loved Dad but was content in her own life, resolute that they were no longer together and that she was able to live her own life. After going through so much during their marriage, including the hurt over the affairs, which diminished their relationship, they still remained friends throughout her life. Maintaining an intellectual intimacy, sharing their art, books and poetry.

In her love life, Mum had a long-term relationship with paediatrician Rob Piggott while she was living at Dural, which started a few years after my father left. With curious irony, the tall, unpretentious and charming Rob was one of Mum's students. Rob had a house at Chinamans Beach, and he found in Valerie a great mentor and lover. It was like the roles had been reversed from her relationship with John. Rob absolutely adored her, caring for Mum very deeply. They had a wonderful relationship, with a shared appreciation of music and prose. Eventually the relationship faded, but they remained close friends.

In her later years, Mum had a relationship with Gilbert 'Gil' Docking, an artist, arts writer and arts administrator. Long-term friends, they started seeing each other some time after the death of Gil's wife, artist Sheila (known as Shay), and were loving companions for the rest of Mum's life.

Gil was highly respected and much loved. A humble man, he was surprised to be awarded an Order of Australia medal for service to the arts, though his contribution was evident through his directorships in Australia and New Zealand. He wrote a definitive, award-winning history of New Zealand art and, after retirement, curated Shay's work, placing her paintings in public and private collections. On his death in 2015, aged 96, Gil donated his art collection to the Newcastle Art Gallery. In a group of works assigned in 2018 were nine by Shay, a John Brack print and (proudly for Louise and me) one painting by Mum, *Afternoon Yarramalong*.[7] Gil is credited with identifying a young Brett Whiteley as a major talent. The Newcastle Art Gallery is the owner of the first Whiteley work to be purchased for a public collection: *Autumn Abstract* (1959), painted when he was only twenty years old.[8] Mum's work is in good company.

Mum's mum, Hazel, was simply wonderful, very kind to Louise and me, treating us with biscuits and sweets. We adored one another. Later in life, mum informed me that Hazel said she had never loved a child as much as she loved me at my birth. Mum was a bit put out! Whenever possible, I would stay with my grandmother; I remember her stroking my hair as I lay on the sofa with my head in her lap. Each afternoon she would have a single cigarette and a glass of sherry, sometimes giving me a sip and a puff. For such a gentle woman, she liked to live danger-ously; in a car, she would never wear a seatbelt.

My grandfather was more reserved, like most men of his generation. There was something broken about him that we could sense, physically and mentally, the visible and hidden scars from wartime. He had been on the beach at Gallipoli for the entire duration of the campaign; he had seen his friend bayoneted in the head. After his second world war, he would sometimes be found roaming outside his property in the highlands of New Guinea naked, and would have to be brought back home by the locals. Like many of his generation, the effects of the war never left him.

When he was having a good day, in a rare sunny mood, he would bump me up and down on his knee, singing 'The Galloping Major': 'Bumpety-bumpety-bumpety-bump / Here comes the Galloping Major.' Other times he would just sit with a drink, tears rolling down his cheeks.

Anzac Day was the saddest day for him. When unable to march anymore, he would watch his surviving mates parade through the streets, tears in his eyes, propped up with a flagon of sherry beside him.

Both of my grandfathers gave away the best part of their youth to go to war. They survived but never recovered, both with the legacy of malaria that affected their ongoing health. Neither of them spoke of their experiences, probably never able to conjure the words to describe how really terrible war was, knowing also how inconceivable it would be to us children. After such extreme and devastating experiences, they felt redundant; when war came to an end, so did a part of them. They blunted their pain and enduring psychological chaos with brandy or beer, and the resultant behavioural disharmony affected everyone around them. Despite this, I completely sympathise with their need to drink to forget those experiences, the haunting thoughts and emotional wounds that never healed. These men have my deepest respect and reverence.

Mum's family lost everything, including her father's World War I medals, when the plantation home in which Mum grew up in New Guinea was burned to the ground. He had to request duplicates from the Australian and Belgium War Offices. Serving in both world wars, Harold had been awarded the 1914–15 Star, the British War Medal, the Victory Medal, the Croix de Guerre (Belgium) and the Diploma of award of the Croix de Guerre before being discharged in 1919. In World War II he was awarded the 1939–45 Star, the Pacific Star and the 1939–45 Australia service medal. It was galling to hear that they made him pay for the replacements, especially when he only wanted them to wear in the annual Anzac march.

I still possess one of my grandfather's medals, and an empty cannon shell he brought back from Gallipoli, a constant reminder that in my lifetime we have had it easy. As drum major of The King's School Junior Band, I remember the pride I felt as we marched up George Street, me twirling my shiny silver mace out the front of the band, honouring him and all of my other relatives who had fought.

Dad, too, has rarely spoken of his own father's experiences, other than to say that he returned from war a broken man. More recently he has opened up, the repressed pain from his child-hood surfacing. Mum, too, was reluctant to talk about her father. Perhaps there were stories she just felt that she did not want to or could not tell. It is no wonder that she found tranquillity in art. War damages the core of families for generations.

Uncle Jim, Mum's brother, became an international pilot. Just a few years from retirement, he was caught up in the Gulf War while living and working in Baghdad. Mum reached out to her friend, Anne Fairbairn, an academic and poet who went to Iraq to campaign for the release of hostages, successfully seeking

Uncle Jim's and another Sydneysider's freedom—the first of over 30 hostages to be released due to their age.[9] He was a humble man. He never received his superannuation or any remuneration from Kuwait Airlines after the war and, returning to Australia as a near 60-year-old, spent the rest of his working life as a taxi driver. Uncle Jim was most saddened that he had had to leave all of his jazz records and collection of aged scotch when he left.

During the Dural years, when Dad's presence seemed almost overpowering, staying with Grandma was my escape, like both of my parents with their studios. Grandma would buy me a six-pack to take to parties when I was underage. The day before she died, she walked all the way to the shops to buy me a sweater as a birthday present. It was her last outing.

The phone rang at Dural shortly after that birthday. Grandma had had a massive heart attack. We rushed to the Mater Hospital where she was taking her last breaths. Louise was too upset to go in; her reluctance to see someone pass away was very understandable. It was an incredibly sad moment but a terribly beautiful one at the same time. It was not long after Dad had left us, and we found ourselves supporting Mum in her last moments with her own dying mother.

In 1926, a gold stream was discovered in New Guinea, just above the Strong plantation in Wau, at Edie Creek, six days walk from Salamaua. A massive gold rush started, attracting prospectors from all over the world, one of whom was a young adventurer called Errol Flynn. The eighteen-year-old Flynn had run off to New Guinea to find his fortune and spent five years bluffing his way into any job, any way he could. A notorious womaniser, he was considered a likeable and capable young man until his rogue behaviour and mountain of debts caught up with him. During one of his expeditions into the jungle, Flynn found himself sharing a tent with an ex-army officer and a very proper Englishman: my grandfather, Mum's father Harold. After two days with the charming young man, he famously wrote to his wife, saying, 'Never, ever introduce my daughter to a man named Errol Flynn!'

One of Mum's favourite quotes was by Elisabeth Kübler-Ross. 'The most beautiful people we have known are those who have known defeat, known suffering, known struggle, known loss, and have found their way out of the depths,' Kubler Ross wrote.[10] 'These persons have an appreciation, a sensitivity, and an understanding of life that fills them with compassion, gentleness, and a deep loving concern. Beautiful people do not just happen.'

That she loved us all immensely was so evident; Mum was so full of love. When we were young she would often say, 'Love is the greatest gift of all. Always love yourself, not in a vain way, but in a way that you can feel happy within yourself. So always: love, love, love.'

10

THE ROOTS OF THE TREE

My father has often been quoted as saying that we are related to the artist Frederick McCubbin, having several McCubbins on the maternal side of the family. When Dad ran into Penny McCubbin, Frederick's granddaughter, at his retrospective at the NGV, he proudly announced the connection. Penny, an avid ancestry researcher herself,[1] remarked afterwards, 'I thought to myself, I don't think so!'

As much as Penny, Dad and I would have liked to prove a direct link to Frederick, I now know enough to confirm that the genetic strains are unfortunately separate branches. We are all McCubbins, though, so I'm still going to claim our hereditary link—art is in the DNA.

Like many Australians, I would have liked to have had a convict or two as an ancestor, but on both sides they were all free settlers, hardworking and industrious. There were strong religious convictions and connections to the Presbyterian Church, too. My ancestors on both sides were responsible for building many churches across New South Wales, and we even have an honest-to-goodness martyr: my eighth great-grandfather on my father's mother's side, Alexander McCubbin, was hanged in 1685 after he refused to take an oath to the Stuart kings. There is a memorial at Irongray, Kirkcudbrightshire,[2] and Alexander is known as the McCubbin Martyr. That beats a convict hands down.

The ancestry of Alfred Olsen, my great-grandfather, was always a mystery. Aside from him being Swedish, we knew nothing else and had been unsuccessful in tracking him down. The name Olsen didn't help; it is one of the most common names in Sweden, and the search was complicated by the patronymic naming conventions. Also, any name too 'Swedish' would be changed if a person or family emigrated; others simply chose their own moniker for their new life.

But, thanks to a DNA ancestry test, I managed to eventually track down Alfred by matching back to some third cousins in Sweden, then back further still. Fortunately I have a diligent researcher. Alfred was born Jonas Alfred Olsson, the youngest son of a family of eight, in Levar, on the eastern coast of Sweden, in 1864. His father worked on the land without owning the property, and Alfred had lost both of his parents by the age of seven. The siblings scattered, some marrying and moving away, while Alfred and another brother went to sea. From 1881, he was marked as 'whereabouts unknown' in Sweden[3] and never returned. He arrived in Australia as a crew member on a boat from Norway, listed as J.A. Olson, a fettler (steel worker), and disembarked in Adelaide as Alfred Olsen, then rejoined and stayed with the boat until reaching Newcastle, where he jumped ship. I had always wondered how Alfred had ended up there and now it was so obvious—the empty barque had to reload with Newcastle coal before making the return journey.

He met the spirited Fanny Dorrington, and they married in Tamworth in 1894. A year later he was naturalised in Sydney.

They went on to have five children; the youngest was Dad's father, my grandfather Harry Olsen. But Alfred really had no success in Australia, and Fanny left him in 1907. 'It was something that was never talked about,' Dad said. 'His name was never spoken.'

Dad only remembers seeing his grandfather once. Alfred was living in Tingha, in squalid conditions in a miner's humpy. He died shortly after.

When talking with Dad about my discoveries, he actually said that he would have preferred to have his name spelled 'Jon', the Swedish way, rather than 'John'. Neither Dad nor I have ever visited Sweden. Maybe that will change now.

Researching Mum's side of the family revealed so much more than Louise and I knew. We had heard many stories, the lore, and a few solid facts, but had nothing like the depth of knowledge, aural and written, that we had for Dad's side of the family.

Dad was always a little dismissive of Mum's side, assuming his side of the family was so much more 'colourful'. I have since come to realise how erroneous this was, and I had also been just as guilty of barely scratching the surface of my mother's ancestry. My research has since unveiled a rich and varied cast of fascinating characters, men and women of intelligence, resilience, industry and ambition. I am proud to now fully embrace my maternal heritage.

Of English and, further back, Irish ancestry, my grandmother Hazel's family was made up of decorated war heroes, a politician, a rebellious trade unionist and jailed conscientious objector (who also happened to be a writer), and a doctor—and that was just in one generation of the Marshalls, headed by my great-grandfather, the Reverend James Marshall, a Presbyterian minister.[4]

Born at Pola Creek on the Macleay River in 1855, the Reverend was to become a leading figure in the establishment and growth of the Presbyterian Church in New South Wales. Ordained at 28, he married and, after several postings, finally moved to Sydney's North Shore and the Hornsby parish, his task to establish worship centres in the suburbs along the newly built train line. He ended up building seven churches, all paid for by donations from his expanding brood of happy parishioners.[5] James and his wife, Agnes, also managed to fit in raising eight children including, of course, my grandmother Hazel.

The Reverend didn't stop working, though; he continued in other parishes before finally retiring in 1920 due to ill health. He died in 1930. My son, James, is named in his memory, as my uncle was, too.

Hazel's brother Augustine Campbell Marshall, known as 'Campbell', applied for a homestead and 820 acres of land in the Hunter Valley region of New South Wales under the soldier resettlement scheme after World War I. He hit the jackpot: the Marshalls became landed gentry, pillars of the community, and the homestead became home to the extended family. My grandmother Hazel lived there until her marriage, and Ravensworth became a childhood rural holiday destination.

We loved going on trips anywhere with Mum, but the visits to Ravensworth were always a little unnerving. To start with, everyone seemed really, really old, and Great-Uncle Campbell was frankly scary. Very formal, he was a stickler for proper table manners and protocol. At meals he would watch us eat, glowering at the head of the table, and if our manners were not up to scratch, he would tap our legs with a small stick under the table.

We were also struck by the strange, eerie feel of the property. We were convinced it was haunted, full of ghosts—even Mum, who swore she used to play with the spirit of a little girl there years before. Louise and I would get goosebumps just thinking about the place, and would scare ourselves stupid every night. Just recently we discovered the backstory that made all of those ghostly feelings disturbingly poignant: the property had once belonged to a family called White, and their daughter was brutally murdered by bushrangers.[6] Her inscribed gravestone can still be seen near the original homestead. The White family left, selling to James Bowman, who went on to build the existing home.

It was during Bowman's ownership that the next tragedy struck. The local Aboriginal people, the Wonnarua, had become increasingly resentful of the encroaching white settlement and the lack of respect for their land ownership and access. A series of violent collisions occurred in the area and, in late 1826, a posse of mounted police and settlers hunted down and massacred a group of eighteen Aboriginal people in what is now called the Ravensworth Massacre.[7]

A couple of years ago I visited artist Dale Frank just outside Singleton, near Ravensworth, to finalise an exhibition. Dale had a 'Ravensworthesque' homestead as well, at the end of a long, winding driveway, with a large garden filled with prehistoric-looking plants: mixing palms with spinifexes, and an array of succulents. An artist and eccentric, Dale had a large room full of taxidermy. The place was a stationery zoo, packed full of motionless beasts: zebras, lions, hyenas, elephant and buffalo heads mounted on the walls, even a giraffe.

During the visit I compared his home to Ravensworth, and

he told me how the old homestead was in a terrible state of disrepair: the windows were all boarded up and it was surrounded by a wire fence. He said, 'You would be devastated to see what they have done to your family's property.' Hearing how the house had gone to rack and ruin, I thought Louise and I might buy it back and restore it to its former glory as the family holiday home, a rural Pearl Beach. However, since researching the macabre history of the homestead and still, even now, believing it to be haunted—Louise does, too—I have misgivings about owning a place that has such a disturbing history.

In the 1960s and '70s, half of the Marshalls' holding was requisitioned for the Liddell Power Station after vast seams of coal were discovered.[8] Campbell Marshall managed to purchase the remainder of the property. The family sold the balance of the estate in 1997 and the now heritage-listed homestead is smack bang in the middle of the open-cut mining project. Acknowledged as a site of local historical significance, the homestead is being painstakingly restored. Unfortunately, the surrounding countryside is not getting the same treatment.

Another great-uncle, James Vance Marshall, was the black sheep of the Marshall family,[9] an activist, adventurer, writer, journalist, passionate trade unionist, prison reformer, conscientious objector and multiple felon. Known as Vance, he was a friend of Henry Lawson, described by *The Sydney Morning Herald* as an 'Australian personality'. After his three stints as a political prisoner, he wrote *World of the Living Dead*,[10] about the torture of the prison system, with a preface by Lawson.

Vance wrote for various newspapers and journals about everything and anything that caught his eye, including his travels, his experiences when he moved to England and the trade union movement. The 1959 book *Walkabout*, a modern-day Australian classic, was based upon Vance's intricate travel notes and diaries, and I had always known the book as his creation alone. Later I found out that the book was actually co-written by Donald Gordon Payne, who had taken James's name as a pseudonym. Vance always claimed that he had written the first draft and over the years, at various times, both Vance and Payne took full credit. A status of co-written was agreed upon, and after Vance's death in 1964, with the permission of the Marshall family, Payne continued to publish another six works using the name 'James Vance Marshall'.

The book tells the story about the survival of two 'amazingly helpless' children stranded in the outback who are saved by a young Aboriginal boy, and was renowned for its vivid descriptions of the harsh landscape and native flora and fauna. This is one reason why the shared authorship of the book niggles me; in theory, it is still under dispute and I have to concur. Vance spent years in the Northern Territory and travelled all over the country. He had in-depth knowledge of the flora and fauna of the outback, had lived closely with Aboriginal people, and was familiar with their beliefs, traditions and way of life. I find it hard to reconcile that Payne, an Englishman who had never visited the outback, could possibly write so intimately about outback Australia, capturing the oppressive heat, the light, the sense of primitive desolation and the silence.

Art is an important vehicle in changing popular beliefs: in his writings, Vance humanised Indigenous people for audiences in the Northern Hemisphere, depicting them as a race of humility and integrity. *Walkabout* has been continually in print since 1959 and the film of the same name, directed by Nicolas Roeg and released in 1971, is considered an Australian classic.

My uncle's family had no idea that the book, first published just five years before his death, would become a worldwide best-seller, let alone spawn the movie. Just think about the royalties.

Culture is not just about art, money or religion, nor solely about the decorative. It is not about the songs, the poetry or the prayers we utter, or the writings we leave behind. Culture is about a body of moral and ethical values that can surround each individual who descends from us.

The maintenance of cultural integrity is the maintenance of human civilisation itself. How fortunate I am, having been brought up in a family that has shown me this.

PART TWO

11

IF YOU CAN REMEMBER ART SCHOOL

On returning from a gap year spent travelling around Europe at nineteen, I had absolutely no idea what I wanted to do. A job—or, more accurately, an occupation—was needed, but I had no inclination at the time to pursue tertiary study, like my friends all were doing. The Sydney I re-entered was on the cusp of another era: the Emerald City was crystallised by harder values and far less poetry.

Fabric manufacturer Max Franks was a friend of Dad's and a collector of his work. One evening we were visiting him and his wife, and they asked me what I wanted to do with my life. Dad said immediately: 'What Tim needs is a good solid job.' When Max offered me a position at his company, I agreed. Starting at the bottom, I learned what textile was what by cutting lengths, and eventually became a sales representative, taking swatches to upholsterers around the city, getting to know the streets of Sydney like the back of my hand.

Although grateful for the opportunity, my heart was not in the work. Aesthetically it was the antithesis of what I had witnessed being created at home. Bored, miserable and unsatisfied, I was—not surprisingly—eventually sacked. I took the next job offered, though again in the rag trade, this time with John Kaldor, another friend of Dad's.

The textile design and manufacturing company John Kaldor Fabricmaker was well established, but I found myself back in a soulless storeroom, again cutting endless lengths of fabric. Kaldor was a well-known collector of contemporary art by then, having started collecting and commissioning in the 1950s, and had great vision. In 1968–9 he had invited artists Christo and Jeanne-Claude to Sydney to create the first John Kaldor Public Art Project, *Wrapped Coast—One Million Square Feet*, at Little Bay. It was the artists' first large-scale environmental project and put them on the art map. By the time I was working for Kaldor he was up to project number eight, having captured the attention and the imagination of the Australian public with innovative installations and performance art. By the time he was curating *An Australian Accent*, an exhibition of Australian art in New York in 1984, Kaldor had changed the landscape of contemporary Australian art internationally.

While all of this was happening, I was stuck in the bowels of a building, hating every moment of my working day, never even laying eyes on John Kaldor himself. Needless to say, I was soon let go. Working in the wrong job in the wrong industry was soul destroying. I realised that work had to be something that inspired me, and I simply was not a nine-to-five person. It was obvious, really: the only place for me was in the art world.

Mum and Louise were still at Dural then, and I moved back in. Dad bought me a Honda hatchback, and I enrolled in a two-year art certificate at Hornsby Technical College. It was back to basics: twelve hours of drawing a week, coupled with photography and printmaking classes. These provided the discipline and space for me to find my identity through the axis of art making. After a lifetime of listening to people talking about art, I was now immersed in the process.

Now Hornsby TAFE, the Technical College had one of the most underestimated art schools in the country. My understanding of the basis of painting slowly grew, largely thanks to Peter Upward, Margaret Woodward and Clem Millward, who were all inspiring teachers. Clem and Margaret never rose to fame as outstanding painters, but their ability to draw was exemplary. The idiosyncratic and nuanced painter Elisabeth Cummings received her (very worthy and belated) public recognition more recently, but fortunately was still teaching during my time.

The humility of an art apprenticeship was far more preferable to the abject misery of an unsatisfying job. Being at art school balanced my energies and I was, for the first time, starting to find my niche. Whatever direction art was going to take me in, it was inevitably my terminus.

Back at home, Dad's departure was sorely felt, and there were reminders of him everywhere. There was a subtle exchange of roles as Mum took on Dad's responsibilities, becoming the head of the family. Louise and Mum had an intimacy that, as the lone male, made me feel intrusive, perhaps unintentionally reminding them of Dad's departure, even in the physical resemblance we shared. We were all missing Dad desperately in so many ways, not least because of the food: his heartwarming paellas and delicious stews had been replaced by Mum's macrobiotic cooking and endless pots of lentils—without the pork knuckle to spice them up, despite my pleading. There was an emptiness that everyone felt.

Louise remembers us 'sitting in' on Dad's art classes at The Bakery when our feet could hardly touch the floor. But, really, our kitchen table was an informal art academy, crowded with empty wine glasses, clashing egos and bold-face names arguing their point, with a deep respect for the visual at the heart of every argument. My decision to enrol at the National Art School (or East Sydney Tech, as it was known) was therefore somewhat misguided. Expecting a continuation of the didactic, intergenerational conversation of my upbringing—a seat at the world's longest bottle-strewn dinner table, if you will—I was in for a shock.

The Darlinghurst school has been in operation in various forms since 1922, located in the historic sandstone jail site. When I enrolled in 1983, artistically Sydney was changing guard. The soundtrack was Joy Division and Talking Heads. Postmodernism, semiotics, post-Lacanian analysis, photography and video ruled from the head rather than the body, a vibe beautifully articulated in a scrawl of graffiti in a local alleyway: 'FUCK ART LET'S DANCE'. Louise had already been at the art school for a year, having first gone to Hornsby Tech straight out of Tara Anglican School for Girls.

Irony and intellect were the reflexes of the fashionable that year, and painting was dead. In class, everything was post-this and post-that, as we stripped art of its romantic connotations and meditated on the banality of semiotics. Some teachers held fast to classical principles, technical finesse and the sheer grit of techniques revered in the nineteenth century, but overwhelmingly the sentiment was the same, a refrain I had heard many times before, even by then: painting was an old medium with an old message, or just off trend.

Yet somehow painting always redeems itself, and the cycle begins again. Larry Gagosian, the American art dealer behind the

Gagosian Galleries, even based a show on this idea of death and rebirth in his London outpost in 2013. Art critic Jonathan Jones's memorable critique captured it perfectly: '*The Show is Over* seems to contradict its own premise—by showing the fearless living glory of painters such as Ed Ruscha and Richard Wright.'[1]

At art school I struggled to calibrate the message. Possibly because painting was so contentious, I decided to major in print-making, mastering sugar lift, aquatint and soft-ground etching. I enjoyed the medium's paradoxes, the discipline and the craft, the way it was often enriched by its aberrations, and I became obsessed with each process because of its unpredictability. There is joy in making artwork embedded in the nature of mistakes, the unforeseen circumstances that determine the quality of the image. The practical bedrock of technique gave me a respect for discipline that has never left me.

Black-and-white photojournalism was another form I was drawn to, one that portrays ordinary people who may be invisible in society. It helped me to understand T.S. Eliot's image of 'the still point of the turning world', the point where 'the dance is'. It is the non-staged aspects of life that hold the truth, quite contrary to the life in art I witnessed growing up as I watched so many people seeking success steered by ambition.

Creative disciplines can carry a certain stigma socially. Studying art for any length of time attracts the clichéd refrain to 'get a real job', but what I learned at art school was that creativity *is* reality. Art represents living in the real world much more palpably than servicing a 'real' job. Once you create your own alternate universe, it is an easier place to live and survive—and some artists are simply unemployable in any other way. A creative mindset can be applied to many other vocations, but often an artist's unique skills are not properly valued or understood.

The other pleasure was developing my own taste, and I was surprised at the sort of artists I gravitated towards. The simple drawings of Godfrey Miller were a great inspiration, as was the subdued palette of John Passmore and the natural, haphazard materials applied by Ian Fairweather. To me, there was a selfless quality in their work. Having grown up around such gregarious larger-than-life artists, it was refreshing to discover a wealth of artists who communicated more humbly but no less effectively. My mother included.

Introverted artists such as Giorgio Morandi and my former teachers, Royston Harpur and Peter Upward, were brilliant but by no means critically exalted in their time. They were not making 'major' statements but rather creating almost incidentally, not driven by any perception of themselves existing within a canon. These artists were not driven by worldly fame but remain pertinent. For them, art was something of an internal odyssey.

Although wisely deciding not to pursue a career as an artist, art school planted the seeds for my life as an art dealer, giving me an understanding of the importance of the dealer's intermediary role between the artist and their public. It was part of the subconscious visual learning process that had begun as I grew up surrounded by art. In my early youth, all this crazy stuff lying around the house did not really make sense to me, but in adult life it did. It was a privilege that took me years to appreciate. The Chinese masters believed that you look at the bamboo for two years, then draw the bamboo for ten years, then forget the bamboo; only after that you may know something about the art of the bamboo. Drawing is an empathetic act where you become the object you are looking at.

Furthermore, some of my oldest friendships developed there, evolving into professional relationships when my own gallery eventuated. Matthew Johnson, the son of artist Michael Johnson and brother of my friend Anna, and I became close friends during those art-school years. As the sons of artists in the public eye, we were conscious of our artistic lineage and felt an implied expectation of artistic success. I identified with Matthew's desire to get out of his father's orbit and make his own mark—at least my father wasn't always around campus teaching classes like his was. We shared a big draughty studio in a former cell block, along with dry humour, a love of paint and a bit of a drink.

When Matthew branched out as a painter, I watched his dogged tenacity for over 30 years. He has emerged, metaphorically and physically, from his muddy earlier works to become one of the most beautiful colourists. His equations of colour and painted dots are pure abstraction and yet they can bestow the most delightful sense of transcendence. He was painting coloured dots decades before Damien Hirst. I have represented Matthew since the early 2000s, and we remain close friends to this day.

At art school, my paint palettes were renowned. Clem Millward had taught me how to devise the limited palette that was often applied to Cubism, where you create primary colours with a mid-tone grey, adding more and more primary in scales so that you end up with huge colour fields. When working on paintings for days at a time, the palettes would have to be covered in cling wrap. Some said that my palettes were paintings in themselves. I taught Matthew my impressionist method, and he still paints using the technique. I remain relaxed about having made better palettes than paintings.

Enrolling at art school is only ever Act 1. Some kids enrolled at art school to piss off their (usually accomplished, middle-class)

parents, or simply because they did not know what else to do. In my case, it was like joining the family business, and the expectation that accompanies such privilege was predictably present.

Still, there was something about the discipline of drawing that felt natural, and on the page I was able to express feelings in a way that felt personal. The combination of marks and colours I made were mine alone and, standing back from a sheet of paper or canvas, there was a 'me' who was different to everybody else, including my father. Creativity is a by-product of identity, and it was such a relief to see my own discriminations and aesthetic aspirations.

In the Renaissance and beyond, artists were traditionally trained as artists, not as intellectuals. I think that many students today are asked to interrogate too much philosophy and take on an activism agenda well before they even learn to draw properly or keep a journal. When this happens, they end up with few skills to effectively facilitate or articulate their ideas. Fortunately, my teachers drummed into me the skills of drawing, painting and printmaking. These gave me the ability to express my own ideas with some formality, and from there I could articulate and expand my maverick ideas within those forms. Act 2.

While never being into the academic, preferring practice to theory, I also began to understand the machinery of art history. I could see where the greats stood in relation to each other, and where my father stood in relation to them, and subsequently came to the stark realisation that I would not have a place among them.

At home I had learned to appreciate art but not to master the making of it, the creative process. At art school I discovered that making art requires both courage and vulnerability. The desire to make art is usually a calling; then comes the belief that you have something to say; and, finally, there is the courage and skill to actually say it. By that time, my whole life had felt like it was on display—but making art was something different altogether.

The third act is realising that art school might not be the place to become an artist. Education was necessary for technique and implementation, but self-motivation is probably the most important driver for any artist. I went to art school for answers and found questions that drove me to examine my motives and those of the artists around me. Call me stubborn, but it took me seven years there to realise that I was neither an artist nor an art teacher by nature or temperament.

I worked throughout my student years, at weekends, nights and through the holidays. While most of my early work was in the hospitality industry, I did manage to work in the arts whenever possible. For a time, I worked for Rex Irwin at his upstairs gallery on Queen Street, Woollahra, on Saturdays for twenty dollars a day, but I loved being around the work of Frank Auerbach, Lucian Freud, Henry Moore and David Hockney. Rex brought Cork Street to Sydney—quite an achievement at a time when Australian collectors were inward looking in terms of international art investment.

While I was a student, I spent an uncomfortable weekend in jail after accumulating $2000 of parking fines. I was living up at 'the Cross' (Sydney's Kings Cross, a notorious nightclub and red-light district, now sanitised after the lockout laws from 2014), where parking, like most places in inner Sydney, is a nightmare. While living it up to the full and relishing student life, I had clocked up the fines without noticing (or simply ignoring) their number. It was either a weekend in the slammer or the fines.

Keeping it quiet from the family, I chose the slammer, spending an informative night with a renowned heroin dealer. I had been frantically saving for my own grand tour of Europe and was not going to let that dream escape. Unlike my great-uncle, James Vance Marshall, to my relief I have no criminal record, though, and that was the grand extent of my criminal past. Just the thought of having to face my mother, let alone relive that experience for a longer timeframe, was well and truly deterrent enough.

There were other firsts in those student years, too. After breaking my nose for the third time, it was time to retire from rugby and find a different sort of athletic pursuit. I was never one to play cricket, and rowing, rather like golf, required too much of a time commitment. My sister had told me how she had joined a dance company and found it an effective and fun way to keep fit. Since emulating flamenco as a small boy living in Spain, I had loved to dance at any opportunity. With such a favourable male-to-female ratio (something rugby certainly didn't offer), it was not long before I jumped ship and tackled the art of modern dance with The Margaret Barr Dance Drama Group.

Margaret, by then in her late seventies had once been a protégé of the American contemporary dance diva Martha Graham. Despite her tiny frame, Margaret was strongly built and more merciless than any rugby coach. Age had not softened this Fonteyn. She was a strict disciplinarian and a demanding choreographer, tyrannical and as tough as nails. I respected her enormously.

After my first class, I couldn't walk for a week. But, week in and week out, I embraced this new discipline and, in the process, found a new creative outlet, a level of flexibility and a subtle fitness that rugby had never matched.

I was soon part of a production choreographed around the

life of Mahatma Gandhi, a contemporary Bollywood-style dance and drama. Today I still do not know whether to take it personally, but Margaret cast me as Gandhi's assassin. We performed to three sell-out crowds and received a rave review in *The Sydney Morning Herald*.

Margaret soon retired, so I found a new dance outlet in the Sydney Dance Company classes instructed by Paul Saliba. I still love dancing and can always be called upon to dance with the wives at weddings while the men drink at the bar. Dom, my second wife, has said that she fell in love with me after watching me dance.

In the history of modern art it is the act, not the study, that makes the artist great. Monet was not a masterful impressionist because he thought about how to convey the essence of a lily; it was because he painted all of his feelings onto soaring canvases that quivered with a translucence that was more expressive than the lilies in his pond. Many great artists were similarly self-motivated. Cézanne and Matisse became rich, and Modigliani and Basquiat soaked themselves to death in absinthe and morphine, but what they have in common is training grounded in sensory exploration and the use of their hands rather than in theory. At art school, like most students, I learned best through application, the repetition of processes, fine-tuning that end. That same tactile appreciation is present in the artists I represent. Instead of the corporatised, hyper-marketed art that dominates today, I search out artists with feeling.

There are some of my works in a drawer at the gallery, mainly etchings, and some still-life paintings and drawings. There is one particular painting, a landscape of the Hawkesbury, that I am most proud of; it was bought by painter Genevieve de Couvreur. After graduation, I had two sell-out shows, a solo exhibition at The Gallery Cafe in Darlinghurst and a two-man show at Galaxy Gallery in Balmain, and it was while working towards these shows that my shortcomings as an artist became apparent. It was all too isolating an existence for me. Art is hard, and the life of an artist is not a glamorous one. It can be lonely. Even great talent, combined with social connections, can only get you so far. To go to a studio and stay there requires discipline and commitment. Studio discipline is vital.

Dad's generation in many ways had a freedom and spontaneity that perhaps ours lacked. There was such a thirst for life then, as society was changing so dramatically; perhaps we have missed out in a way. When Dad talks about his time at art school, he certainly seemed to have had a more exciting experience than we did.

Speaking recently of his first year at the National Art School, Dad said: 'We just loved being finally free to be art students and unashamedly make art. At graduation exhibitions there were lots of energetic and bright young people, from both working and middle-class backgrounds. All aspiring to be noble bohemians. We may have been poor, but we were very sexy.'

12

BEAUTIFUL PEOPLE

Life has always been about extremes for me. In my art-school years, my life propelled me between the bohemia of young painters and the Eastern Suburbs cocktail set. After graduating from art school, I had gone straight to The University of New South Wales to continue my focus on painting and printmaking and decided to do a teaching degree on the side, specialising in child psychology and cognitive development. This was Mum's suggestion; I should be an art teacher like her. However, my short-lived career as a teacher only involved short placements at Sydney Grammar School, Galston High School and St. Catherine's School before I realised my true calling.

I ended up working as a waiter at Arthur's on Victoria Street, Darlinghurst, owned by namesake Arthur Karvan and his wife Gabrielle (mother of actress Claudia Karvan), running drinks and meals by night and studying and printmaking during the day at UNSW. Arthur's was not far from Dad's own stomping ground as a young artist, when he had lived in the crumbly Victorian houses overlooking Woolloomooloo in the company of Laurie Thomas, Robert Hughes and Paul Haefliger.

Arthur's could only be described as a feral fusion of Studio 54, Max's Kansas City and perhaps Ronnie Scott's in London. It was the bar where people were beautiful, famous or shady. On any one night, Tiny Tim, Brett Whiteley and The Rolling Stones would be there. Another night, Tina Turner walked into the glass doors and left the impression of her lips, like a crushed peach. If people were having sex in the toilets, high on Quaaludes, and Engelbert Humperdinck was on the dance floor, it was just another night at Arthur's. This was the eye of the storm: a post-punk/new wave apocalypse where everyone seemed to have sticky fingers, leaving a trail of coke, cigarette smoke or Chanel No. 5 in their wake; it was a meeting place for actors, artists, filmmakers, writers, and anyone and everyone who was considered creative.

I was a glorified busboy in this environment, but in 1984 it seemed the perfect place to hang out. Arthur and Gabrielle liked to have interesting, good-looking people around, and at one stage it was the hardest place to get into in Sydney. It was a sexy hot mess of a bar: older women came for a champagne, left $200 tips and propositioned the waiters. Everyone was agitated and horny, acting as if the cameras were rolling. It was hedonistic mayhem.

We'd hardly seen Dad during the years of his marriage to Noela, but now he was back in Sydney. In fact, I was only informed of his upcoming marriage by chef Tony Bilson, and he recalls my bursting into tears at the shock. They had had a Hindu ceremony, then in 1986 were legally married in a last-ditch attempt to save the relationship. His relationship with Noela deteriorated and became unworkable. They were fighting constantly, and Noela even damaged one of Dad's paintings in her fury during one of their altercations. His relationship with Noela's daughter was strained, which didn't help; neither did the affair Noela was having with a former lover. Dad had really wanted to make it work. At Clarendon he had found his Provence of Australia—its rolling hills and vineyards inspired some of his greatest works and a new oeuvre in terms of colour.

The final straw came one day when Noela walked into the studio demanding, 'Where's my dinner?' Dad walked out, his box of watercolours under his arm, and returned to Sydney. A few days later, Dad was reaching into a bookshelf when his wedding ring snapped in half as though it had been frozen. It was a high-quality ring, made by renowned jeweller Tony White. Dad took the breakage as a sign: the marriage was well and truly over.

An artist's work is their life. A relationship with someone who is not sympathetic to what they do, who does not appreciate how important art is, simply will not work. Artists' relationships are not so different from any other where work is paramount. If an artist has to stop working, it is like cutting off their lifeblood. Dad feels that Noela tried to use him to further her career, to put her on the artist map of Australia, and then resented him for still being the more successful. She even wanted to stop him working and was highly competitive. The best relationships Dad has had have been those that have enabled him to work, whether by supporting him totally like Mum did, or simply leaving him alone to work, like Katharine did.

By 1988 I was still a student and working part-time at Arthur's. Dad was in Sydney, living in McDonald Street, Paddington, renting a terrace house—almost like he had in his own starving artist years. A few years later he painted *Barcelona—Living in Small Rented Quarters*, one of his greatest works and a metaphor for this period in his life when, after building several houses and going through two divorces in quick succession, he was now feeling the financial after-effects. He was back to the transitory lifestyle of the renter. No matter how restless his spirit, John liked to have a home.

One evening, when I was serving drinks and running the balcony tables, a statuesque red-headed woman walked into the bar with a friend. They sat on the balcony where I was serving, and my ears pricked up at the mention of 'John Wolseley' and 'Alistair McAlpine', both of whom were friends of my father. Sydney is a city where whispers are usually louder than necessary. It wasn't hard to ascertain that the focus of their conversation was falling upon the 'market' of love. Flitting in and out, I overheard a story about how things had not worked out between the redhead and John Wolseley. Her friend said: 'John Olsen is back in town.'

She replied swiftly, 'Well, you know that I am after a successful artist . . .'

Her friend interjected, 'Well, it doesn't get any better than John Olsen!'

The next thing I heard was that writer and academic Christopher Leonard, who knew the redhead, was introducing them at her request. Her name was Katharine Howard, and she was the owner of a bed and breakfast at Wentworth Falls in the Blue Mountains. I did not think much of it at the time: dinner parties, lunches and assignations were the background noise all my life. Typically, I underestimated the passion of the affairs of the older generation.

Shortly after meeting Katharine, Dad, knowing Noela was away, returned to Clarendon with artist Jolly Koh and Katharine to retrieve his studio contents and the rest of his belongings.

Finding the house locked, Dad and Jolly started to walk away only to hear a strange noise. Turning around, they were amazed to see Katharine's feet disappearing through a window, having scrabbled up the drainpipe, and Katherine appearing moments later triumphantly at the open door.

The attraction between Dad and Katharine was immediate and mutual; they seduced each other. Three weeks later they were in Paris and, not long after, my father told me that he was going to marry her. Nine months after they met, he did.

This was one wedding to which we were invited. It was held in the barn-like studio at Wentworth Falls that Dad swiftly built after moving in with Katharine. He was dressed like a country squire on the day.

We had no idea how great an influence Katharine would have upon John, both emotionally and financially. This was a turning point in our lives, in a way, as devastating as when Dad had first left with Noela, only this time the relationship endured for nearly a quarter of a century. We were living our own lives, but Dad was increasingly withdrawn and involved in his own. The small stipend that had been made available to Louise and me as students through the family company suddenly disappeared. Slowly but surely, Katharine came between us, subtly and irrevocably.

13

MENTORS

In my years as an art student, Dad was almost invisible to us, so I found other mentors. First, I worked with the esteemed restaurateur Anders Ousback. A man with an innate sense of style and good taste, Anders was responsible for revivifying some of the gastronomic hot spots of Sydney. He was a cultivated man, and it represented a graduation for me when I went to work for him.

Known as the 'Mr Fixit' of the Sydney restaurant scene, Anders, like Dad, recognised the synergy between food and art, the passion in both, and he relished the way the two influenced each other. When he retired, he became a skilled potter by vocation. As a spiritual protégé of the British potter Lucie Rie, he dug and processed his own clay and directed it to pleasingly ascetic effect.

'Both cooking and clay have their origins in the application of heat, a chemical change, the taking of raw produce and its transformation,' he said at a ceramics conference in 1993. 'The kitchen is divided into the savoury and the sweet. The former, like creating with clay, is its fullest expression. The sweet kitchen with its exactitudes and demands of proportions equals the glaze.'[1]

When I worked for Anders he was overseeing the Hyde Park Barracks Restaurant on Oxford Street, and later the Wharf Restaurant at Walsh Bay. It was the late 1980s, and the Barracks Restaurant was under Australia's first dome, designed by Francis Greenway, in the original convict barracks. I started ferrying plates to society ladies and friends of my father, eventually working my way up to manager.

I seldom use this word but Anders was a bona fide genius, an opinion reinforced by his friends and colleagues. For Anders, it was all about getting the feeling right. Restaurant critic Leo Schofield said that he had 'a sixth sense about food tastes'; John Newton noted that 'wherever Sydney dining has moved, at the point where you can mark a change for the better, a move away from the parochial, there you'll find the hand of Anders Ousback.'[2] Anders taught me about quality, presentation detail and the importance of doing anything (and everything) properly.

Anders was very understated but had great style: he knew that the tiny things done well can often make the biggest noise. His eye was acute, his emotional alertness intimidating. Many have spoken of his 'perfect timing', but I was in awe of the feeling he got just 'right'. I have tried to carry that skill into my work as a gallerist. A sentiment echoed by Dad.

Anders could be a contradictory misanthrope but, paradoxically, was also an incredible entertainer. He shied away from publicity and being photographed but, on his own with a small audience, he was the star, an incredible conversationalist. At the Sydney Theatre Company Wharf Restaurant, after the early sitting for the theatregoers, a more serious dining crowd would appear. Anders would saunter out of the kitchen in his clogs, throw his apron on the piano like a diva with a mink coat and break into Leider. There he would be, in his checked pants and white T-shirt, belting out in his tenor voice the love sonnets of Schumann or Schubert, accompanied by pianist Max Lambert resplendent in a bright silk shirt. At the staff Christmas party one year, Anders arrived high up in a cherry picker, dressed as the Pope. He signalled and blessed us with the sign of the cross as he was slowly lowered into the revellers.

Giving him a lift one day in my car, I found out that Anders was driven to success by the rejection of his father who did not understand him. He told me how one evening he was having dinner at his mother's and the urn of his deceased father had fallen over and smashed. The ashes went everywhere. Everyone was horrified, but Anders laughed hysterically, saying, 'Not even in death can Dad hold it together.' I nearly had a car accident, not knowing whether to laugh or sympathise. That is how Anders loved to entertain: for the shock reaction. He deplored mediocrity of any kind, even in his humour. Once, driving by my gallery in his old cream-coloured Morris Minor, he spotted me out the front and called out: 'Tim, you look like an ego-gallertarian.' He was quick, apt and hilarious.

When he committed suicide, it seemed a terrible irony.

If only he could have learned how to love himself as much as we loved him. He suffered from manic depression, now known as being bipolar, refused to take any medication, and despite his success and intellect was plagued with feelings of failure. After managing the Barracks cafe one weekend, at the Wharf on the Monday I approached him, asking, 'Did you think everything went alright at the Barracks on the weekend?'

He turned and said, 'Why should you ask?'

'Perhaps I'm being paranoid,' I replied.

He looked at me and said, 'The whole universe is paranoid.'

In 1995, Anders had his first critically acclaimed ceramics

exhibition, *White Bowls*, at Rex Irwin's Woollahra gallery,[3] fulfilling another dream. His works were bought by the Powerhouse Museum and the National Gallery of Australia (NGA). Rex said, 'His pots were beautiful and austere and sophisticated—which is what people also said about his restaurants.'[4]

The day in 2004 that I was told he had killed himself in his home at Wombarra, north of Wollongong, at only 54, I thought, 'What a waste.' Having experienced depression through my own addiction issues, I can empathise with the sense of desolate hopelessness he must have felt to resort to that final act. He was full of great spirit and intellect, but overwhelmed with self-judgement, perfectionism and a kind of self-loathing, in denial about all his success and the accolades he drew from his work. Even his parting note pinned on his door ('Do not enter—suicide')[5] was written with panache. He had sent farewell letters to 21 of his close friends.

'When my time comes to an end,' Anders wrote in 1987, 'I have a feeling that I will arrive at that netherworld and the land-scape of my culinary life will be laid out before me.'[6]

Later, when things got really bad for me, I realised exactly what depression feels like: as though it would be a rational decision to take your own life. That feels like the only escape. You lose sight of the suffering your actions may cause others. Luckily, I was able to identify that suicide really is a long-term solution to a short-term problem. You lose sight of the love that so many people have for you. For me, it was my love for my son James and my belief in the existence of a higher power that cared for me, that saved me.

Depression is well known to have a genetic component. I know that my mother suffered, and my father's mother also.

Dad, too, has his moments, and has told me that he uses creativity to work through it. Rumination is one of my weaknesses. Resentment, a false sense of childhood rejection, not being able to let go of stress, and a tendency to think that people are always against me have been obstacles. Those constant thoughts obstructed my ability to move forward mentally and to be more positive, diminish my mistrust of people and, most importantly, to forgive.

Another mentor was Christopher Leonard: an aesthete, writer and academic; a thespian with an Oscar Wilde persona; and, most poignantly, a friend and another father figure to me in Dad's absence.

When I had a day off we would often dine at Kinselas in Darlinghurst, or go skiing at Charlotte Pass where he was a member of a small lodge. Christopher was a big drinker with a vast knowledge of things that I found interesting. He provided the paternal depth that I was used to from my father, and his knowledge of art history, particularly Romanticism, and classical music filtered into my receptive consciousness. It was a strong platonic bond that filled a huge gap. Christopher set me up with a sense of a deeper civilisation that would lay the platform for a confident education; unfortunately, it also set me up (along with working in fine dining restaurants) as a pseudo bon vivant, believing that drinking a bottle or two of wine in an evening was quite a normal thing to do. With alcoholism being a progressive disease, the older I got, the more it got a savage grip on me.

It is one of the stranger aspects of my education that I learned a great deal about art from non-artists. Anders and Christopher

'Undiscovered Australian beauties: Valerie Strong, of Sydney', *The Australian Women's Weekly*, 25 July 1951. (Photo: J.C. Young/Courtesy Bauer Media)

Valerie Strong, c. 1954.

Harry Olsen, John's father, 1930s.

Hazel Strong, Valerie's mother, late 1920s.

John Olsen, c. 1960.

Valerie, c. 1959.

Hazel Strong with her grandson, baby Tim, in 1962.

Tim with his godfather Robert Hughes at Hill End, New South Wales, 1962.

Three-month-old Tim with John at the opening of Macquarie Galleries' Ian Fairweather exhibition, August 1962. (Courtesy *The Sydney Morning Herald*)

Hill End, September 1962: John, Valerie and four-month-old Tim in front of Haefligers Cottage, the artists' residence that was once the home of Paul Haefliger and Jean Bellette.

Valerie and John in front of *Tree of Life*, Clune Galleries, Sydney. The painting won the inaugural Georges Invitation Art Prize in 1963.

Valerie with two-year-old Tim, 1964.

Tim, Valerie and Louise before leaving for Europe in 1965.

Valerie and Louise in France, 1965.

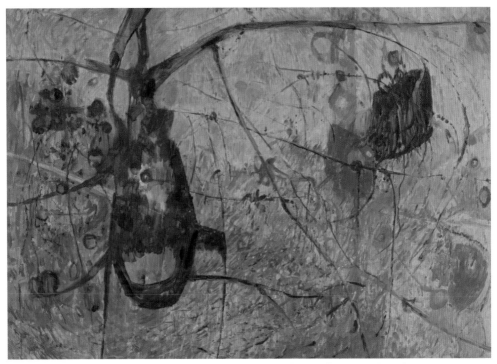

Valerie Strong, *Afternoon Yarramalong*, 1963. Newcastle Art Gallery Collection, Gil Docking Bequest 2018, NAG.2018016. (Courtesy Newcastle Art Gallery)

John Olsen, *Tim going into his room for being naughty*, c. 1965. Collection of Tim Olsen.

Tim (left), with baby Louise on John's knee, Watsons Bay, 1964. (Photo: Robert Walker)

Tim and Louise in Hyde Park, London, 1966.

Valerie in Madrid,
Spain, c. 1966.

Louise in England, 1966.

Tim (far right) with Spanish schoolmates, 1966.

Tim at Stonehenge, Wiltshire, England in 1966.
This photo, taken by Len French, was sent as a
Christmas card.

Valerie, Louise and Tim with John in Spain, 1967.

A beret-clad Tim in France, 1966.

John Olsen, *Tim by Dad*, 1966. Collection of
Tim Olsen.

Louise at The Bakery art school, Paddington, Sydney, 1969.

John and Valerie on Camp Cove beach, 1968. (Photo: Robert McFarlane/Courtesy Josef Lebovic Gallery)

John Olsen, *Tim looking at TV*, 1969. Collection of Tim Olsen.

John Olsen, *Louise and Tim looking at a Pike*, c. 1969. Collection of Louise Olsen.

Louise and Tim on the beach at Watsons Bay, c. 1968.

Tim and Louise with Tim's tortoise on the beach at Camp Cove, c. 1968. (Photo: Robert McFarlane/Courtesy Josef Lebovic Gallery)

Tim, aged six, in the backyard at Watsons Bay, standing next to a bark painting that John acquired on a visit to Arnhem Land.

Outside painter John Bell's studio at Dunmoochin, Victoria, 1969. Louise is on the car; Tim, at far right, stands behind John.

John painting *Love in the Kitchen* at Dunmoochin, 1969. (Photo: Mark Strizic)

Valerie in John's studio at Dunmoochin, 1970. Valerie's *Autumn Pond*, 1970 (far left) and John's *Two Eyes of the Dam*, 1970 (in the middle, rotated 90 degrees) and *Love in the Kitchen*, 1969 (right) hang in the background.

Tim in his Cranbrook school uniform, 1971.

John Olsen, *Salute to Five Bells*, 1971–72, Sydney Opera House. (Courtesy Sydney Opera House Trust)

Valerie and John at the opening of *John Olsen 1971* at the Rudy Komon Art Gallery, in front of the tapestry *Eastern World*, woven by Bruce Arthur and Deanna Conti on Dunk Island, 1969.

Tim with John and Valerie at Watsons Bay, 1973.

20 October 1973: Valerie (at left) with Queen Elizabeth II, when she attended the opening of the Sydney Opera House with Prince Philip.

John with Rudy Komon in front of *Salute to Five Bells*, the Sydney Opera House mural.

Valerie, in Tim's favourite photo of her. (Photo: Robert Raymond)

Valerie in the living room, early 1970s, with John's *Lake Hindmarsh, the Wimmera*, 1970, behind her.

Valerie Strong, *Roofs over Watsons Bay I* and *II*, 1965. Collection of Tim Olsen.

Jane Olsen, early 1970s.

John, Louise, Valerie and Tim at Watsons Bay in the mid-1970s.

Louise, Tim, Clay the dog (named after boxer Muhammad Ali, formerly Cassius Clay) and John, Camp Cove beach, 1975. (Photo: Robert Walker)

Valerie and John with Luke the dog at Dural, late 1970s.

Vincent Serventy with John during *The Land Beyond Time* expedition in Western Australia, 1982.

John and Valerie in the studio, Dural, late 1970s.

Valerie and Tim at Dural.

Valerie and John in the Dural kitchen.

Louise with Valerie's mother Hazel on a family picnic before the move to Dural, c. 1970.

Louise, Valerie and Tim at Pearl Beach, c. 1983. (Photo: Jon Lewis)

John and Louise in front of his studio in Clarendon, South Australia, c. 1982–83. (Photo: Jon Lewis)

Early 1980s: Louise, Valerie, Sarah-Jane McCubbin (John's grandmother), Pamela (John's sister) and Esma (John's mother).

Tim with Valerie at his 21st birthday party, 1983.

Valerie drawing in the Blue Mountains, New South Wales, mid-1980s.

were aesthetes who imbued every moment with creative intensity. They taught me that the approach is such a huge part of the whole. Everything dwells inside the intention.

The most inspiring trips of my life were often full of misadventure. In the late 1980s I went to Spain with Philippe Roussel, a childhood buddy. Travelling with a man or travelling with a woman matters less than travelling with a smoker: it was an agony perpetually waiting for Philippe to finish his cigarette. We got terribly drunk and God knows how we were not killed, continually finding ourselves in underground nightclubs and in bed with strange Spanish women.

I met a beautiful girl called Carmencita in Andalucía. She and her girlfriend took us around the Seville Cathedral. She was like a delicate femme fatale, a diminutive but passionate Carmen straight out of Bizet's opera. Carmencita was studying literature at university, and we spoke at length about Ernest Hemingway and *For Whom the Bell Tolls*. On my return to Australia I found that Dad had a copy. Thoughtfully and with great pride I sent it to her, thinking that it would impress her and help improve her English. She was obviously a very strict Catholic, as some weeks later she returned the book, saying, 'You have offended me with your vulgarity.' At first, I blamed it on Hemingway but then, flicking through the book, I discovered tiny life drawings that Dad had left in the margins—little vignettes of women with their legs spread. Dad! He'd done it again. He gets me in trouble even when he's not even in the room. Carmencita and I had got off to such a pure start at the base of the cathedral, but it all ended on a somewhat pornographic note. 'Dad,' I moaned, 'you fucked it up again.'

He just replied, 'If she's not ready for that, she's not ready for you.'

There are a few lines in that book about the primal truths of nature taught by the patriarch:

I had an inheritance from my father,
It was the moon and the sun.
And though I roam all over the world,
The spending of it's never done.[7]

A tiny pocket of that inheritance was scribbled in the pages of that book. One person's vulgarity is certainly another's elemental sun-and-moon treasure.

Sometimes I travel for light. Australian light beats down with a naked truth that feels exposing and relentless after a while, whereas in Italy it is like walking into a watercolour. After a somewhat hippie childhood, I have to admit to being an extravagant traveller. I love a hotel room with a tall ceiling and opulent furnishings; to feel as if I'm in Versailles, probably because of many years of Zebra motor inns and crunchy commune living. A bottle of Acqua di Parma goes everywhere with me, because people smell you before they see you. I've learned that the best introductions can happen in seconds and that it is the initial apprehension that matters. I have met some of the most important people in my life by chance in hotel lobbies.

My life has been marked by many an art fair and many a strange small town glazed in Mediterranean light, but I am actually a failed vagabond. This apple fell quite far from the tree. Don't tell anyone, but I am a homebody.

When I was around eight or nine, Dad took me with him on a visit to the art dealer Rudy Komon at his gallery on Jersey Road, Paddington. During the conversation Dad mused whether I, too, would become an artist, whereupon Rudy interjected in his thick accent, 'No, the boy will become da dealer!' We left, and as we drove down Jersey Road I remember noticing a tall white building, a cane furniture shop, adjacent to a small reserve, and thinking, 'That would make a great gallery.' Little did I know that premonition would come true.

Rudy, born in Vienna to Czech parents, was an innovative gallery director, art benefactor, patron, bon vivant, wine connoisseur and wine judge.[8] Dad called him 'the doyen of Australian dealers'. He had started art dealing during the war years when he was active in the Czech resistance while working as a journalist— sometimes trading paintings for fresh vegetables out of necessity.[9] He rarely spoke of his wartime years. In 1950 he immigrated to Australia where he started selling antiques, specialising in paintings, then focusing on traditional and contemporary art alone.[10]

Rudy's bravado and vision revolutionised the Australian art scene, sweeping away parochial attitudes and establishing our art on an international level. He converted a former wine shop on Jersey Road into Paddington's first art gallery, the Rudy Komon Art Gallery, choosing Paddington because it was close to transport, the city and the suburbs where 'the rich people lived'. The gallery was opened by his friend Harold Holt, at the time Australia's treasurer and later our seventeenth prime minister, only to be presumed drowned when he mysteriously disappeared while spearfishing off a Melbourne beach in 1967. The night was a triumph, packed with artists and the social elite.

Committed to his artists, Rudy supported and nurtured their careers. He was interested in them on a personal level, in their lives, their problems, wanting to help them, not just gain from them. Childless himself and a father figure to many, he provided his artists with a sanctuary and stability. By instigating European marketing techniques and practices, such as the creation of a 'stable' where artists are nurtured and supported, his reputation grew and his stable included the leading names of the day: Dobell, Williams, Leach-Jones, Drysdale, Whiteley, Nolan, Dickerson, Brack, Pugh and, needless to say, Olsen. Not one to believe in contracts, a handshake was sufficient in Dad's time, but he did demand total allegiance to his gallery. Financially astute, he was generous and benevolent yet would haggle with artists relentlessly over their prices. He believed that Whiteley's pricing of his works was 'absurd'. A modest-living man in many ways, he preferred to own his art stock than live ostentatiously, and paid out some exhibitions of his artists to protect their market. Although he always drank good wines.

Rudy was one of the first gallerists to establish a regular payments system for his artists, a system I still follow today. In the late 1970s he instigated his own royalties system on the reselling of works, paying his artists 10 per cent long before Australia implemented the artists' resale royalty scheme in 2010. He had a visionary eye for quality and talent, and was a man of conviction. 'I will never compromise with the new gimmick art,' he said, loathing conceptualism, performance work and video art.

The friendships Rudy nurtured with all of his artists were enduring. The gallery door was open to his artists, friends and clients, and there were always platters of brawn and sausages on the table, accompanied by wines from his cellar in the upstairs back room. Perpetually hospitable and revelling in good company, Rudy pioneered the gallery lunch; his friends not only included his artists but also prime ministers, captains of industry, restaurateurs, winegrowers, providores, journalists and furniture makers—anyone interesting, as long as they appreciated art, food and wine. He had the capacity to engage in any conversation on any subject, then bring it back to art and the subsequent sale.

The Komons lived in an unassuming house in Watsons Bay not far from us. Patrick White, visiting Rudy for lunch, described his house as 'a decrepit looking semi-detached brick villa on the waterfront . . . We ate a mass of delicatessen and drank several bottles of wine,' White wrote, 'but it was the paintings which made me drunk.'

Dad had a sometimes testy relationship with Rudy—he has said that their relationship was always somewhat tenuous—but they remained friends throughout Rudy's life, even when Dad moved on to David Reid, then Barry Stern. He had felt that Rudy had simply stopped trying in the gallery, with Fred Williams providing him sufficient income with which to relax. He also had an opening of John's, then flew off to Europe the following day, leaving the exhibition unto itself.

The only complaint ever heard about the ebullient Rudy was that, in company, he would keep a personal bottle of great wine at his feet under the table. My father once asked why he wouldn't share his bottle of Grange with everyone, and he replied, 'Because I'm not sharing it with you bloody barbarians!' It was a favourite word of his.

To buy the best, you had to pass a kind of cultural initiation with Rudy. His philosophy was that art was a rare object, and he cared where—or, more specifically, with whom—a work would reside. He was before his time in this belief, a practice prevalent in the major international galleries today: if you want to buy an Anselm Kiefer from Gagosian, for example, you have to have earned your stripes. Being wealthy is not always a passport to buying whatever you like when it comes to high-end art—unless you are prepared to pay well above the market price, of course!

If Rudy did not consider a would-be purchaser worthy of a good picture, he would refuse to sell the work, saying, 'You are not ready yet.' He would often take a client down a meandering path of buying smaller works or works by lesser artists to educate them before they were allowed to graduate to the calibre of the one they initially wanted. This was his approach with the 'big-name' artists such as Williams, when he famously said to one potential buyer, 'I would not sell it [to you]. The painting is too good for you.' Yet buying from an exhibition of an array of an artist's work gives the purchaser an opportunity to compare and contrast, to decide which works are stronger than others. Without the help of an experienced eye, a novice collector may not obtain a good example of an artist's work, or a work from a strong period in their career.

It took some clout and authority to be able to address rich or important collectors this way, not to mention a belief in the deeper virtues of good art not being sold off to 'barbarians'. At one Drysdale opening there was a flurry of sales, red dots appearing everywhere. He loudly instructed his long-term assistant: 'Gwen, Gwen, stop them! They are buying all our stock!'

Rudy is now revered as the innovator he was, a man who left an indelible mark upon both Australian art and the wine industry. Rudy was Cellarmaster of the Wine and Food Society of New South Wales and a judge at the Royal Easter Show for twenty years, and at wine shows across the country with his good friend Len Evans. The Rudy Komon Memorial Perpetual Trophy is still awarded annually at the Sydney Royal Wine Show.[11]

A favourite story of Dad's involved Rudy, with Fred Williams and his wife, having an extended stay at Len Evans's chateau in Bordeaux,[12] where they drank all of his champagne, usually retained for guests at vintage times. When Len met them on their return at the airport, he shouted, 'You bastards! You drank all my champagne!'

Rudy paused, looked Len straight in the eye and responded, expressionless, 'But what else was it for?' With a blunt response like that, there was nothing that Len could say without being accused of being a stingy bastard.

When Rudy died in 1982, he left so much art and his extensive wine cellar behind. His wake, in a large gallery space next to Rex Irwin's gallery, was full of politicians, artists and collectors, the elite of Sydney society. In one of the eulogies, it was said that Rudy's eyes were donated as organs. I'm sure that they were great eyes, but not as perceptive without his experienced mind behind them.

Ruth Komon, Rudy's widow, went on to establish the Rudy Komon Memorial Fund with the AGNSW to support young local artists of new generations, ensuring Rudy's legacy lives on. There is now a plaque dedicated to him at his old gallery premises on Jersey Road, a fitting tribute to a truly memorable man.[13]

To me, Rudy had more character, style and personal clout than most major international gallerists today. He was a brilliant art dealer and a true statesman in the company of any dignitary. He is my greatest mentor in my chosen field.

To commemorate my birth, Rudy gave me a special case of wine, to be saved until my 21st birthday. It was a family legend that I would receive this amazing case of wine that Rudy had personally selected for me on that day and, being the wine connoisseur that he was, it would have been fantastic. Robert Shaw, who sponsored Dad's first trip to Europe, said he would store it for me, accusing Dad of being incapable of not drinking it! Years later it transpired that it had been drunk, even though the case had 'For Tim Olsen on his 21st birthday' written all over it. It reminded me of how Rudy always kept his personal bottle of Grange at his feet under the table, not to be shared, away from all those barbarians.

I thought it was still a brilliant idea so did the same thing for my godson, Tibbo, at his birth, buying a case of the best Australian shiraz that would be at its optimum to drink in 21 years. This time, though, I insisted on leaving the case with his grandmother for safekeeping, and on his 21st he received it.

14

LUNCH WITH DONALD FRIEND

Artist Donald Friend had a close friendship with Margaret Olley. Friend's diaries, published in 2010 after his death, openly discussed his inappropriate relationships with underage boys when living in Bali from 1967–80. While Friend was never charged by authorities, Balinese victims have corroborated his accounts of these events. It is not known if Olley knew of these activities, however this information warrants declaration in a contemporary retelling of history.

—Queensland Gallery of Modern Art, exhibition label, 2019

In June 2019, the Queensland Gallery of Modern Art placed the label text above next to two Donald Friend works included as part of the major exhibition devoted to Margaret Olley.[1] I cannot lay claim to the same level of friendship that Olley had with Donald, but will state categorically that I was completely unaware of his inappropriate relationships when I commenced a series of interviews with him in the late 1980s.

In my last year of visual arts study, I met with Donald Friend and held some informal interviews with him. After six and a half years of hard slog at art school, I still had questions banking up. In this regard, I could possibly describe him as my last mentor in an (in)formal education.

It was a privilege to take tea with Australian art's greatest draughtsman and diarist, but it did not seem a huge deal at the time. Donald Friend, in his later years, was out of fashion. He was underground, living lean but still drawing every day. Outside of the argument about current trends, he was occupying his own continuum, arguing with the great figurative masters and flâneurs, taking notes. The stark loneliness of his last diary entries was not just made manifest by the obvious limitations of old age, ill health or beckoning mortality; I saw them as occupying that cold place of being outside the stream of ideas. The bright young thing of the 1940s was an outsider by the late 1980s, but I have consistently backed the outsider.

It seemed like Donald Friend had always been around. In the 1950s, his wartime friendship with Russell Drysdale led to the establishment of Hill End as an artists' colony, and he was a regular presence in our lives when not off travelling the world. He would blow into our Watsons Bay cottage on a plume of clove cigarette smoke in a loud batik shirt, usually accompanied by a young Balinese man in need of health care. Since the publication of his diaries, much has been made—and rightly so—of Donald's boy models, his lovers and his unconventional living arrangements in Bali. Among the stories of the lavish entertaining of A-list international visitors at his compound (Rupert Murdoch, Mick Jagger, Gore Vidal, to name a few), his journals unashamedly recounted his sexual liaisons with adolescent boys, accompanied by drawings of them.

I do not support the life choices he made. I deplore many of them. Yet what I remember about him from when I was young was his real altruism, his kindness, a consistent dedication to charitable action at a grassroots level. My parents found him wise and entertaining, with a biting wit and wicked sense of humour. He had the most satirical and unpretentious way of dealing with the truth of art—and its many falsehoods.

When we met again in 1987, Friend was so much older, living in damp bohemian digs in a laneway in Woollahra sourced for him by long-term friend Margaret Olley (who, famously, had once proposed marriage to him). I found him chain-smoking, making frequent trips to the lavatory and generally living out what looked like his ninth life in his own art history.

Sacred monsters are at their most vulnerable in old age. The flamboyance of his grand Sanur residence, the journeys to Italy in the blazing 1960s, the whiff of scandal that always seemed to shadow him, and even the extreme vagaries of fame and reputation now all seemed like evaporating smoke rings in his fragile presence. His later diaries testify to the remorse and rage of a declining vitality, the continual self-doubt of the serious artist and a bemused bird's-eye view of an art world he viewed as spilling over, like a runaway experiment from a Petri dish.

It seemed obvious then, and even more so now, that we were divided by two generations, but that never bothered Friend. This was the man who preferred the company of the post-punk layabouts at his local, the London Tavern in Paddington, to the exalted dinner parties that he found pretentious, routine and exhausting. I went to him with pockets full of questions, and instead of pat answers he threw a pile of questions back at me. The answer, he stressed, again and again, was not in the posture or even the desire for art, but the sheer bloody-minded application. It was a position that could only be adopted after a lifetime in art, and in gossip and love and disappointment, in rare success and daily failure. It was revealing to me to connect across generations, and I had to do that to fully understand just what Friend had contributed to Australian art.

'Until the time I went to England,' he told me bluntly, 'all my ideas of the great masters' work, modern and ancient, were entirely from reproductions in art books':

> At that time the reproductions were inclined to be a bit yellow, and you'll see in the works of people like Perceval, and those ones who were then tremendously influenced by old masters and so on, that they even painted with a lot of yellow in their work, to yellow it up a bit, because they thought that was the proper thing—not realising it was just a fault of reproduction. It is not until you see the actual painting that you get this appalling primal shock of seeing the paint itself being so marvellous, practically edible looking, in some of the works.

Every conversation we had inspired me far more than the art-history lectures I was attending, as he spoke of the artists that had interested or maybe even influenced him: the Greeks, Dürer, the madness of Bosch, the decadence of Jean-Antoine Watteau. He said that the satire of his work came from nineteenth-century English illustration and a love of vaudeville. He turned to the Egyptians for an understanding of refining the human form, the ancient Egyptian art that highly influenced the Cubists: Picasso's *Les Demoiselles d'Avignon* really depicts women like tall Egyptian figures. Primitive art may have played its part, too, but the Egyptians were the original minimalists of art. Likewise, he found that African sculpture had the same simplicity.

'The Greeks and the Italians were the sophisticates of the human form,' he told me. 'The beauty of figure derived from the breakthrough in understanding the physiology of the figure, started by da Vinci, is what helped me tremendously when I was a young artist. Masaccio, et cetera.' I was transfixed.

I can well imagine Donald wanting to gobble up an old master, especially if there was a nude inside the picture. 'The nude!' he almost exploded. 'The nude is delectable and ever desirable—it once embraced my whole life and art. The nude is youth, love and the core of happiness.' Whatever people say about his nudes now, Friend was certainly a trailblazing master of the male erotic, well before the Tate placed a penis on its catalogue cover. Art critic Robert Hughes described him as 'one of the two finest draughtsmen of the nude in Australia'.[2]

Talking to this spiky character could be peaceful and confronting in turns. Friend was the master of the cutting final remark, and few escaped the scalpel. But time and a walk through his diaries exposed the fact that Friend saved his harshest criticisms for himself. Mortality, in his view, was potently physical but also aesthetic. His idea of tragedy was to see the muse die before the body followed. From the vantage point of middle age, it is so much more poignant now to see how generously he shared his ideas with me and how his wit (if not hope) never left him.

Dad visited Friend in Bali several times, including with my mother in 1973, as did gallerist Stuart Purves, and artists Ian Rose and Peter Upward. They brought Donald much-needed art supplies. Dad wrote in his journals that 'Friend's work seems to be an idealisation of the people, beautiful and handsome though they are, and he has placed them in an environment of his own, with sculptures, paintings and masks, done in a manner which exemplifies Friend's own taste and discrimination, his wit and (at times) Georgian humanity and sympathy.'

A retrospective of his life's work in 1989 at the AGNSW was staged less than a year after his death, and curator Barry Pearce's accompanying monograph raised the main question of his attainments: was Friend a master or dilettante?[3] To make the leap from confident drawing to important painting is a great hurdle. I feel Friend's figurative work is up there with Michelangelo and the masters, but I do not think he was a particularly great painter. Over time this seems to me less and less of an impediment. The legacy of his journals, the raw cleaving quality of his wit and the dogged principle of pure draughtsmanship all serve as major contributions. Friend remains an exemplar of concentration in an age of abundant distraction.

My most successful artists hold to the rigour of their practice, whether after a sell-out show or in a fallow season. And though I had great teachers, the last one, the least expected one, left the most enduring impression. It was difficult to get a straight answer out of Donald Friend, and you were not meant to. He could be direct and illuminating or vague and confusing. Like a Zen kōan that takes years to decode, his deliberately opaque and often blatantly evasive conversation style was like a stone tossed into a well. Money was a mildly offensive necessity. Abstract art was a peripheral sensation. Disappointment was normal, but the quest was sacred and intensely personal.

By then I had heard so many conflicting theories about art, but Friend seemed to bring everything back to base for me as he urged me to simply carry a sketch pad and put the world in the palm of my hand. 'The world is my tiny universe,' he said with some urgency, 'and a young artist has to create their own tiny universe and immerse themselves within it. The absolute focus is subtlety of line. The searching line sometimes close to a kind of calligraphy, allows for delicacy, strength and flexibility. Find your line!'

The other aspect was to do with discipline and the idea that if you're an artist you have a natural inclination to draw every day. I asked him what the crux was of being a better artist and he replied, 'Just do a bloody drawing a day.' Like learning to play a violin, it is the greatest tip for becoming a better draughtsman. A simple message, really, and it highlights how many people complicate everything, and the importance of maintaining a direct approach. He said that, for most students learning how to draw, it is about hard discipline and repetition. For me, right from the beginning, it was a joy. It was all I wanted to do.

Friend's creative principles have not dated. He attributed to great works of art a quality that he called, 'authority', and he believed that it was an essence that needed no frame, no cata-logue essay and no government grant. 'It should,' he thundered at me, 'be instantly recognisable.' I probably just nodded, but it is a quality I have let guide me ever since. No amount of pomp can disguise the truth of an artwork. It is self-evident. It is there or it is absolutely not present. It was a quality he looked for in every corner of life.

A dedicated diarist since the age of fourteen, Friend's journals were published posthumously, in four volumes, by the National Library of Australia (NLA), a chronicle of a life in art. 'Our sensory experiences and thoughts are all part of our development,' he told me. His diaries were central to that development, he said: 'Our mind expands and creative thought can only blossom the more we retain and journal our sensory interaction of the world.'

Another message that came through was that your intellec-tual growth should mirror your creative growth. Some artists often do not read enough. Other artists do not really explore fertilising their own minds by being interested in the way others think, the way others look at pictures. An inquiring mind is a fertile garden of ideas. Simply, to read more avidly is to be better informed about the world and, subsequently, about yourself. It is your disposition and your interaction with your surroundings that make you become a better artist and a better person.

My ultimate hopes for those conversations with Friend were that they would become a book. Its tentative title was *What They Don't Teach You at Art School*. As the revelations of paedophilia unfolded, though, I quickly realised that this would be impossible and unwise. Friend's actions would now be irrevocably joined to his art.

Friend had donated his diaries to the NLA on the proviso that they be published. In 2006, seven years after his death, the fourth and final volume, *The Bali Diaries*, was released. It covered the last 22 years of his life and included descriptions of his sexual trysts with young boys. Injudiciously the editors neglected to omit the names of these boys, and at least one sought compensation from the NLA.[4]

In the diaries Friend was brutally honest but unrepentant, describing himself as 'a middle-aged pederast who's going to seed'. It was unforgivable, a confession from the grave. He was always an enigma and condemned himself posthumously in a way that was typical of his sarcasm for society. He was placed immediately and eternally on the wrong side of art history.

The debate on morally compromised artists is increasingly complex. Certain Australian museums have decided to remove Friend's artwork from public view. The list of artists who were perpetrators of crimes and heinous acts is long and old: Caravaggio committed murder ('it was manslaughter' has been the defence); the racist and syphilitic Gauguin, Chuck Close and, yes, Picasso have all behaved deplorably. When artist Dennis Nona was jailed for sex with two underage girls, his work was immediately removed from public display and remains so.[5] In the cases of Roman Polanski and a long list of perpetrators now exposed through the #MeToo movement, there are people who defend or excuse a 'famous' sexual predator, separating their acts from their art. I find it impossible to do so.

People may frown at a Donald Friend work as they walk past in a museum, but the next weekend they will be dancing at a wedding to a Michael Jackson song or watching a film by Polanski that night. It is extremely difficult to live by our convictions without our lives becoming one long demonstration. When looking at Friend's work I still struggle, torn between admiration for his mastery as a draughtsman and disappointment at his behaviour. If publicly 'outing' an artist's abuses alongside their work is the answer—a full transparency to ensure our history, art or otherwise, does not lose relevance—then so be it. I do not think that something well crafted should be admonished because of its creator. The conversation about the separation of the artist's actions or accusations from their art, whatever the medium, will continue.

When I look back on those meetings with Friend, I smile to think of what he would make of my career now. His views on art dealers were well known and, with his acerbic wit, he was scathing:

Dealers. I don't pretend they're all alike, but it does them a power of good if one is blatantly unfair about them occasionally, as a tribe. One of the essential techniques of art dealing consists of baiting mouse traps with cat's flesh. A surprising number of dealers themselves suffer from sore paws. From the artist's side of the fence, it is often a simple love–hate convenience situation which sometimes expands to a love-money, hate-too-much-work-convenient-if-possible-to-be-paid-in-advance situation. They have their problems.

Just before this book went to press, I attended a lunch at Lucio's with Dad, Tim Storrier, Lou Klepac and Nicholas Pounder. Klepac, who is an authority on Friend,[6] raised the continual controversary. One point made was regarding Friend's irrefutable wit. Klepac pointed out that this was his Jewish heritage (his great great-grandfather, convict Uriah Moses,[7] had converted from Judaism just eleven days before his death; Friend was born Donald Moses). Jewish wit is synonymous with the people.

The conversation at the lunches is always intoxicating, arguments about art, politics and life, sometimes heated to the point of causing a minor disturbance. I am now honoured to often be included, not just as John's son, but as one who has earned his right to sit at the table. To listen and be able to contribute to the discourse is a privilege. I did not imagine as a small boy sitting under the table that one day my own place would be set. I walk away from the lunches invigorated, wiser and frequently highly amused at the erudite exchange. It is fantastic to add the word 'colour' to debate at the table.

15

THE GODFATHER

My first real trip to New York as a 'nobody' in the early 1990s was a revealing one. I had been coming at art every which way, through years of study and through friendships. Now, finally, I was an emergent dealer, armed with a few phone numbers and a portfolio of Dad's etchings under my arm. Dad been drip-feeding me prints to sell since my early student days, nudging me towards dealing under the guise of financial necessity. Rather than just giving me money, he wanted me to earn it. It was to take years for me to realise how insightful and fortuitous this was. It was never going to be educational institutions that would form the basis of my career but raw living and experience.

Holding me up on arrival at JFK airport, customs agents grilled me about the contents of the folio and scrolled through my father's work. Because my middle name is John, I was able to convince them that it was my work and that I was in New York trying to find a gallery. Staring me in the eye, one wizened agent asked, 'Is this what you call modern art? Son, if you can make a living out of these, good luck to you!'

As a result of a series of dinners and lunches with expat

friends, I managed to quickly sell all the prints and came home with more money than I had left with.

While there, I organised a meeting at the M. Knoedler & Co. Gallery, then one of the oldest and most respected art galleries in New York, having opened its doors in 1846. Meeting with the gallery's director, Ann Freedman, I presented a book on my father by the art writer and curator Deborah Hart. She looked at the work; I mentioned that John was a close friend of Robert Hughes and was already in several important American collections. She said, 'It is all too hard and too far to show an artist from Australia.' It was the first time that I got a true perspective on how irrelevant Australian art was to the international art market then. They just thought that even a great artist like my father John was too geographically removed to put their energy behind. Going to New York to pitch Australian art was like being Copernicus trying to convince the clergy that the Earth is not flat and doesn't fall away south of the Brooklyn Bridge.

Knoedler represented the Boston-based artist John Walker— an old friend of my father's from more than a decade earlier, when Walker had taught painting at the Victorian College of the Arts in Melbourne. I knew that glowing references from John Walker and Robert Hughes could convince them that Dad was worth a punt, but it never eventuated.

I realised in that moment that if I ever wanted to show our art to New York I would have to do it myself. I came home with mixed feelings, only dreaming that I would open a gallery there twenty years later.

I was truly blessed to have two godfathers, neither one of them official. My very unofficial 'christening' was at the local pub in Hill End, when Dad poured beer over my forehead and his friends all cheered—Robert Hughes and Russell 'Tas' Drysdale proudly standing in as godfathers, with Donald Friend in attendance. I was named after Russell's son Tim, who tragically suicided far too young. Dad says, 'There was much jollity on the day!' I had always thought that my baptism was with red wine so was a little disappointed to hear recently that it was beer, not a vintage Grange Hermitage, that had anointed me.

A godfather can be an integral part of your life or famously absent. Whenever Dad was at lunch with Bob Hughes, they would call me; we would chat about what I was up to, Bob would express his pride and, as I got older (and had something to say), we developed a relationship over the phone. When it came to the crunch, though, he rarely had the time for peripheral children, or even for his own son, Danton. By the early 1990s, he was an internationally renowned art critic and writer. *The Fatal Shore*, published in 1986, was a bestseller, and he was well on the way to being 'the most famous art critic in the world', a title bestowed on him by Robert Boynton of *The New York Times* in 1997.

Hughes had two godsons: the other was Alex, the son of Malcolm and Lucy Turnbull. One day, in the late 1990s, I got a call from Dad. He was having lunch with Hughes and the Turnbulls and invited me to join them. It was a very special afternoon and, at the end of it, Hughes said, 'There is one thing I'd like to do. I've never had a photograph with both my godsons.' Alex and I stood on either side of him for the shot. I do not have a copy of that photograph but hope that one day it might turn up. One of Hughes's favourite mottos is still particularly vivid: 'I couldn't give a flying fuck through a rolling doughnut.' That wound up being the best advice he ever imparted to me.

Hughes had left Australia for Europe in the mid-1960s. He settled in London, where his career in art criticism began and he wrote the first of his books, *The Art of Australia*, before moving to New York as art critic for *Time Magazine*. He blended scholarship with a meticulous memory and the rakish spark of the vernacular. Hughes used his acerbic wit to tear apart the phonies in the art scene: the top three on his hit list were Andy Warhol, Jean-Michel Basquiat and Julian Schnabel. He said of Schnable: 'The art looked radical without being so; it was merely novel, and that quality soon outwears itself. However, in 1980 the uncertainty of new-market taste was such that if someone stood up to assert loudly and repeatedly that he was a genius, there was a chance he would be believed.'[1]

Of the three, only Schnabel is no longer so deeply revered (as a painter), but he moved on to filmmaking and made a film about Basquiat—one that Hughes detested, calling it 'a sentimental piece of myth-mongering mixed with self-aggrandizement'. 'The worst living American painter does a film about the worst dead one' was his pithy, memorable description.[2]

Schnabel seems a bit more benign now, almost prescient. In 1988, it was almost scandalous to move seamlessly from painter to filmmaker to hotel decorator and property developer as Schnabel did, and yet to the millennial this is not just the norm but the aspiration. Art continues to chase its own tail, but Hughes ate poseurs for breakfast and smartly made them his bread and butter.

He also had a photographic memory. He could read a page and remember every word. He had not only a huge grasp of art and world history but also an attuned and acute knowledge and intuition about art, and he could pinpoint a good or a bad handler of the brush. He could describe art using the tongue of a poet, with the twist of a cultivated larrikin. He baffled many of the art world's elite, who could not believe an Australian could rise to such an important position in international art criticism.

Hughes's prophecy that the New York art world would implode for lack of content did not come to pass and, as Patrick McCaughey sagely noted in 2016, sometimes he had more spite in him than affection: 'Rancor becomes the enemy of Hughes' wit. An undercurrent of abuse runs through his writings on art.'[3]

I don't have a signed copy of *Nothing if Not Critical* or *The Shock of the New* on my bookshelf but I do have a searing portrait of his face, ragged with the vicissitudes of the sun, steak and scotch.

I had spent most of my earlier life searching for father figures, never finding them in the inner circle of my own father, and I lacked the fruity anecdotes and rhetorical smarts to joust with a generation who kept intricate journals and had a true intellectual ambition to shatter provincialism with experience. In that sort of company, my initiation was always going to be a long one. I was not the only child of the 1960s to feel inferior to our parents' generation, and Hughes himself wrote of the damage that the 'Swinging Sixties' had brought to many families.

It was easy to side with Hughes when he was in the middle of a tear-down because he often chose artists of such extreme contrast that the senior of the crew could not help but seem the wiser. Savagely he sliced through the Brit Pack, using Lucian Freud as his scythe: 'At 81, Freud is so much younger than any of the Brit-art pack installed on the other side of the Thames: younger than Damien Hirst's slowly rotting shark in its tank of murky formaldehyde; weirder than David Falconer's *Vermin*

Death Star, which is composed of thousands of cast-metal rats; and about a hundred times sexier than Tracey Emin's stale icon of sluttish housekeeping, her much-reproduced bed.'

Hughes was like a locomotive in perpetual motion, with an ability to write prose that was dense and loaded. Yet if he sensed even the slightest weakness or frailty of character, his vitriol was unlimited.

The example he set for so many younger Australians, though, was that one Antipodean voice could rise above the clatter and the cultural cringe and seriously make it. I like to think that we would have a lot to talk about now if we were to meet again today.

The baton of Australian art criticism passed from Hughes to Sebastian Smee, journalist, art critic and Pulitzer Prize winner.

Sebastian's father was a great scholar and was once my history teacher at King's, and a house master of one of the boarding houses. I remember Sebastian as a small blond-haired boy, like me. One afternoon he chased a few of us with a blasting hose as we passed by his house on the school property.

After graduating from The University of Sydney with Honours in Fine Arts, Sebastian immediately made his mark as a critic with his beautifully written and engaging reviews. At lunch with Dad and me once, when he was a local arts critic in Sydney, Dad said to him, 'If you really want to be important, you've got to do what Bob Hughes did: leave Australia.'

And he did just that, leaving for the United Kingdom soon after, working at *The Art Newspaper*, and writing for *The Times*, *The Guardian*, *The Independent*—in fact, nearly all of the daily newspapers. During the four years he spent in London, Sebastian befriended artist Lucian Freud, and wrote the accompanying essays to five books on Freud's work, along with essays for books on Mark Bradford, Fred Williams and photographer Max Dupain.

Returning to Australia, Sebastian became the national art critic for *The Australian* until 2008 when he joined *The Boston Globe*. It was while working at the *Globe* that he won the Pulitzer Prize for Criticism in 2011, praised for his 'vivid and exuberant writing about art, often bringing great works to life with love and appreciation'.[4]

Sebastian met Robert Hughes only once, when he was the arts critic for *The Australian* in 1996, just after Hughes had completed his history of American art, *American Visions*, and was visiting Australia. Writing about their meeting after Hughes's death, Sebastian described Hughes as 'warm, brilliant, and generous', taking the time after the interview to speak with some schoolchildren, engaging and charming. He captured the Robert Hughes that Dad remembers, 'the liveliest, most influential art critic Australia has produced . . . a brilliant popular historian, a polemicist, a critic-at-large, and even a congenial memoirist'. Sebastian pinpointed Hughes's appetite for knowledge, argument and experience, his ability to 'convert sensuous experience (and especially visual experience) into brilliant, vital prose—prose that popped'.[5]

In his insightful 2016 book *The Art of Rivalry*, Sebastian examined the 'relationships at the roots of artistic genius' of frenemies Matisse and Picasso, Manet and Degas, de Kooning and Pollock, Freud and Bacon.[6] I saw similarities in the friendships of Dad and his contemporaries, a fine line between mateship and artistic rivalry, artists who inspired and stimulated while sometimes annoying the hell out of each other. It is an engrossing read.

Art is a visual rather than verbal language. Sometimes it whispers.

Without mentioning my father, my favourite artists of all time are Agnes Martin, Giorgio Morandi and Ian Fairweather. They are all artists who created reduced images possessing an inner power beyond any art. In trying to describe one thing, they say everything. They provide a portal for my soul, a contrast to the complex, chaotic art I grew up around for most of my life. It was my mother who taught me the value of subtlety. She often said, 'What is felt is better left unsaid.'

It is not what's in the art, it is what's in me that enables me to interpret it and then in turn to interpret myself, an exchange of energies that these artists are able to nourish. They represent a place of peace, of solitude and contemplation, with the inner workings that give solidarity to my thoughts and feelings. The works that move me are a conduit for something more monumental. When an artist gets it right, it can be a kind of spiritual experience.

One of the most life-changing exhibitions I have ever seen was the Agnes Martin exhibition at the Dia Beacon museum outside New York.[7] Her serene, simplistic, repetitive geometric patterns and grids capture the spiritual nature of the landscape in the ideal of classical perfection; the light grey washes and pastels seem to emanate light. There were her earlier works before she sought refuge in a remote New Mexico desert, and later works from just before her death in 2004. It was a sublime experience that left me paralysed in psychological amazement the whole way back along the Hudson River, on the hour-long train ride back to the city.

In the simple still lifes of Giorgio Morandi, the bottles and clay pots might just be objects, yet in a sense I feel that they seek an inner structure and solace. This is art that does not dictate to me how I should feel; these are artists obsessed with making art for art's sake. Beyond the simplicity, there is an elevation of consciousness.

Ian Fairweather's beauty dwells in his contradictions: in a reactive demonstration against his British teachers, he rejected Cubism but painted tonally; he denied abstraction but pushed Australian painting (finally) out of landscape and into Modernism. He was obsessed by Cézanne. He was a quiet man who painted raw figurative work using poor materials, works that combined worldly sophistication with an educated innocence.

If you want to talk about the artist as a purist, Fairweather was an undeclared saint, probably the purest artist Australia has ever produced, even if he was born and raised in the United Kingdom. Despite his misanthropic behaviour, Fairweather was an artist of true integrity, creating in the spirit of selflessness, in the unadulterated true love of just making art. He never was concerned about impressing or pleasing anyone. The lucidity he created in his art, the underlying internal construct, is the internal mechanism I aspire to.[8]

Fairweather was a hero and mentor to Dad. He first visited Fairweather on Bribie Island the year before I was born. Dad was doing a series of portraits of the artists whom he admired: Fairweather, John Passmore, Lloyd Rees. Transfixed by the man, he was nonetheless appalled at the squalor of Fairweather's life: the artist was living off tinned food; his depressing, uncomfortable shack was swarming with mosquitoes; he was existing (not living) like a derelict, a modern-day castaway. Dad described him as having 'a presence like no one else' he had ever met, with 'a beautiful, cultured voice, the voice of a gentleman'.

Fairweather would paint on newspaper, without archival concerns. He did not care about art as a timeless object; it was for personal gratification. A potential audience in a museum or a national gallery like the Tate was the least of his concerns. Macquarie Galleries would send up canvases for him to work on instead, to extend the perpetuity of his art through quality materials, and would be exasperated to discover that the canvas had not ended up on an easel, but rather had become a roof for his tropical shack. A calico ceiling was as gentrified as his home ever got, hardly a safe retreat should a cyclone hit.

I love Fairweather's work from China the most, when he was living in the former American concession building overlooking the bustling, chaotic Soochow Creek, travelling to towns such as Suzhou where he was enchanted by the contrasting tranquillity and spirituality. The feel, touch and palette of these works are so subtle and egoless. One of the works from this time was gifted to Louise by Dad, who had received it in lieu of payment from Rudy Komon. At the time, Dad gave me a Fred Williams.

To my mind, Ian Fairweather is the antithesis of contemporary art's decadence and greed.

As prices in the international art market soar to astounding heights, the vulnerability to fraud, forgeries, price ramping and breach of fiduciary duty increases across all markets, from the most respected galleries and art dealers in the world to the blatant knock-offs found online. The art world is not governed by the same laws as other industries. The responsibility of authenticity and provenance is essential. Trust in the integrity of your art dealer is paramount.

It is estimated that 80 per cent of all art crime is fraud, fakes and forgeries, not art theft, though art heists do make great movies. It is up to the gallery, dealer or auction house—or the family, as in the case of Picasso—to ensure a work's validity. The compilation and continuation of a formal catalogue raisonné provides a means of identification and reliable reference. Brett Whiteley's seven-volume, 2400-page catalogue raisonné was recently completed, a mammoth seven years in the collation by art historian Kathie Sutherland.[9] Dad's own catalogue raisonné is well underway by Kylie Norton, in both an online version and a multi-volume fine-art print edition.

The exhaustive 33-volume Picasso catalogue raisonné by Christian Zervos is now hailed as a masterpiece. Zervos commenced the monumental project in the early 1930s, listing over 16,000 of Picasso's paintings and drawings. The final volume was published in 1978, after the death of both its author and subject. Original versions of the elusive catalogue have fetched up to $200,000 at auction. A limited edition republished in 2013 was the first English translation; it sells for around €20,000.

A few decades after my unfruitful visit to M. Knoedler & Co. in New York, the gallery's doors closed permanently and abruptly, in 2011. A high-profile scandal involving more than twenty fake paintings, including several Jackson Pollocks and an infamous Rothko, had forced its closure. Even uber-gallerist Larry Gagosian has been caught up in fraud scandals, with two lawsuits for fraud and unjust enrichment over a Jeff Koons Popeye sculpture and a Roy Lichtenstein painting.

Artists can be naive, trusting souls. Very few have the canny business minds of the Young British Artists of the 1980s and '90s. As an artist gets older, they risk being exploited by their own families, their carers or their representatives who want to benefit from their estates. In the art world, this abuse has seen fraudulent works produced, such as Robert Indiana's iconic *LOVE*; unscrupulous art dealers or consultants stealing works or mementos from a deceased artist's studio, locking out the family; the gift or reduced-value sale of works; and contracts and agreements forcibly signed by the trusting, medicated or infirm.

My favourite sculpture is *Mug Lair* by Mike Brown. 'Mug lair' is derogatory Australian slang for a person who is stupid and vulgar. I grew up fascinated by this anti-formalist work. As a three- or four-year-old child, I related more to this than my father's work. For me, this sculpture was like a totem at play, accessible and tactile. The son of an upper-middle-class family, the brilliant, controversial Brown dropped out of East Sydney Tech where he was studying art, aimlessly drifting until he joined Colin Lanceley, Magda Kohn and Ross Crothall working from a dilapidated terrace in Annandale. They became known as The Annandale School, launching the short-lived 'imitation realist' movement, which his biographer, Richard Haese, claims to be the 'third important movement in Australian art' after the Heidelberg School in the 1880s and '90s, and Sidney Nolan and Albert Tucker's Angry Penguins group in the 1940s.[10]

During his prolific career, Brown encompassed virtually every aspect of contemporary art, working in all styles and directions as epitomised in *Embracing Chaos*, the title of his first retrospective survey exhibition at the NGA. Always the misfit, Brown had a personal life that mirrored his art, a mess of disastrous relationships, substance abuse and the drug addiction that aggravated his psychological problems.

'What-the-hell are you people doing in an art gallery, anyway??' he wrote in 1972. 'If you're looking for art, you won't find it here. You might as well hope to find religion in a church, health in a pill-bottle, youth in a jar of cosmetics, or true-love in a brothel.'[11]

He led a scandalous life (even to his contemporaries) until his death in 1997, being proudly the only Australian artist to be successfully prosecuted for obscenity. (The obscenity convictions of the *OZ* trio—Richard Walsh, Richard Neville and Martin Sharp—were quashed, and Bill Henson didn't make the cut.)

The man could also write, when he was not being purely splenetic or rancorous. His catalogue essay for his exhibition at Watters Gallery in 1972 was incisive, and to me as relevant today as it was nearly 50 years ago:

> We have forgotten that art isn't some special condiment you splash on life to make it taste a little better: if it is anything at all, it is everything there is, or was or will be, everything that a person can do, think or say to another. It is a way of living and thinking, a way for me to transmit to you the totality of my being and for you to transmit your totality to me.[12]

Yet he could also spew forth bitterness. His 1964 work *Kite*, a handwritten diatribe now in the collection of the Heide Museum of Modern Art, Victoria, is a raging manifesto on what he saw as the commercialisation and rarefied aesthetics of the Sydney art scene. In it, he declared that art in Sydney was like 'a cancer which won't stop flourishing until it has eaten the heart out of its own futile existence'.[13]

The work incorporated a photograph of twelve artists featured in an exhibition at Hungry Horse Gallery in Paddington the year before. In the exhibition catalogue, each of the artists had their own page featuring one of their works. Brown singled out Dad: 'John Olsen is there, of course, with a painting which amply illustrates the fact that, now that the abstract revolution has been won in Sydney, Olsen has no further function and nothing more to say. Being a purely derivative painter, he is doomed to ride his chosen bandwagon until it crashes.'

Kite was seen as a personal attack on Rudy Komon and the other Sydney gallery owners of the time. It was disappointing considering Rudy's integrity in his dealings with artists and their work, and his commitment to nurturing the arts. Dad was particularly irked by it, having opened our home to Brown as an artist and friend on many occasions.

Brown abandoned Sydney for Melbourne in protest. I can only wonder what he would think of the art scene now, but my father certainly had the last laugh: that bandwagon hasn't crashed yet!

The reclusive Ian Fairweather climbed aboard a homemade boat on a beach near Darwin on 29 April 1952. Drifting off into the Timor Sea, he had only a limited supply of bread and a compass. This has been interpreted as an act of deliberate finality for the 60-year-old, who was said to be desperately trying to retrieve a shipment of paintings that had gone astray. However, an interview in 1962 offers a different version: 'I wanted to get to Portuguese Timor, as the next best thing to Bali, where I had done the best painting of my life.' When a pearling lugger spotted him about 50 kilometres from land and asked him if he wanted a lift back to Darwin, he replied: 'No, I'm going to Timor. Is this the right road?'[14] The search planes gave him up for dead a week or so later.

Somehow he survived, reaching shore sixteen days later, irreversibly changed, with a new lease on life. He went on to become one of our most original and respected artists, one of the first Australian artists to be hung in the Tate with his work *Bathing Scene, Bali*. Always trust an artist who reaches the shore without a map.

PART
THREE

16

THE BOY IN THE BACK ROOM

The day after I finished my degree, I went to lunch with Dad and Stuart Purves of Australian Galleries. John had just signed up with Stuart in Sydney after having shown in Melbourne with them for many years. By the end of lunch, Stuart had offered me a job as part of their foray into the Sydney art scene in 1989, having established themselves in Melbourne in 1956.

After lunch we went back to my rented studio so I could show Dad the works I had completed for my final examinations. There was a box full of oil paints on the table. Dad said, 'I'm taking these—you won't need them anymore. You have the ability to become a good art dealer.' It seemed Dad had the final say in my vocation and out the door went my paints and brushes.

Every moment of my life up to that point had been in contact with visual art. I had made some fine etchings, had drawn from life models for what felt like decades, and primed and daubed and finished canvases, but sadly, no, I did not have the calling. There are many career artists, but art is not a career. It is a compulsion. I was diligent, but without that essential spark. Dad has always said, 'To be a successful artist, you either need to be bloody good or forget it.' The art world still called me. For the purists at art school, working for a commercial gallery was like selling your soul.

Australian Galleries was considered at the forefront of Australian art when I joined them. It was the most appropriate position for a trainee dealer. They were one of the first serious galleries and had a stable that included Brett Whiteley, Arthur Boyd, Jeffrey Smart and, of course, my father, among others. The boom of the late 1980s had peaked, and there was a plethora of artists who were selling regularly above the $50,000 mark. It was no wonder the directors—Stuart Purves and his mother Anne— could justify opening in Sydney. By having galleries in both cities they could have both important art-buying centres covered; by getting the Melbourne-represented artists to join them in Sydney, they effectively had two bites of the cherry and artist exclusivity.

I worked for Stuart for three years, living in Melbourne for the first six months in an original art deco–style apartment block with my friend Don Bennetts, a film producer and an ex-heartthrob from the 1950s TV show *Hit Parade*. Don had also just made a film about Dad, Donald Friend and Lloyd Rees. Melbourne was an amazing experience: while I worked hard, the night life offered new attractions and I discovered that being able to dance was a great way to meet women in a new city.

Australian Galleries is situated in what was then the unfashionable suburb of Collingwood, away from Toorak and the esteemed wealth belt of Melbourne. Like any novice, I had to learn from the bottom up. Working in galleries takes footwork. Working with people like Stuart, I learned how enthusiasm is infectious. Enthusiasm about an artist, and an artist's work, makes you need and want to be involved. To own a piece of art enriches your life; it brings a positivity. Owning an artwork goes beyond decoration. It gives personal kudos—what the artwork says about you to society, to your friends or to your contemporaries. You either buy art for deeply personal reasons, to lose yourself in it, or you buy it to make a statement. It is a way of expressing the spiritual side of yourself. I would include books in that, too. My writer friend Angela Mollard once said to me, 'Objects are to homes what anecdotes are to storytelling.' I have always believed that a house without art and books lacks substance.

The success of the Purveses was built on their ability to create a serious gallery. Their approach to business systems and administration had not been seen before in the local art world. They were probably one of the first galleries to use computers. They made art an elite, elegant experience, attracting the wealthy buyers and the blue-chip artists to match. At one stage, the Purveses represented every major artist in Australia in what was then a dour industrial suburb, making the gallery a 'destination'. Their exhibition history was exemplary. Only John Brack and Fred Williams come to mind as artists who never exhibited with them, at least in their lifetimes.

The Purveses did not have an adventurous, risk-taking approach, and I doubt that they would have represented my father in his early career, but they brought professionalism and style to the way a gallery could operate. While working for them in Collingwood, I constantly imagined putting a business like theirs in an area with more foot traffic, located closer to more affluent suburbs. Which is exactly what I ultimately did.

Anne Purves was the grande dame of Australian art, an immaculate and stylish woman dressed in haute couture that was beyond any leading department store in Australia at the time. She adored her golden boy Stuart and had implicit trust and faith in him running the gallery: not once did I witness her instructing, publicly mothering or castigating Stuart in any way, despite his flash and sometimes high-flying tendencies.

Stuart well and truly became the future of the gallery after his father Tam, the gallery's co-founder, died in 1969. He was a perfectionist and was constantly renovating the gallery. The hammers never stopped. My father often told him he should be putting his money back into his artists, not into marble bathrooms at the gallery.

Tam was a New Zealand businessman and a conservative man. When one opening got a little too rowdy and drunken, he asked the exhibiting artist to quieten his arty crew and promptly shut the bar. 'Reopen the bar or I will be taking my friends down to the local pub,' the artist demanded. 'And I'll be picking up my paintings tomorrow!' Tam instructed the waiters to put the large flagons of white wine back. One guess who the artist was! Stuart still laughs about it.

Anne did not rate women artists as highly as their male counterparts, purely on a commercial basis. As in all pre-21st-century societies, works by female artists did not reach the returns of works by their male counterparts. There was the same gendered disparity among Indigenous artists' work, the exception being the Queen of the Desert, Emily Kame Kngwarreye.

Anne's favourite artist was Arthur Boyd, with whom she had a very close friendship. She respected my father, but I sensed that she thought of him more as a working-class larrikin—and she was right. Out of all the Australian Galleries artists, Arthur was certainly the most remunerative. Today his prices still exceed those of his modern master brothers. When Arthur was in town, he would escort Mrs Purves to the opera and they would dine together after. The first sign that 'King Arthur' was in town was that Anne would spend the afternoon at the hairdresser. At the mere mention of his name, her eyes would light up.

On one of Dad's early trips to Lake Eyre, Stuart accompanied the group, setting off in a white four-wheel drive, a dinghy strapped to the roof. After a few days, they ran out of grog and Stuart was sent to replenish the supplies. A few days later he was spotted on the horizon, a tiny ball of dust gradually increasing in size as he drew closer, and met with jubilant cheers on his arrival—crisis averted. In the scrapbook in the Australian Galleries archive there is a series of three polaroid photographs showing the approaching vehicle, materialising like an arenaceous beast.

My father has had a long association with Lake Eyre. For years its dry salt pan was known as the place where the land-speed record had been broken. Yet when two northern rivers flood simultaneously, it fills to form an inland sea, a display of the rise and fall of an ecosystem that usually only happens a few times each century. Then the inland desert sea is suddenly abundant with life—the migration of birds and fish, and the emergence of underground hibernating frogs—only to decline as the bed salt slowly infiltrates the fresh water from the rivers. Just as suddenly, death is omnipresent: dead pelican chicks, dead fish. Nothing can survive. Over a few years, the land resumes its usual existence as a salt pan. Dad was fascinated by this. Flying above the lake, he loved observing the contrasting colours of bleaching white sand with pink salt, and the red-ochre earth. It was a delicious, beautiful palette for an artist to salivate over, one unique to the Australian continent.

Another highlight of the Australian Galleries archive is a series of photographs of a notorious artist lunch at the Galleries in 1983, including Dad, John Firth-Smith, Jeffrey Makin, Geoff Dupree and a gatecrasher, John Walker. The lunch rapidly deteriorated and ended up in fisticuffs, two of the artists rolling around on the floor, locked in combat. Their contrite letters of apology to Anne Purves are pasted into the beautifully bound archival scrapbooks, each embossed with the year.

Excited at selling an expensive picture one day, I reported it to Stuart. 'We have a saying around here,' he said. 'The picture's not sold until the money's in the bank and you've spent it.' Stuart had another philosophy: 'Never let the client into the artist's studio. More often than not, the client will go back and try to do a deal direct.' How true I have since found that to be.

He sent me a message recently: 'Don't dwell on things that you can't change, only dwell on things that you can.' We'd had a coffee together that morning and often catch up at events, standing side by side at a recent Archibald announcement. He remains an enormous mentor to me, except our taste in footwear differs! His shoes are either shiny fire-engine red or lemon yellow.

It is a privilege to be able to buy art. Buying art is a want not a need. People do not die if they don't buy art. I quickly learned that you need to convert art from a want to a need. Art can enhance your life not only visually, but also for some spiritually and intellectually.

During his twenty-year relationship with Australian Galleries, Dad's career went from strength to strength. As well as exhibiting annually and in numerous touring exhibitions, he published a series of print portfolios and books on his etchings. In 1984, he was commissioned by the Arts Centre Melbourne to paint a series of works based on operatic themes, which suited John's imaginative work. In 1985, he was awarded the Wynne Prize for the work *A Road to Clarendon: Autumn*, then the Sulman Prize in 1989 with *Don Quixote Enters the Inn*. This period culminated with the 1991–2 retrospective curated by Deborah Hart and its superb accompanying publication *John Olsen*, still considered the ultimate monograph of his work. In 1997 came the long-awaited publication of his journals, *Drawn from Life*, judiciously edited yet still riveting. Dad was now 'the maestro'. He had become 'Australia's greatest living artist'.

17

FIRST LOVE AND
ARTISTIC RIVALRY

The memory of my first real kiss stayed with me for more than twenty years. My initial love, the girl I had silently adored, was Arkie Whiteley, the beautiful blonde, blue-eyed daughter of Brett and Wendy Whiteley.

We met for the first time when I was seven and she was four, a tiny sage dressed in Biba. Arkie was just back from living at the Chelsea Hotel in New York where Janis Joplin was her babysitter and Bob Dylan her neighbour. Although I do not recall that encounter very well, I do remember vividly the kiss we shared the next time we met.

It was 1975; I was thirteen years old. As children of artists, Arkie and I were guests by proxy at a party at Bundanon in the Southern Highlands, a two-storey 1860s sandstone homestead overlooking the Shoalhaven River, at the time owned by art dealer Frank McDonald with Tony and Sandra McGrath (the art critic and author who created the definitive monograph on Brett). Bundanon was later to become the home of Arthur Boyd and was gifted to the nation on his death, becoming an artist's retreat in his name.

Apart from her friend Sarah Ducker, who witnessed it, I never told anyone about the kiss we shared that weekend on the verandah of the shearers' quarters. It was an educated, proper kiss, a French kiss, adult in comparison to my previous fumbling attempts. I was besotted.

The children of artists can seem to orbit their parents in a sometimes dark universe. Occasionally planets collide. Arkie and I liked each other and were able to relate. Despite having had a liberated, artistic childhood, I was still incredibly shy and naive whereas Arkie was confident, if not precocious for her age. Like her father and mine, she always had the compelling and perplexing need to have the last word.

Arkie handled her unorthodox upbringing so much better than I handled mine. She had experienced so much in her life by that point. My mother and others had told me how she had, on occasion, returned home from school to find both of her parents unconscious on the couch. Afraid of calling the police, she would rollerskate over Sydney Harbour Bridge from Lavender Bay to her grandmother's in the east to get help. It would have been a confronting situation for anyone, let alone for a child.

The Whiteleys returned to New York, and Arkie moved to London to study drama, evolving into an accomplished and hauntingly beautiful actor. Our paths didn't cross again until years later at her father's funeral in 1992, where her heart-wrenching eulogy had the rhythm of a soliloquy.

Like Arkie, Louise and I, too, have been caught up in our parents' dramas, relationships and disputes over wills,[1] with every aspect played out in the public eye. This exposure affected Arkie, and she was known to be 'wary and aloof in her dealings with many people, trusting only a small inner core'.[2] Knowing what it was like to be known as 'the SON of . . .', I could again relate. In England, Arkie was able to be her own person, much as I can be now in New York.

She was on a pre-honeymoon trip with her fiancé Jim Elliott when she felt ill, and was subsequently diagnosed with advanced-stage cancer. They quickly married but she was tragically to die just two weeks after their wedding, aged only 37.[3] Her rapid demise devastated everyone who had known her. Her mother said, 'The energy and creativity in Brett's art has always been a kind of memorial to his life and Arkie was always a very important part of it, and always will be.'

As a child, when John walked into a room, for me it was like the sun came shining in with him. Arkie had a similar bond with her father. 'There was a great beam shining between us,' she said.[4]

During my early apprenticeship at Australian Galleries in Sydney, I was asked to go around to the Whiteley studio to collect a sculpture for his new exhibition, a show of a series of small landscapes featuring exotic birds. I arrived at his studio door and was taken into his vast atelier then directed to a white plinth, 3 metres tall, upon which was a nest of twigs fit for an eagle. Resting upon that was a large shiny Brâncuşi sculpture, like a smooth, chalky white plaster egg. Brett set up a ladder and then instructed me to carry it down, put it in a protective box and take it back to the gallery. As I was climbing down, desperately trying to keep my balance while cradling this huge object, I heard voices. Halfway down the ladder I looked sideways and there, sitting around a book-covered coffee table, were Mark Knopfler and John Illsley from Dire Straits, plus another man with dark curly hair who resembled Bob Dylan.

In my shock I slipped down several rungs and landed on my back, bumping my head on the concrete in the process. I looked over to see that it actually was Bob Dylan, nonchalantly looking over his shoulder with disbelief—I had managed to save that great, fragile egg at my own peril. He remarked, in his laconic drawl, 'Son, you nearly got egg on your face.' Mortified, I quickly packed it into a box and escaped as hastily as possible.

Never underestimate what a day working in an art gallery can present you.

Brett Whiteley was the guru, a kind of 1960s Australian art cult figure. He kept company with some of the most famous legends of modern music. At the time, he was the rock star of Australian art. My father likened his appearance to a yogi Harpo Marx, with his loose white cotton pants and red afro. But when it came to drawing, he had a deft gift and a mesmerising touch.

Rivalries run deep in the art world. Imagine a commercial rivalry between two artists to whom fame came for very different reasons. 'Olsen vs Whiteley' seems hardly relevant now: Brett Whiteley was a freakish enigma, John Olsen a landscape poet. Yet my father's success was very broad, his experimentation under-estimated in the context of art trends that burned bright and then extinguished just as swiftly: pop art, colour field, political art, performance. In a strange way, there are threads of all those thoughts in my father's oeuvre: he is capable of searing wit and contemplative minimalism; he is an intense colourist and has the calligraphic energy to burn.

So any curator on Earth would see the affinities between them in the sheer love they had for landscape, calligraphy, colour, painting and especially the nude; for the line, quivering and electric; for ink alone, as both mastered a tache or a Zen mark, without striking a false note, that only nature itself could otherwise emulate. There was an intensity in their work, and their unexpected, complementary prose, from their draughtsmanship to their beautiful handwriting. One could recognise that they were more kindred spirits than intergenerational combatants. But, all that said, an Olsen/Whiteley union was as unthinkable as a Capulet/Montague one, without a hint of disrespect for either side.

Brett once, however, crossed the line with Dad. His Spanish studio manager, part-time dealer and friend, Christian Quintas, purchased a landscape oil painting directly from Dad and stored it in Brett's studio. In an impulsive moment, Brett decided to embellish the work with his own markings—ironically, much as I had done the same at Watsons Bay as a child. The painting eventually was to hang in Barry Stern's Paddington gallery; John walked in one day, saw it and nearly fell over in disgust. He felt it was an unforgivable, disrespectful act.

John was later to forgive Brett, much as he had forgiven me as a child. My father admired Brett's talent; his only criticism was that Brett could have been an even better artist if he was a more avid reader. As far as I know, Brett did like the imagery provoked by the intoxicating poems of Baudelaire and had a pretty good array of ideas—'subject matter' or 'circus animals', as my father called them. While Brett's work was clever and possessed a 'wow' factor, Dad thought that if he had read more it could have enriched his work profoundly. His occasional references were interesting but were too based around popular culture for Dad's tastes.

John also thought that Brett's journey into addiction was triggered by the disappointment and failure of his work to gain traction in New York, when he and Wendy lived there in the 1960s. I'm sure today it would all be different. I recently learned that Larry Gagosian had approached Wendy to mount an exhibition of Brett's work.

Brett was a perfectionist. When putting his show for Australian Galleries together, everything was already visualised, whether placing the sculptures or hanging the pictures. In his mind he knew the scale of the space, and the dialogue he wanted to create between the artworks, all of which would provide a conversation beyond each individual work and its own message. He had his own version of exhibition feng shui that made a room sing. Brett also used that exhibition to express a resentment for a past bad review. On the occasion I hung his exhibition, he stuck up a little typed sign that read, 'This exhibition is not dedicated to John McDonald, the visual cretin.' He also used to say, 'Critics are the dildoes [*sic*] of art.'

Brett would visit me occasionally on Sunday mornings, after his Narcotics Anonymous (NA) meeting in Kings Cross. Little did I realise then that I would become a member of Alcoholics Anonymous myself; at that stage, no one would have considered me a problem drinker. We would sit out on my apartment balcony in Darling Point overlooking the harbour, before us a huge Moreton Bay fig tree with its curly twisted limbs and nodules. He would point to the tree and say: 'Tim, look where the tree limb connects to the bower. It looks like a vagina, and above could be a breast.' As in his work, he saw the whole world as crowded with sexual metaphor.

When Brett went to spend time in Paris, he asked if I would take care of his bonsai tree. The next day, an art mover carefully carried in a dwarf Moreton Bay fig on a copper tray, like a huge cake. Without having uttered a word to me, Brett had also arranged the delivery of ten of his major seminal works, including nudes, landscapes and a huge portrait of Rembrandt, a homage, and moulded into the work was his signature bulbous nose cast in papier-mâché. Brett was paranoid that while he was away someone would break into his studio. The next evening,

I had a dinner party; every jaw dropped as the guests entered my tiny apartment and saw the row of canvases. In today's terms, I had many millions of dollars' worth of art stored in my bachelor living room.

Later, Christian Quintas consigned me a Whiteley charcoal nude on paper. This was in my early art-dealing days, working from home, having finally gone out on my own. I sold the work shortly after. The following day, I heard the news that Brett had overdosed in a small hotel in Thirroul. Hours later, I received a phone call from his girlfriend, Janice Spencer, asking me for the work back, informing me that she was actually the owner. I told her that the deal was done and the new owner had every right not to return it. It was an intensely emotional conversation and, despite the facts, I felt deeply compromised.

Brett and Wendy had divorced in 1989. Janice had met Brett at an NA meeting, where their romance blossomed. She became his muse, just as Wendy had. Both were very curvaceous, sensuous, mystical-looking women. Janice, too, was to fatefully relapse, and overdosed several years later.

After Brett's tragic death, and having witnessed the fate of many other talented artists, I can see the extremes of art failure and success, where success masks the throes of addiction and self-destructive behaviour. Dad has often talked about Brett's downward spiral, seduced by his own success and the myth of invincibility. The Whiteleys were fêted and adored, seducing the media and other people alike—everyone wanted to be as cool as them. While the drugs were his downfall, it was his compulsive hubris that was his ultimate Achilles heel: he thought that he could handle anything.

Dad remembers waking up from a siesta one hot January day at Watsons Bay to find Brett sitting beside the bed in a singlet and cotton pants, barefoot in the heat. Just back from New York, Brett was keen to reconnect and, finding the house dormant, had crawled through the window, flowing in with the warm afternoon harbour breeze.

'Man, you've got to try this heroin. I've just got back from New York. Everybody's doing it, man, everyone's handling it, no problem,' he said immediately, adding enticingly, 'You'll see new things in your work.'

For John, wine and food have always been integral parts of his life, his nourishment and enjoyment (albeit sometimes a little excessively). He has never wanted or needed any other drug. Brett was by then sitting in the lotus position. Dad replied, trying to dissuade him, 'Brett, God gave us wine. We can barely handle that. I don't think we can take another thing on.'

Mum felt much the same. In her 1965 interview with Hazel de Berg, she said, 'You must have a conversation with your painting, just go on and on with the dialogue. Then out of this can come the most fantastic exhilaration. I can never understand why some artists revert to drugs such as mescaline or marijuana, because I think this is the effect that comes over one, one is completely drugged in this world of form and colour.'

Art was her drug.

Among Mum's papers, I recently found numerous notepads and small books that my parents continually used, whether as journals or for shopping lists, poems, inspirational notes or reminders. Some were John's, some Mum's, some shared, one hand merging into another, my father's distinctive hand instantly recognisable. These were not like Dad's beautifully executed journals, but sometimes uncharacteristic scrawls, sometimes in biro (which he now loathes) or pencil. One note from the early 1960s caught my eye: '26th. Whiteley here. Quick, intuitive, poetry in conversation brilliant talker. I haven't heard anyone as good since [Len] French. He talked of environments. Cicadas. Valerie very impressed.'

Whiteley was persuasive, and he drew others with him into addiction. Robert Hughes never forgave him for introducing his first wife, Danne Emerson, to heroin. In 1978, Whiteley's controversial self-portrait *Art, Life and the Other Thing* was awarded the Archibald Prize. The brutal throes of addiction were clearly depicted with the grotesquely howling baboon on one side, screaming at the approach of a syringe. The salute to Dobell's portrait of Joshua Smith was in the centre, with an elongated, distorted self-portrait; lastly, there was a mischievous-looking photograph of himself, appearing quite normal.

Today I share a good relationship with Wendy, who has been clean for decades, and have much admiration for her. Despite the way her life with Brett ended, she sustained her deep love and respect for him. She has perpetuated his legacy: Brett's Surry Hills studio is now run as a studio museum, managed by the AGNSW. His work continues to capture the imagination of the public and the art world. He will be forever remembered as an incredible artist, if a flawed human being.

Wendy established a beautiful public garden by the harbour, below the Lavender Bay family home. Called Wendy's Secret Garden, the ashes of both Arkie and Brett are buried there in an undisclosed location.

18

CONCEPTUAL ART

After three years at Australian Galleries, I was poached by Roslyn Oxley9 Gallery in Paddington. This was a shift to contemporary art, and a promotion to gallery manager, that I saw as a bit of a feather in my cap. My job description included the hanging of exhibitions and selling works as I had done with Stuart, but now my title and salary reflected my input. The hanging part was easy; it was something I found intensely satisfying and had a natural aptitude for, although hanging paintings was quite different to working with some of the conceptual works I had to grapple with at Ros's gallery. My role also entailed cooking dinner for the artists and important collectors after openings, back at the Oxleys' harbourside mansion. I accepted this and the overtime it involved without thought, although now I think how amazed my own staff would be if I asked the same of them. It was also fortunate that I could actually cook!

Ros and Tony Oxley ran one of the first fashionable post-modern galleries since Gallery A in Sydney that tinkered with the new avant-garde of Australian art. Ros had started her career as an interior designer before becoming an art dealer, and both she and

Tony came from privileged backgrounds with an inheritance to boot, being respectively the heirs to the Waltons department store and Bushell's tea fortunes. Being independently wealthy, they could afford to represent conceptual art in a slim contemporary art market and run what was essentially an experimental gallery. For every successful exhibition there were far more that were not financially viable. Eventually they began to succeed, and today I respect their vision (and deep pockets). Some of their artists have become important in recent Australian art history—Tracey Moffatt, Fiona Hall, Del Kathryn Barton, Rosalie Gascoigne, Dale Frank and, of course, Bill Henson.

Established in 1982, the gallery is now considered one of the most influential galleries in Australia, perhaps, it has been said, in part due to its strong representation in the Australian Pavilion at the Venice Biennale when compared to other galleries. The Oxleys have fostered the careers of their artists, exhibiting regularly at international art fairs, and have a strong history of supporting contemporary international and Australian artists.

During my brief time there, I tried to implement a lot of the administrative systems and processes instilled in me at Australian Galleries, but Ros saw method in the chaos that could not be changed. I found much of the conceptual art unenduring, a bit hit-and-miss, and many of the artists from that time did not progress—aside from those aforementioned, along with Mike Parr and Bronwyn Oliver. Roslyn's gallery, too, has evolved over the years and now has an enviable stable at an international level.

Visiting Sydney from the Blue Mountains one day, my father came into the gallery to see me. 'John, why don't you show here?' Ros asked him.

My father, the never-ending Modernist, replied, 'But Ros, there is hardly anything for sale. I'd be lonely.' Dad had come down to see Katharine's cattle in the Royal Agricultural Show, where all three won prizes. He noted in his journal: 'Pleasing, also, that my son Tim is doing so well in his new job at Roslyn Oxley's.'

Overall, my experience with Ros was as valuable as my time with Australian Galleries, Rex Irwin and my earlier mentors in the restaurant industry. I have been fortunate to be surrounded by incredible people in my life, celebrities or otherwise, all of whom taught me something pertinent or presented something that has moved me towards the truth of things. I now have a tremendous respect for conceptual art and have every desire to work with particular conceptual artists in the future.

Today I strive continuously to morph my gallery into one that possesses and marries both formulas: a juggling act between collectable and curatorial, where old-school meets what is new and pertinent in art. 'Newness' seems to be a recurring term in contemporary art that is overused, especially when the newness looks derivative. John once said that some conceptual art has little perpetuity or lasting interest: 'It may be clever to watch someone fart through a keyhole, but do you really want to come back for more? Probably not,' he said. 'Seen it, done it. The avant-garde that emerged from the early part of the last century, Duchamp and Man Ray, paved a way for many young artists today, but please don't refer to this work in terms of "newness" because it isn't.'

Ultimately I was sacked from Ros's gallery, which did me a huge favour as I was terribly unhappy, at the time a Modernist fish out of water. The cultural crucifixion of working for Ros was brought to an end by an unexpected conversation with Christian Quintas, who said: 'Tim, with your experience, you know more about art than many other dealers. It doesn't matter if your taste differs. That's what makes people trust you.' It was his faith and that brief exchange that changed my course. Christian provided me with the stimulus. I just had to have the confidence.

From there my independent foray into starting my own gallery began, with my initial art-consultancy business. My first real, big client was Christina Goulandris, the Greek shipping heiress. Christine had a great appetite for my father's work, and it was a huge step up to be selling major oils to her. I made more in one sale than I would have in three years working for another gallery. I had a taste for the big game and knew it could only get better.

Showing highly uncommercial conceptual art is still usually the privilege of the wealthy—those affluent enough to run their business off their personal wealth—or of other established businesses. Without these galleries, some artists would never have been given a chance; regrettably, such galleries are the exception not the rule. Running a gallery involves a certain amount of philanthropy towards artists. Like most galleries, we cannot afford to run at a loss for a long period of time. A certain budget needs to be reached each month and sometimes we fail, but I know in the back of my mind that another exhibition or artist will offset this down the track.

In New York and London, great painting is very much part of the conceptual art scene. In Australia, there seems to be a divide between curatorial and/or institutional credibility and commercial success. What the elite and the general public want and will pay for is usually not lacking in integrity or intellectual substance. As my father always says, 'There is nothing wrong with what the people like.' Sometimes I hear that my eye and taste are either too commercial or too abstract and abstruse, although it would be commercial suicide to try to please everyone.

Some considered it incongruous to even consider hanging conceptual or contemporary art with classical or modern art, but it was also once regarded the same to hang impressionist works with Renaissance art. Time distils and integrates art; all things come together as part of the course of anthropological thinking and human civilisation.

Many collectors who make purchasing decisions based on factors beyond pure aesthetic beauty are not as likely to pay top dollar for work by artists who do not show strong institutional support in their CVs. With those points on a CV, an international artist has a better chance of being purchased with a higher price point because they are institutionally vetted: there is more authority backing their value in the market. This helps us and buyers rationalise the price tag and, in turn, to close the sale. New York collectors tend to be an intellectual crowd, and this appeals to them; it even encourages them to trust a gallery more.

We need to focus on getting our Australian artists into institutions more. These artists need to be shown in more art fairs, to have them in more curated shows, as, quite simply, most of these curators will just not come to Australia. The brand of the gallery is just as important as the brand of the artist.

No one expects to marry more than once. That's not the plan, especially when your father is something of a serial husband. I was 29 when I met Harriet France. She was very pretty and polished.

I was on the rebound from a relationship with Josephine Elworthy, the daughter of prominent Kiwi farmer–businessman Sir Peter. Josephine was a well-read and articulate law student.

When visiting her family's estate in New Zealand, I had felt that her father did not really approve of me, although her mother, who was artistic and creative, adored me. Her father's hobby was flying his own Tiger Moth all over the 4000-hectare property where they ran countless cattle, sheep and deer—he nearly ran over me in it one day at an air show. This was the English gentry in New Zealand.

Still, when our relationship came to an end, I was quite heartbroken. Josephine instilled in me that intellectual substance was as important as beauty in my quest for the complete woman.

It took a good woman to cure me, and Harriet certainly did. I can see the similarities in both women, and to my father's own taste: we are both attracted to refined, dignified women with good minds. Dad once said, not without irony about his own origins, 'Never fuck outside your class', even though he was punching way above his weight with Mum.

Harriet's father Stephen was the classic English gent. Her mother Christine was an art critic and author. I really loved her parents, and they were so kind to me. In a strange demonstration of how cyclical life is, they lived in the house John Passmore had once rented on Edgecliff Road. Harriet was an equestrian, so I picked up my horseriding again; I had done much childhood riding in Dunmoochin on my little white pony, Etela. We bonded over our horses: mine was called Heathcliff and Harriet's was La Questionnaire.

I certainly scraped the mud off my boots in the relationship, polishing whatever social airs and graces I had scraped together from school. I think I was craving a bit more style and can admit it now that, generationally speaking, we were shameless and unreconstructed yuppies in an era when we considered that to be cool. We were probably a bit too Ralph Lauren for our own good.

We married quickly (she said that she didn't want to marry a man over 30) in a beautiful society wedding at Darling Point, exchanging vows at the upper-crust chapel of choice, St Mark's. Artist Margaret Olley said that we were the most good-looking couple she'd ever seen at a wedding, but I just remember standing at the altar feeling that the whole thing was not quite authentic, that I was not being honest with myself—or anyone else—about truly being deeply 'in love'. I simply did not feel true to myself and felt ashamed, as I could not fault Harriet in any way.

Harriet and I looked regal as we trotted along William Street in a glorious white-and-silver carriage, with Percheron horses prancing in high action, on our way to the reception at The Rocks. Travelling along the fringes of Sydney's red-light district of Darlinghurst, prostitutes were waving at us and cars were honking their horns; it was completely over-the-top. Her parents had spared nothing in giving their only child the wedding of her life, yet I felt like I was tagging along in a fairytale.

We ended up in the ballroom at the Museum of Contemporary Art (MCA) with a reception for several hundred people. I made a charming speech about how our courtship was enriched by our love of horseriding together around Centennial Park. Quoting from The Rolling Stones, I actually said: 'It took two horses to bring us together, but it would take 10,000 wild horses to drag us apart.'

We started married life in a beautiful house on Edgecliff Road but, regrettably, Harriet and I drifted apart very quickly. It was a bit like an F. Scott Fitzgerald short story where everything appears so much better than it is. In marrying each other, we were not really living our true destiny. The marriage was over in eighteen months.

'It was more like an arranged marriage, even though we arranged it ourselves!' says Harriet; today we are very good friends. In a strange twist, it was she who brokered the sale of our cottage at Watsons Bay. Wryly, we call the whole adventure 'the one-night stand that got out of hand'.

I still think of Harriet's parents, Stephen and Christine, with tender fondness, and they had a lovely relationship with Mum, too. Perhaps, in a way, I was marrying them, not really Harriet. I think her parents were more distressed by the failure of our marriage than we were.

Just before the wedding, after not hearing from our half-sister Jane for nearly twenty years, she suddenly rejoined the family. By this time, Dad had gone from being a well-known artist to a very famous one. Jane must have seen her father on television; she certainly would have read articles and reviews about him. Knowing how it had felt for Louise and me after Dad left Mum, I knew that Jane had missed out on so much more, especially growing up.

Jane got back in touch with Louise after a newspaper article about Dad and the family was published that mistakenly named Valerie as Dad's first wife. Naturally upset, Jane wrote to point out that it was her mother who was Dad's first wife; it had been a journalistic error. Louise, upset at the hurt this mistake had caused and struck with a yearning to be reunited with her sister, wrote back immediately to apologise. A visiting friend, Jolly Koh, hand-delivered the letter to Jane while Louise waited in the car. Fortunately, Jane was home. Jolly handed her the letter, mentioned that Louise was waiting, and the next thing Louise knew was that he was outside the car window, saying, 'Jane wants to see you.' It was a very emotional reunion for both of them, and they reconnected immediately. Louise met Jane's children, Georgia and Augustus (Gus), and they became close friends again, sisters reunited. Bizarrely, they had been living just down the road from one another all that time.

I met Jane again soon after, then it was Dad's turn. At first he was reticent, but Louise persevered and organised a meeting— and, after hugs and tears, Jane was our sister again.

With Jane's relationship with Dad restored, he gave her two of his early paintings, which I sold for her as the deposit on her home in Bega. Dad really did try to make amends. It was not just out of love, compassion and care; it was also strategic to how he felt about himself.

This time, Jane and her children stayed in our lives. During her absence she had worked as a hand model (her hands were in a famous Palmolive dishwashing detergent ad) and become an artist, teacher, ardent gardener (calling herself a 'brown thumb') and organic cook. Determined to never have her own children feel the neglect that she had experienced, she was a loving, devoted mother and a sensitive teacher. Without being in Dad's orbit, she had made her own life in the arts community, completely out of his shadow.

19

EARLY INSTINCTS

The decision to start my own gallery was inevitable. I had started dealing out of the house Harriet and I shared in Woollahra, a classic Victorian with lofty ceilings and elegant roses on the cornices; it reminded me of a stately London apartment. It was the perfect backdrop to showcase art but did not have any street presence and, with the business rapidly expanding, it was time to move on.

Deciding to go into partnership with my friend Michael Carr was unexpected, though. Michael was a corporate lawyer and, although an art lover, had never considered art as a career until we got together. Australia—and Sydney in particular—can be socially miniscule, with friendships and relationships closely interwoven. I had met Michael through Paige Henty, a family friend from our Watsons Bay neighbourhood years before. The connections were set, and the line between the corporate and art worlds was blurring.

The start of the business partnership between Michael and me really did come out of the blue. We were having lunch in the front room at Lucio's in Paddington, talking about his corporate legal connections and thinking that those connections, along with my knowledge and experience, would be a winning combination in an art partnership. We looked across the park and there on the corner, at 72a Windsor Street, opposite the Windsor Castle pub, was an empty shopfront. With the close proximity to fashionable Paddington and the other Eastern Suburbs, plus the attraction of Lucio's—an institution that has spanned all art generations—it was a prime location for art. Remembering my days at Australian Galleries, I was determined to get the location right from the start.

Olsen Carr Art Dealers opened its doors on the Sydney art scene in 1993. We started showing the conceptualist Billy Rose, a kind of Kazimir Malevich who was part of the new direction movement in response to Cubism. His works were very architectural and mathematical, almost inhuman, which was paradoxical considering that he always worked listening to classical music—Beethoven in particular. He was producing work of an international conceptual standard but in a country without a sophisticated market that could generate prices to match. His work was idiosyncratic and before its time. If it was being done today, he would be snapped up by a conceptual gallery; the minimalist, geometric quality of his work could easily come back into fashion again. In a sense, he made psychological landscapes in much the same way that Kandinsky used music to create his own mindscapes.

We then showed a posthumous exhibition for Guy Grey-Smith, the Western Australian landscape painter, printmaker and ceramicist who, like Ian Fairweather, had started drawing while a prisoner of war.[1] The World War II POW camp was also where he contracted the tuberculosis that would debilitate him and eventually end his life. Other artists included Michael's mother, expressionist Pat Harry, who showed with us over three years; sculptor Kevin Norton; and Brett McMahon.

Over a six-year period, our reputation and stable exploded. We were soon showcasing major and emerging artists, including my longtime friend Matthew Johnson, George Raftopoulos, a young Jason Benjamin, David Band, Marie Hagerty, Angus McDonald, Louise Tuckwell and more. Some of these artists are still showing with me today. And eventually, of course, Dad would join us.

We outgrew the shoebox almost immediately and moved up the road to a space on the corner of Windsor Street and Paddington Street. Our reputation was now well established, and we continued to thrive. Dad was showing his paintings with Sherman Galleries at the time, while I had his works on paper. For Dad, it was essential that I build my own stable of artists, a stable he would fit into, before he showed with me. He never wanted my business to look like nepotism, or for my gallery to be focused solely upon him. But with our new premises, the time had come for him to choose which gallery would represent him in Sydney, and he chose mine. It is gratifying that he felt the gallery had become established enough to join me, and that my experience as an art dealer was now confirmed in his eyes.

While never taking our relationship for granted, those early years were not easy, especially when I would see fantastic new works of Dad's that I would have loved to exhibit myself being sent interstate to other galleries. It did mean that so many others were able to enjoy Dad's work across the nation, though. It also necessitated growing the quality and appeal of my own stable of artists, and allowing my own standing as an art dealer to progress.

During this period I was also building a reputation as an art consultant and advisor with corporate and personal clients, the highlight being brokering the acquisition of a sixteenth-century Agnolo Bronzino portrait by the AGNSW.

In March 1996, Michael spotted a painting in Martin Cook's Queen Street antique establishment and thought immediately 'that looks like a Bronzino'. It was the subject matter and the attention to detail in the costume, jewellery and decoration that had caught his eye. To our delight, Martin confirmed it was. He had brought the work, *Cosimo I de' Medici in Armour* (c. 1545), out from London on loan for a client who was slow to commit.

Michael Carr and I thought this would be a great addition to the AGNSW's collection and proceeded to broker the deal. The gallery's director at the time, the flamboyant Edmund Capon, flew to London to authenticate the painting, where it had been on loan to the National Gallery in 1990. In the blink of an eye, the Bronzino became a highlight of the gallery's collection.

The oil depicts Bronzino's principal patron—Cosimo I de' Medici, the Grand Duke of Tuscany—as resplendent in shiny, skilfully rendered armour. The Duke had commissioned his official portrait to show his immense wealth and power, and multiple copies had been distributed in a 1500s propaganda campaign. As the AGNSW describes it: 'The painter displays a perfectionism it is hard not to think obsessive. Riven with reflections, highlights and shadows, Cosimo's armour alone is an article of transfixing interest: almost reason enough for the painting.'[2]

I feel it was all serendipitous. Trust your eye. You never know what you might find.

Some client requests can be challenging, at the very least interesting. Ann Gyngell, Kerry Packer's interior decorator, wanted me to find a painting for one of his homes. Ann's brief was that if it was a painting of a tree, for example, it had to look like a tree. 'Don't show me something and tell me it's a tree if it doesn't look like one,' Packer had reinforced. He went on to say that he loved paintings featuring animals, in particular horses (expected in a polo enthusiast) or wild beasts devouring other animals.

Michael and I were finding it difficult to source a picture of that nature, then stumbled upon a rural scene of a French horse fair, attributed to Rosa Bonheur, a nineteenth-century painter. At a time when females were banned from such places, Bonheur would dress up as a young male horse-hand and find her way into the horse market to sketch and draw. She had permission from the police to dress as a man. Packer was completely enamoured with the picture. He did not care about the provenance or anything about the artist, just what he saw.

I still wonder what he would think if he knew about the artist, that in his male-dominated world of horseracing and polo, his favourite equine picture was painted by a woman and reputably a lesbian. Reviews of her work at the time expressed surprise at a woman painting such a masculine picture.

Marie Hagerty is one of the artists who has been with me from the start, and it has been my pleasure to work with her. She has shown almost annually with me, including in New York with her husband, the sculptor Peter Vandermark.

Marie worked at Rosalie Gascoigne's sculptors' studio and is a consummate technician in the manner of the old masters. She is an extremely talented artist who emphasises painting as an extension of sculpture, rather than the other way around as is normally perceived, part of the influence of working with Rosalie.

She won the John McCaughey Prize in 2004 for contemporary painting, joining alumni of the calibre of John Perceval, Ian Fairweather and John Firth-Smith.

Marie has some very interesting curators and collectors who love her work, and is in public collections nationwide. She is on the 'curators' radar'. As Sebastian Smee wrote of her work, 'what really makes these works so effective is the optical trickery they employ. By the subtle shading of the squares and a clever manipulation of the black lines separating them, Hagerty creates a beguiling impression of three dimensionality. As you stand there, each plane seems to push out from the one "behind" it, so that each painting has its own aura of quiet movement and mystery.'

In the mid-1990s, the highly esteemed curator Nick Waterlow was teaching the gallery administration course at the College of Fine Arts (COFA) and mentioned that he had a particularly brilliant student, Katrina Arent. Always on the lookout for new talent, I asked Katrina to come in for an interview. She was so eager and excited to work in a commercial gallery that she swept the entire space out on her first day without being asked. Within a week she was working at the gallery full-time. Katrina took a deeply custodial responsibility for the space and the mood of the gallery, and I could see straightaway that she genuinely connected to almost every artist on a uniquely personal level. Not everyone can communicate with artists. They can be sensitive, quixotic, highly strung, vulnerable and, at times, completely impossible. Katrina speaks their language and sometimes translates it back to me.

Katrina has been with me ever since and is my long-term gallery manager. While we were at Paddington Street, Katrina gave birth to both of her sons. Before paid maternity leave was the norm and a legal requirement, I made sure she was looked after financially. Keeping good staff is as important as finding them. The Katrinas of the world are true rarities.

Twenty years ago, I did not imagine she would become such an integral part of the business and, on many occasions, my unofficial 'art wife', able to convey a complex rebuke, doubt or a subtle 'Shut up, Tim!' with a single look.

Katrina is a people-pleaser and sometimes, politically or diplomatically, that can be a double-edged sword. But she instinctively knows how to defuse the most outrageous situations. When I was drinking heavily, it was Katrina who held it together—along with the deep patience of my wife Dominique. Katrina was put in a position that many could not, and should not have to, sustain. Very often, in the tense prelude to a show being hung, a deft emotional intelligence is needed to lift the occasion.

Katrina calls me 'Timothy'. It is a privilege she shares with my parents and perhaps two others who are very intimate within my circle. It is, I am well aware, laced with irony, occasional impatience, sarcasm and much affection. Katrina's warmth sets the tone, that feeling of entering the space and looking at art in an atmosphere that is respectful and rarely tense. I am fortunate to have her in the gallery and in my life. Every gallery business needs a Katrina.

Nick Waterlow was a fine man: an Englishman who was highly enthusiastic about Australian art and Indigenous art; an astute curator and art historian with a rare sensibility for the understated, the art that other people might pass over. Remembered for his mentorship of students, he also curated three Sydney Biennales and the 1997 exhibition *Spirit & Place: Art in Australia 1861–1996*—the first time Dad had had a work exhibited at the MCA. Nick was passionate about all art and was never swayed by contemporary art fashion. He sought to break free of provincialism, presenting Australian art in an international setting.

On visits to England, I coincidentally would run into him from time to time at the Tate Modern—a must-visit for me when in the United Kingdom. We would quickly discuss the art exhibits, rugby and cricket, and then part ways, moving into different rooms. The last time that happened was when he was squeezing in a quick visit before going on to a day's cricket at Lord's cricket ground, where he was a member.

Nick bought many artworks from my gallery for the Macquarie Bank Collection (now part of the Macquarie Group). His funeral service in 2009 reminded me of some thoughts that Nick had told me personally that were pertinent to me and a message for any curator: to maintain 'an eye for discernment'. This became my mantra for the future, and when choosing artists to represent.

In 1997, Malcolm and Lucy Turnbull commissioned Dad to create a seascape of Sydney Harbour. After first hanging in their home, *Sydney Seaport Table* then accompanied Malcolm to each of his parliamentary offices. In the painting, Malcolm had wanted Dad to include him in his kayak being chased by a shark, but Lucy vetoed that.[3]

The Turnbulls have always been supportive of the arts and are passionate collectors. Both have opened exhibitions for Dad and, when prime minister, Malcolm unveiled one of John's frog sculptures in the entranceway to the harbourside restaurant Catalina,[4] a favourite lunch venue of my father's. Their art collection was chosen by Lucy, and it has been much admired. There is only one work in it that has not been well received: a 1963 oil painting, *Mineshafts*, by Robert Hughes.

I must confess to finding Lucy and Malcolm rather intimidating when I was younger. In my alcoholic days, this exacerbated my anxiety and I would drink more than I should have whenever I was in their company. Both highly intelligent individuals, the Turnbulls can be rather daunting. Now sober, and hopefully wiser and more self-confident, I can offer this advice: never go toe to toe with anyone who unnerves you, especially if they don't suffer fools. Know yourself well enough to know when saying nothing is genius. Listen and learn. If you can't front up, shut up. It is not the man who says the most who has the most to say.

In the 1960s, Dad left some paintings in London with an old friend, Margaret Ingram, for safekeeping when he left for Mallorca. Margaret had been a librarian at the National Art School, and I suspect they had a romantic tryst at some stage. The paintings had now become a burden and, in 2002, Margaret wrote asking me to collect them. I was flying to London, so decided to pay her a visit, curious about these mystery works.

Margaret was living in a first-floor flat of a rundown old house in Holland Park. The door was answered by an elderly, bow-legged man who lived downstairs, who led me up to her apartment and let me in. He then remained standing outside the door, like a sentry. Margaret was sitting at a table covered in newspapers and old books, with a tray ready to serve tea.

We spoke for some time as she reflected at length on how she was still fond of John. 'He is so talented, but . . . he belonged to the world and everyone else, it seems,' she lamented.

At John's insistence I had arrived with £2000 in my pocket, a letter and a large monograph from his recent retrospective in hand. I explained that the money, letter and signed book were from John to thank her for looking after the paintings for so long. She teased me for two hours, saying that they were in a cupboard and that she wasn't sure if she was ready to give them up yet. After much back and forth, while trying to explain that I was there as John's son, not as an art dealer, she still would not relent. She continued to recount old romantic stories about John and their early days at the National Art School, and to ask why he had never returned. I sat politely listening, just wanting to see the paintings. After some time, my patience lost, I headed for the door, leaving the book and the letter but refusing to hand over the cash. Margaret piped up, 'I don't feel right giving them to you. Tell your sister Louise that she can pick them up. You're an art dealer.'

On every subsequent visit to England I would reach out to her, but still she refused to pass on the works. It was beginning to appear that this was a game to her, a strange kind of power trip to tease my father.

Ultimately, ten years later, a letter arrived advising that she was in an aged care home and was now ready, at long last, to release the artworks. Our worst fear was that she would pass away and the works would be thrown out, their worth unrecognised. We sat together at the hospice for another couple of hours before she instructed me that a caretaker would be back at the Holland Park apartment. If handed £200, he would relinquish the paintings.

After finally collecting them, I raced excitedly back to my hotel. Carefully sliding the works out of dusty old cardboard tubes, I found two early abstract oils: *The Fish Cart* and *Majorca Market*, both circa 1958. Characteristically early works and in drastic need of restoration—as Dad would say, 'the oil paint needs a drink of linseed'—they were both precursors to the *You Beaut Country* series. I felt something like what Dad must have felt when he walked into his retrospective at the AGNSW in 2017 and said to his paintings, 'Hello, my lovelies.'

When researching for Dad's catalogue raisonné, we came across a letter from Dad in Rudy Komon's papers, asking Rudy to pick up some works from 1957–60 that had been left in Pat and Penelope Allen's basement in London in the days when he was painting their ceiling—just before our young family left to travel to Portugal. Dad had left other works for safekeeping, but this roll of works was a mystery. Coincidentally, two works turned up at auction in late 2018 and, investigating further, two more were discovered. I had been in transit to the United States when the auction house sent the works for review, missing the email completely, so hearing about them came as a total surprise.

It turned out that these were the missing paintings Dad had mentioned in the letter to Rudy: there were five works, all in dire need of restoration, with stress cracks, that had been rolled up for nearly 60 years (the fifth turned up at another auction in 2020). The auction house and restorer had assumed that these were works sent back to Australia for inclusion in the now legendary first exhibition at the Terry Clune Galleries in 1960. In reality, they had never been exhibited, left to languish, eventually given by the Allens to Dad's then-dealer, the notorious

Frank McDonald. McDonald had kept them despite not having ownership, and they passed by descent to his family who had transported them to a property in Yass after his death in 2011. Unknowingly, the new custodian had assumed they were part of Frank's considerable estate and put them to sale by auction.

After tracking down the seller, we were able to make the connection and Dad confirmed their provenance. Just pleased to know the works had survived and some had already been restored, he shrugged his shoulders and merely commented on the sometimes dubious tactics of McDonald, the same dealer who had kept us waiting desperately for payment while we were recuperating after our car accident in France. One of the works was inscribed on the verso 'One of my favourites', which Dad immediately said was not his addition and that Frank must have written that himself, being a dab hand at copying handwriting, too.

John's *Five Bells* (1963) was a commission from George and Eva Clarke soon after he had completed his first ceiling paintings, and was the first to be painted on a wall in situ as a mural. A wall must have been a welcome relief from the back-breaking ceilings. Dad was by then completely enamoured by poetry and drew for the first time upon Kenneth Slessor's poem, the harbour and his life with us as a young family at Watsons Bay, a theme that would continue with the Sydney Opera House mural. Here the mandala is a rock pool, overflowing with gullies and rocks, plant and animal life, fish and sea anemones, full of movement, the ebb and flow of the harbour. If you look closely in the centre, there are three sails—the Sydney Opera House, nearly a decade before it was completed.

In 1999, Tim Goodman conducted an auction at the Australian Jockey Club where he sold the huge work *Spanish*

Kitchen (1992), reaching a new record for an Olsen. On the same night I was approached by George Clarke, who was attending the auction as an interested observer, to assist in the sale of *Five Bells*.

We removed the mural from the wall, had it restored and made a video, where Dad got on board. The work was auctioned in August 1999 and was purchased by the AGNSW. It is a high-light of the gallery's collection and now owned by everyone.

In 1999, Michael and I parted company professionally, having realised different paths, and Olsen Carr became the Tim Olsen Gallery. I was soon approached by a rush of people wanting to invest in the gallery. There was one such friend I did trust: Mike Hale, who had a very successful advertising agency. He loaned me a substantial sum to invest in art, which was repaid within six months at a 50 per cent profit. We remain great friends today, and I am forever grateful to him for supporting me with the capital that the gallery needed to move forward at that time. Fortunately, I have never had to call upon him, or anyone else, again.

In the excitement and rush of building the gallery, I had failed to notice how crucial alcohol had become in my life. Every step of my career was now oiled with booze. While Paddington was the perfect location for art, it was also a prime setting for a budding alcoholic.

In art school, everyone had had a glass in one hand and a cigarette in the other. By my thirties I found myself surrounded by enabling alcoholics. Most of my mentors, the most pivotal thinkers, were brilliant bon vivants. A common perception about alcohol is that people drink for pleasure, but many more drink from pain. At the time I did not consider myself to be a problem drinker but, without realising it, through drinking I was slowly becoming more isolated and lonely. The din of an intense art opening was softened by the fourth drink, rendered noiseless by the fifth. As F. Scott Fitzgerald quipped: 'First you take a drink, then the drink takes a drink, then the drink takes you.' I can easily draw analogies between Sydney during the art boom of the 1990s and early 2000s, and the roaring 1920s. When you are young and not yet mature enough to face the potential for your own failure, every night feels like Friday night—especially in an art gallery when there is opening night, closing drinks and a hundred boozy lunches to sell the pictures in between.

In some ways, I was always brought up to view alcohol as a social lubricant, and in my business it went hand in hand with selling pictures. The image of my father in the press was almost always with a glass of red in hand. The dinners where it all went down in the 1960s and '70s were Dionysian. The ghost of my grandfather Harry Olsen, the destitute drunkard, seemed to be buried by a far more socially mobile and worldly image of drinking held up by his son. Somehow Dad used his wine bottle as a shield against the slings and arrows of being an out-there painter in ultra-conservative, xenophobic Australia. Drinking in this country engenders trust across social divides. The culture of drinking in Australia pivots on the idea that everyone is equal when they stand at the bar. So many politicians pose for the mandatory sleeves-rolled-up, beer-swilling photo op at the pub as they down a cold one: to drink beer is to pledge allegiance to 'ocker' integrity.

For me personally, drinking really was a bridge between bohemia, high society, the lover's bedroom and the rugby field. The flow of booze kept it all moving. Image-wise, so few people saw alcohol as a killer then. Somehow, despite the statistics on road deaths, domestic battery, suicide, the co-addiction of gambling, obesity, liver failure and cancer, this substance still held on to its sheen. Cleverly, it seemed to find a niche for every aspiration: for the foodies, it's an accompaniment to a degustation, and for the teenagers, a soft drink with a mighty sting. To an Australian man, it is still hard to turn down a drink without looking like a bore, even with the lockout laws and initiatives like Dry July. Our national image is embedded somewhere within the strange split between convicts and Irish rebels, and colonial British decadence. As a result, there is always a reason to get rinsed and always a social identity to match the moment: drinking is sophisticated and larrikin, sensual and intellectual, civilised and pagan, accepted and naughty, youthful and yet mature enough for the wine snobs. It is fun until the fun runs out and you're a fat sugar junkie standing in front of the fridge at 3 a.m. taking a slug of vodka to help you sleep.

Just a decade after striking out with my own gallery, that was me.

20

GOING IT ALONE

I relished the freedom of being completely in control of my own gallery at last. Our stable continued to expand, and we had some fantastic shows. In autumn 2002 we opened the Annex Gallery on the corner of Windsor Street, opposite Lucio's, and a further space on Queen Street in 2006.

The Annex was initially opened as a small works gallery, then transformed into the Tim Olsen Works on Paper Gallery to reflect my passion for works on paper, whether originals, prints or drawings.

I am not obsessed with high art, which is why works on paper are so appealing to me. Many art dealers avoid etchings and other prints because they are art forms that are selfless— never about making money, but about connecting with the earth via a mechanical, disconnected technique. At art school, I loved making etchings. The beauty of it is in the processes of working with metal plates, and with beautiful handmade papers and inks. You engage in an alchemy where you never really know what you are going to end up with. It is a creative process that I found extremely therapeutic. Today I still treasure the works I made, and if I were to go back to art, I would love to make more. A successful etching is one that arises from chance—the chance of emulating the markings of the natural world—yet it is a world that has to exist within you to begin with. It is a mysterious medium that does not attract the respect it deserves. Few art lovers know how difficult it is to make a magical one.

My passion for works on paper was one inspiration behind establishing the Tim Olsen Drawing Prize in 2000. The other was more practical. When I first left school to go and live in Europe, Dad had promised me $5000. Unfortunately, the money never arrived so I'd had to earn my own sabbatical—in hindsight not a bad thing—and I managed to get to Europe a few years later. This was the stimulus for me to set up the drawing prize, encouraging excellence in drawing at the City Art Institute, now UNSW Art, Architecture & Design. Having known what it was like to have to postpone an opportunity due to finances, I thought that the prize would be able to help young artists to travel overseas and experience, most for the first time, the artistic stimulus of Europe—the art and architecture but also the people, food and languages, enabling the total experience of spending an extended period of time in a country rather than a fleeting visit. As Robert Hughes once said, drawing responds to an innate human need: 'Drawing never dies, it holds on by the skin of its teeth, because the hunger it satisfies—the desire for an active, investigative, manually vivid relation with the things we see and yearn to know about—is apparently immortal.'[1]

My philosophy has always been to support artists who embrace the traditional practices of drawing and painting as time-less and pertinent today. Consequently, many serious collectors and institutions are still acquiring the works of artists who have won the prize as part of their otherwise conceptual contemporary collections. Collectively valued at (without irony) $5000, the prize has now been running consistently since inception, in collaboration UNSW. I am pleased to have seen so many talented recipients of the award go on to have substantial careers, showing in biennales and with national representation. The postgraduate candidates are selected by a panel of lecturers, and the prize is always judged by a guest curator or artist. While I have never used the prize to fish for new talent to feather my own nest (or stable), I will be keeping my eye on a few of them in the future.

In the late 1990s I would see Dominique Ogilvie at parties, but there was something about her half-Scottish, half-Italian looks that made her stand out when I spotted her at the infamous Cointreau Ball on Bastille Day in 1999. I felt immediately that she would be part of my life somehow. She was glamorous, charismatic and dynamic, with an obvious intelligence and independence, and was running her own successful fashion business. Both of us had had a history, but we each felt ready to commit.

Our first date was unconventional at best, and the mood of the relationship from the first encounter was one of fun for fun's sake, two complicit partners in crime driven by hard work and hard revelry. My proper courtship of Dom, once it began, was elaborate. We went to the Hotel Danieli in Venice and played backgammon in the atrium rather like the hotel in *Death in Venice*. It was a high-flying romance. Dom was a power blonde with a huge coterie of friends who fortunately all approved of me, and we were engaged within a month. I had a feeling that, as she was a strong woman, we would support one another in our careers.

Nearly six months later, on 31 December 1999, we decided to have New Year's Eve in Sydney and then fly to New York for

New Year's Day. Crossing the International Date Line, there were perpetual champagne corks popping. We stayed at The Pierre opposite Central Park, a prize we had won at a charity auction, and both decided we should elope.

After quick stops at Tiffany's and Armani on Fifth Avenue, we flew to Aspen where Dom was able to gather her family and friends who were already holidaying there, and we married in the Prince of Peace Chapel. This was a place that could convert itself from a synagogue to a Protestant place of worship with the quick exchange of a cross for the menorah.

Our wedding photographs show us standing ankle deep in snow, Dom dressed in white silk and me in dark cashmere. We were both at the pinnacle of professional success: my own as an art dealer in a heady market of rich young collectors, and Dom's as a fashion powerbroker at the top of her game. The reception at The Little Nell hotel at the bottom of the ski slopes was scenically beautiful and spontaneously lavish. The reality was that I was living like a Gatsby millionaire with a modest cash flow.

Louise, Mum and Dad did not make it. Having already had a white wedding a decade earlier with Harriet, I think this time my family was simply relieved that I was content, and that our decision to elope meant we did not need any pomp and ceremony. Louise in particular was very happy for us, and everyone knew that Dom had a grounding influence on me despite the fact that I was still, at times, drinking to excess. She stabilised me yet enabled me at the same time. However, as her anxiety about my alcoholism grew, so did my consumption.

As newlyweds we bought a house in Queen Street in Woollahra, part of the art and fashion village of Sydney, and started trying for a child. It took us two years to conceive. Dom lost too many pregnancies. I still find it hard to think of and almost impossible to write about. It is probably one of the greatest omissions of our society that we can minimise the impact of miscarriage. It is such a crushing blow. The vulnerability, the hope and then the desolation when that moment comes. Dom endured so much, and I feel for her deeply. It is devastating for a woman to go through, physically and mentally. As her partner, I felt powerless as well as heartbroken. Our sense of loss was overwhelming.

We grieved, healed and tried again.

For me, the grief was not about the male ego, a man's desire to procreate and spread his seed. It was the emotion, the effort, that goes into making a child; the fear of another month without fertilisation, the dread of another miscarriage. The pressure to perform becomes overwhelming, until the process becomes technical and moves outside your secret, intimate realm of lovemaking. When we tried IVF, it felt as if our bedroom doors had been ripped off and thrown into the street. I felt exposed and stressed in the quest to conceive, in having to express myself into a test tube. I had been spontaneously conceived, a child created in love, whereas now we were trying to create a very much wanted child in the sterile confines of a Petri dish.

Still, I am eternally grateful to modern science and stand in empathy with the couples who pursue the procedure. One of the happiest days of my life was when Dom told me that she was pregnant; another was the day of my son's birth.

From that moment on, we were on tenterhooks. We wanted to make sure we kept the baby. Nothing was done by halves. During her pregnancy, Dom had a serious nesting 'affliction' and we decided to renovate the house. We moved into James Street during the renovations—ironically, the name of our son. (My father quipped, 'Well, thank God you moved out of Queen!')

I was present at James's delivery with obstetrician Robert Lyneham, a friend and art collector, essentially helping to bring him into the world. I remember bursting into tears before leaving the room to call family and friends. It was the most powerful moment of unadulterated joy in my life when I held James for the first time, like the moving epiphany of great art or romance, the instant realisation of what a true gift was: our own son's life. My life now was less important to me, as James was now my focus.

It gave me great pleasure to say to Dad: 'It's a boy!' I was floating on air.

After a long pause, Dad responded with, 'Here comes another 100 years.' The ego of men! It is a very primal thing to produce an heir. We were all celebrating after the birth. Despite a painful invasive caesarean for poor Dom, with James in breech before his birth, she was radiant, beaming.

With the welcome addition of James, our life continued in a gilded way. The art market was buoyant, and I caught the wave. Apart from exhibiting my father, I had a collective of artists who painted large decorative works at a good price point, perfect for the new homes of our peers and school friends who were also nesting. We targeted our PR to focus on interior design and lifestyle magazines to appeal accordingly. The independent woman in a relationship is usually the person who spearheads an art collection.

We had built up a good stable of artists, some of whom were taken more seriously than others, and they provided a constant flow of sales. In the style of London's Cork Street, I was the first Sydney gallerist to place a painting in the front gallery window. Many art purists still find this a highly commercial act for a serious gallery. This became core to my philosophy and branding: that art should beckon you and invite you in. No gallery needs a cold façade.

I had a successful gallery, a beautiful wife and a gorgeous baby boy, and yet I was still self-sabotaging like mad. Even with all the trappings, I was unfulfilled and unhappy.

Clichés are based on reality and, although it is hard for many people to relate to misery within the privileged, I was an obese alcoholic who could not cherish his wife or father his son properly. Numb, even with everything I loved, I could not love myself. Slowly I was gaining more and more weight. Daily I was finding reasons to drink earlier and earlier.

Dad broke another record in 2006 for the sale of a work by a living Australian artist with his work *Love in the Kitchen* (1969), which fetched nearly $1.08 million,[2] double its original estimate by Paul Sumner, at that time the director of auction house Mossgreen. The painting was sold as part of the collection of Tasmanian dealer Nevin Hurst and his wife Rose, who (along with two other investors) had paid $486,000 for the painting in June 2003.

Mossgreen had heavily promoted the sale: a brochure was sent to all the potential buyers, and the painting was toured nationally. It was a phenomenal result and a genuine one; with five or six serious bidders in the room, it was a battle of an auction.

Dad's painting was bought by Melbourne property developer Ted Lustig, with former Metro 5 Gallery director Brian Kino bidding on his behalf. With seemingly bottomless pockets, Ted was blindly passionate in his intent to build his contemporary art collection, the Ted Lustig Collection. He had just set another record the previous month by paying $2.04 million for Brett Whiteley's *Frangipani and Humming Bird—Japanese: Summer*.

Three years later, the curator of the Ted Lustig Collection suggested that they sell a number of works, including *Love in the Kitchen*. The sale was handled very poorly; no one was really aware that the work was coming back on the market so quickly, or why. One of the original bidders from the first sale bought it for a fraction of its worth, and it is now in a private collection in Melbourne. The new owner, the late Dr Sam Shub, contacted me afterwards to say that, as it was such a meaningful work to the family, that if we ever wanted to look at it again he would open his home to us. Louise and I were very touched by that.

Since the sale of *Love in the Kitchen*, John has had an extremely healthy market at auction and it is getting stronger, even though it hasn't matched those heady pre-GFC days, or even neared that singular result until recently. The sad demise of Charles Blackman has left John remaining as the last great Modernist, and people acknowledge that we are clinging to our last truly great master.

We decorated the space in Queen Street like a French salon for a survey of John's lithographs one year. There were prints from floor to ceiling, not an inch of spare wall space anywhere. It was a celebration of the art of printmaking.

Edward de Bono, the father of lateral thinking, was in Australia on his worldwide corporate tour spreading his gospel of 'thinking outside the box'. A friend of mine, Julia Pomirska, was Edward's executive assistant and suggested that Edward and Dad might enjoy one another's company. They ended up lunching at Lucio's. John's lateral ideas on art and Edward's on logic melded into an interesting conversation. They became friends, and Dad asked Edward to open the show.

Edward made an extremely eloquent speech on the night but

ended it, oddly, by telling a sexist blonde joke. It was irrelevant and inappropriate. Dad, normally an advocate for the absurd, was taken aback and refers to him to this day as 'Edward de Bonkers'.

On the subject of the absurd, in 2007 the TV comedy *The Chaser's War on Everything* thought it had found a way for people to get rid of their junk in between council clean-ups. Simple, they thought: most modern art galleries are full of garbage anyway, so would it be noticed if they put their own rubbish into a gallery and pretended it was art?

They went to a few galleries, creating installations literally made from rubbish, complete with labels, then filmed the results, unbeknown to the galleries themselves. First, a bunch of unwanted palm fronds on a plinth was labelled as *Lord of the Plants*, and gallery visitors were filmed as they paused to inspect it. 'DUMPED' was stamped across the screen. A discarded computer was the next subterfuge. When challenged by a gallery attendant, he was told that it was a new shipment. 'That's fine,' the attendant replied. 'DUMPED' again!

The third item, a broken vacuum cleaner, was then placed in my gallery. I just happened to come through and saw it against the wall, 'What's this?' I demanded. My assistant didn't know. Without hesitation, I picked it up and threw it out onto the footpath, saying, 'This is what you do with rubbish.'

'Hey. That's art,' came the voiceover, before the red stamp appeared: 'REJECTED'. It went on . . . at the MCA with a sullied second-hand mattress, even at the AGNSW.

I was the only gallery not to get DUMPED!

I am not sure if prizes are relevant to the success of an artist or the pertinence of a work. I was proud when Guy Maestri, at that time an artist in our stable, won the Archibald in 2009 with his moving portrait of the singer-songwriter Geoffrey Gurrumul Yunupingu. 'I feel like I'm going to have a heart attack,' he told the ABC on accepting the $50,000 prize. This is said to be a common response to the accolade.

Guy had entered that very famous and media-saturated competition eight times, and he admitted in an interview that he was not a portrait painter. 'I'm one of those guys who does a portrait for the Archibald once a year,' he said bluntly to the press, and I commend him for his signature honesty. I was overseas on the big day; in fact, I was in rehab. The public success of one of my favourite painters was a tremendous inspiration and a milestone that I sadly missed while getting clean, but not even that could detract from the moment. Katrina Arent was crying down the phone when she told me the news, but given my lifelong experience with the Archibald, I remained dry eyed. This was the one Australian art prize that delivered creative justice and, in some cases, politically safe choices in equal measure.

From its earliest days, an aura of complacency and tradition surrounded the Archibald Prize. The scandal over William Dobell's portrait of Joshua Smith would seem so laughable today. Yet in 1943, any deviation from realism was seen as a moral offence. Such was the outcry over Dobell's attenuated limbs that mothers and pregnant women were warned not to look at the painting. Perhaps they were scared that more Modernists might be born. Talented women artists were swiftly scuttled or merely overlooked, as in the case of Grace Crowley's delicate and progressive portrait of Gwen Ridley in 1930.

Dad was part of a demonstration at the AGNSW in 1952 after Bill Dargie was awarded the prize for the seventh time, first winning in 1941. And fair enough. In his book on the history of the Archibald, Peter Ross reports how the gallery's director at the time, Hal Missingham, was widely thought to have prepared a congratulatory telegram to Dargie well in advance of the judging.[3] This ugly pocket in our art history reflects the complacent conservatism of the Menzies era and an art establishment allergic to change. No wonder Dad jumped on a boat to Europe.

This said, the prize still held a strange power over my father and artists of his generation. There is no denying the buzz of the Archibald. The public swarm the gallery to see the winning work, and it is probably the one day of the year when the mainstream Australian media reports about art. This anomaly is probably due to how much this particular art prize resembles the Melbourne Cup or the State of Origin, the major public sporting events where bets are laid and people claim allegiance to this or that horse or titan. Even John McDonald caught the vibe, writing in 1989, 'They're off and running in the annual Archibald Stakes.'[4]

With the Archibald, Wynne and Sulman, John Olsen has form. In 1989, I had watched Dad reach elation as he was built up to believe that he was to win the Archibald (the bookie, Darren Knight's favourite with odds of 7-4) only to be surprised by the judges' far more predictably conventional choice of yet another realistic portrait. Although he was elated to win the Sulman. Instead, the Archibald was awarded to Bryan Westwood for his mirror image *Portrait of Elwyn Lynn*.

On the eve of the announcement, Dad was told to come to Sydney and await a phone call, and then come to the gallery. When he arrived, he and Katharine had to push through a melee of press and punters, then were taken aside and told that he had not won. Edmund Capon made it very clear to Dad that he did not agree with the decision.

By a stroke of irony, the work he had entered was titled *Donde Voy? Self-portrait in Moments of Doubt*. It was a magnificent, sprawling diptych painted in the style of his nocturnal and highly experimental Spanish paintings, those works that had been inspired by Goya, Velásquez and Tàpies, yet evoked the existential pain of Bacon. This was the sort of experimental, difficult artwork that pushes the painting dialogue in Australia forward, a powerful fusion of both portraiture and abstraction.

John's interpretation of the self-portrait has always been a circumspect exercise. Although he has been depicted many times in oil portraits as a jolly bon vivant, his own image of himself is so much darker and less concrete. The playful persona and the creator of such majestic landscapes is far less whimsical when it comes to the self. It's not what the public expected, which I found brave.

The painting he entered in 2005, *Self-Portrait Janus-Faced*, might be one of the most abstract works of his oeuvre. In it, his round head and nobly jutting chin are stripped down to a quivering line, and the landscape that engulfs him looks like a scorched riverbed. This work was profound yet, John being John, he was characteristically lighthearted on accepting the award when he joked: 'Janus had the ability to look backwards and look forwards and when you get to my age you have a hell of a lot to think about.'

To be fair, some years yield better crops than others. *The Sydney Morning Herald* mainstay John McDonald has built a comedic thread of art criticism on the pickings of some of the lesser works entered each year. However, many accomplished portraitists have entered, such as William Robinson and Louise

Hearman, and they are recognised for both their artistry and excelling at the genre.

The portrait of me by Richard Dunlop, *Tim Olsen: The Man in Black*, hung in the 2008 Archibald, was my Dorian Gray moment. Once a handsome young man, by then the sins, weaknesses and the decadence of my life were written all over my face, exposed in the most visited exhibition in Australia, for the whole world to see. It is the darkest, most lugubrious version of a beaten-up art dealer who has been poisoned by celebration. Expressing my amazement that it was hung at all to Edmund Capon, he replied: 'It does have a certain likeness. He's really captured you.' It was horrifying to think that was how people saw me—obviously my inner and outer beauty needed attention. This was another reality check. It still took me another four years to get completely sober, but seeing myself through the eyes of the world was confronting.

Dad, Louise and I have all been the subject of Archibald portraits, although none of the previous ones of me were hung. As an artist, Louise was also hung in the Portia Geach Portrait Prize at S.H. Ervin Gallery just after she left art school, entering a portrait of Mum with her cat, titled *Scrap*. Scrap had passed away just before the painting was made. Louise described Scrap as like a ghost in Mum's arms. Louise's talent was evident from a very early age.

Asked how I would like to be portrayed now, I show my favourite portrait by Yvonne East, *Father and Son, After Janus* (2012). It depicts me with James, then aged eight, on my lap, its title a nod to Dad's Archibald-winning self-portrait. It was not selected to be hung in the Archibald but was a finalist in the Portia Geach Portrait Prize and a semi-finalist in the Doug Moran National Portrait Prize. This is a very special painting for the family.

PART
FOUR

OL
SEN

63

21

ART TEMPLE

The most difficult thing in running a gallery is maintaining your relevance. With constantly changing attitudes, tastes and aesthetics, let alone art fashion, it is a constant challenge. Many galleries over time lose their pertinence and simply fall away. No good art dealer or gallerist can afford to take their eye off the ball if they want to stay in business. It requires perpetual reinvention in the fickle art society.

My ideal for a gallery is a composed yet inviting art temple flooded with natural light, graced by an elegant ceiling height. A place where ideas really are sacred, where you can aspire to the spirit beyond the geometric materiality of an art space. For all of these reasons, front of house in the gallery matters. The ancient code in hospitality is 'set the mood and not the table'—or, as Dad always calls it, 'getting the feeling right'. First impressions endure.

When we meet people we subconsciously do a body scan, an energy reading, and that initial feeling we get from people is important in where our energy sits with them. The same applies when you enter an art gallery. You want to feel like you are going to have an experience and be visually and intellectually nourished in some way. If you walk into a gallery (or a restaurant) and someone makes you feel uncomfortable or out of place, leave. I always loved that line in *Absolutely Fabulous* when Eddie Monsoon enters a high-end gallery and tells off the arrogant gallery assistant reeking of art snobbery: 'You only work in a shop, you know. You can drop the attitude.' This assistant is the antithesis of the attitude and approach that I hope to maintain with my own staff. The very few times I have ever had complaints about staff behaving in a similar way, it has upset me profoundly, as the thought of offending anybody horrifies me. With my name on the front of the building, it is my responsibility and I take it very seriously.

When it comes to running a gallery, very few people talk about the language of energy, the energy that affects all walks of life. Energy can be communicated through colours, shapes or symbols and, translated into art, it gives us an innate ability to connect, to relate and to feel.

In late 2006, talking with a friend in real estate, I was asked what my dream building would be, and I said this one: 63 Jersey Road. My friend tracked down the owner, I made a ridiculous offer and, after some negotiation, that 'tall white building' at last became mine. It had an antique dealership downstairs and two businesses upstairs, so the leases had to be paid out, but in real estate terms alone it was a fantastic deal—and in terms of becoming a gallery it was priceless. Dom was instrumental in getting James Dack, the real estate agent, to search title deeds and negotiate the sale, and she also helped to oversee the renovations.

At last I had my ideal gallery—well, the perfect space and location. Turning the raw material into my 'art temple' took a little more time. Designing and overseeing the renovation of the gallery was one of the most rewarding experiences of my life. After a meeting with a leading architectural firm who were talking about spending millions, I ended up working with another architect and we agreed on everything. After a lifetime visiting and working in galleries, my idea of the ideal space was crystal clear, and this was my time. The bare bones were perfect: towering ceilings and the potential for superb light. We gutted the entire building, leaving only the external structure; added a massive skylight upstairs, accessed via a feature staircase; and included engineering throughout the building for a potential third floor. Every inch of space was utilised, leaving only the rear garage with a custom-built pull-out picture storage system and an office space upstairs. Everything was painted a crisp white, the lighting and hanging systems set up for maximum flexibility. This space could showcase all types of artworks. It was a sublime project.

We were still running the Paddington Street gallery, the Annex and Queen Street at the time. All the artists were chafing at the bit to exhibit, and while we were on target, renovations on this scale take time. It had to be perfect, and it was.

The Jersey Road building is an anomaly. In the area there are few other buildings like it. It was crying out to become a gallery for many years, and it even has parking, a rarity in Sydney. Dad thinks that it is one of the best exhibition spaces in the country.

There was only one massive blight on the landscape. By that time I was morbidly obese and a hopeless yet highly functioning alcoholic. The constant lunches and dinners, a professional liability of being a gallerist, were starting to erode both my mental and physical health.

The new gallery space opened in November 2007 with the ultimate exhibition, Dad's truly memorable *A Salute to Sydney*, the tribute to 'the blue bitch goddess' that has inspired his work since the early 1960s when he first returned from Europe.

The previous year he had worked frantically, almost obsessively. It was an incredible output for an artist of any age, with the energy and vibrancy of the works from his prime—every piece electric, brilliant. Betty Churcher described him as 'an unstoppable force'. It was reminiscent of his *You Beaut Country* series, and how those works exploded the view of the Australian landscape at the time, establishing his reputation as one of our greatest contemporary artists.

Stemming from his love affair with the harbour, so often depicted in his work, the explosive works revealed Dad's absolute lust for life, spontaneous and youthful in their execution. They took Louise and me back to our childhood, the idyllic early days at Watsons Bay, the memories of popping bluebottles on the beach, exploring and swimming in the harbour pools, the walks we would take along the water's edge. For Dad and for us, these works were like a childhood revisited. Every aspect we loved and would always reminisce about from our childhood, he had captured perfectly.

It was fitting that this incredible exhibition, a celebration of Dad's 80th birthday, was shown in the new gallery space, the light and vastness allowing the works to be seen at their absolute best. The opening was one of the best commercial gallery openings I have ever experienced, a magical night for Dad and for all of us. The energy was infectious, the gallery packed with friends and family, clients, artists and art lovers. Having Jane with us that night was particularly special; we were all together for the first time to celebrate with Dad, the family coming full circle.

I spoke briefly, called it 'the greatest show on Earth' and thanked John, saying, 'Dad, you don't have to worry about my Christmas present!' It was his most successful exhibition ever and still is today. Every work sold instantly. It was the highest grossing exhibition for a living artist in history.

Dad wrote for the exhibition:

Last year I left the biscuit dry interior of Australia to the arms of that blue bitch goddess named Sydney where I spent my childhood.

Fascinating it is when you visit the caves of memory what comes up. For instance, in January when the south-east winds blow millions of blue-bottles towards the beach and are left on the beach by the receding tide, the children's game was 'popping blue-bottles'. What a game that was! . . . Revealing the vitality of that blue-violet colour against the yellow of the sand.

Throwing caution away with rude cheek and daring we were inevitably stung, our bodies, as an antidote we were painted with gentian-violet.

We radiated barbaric frivolity. Another memory—swimming at Bondi Baths—'The Icebergs'—the sea surge of King Tides spraying over the baths and the swimmers rocking back and forward in the turbulent water.

Above all Sydney sparkles with bouncy light—the hills surrounding the Harbour cradle the light to make a radiant bath. The beach a place of primitive sensuality, bold and brassy, promises freedom if only for a hedonistic moment.

Each of us has memories that stick to us like the paste of time.[1]

Taking advantage of the luxury of having such a large exhibiting space after the confines of the Paddington gallery, we put on a mini survey of works from over the last 45 years, drawing from Dad's personal collection and my own stockroom. It was fascinating to see the response from the viewers, the interest in the past works upstairs versus the irresistible allure of the new below. Some seemed sombre in comparison with the vitality and riotous explosion of colour and joy. For Dad to have produced this body of work at his age, with the rigour of a man younger by generations, was truly remarkable.

The only message of cold reality on the night was when Margaret Olley, sitting on the windowsill outside the gallery and puffing away on a cigarette, said, 'Tim, I want you to come over here, so that I can congratulate you.'

Margaret, who was so adamant that I stop drinking, could probably smell the beers consumed to calm my nerves earlier in the evening. She leaned in, looked me in the eye and said, 'Now that this is over, this is now the time that you really stop drinking completely.' It brought me back to earth with a thud.

As Dad got older and less mobile, he became more reluctant to come up to Sydney to visit the gallery. Knowing that the stairs were a contributing factor, we installed a lift to the second floor, giving easy access to my apartment and upstairs gallery. The first time Dad rode in it, he said, 'I'm loving this. One day you will be able to call it the John Olsen Memorial Lift.'

We had rented the terrace next door to the gallery for several years for storage and additional working space. I wanted to buy the property, knowing it would add so much more to the building and the business by extending the gallery space, so I waited patiently for it to come on the market. The two buildings had been connected previously: the main building had been used for storing horse-drawn trams, and the caretaker had a cottage next door. Eventually it came up for auction.

By then I had begun attempting abstinence, and my awareness of spirituality had grown. After meeting some Buddhist nuns and hearing about the imprisoned monks in Tibet, I offered to lend them the gallery to hold a large exhibition and auction as a fundraiser, to raise money for the incarcerated Tibetans to provide them with reading material. The day before the event, the nuns offered to help me get the next-door building through prayer, the antithesis of doing something sinister like planting a smelly rat under the staircase to scare off potential buyers. They chanted the entire *Bhagavad Gita*—'The Song of God'—taking well over an hour. On the auction day, no one else turned up and the building was mine, with good karma for a fair price. After extensive renovations, the two buildings were once again reunited.

The acquisition not only greatly enhanced the gallery space but also eventually became my home in the apartment upstairs. Rather than being just a rented building, a dogbox used when off on an alcoholic bender, I now owned it in positive growth, a gift from above thanks to staying off the piss.

James and Dad can visit whenever they wish. The lift ensures easy access for John, and I am always close. Walking through the Jersey Road gallery space with its high ceilings and light never fails to give me pleasure. I often walk around at night after we have closed, just to feel the energy, to make sure everything is perfect for the day to come, especially the night before an opening when the atmosphere is palpable. On those nights I walk around the exhibit, stopping by each painting in turn. The next day we frequently make changes that always seem so obvious: how could we have not hung that particular work there? During an exhibit we often move works around internally, and changing the main window work is essential, the portal to the gallery.

I consider each exhibition as a painting as a whole, in a way that they all speak to one another, a dialogue that extends beyond the individual work. You can instantly sense when an artist has worked towards income rather than an idea, more of a commercial venture than an artistic exploration in an exhibition. There has to be a central theme or a metaphor, a show that depicts the artist's struggle with a concept. It cannot be repetitive or it will come undone. There has to be an honesty in the work, a challenge to the audience to think and feel.

Sometimes I crank up the music and dance around the gallery, much to the amusement of the odd passer-by peering through the door to see what is hanging. The funniest moment was when I had forgotten to put the alarm on and ran downstairs in a towel only to slip, dropping the towel, and looked up to see the horrified face of an elderly lady with a poodle at the glass.

Opening up the ground floor and linking through from the main gallery gave us much-needed additional hanging space, a kitchen area and, for staff and clients alike, a small inner sanctum, a Zen courtyard garden with a wall of bamboo, a Buddha and elephant statues, and a table where we hold staff meetings in summer.

Pride of place is my beloved bonsai. Ever since looking after Brett Whiteley's bonsai all those years ago, I have always had one. It is painstakingly maintained every year, when the roots are trimmed and it is given a hefty feed. Some consider the ancient Japanese art of bonsai as cruelty to plants, but mine is much loved. For me they are almost like a breed, perhaps the chihuahua of trees. It is my very special private memento of Brett.

My old boss, John Kaldor, has become one of the most passionate contemporary art collectors in Australia. Collector, patron and philanthropist, his commitment to contemporary art is unparalleled. In 2008, Kaldor shared his passion again with the Australian public when he gifted his immense private collection to the AGNSW.

The late Edmund Capon said that the collection was 'a milestone that happens once in a century' and that it would be 'a transforming experience for the Art Gallery of New South Wales'. It literally was, necessitating a major expansion of the gallery to accommodate the benefaction, the John Kaldor Family Collection.

My personal favourite Kaldor project was Project 10: Jeff Koons's famous *Puppy*, created outside the MCA in 1995 just after Michael Carr and I had opened the first gallery. At 12.4 metres high, the West Highland white terrier puppy was constructed from 'flowering blooms like a monolithic topiary', a 'symbol of love and happiness'.[2] There was a rumour that one of the students working on the project managed to slip in a cannabis plant among the flowers! *Puppy* was probably the most memorable and loved of Kaldor's projects, with universal appeal. I always thought that we should have kept it (for a cool $1 million[3]), but it was relocated permanently to the Guggenheim Museum Bilbao.

Kaldor's contribution to the art scene cannot be underestimated, even if Dad's work does not overly appeal to him! I always thought that my father was the most avant-garde artist, but to

Kaldor my father is a bit conventional. In 1962, Dad had been commissioned to paint a ceiling in Kaldor's mother's home. The two-panel painting was titled *Darlinghurst Cats*. After his mother died, John Kaldor rang me, asking me to remove the mural from the ceiling and sell it on. It came as a surprise as, given the nature of Kaldor's taste in art, I thought that the work would have been a good inclusion in his vast collection. It ended up in the home of a delightful couple, John Grill and Rosie Williams, who live near the gallery. They love it.

Brian Eno and Paul Simon came into the gallery one day. They spent an hour looking at the group showing, and we spoke at length. Simon was such a lovely man. As we walked around the Michael Johnson exhibit, we had a fascinating discussion on how sound can play a part in the creation of visual art, how paintings can reflect sounds.

We discussed Kandinsky's art as being like an abbreviation of a conductor's wand and how Billy Rose's highly underrated constructed works were mostly painted to the mathematical sounds of Beethoven. Wassily Kandinsky, one of the pioneers of abstract art, had been similarly fascinated by the relation-ship between music and the visual arts. Believed to have had synaesthesia—the stimulation of one sense that stimulates another, with colours and marks triggering sound, musical notes provoking imagery and so on—he gave music-inspired titles to the three different categories of his paintings: 'Compositions', 'Improvisations' and 'Impressions'.

A week later, for James's sixth birthday, Dom thought it would be a great idea to have a disco in the gallery for him. It was a weekday afternoon, and Katrina was convinced that an important client would turn up just when we had 50 screaming children and music blaring away. Almost on cue, within half an hour of the party starting, Brian Eno and Paul Simon walked back in.

Paul Simon fell in love with a Michael Johnson painting that we promptly sent to New York. As they were leaving, Eno said, pointedly, 'That music is way too loud for those children.'

I have always admired the work of ceramicist Fiona Myer. She had produced a series of works inspired by Australian ceramic artist Gwyn Hanssen Pigott, and I asked her to collaborate with artist Angus McDonald for a show: Fiona to make the ceramics, and Angus to make them into the subjects for his paintings. Every piece sold out, including one work ordered by a member of the British Royal Family. After my father's experience with the Queen and Prince Philistine, I never thought we would have any further dealings with them. We smartly had the work packed and boxed as if it was a Fabergé egg and sent it off to Buckingham Palace. We received a letter back, thanking us for sending the piece so promptly and so well, which was duly framed.

Shortly after moving into the new gallery space, we were approached by the ABC TV show *Family Fortunes* to tell the Olsen family story.[4] It seemed like a good idea, and Jane, Louise and I were all on board with Dad. It soon became apparent that the *Family Fortunes* team had a very clear agenda: to focus on the saddest aspects of our childhood, trying to almost vilify Dad as a father. Jane was very much a part of the family again after our long estrangement but, instead of celebrating a family reunited as we were expecting, we found ourselves delving back into the heartache of our childhoods.

They started by filming Dad working. He was just starting on the commission for *Seafood Paella*, and they filmed him placing the first brushstrokes: 'This is really quite wonderful, freakishly good,' he says. 'Who knows—this might even turn into a beautiful kind of wok. The law of chance plays a big part.'

Then came the voiceover: *John's children too know the uncertainty of a life driven by art: sometimes swept along by their father's creative passion, sometimes left behind.*

Jane followed, sounding teary and desolate, talking about Dad leaving on the boat when she was four: 'I remember waving him off, thinking we would see him again, and then I didn't see him again for a very, very long time.'

Next up was Louise, speaking about when Dad left Mum for Noela: 'Everything that was the structure of my life at the time all of a sudden sort of crumbled around me.'

Then there was me: 'You have to be a selfish bastard to be a good artist, I think.'

The team obviously thought it made for better television, but the sometimes dubious art of editing can be very damaging.

I could see Dad becoming frustrated at the approach. He lost his temper at one point and yelled at me—I had just called him a selfish bastard! Eventually they moved on, depicting Dad's life and career: his works, awards and accolades, and his many marriages, culminating in the triumphant opening night of his 2007 show.

The TV show ended with depicting us all, reunited and happy, sharing a paella as one happy family, Jane back in the fold. Well, happy for the cameras at least, as Katharine was there.

Jane and her children visited Dad once—at Rydal, just west of Lithgow, where he and Katharine were living—but for some reason Katharine seemed to think that Jane had ulterior motives, monetary ambitions, and did not welcome her into the family. She did not believe that Jane was there out of love and thought that she was only there to put her hand into the 'honey pot'. Having spoken recently to Dad about Katharine's attitude back then, he feels a little ashamed that he allowed her to behave like that, saying, 'It takes one to know one.' Jane, Gus and Georgia would still catch up with Dad regularly for dinner, but never with Katharine.

The sisterly bond between Jane and Louise only continued to grow. In 2002, she helped Louise set up her US store for Dinosaur Designs, in Mott Street, New York, having a similar interest in glass and ceramics. Jane, too, was highly creative and was launching a new design company, Egg V, when she contracted an intestinal virus while on a trip to Indonesia.

Shortly after, she was diagnosed with advanced bowel cancer, dying far too young at only 56 in 2009. Dad was very much there for Jane in her last years, loving, supporting, constantly in contact. When I turned the same age in 2018, I thought again how desperately sad her life had been for so long, filled with feelings of disconnection and abandonment, and, most keenly, I thought about how much we all miss her still.

My niece Georgia is very close to Louise and Louise's husband Stephen, and is in regular contact with Dad. When she was growing up, Dad paid for her school fees for a while, until Katharine found out and stopped it, despite Dad paying the school fees for all three of Katharine's own grandchildren.

Georgia Blake is now a highly talented photographer; her images are beautiful, full of sensitivity. She has worked for the best in Sydney and New York across a variety of genres, including fine art, photojournalism, portraiture and fashion. She, too, followed the Olsen path in studying at the National Art School, then moved to New York and is now living back in Australia with her daughter, Aditi, working primarily as a videographer and film editor for the last six years.

At first, Dad was not as involved with Jane's son Gus. They met and started to build a relationship, and Dad helped where he could with his art tuition at Julian Ashton's, as well as his studies in Europe. But when journalists write without fact-checking, it can cause such heartbreak: in 2004, after James was born, *The Bulletin* wrote about Dad's joy at the birth of his 'first grandson', without acknowledging Gus's existence.

They are much closer now. We all are. Gus is very much his own man, even changing his name to Augustus Firestone. He has become an artist, a painter and sculptor, and a very good cook, hosting the web series *Visual Feasts*. Having worked as an actor, photographer, television producer and film director, Gus can turn his hand to anything. He's even written a children's book.

Dad is now close to all of his grandchildren and, as the family has grown, his great-grandchildren, too: Gus's children Leonardo (Leo) and Olive Jane, and the youngest, Georgia's daughter, Aditi. It was wonderful to have Georgia and Gus join us to celebrate Dad's 90th birthday.

Dad is very proud of Georgia and Gus. Of all his family.

22

AWAKENING

My life as an art dandy in a bespoke Italian suit was deceptively easy. In between running the gallery, it was a continual sunlit lunch at Lucio's. One o'clock in the afternoon and I would be smiling into an empty glass, a full bottle coursing through my blood, the mains not yet on the table. Another bottle would be ordered. I wasn't drunk; I was marinated. A happy Buddha, my pinstripe shirt straining at the buttons. And we were just warming up.

I cannot blame my addiction on my profession, but it certainly did not help. The art world eases you into a life where everything is bought, sold, resolved and discussed over a shared bottle. My success and solid marriage were cushioned inside an illness that became more obvious as the drinks surfaced earlier each day. The inevitable hangover was dealt with by midday at the pub across the street from the gallery by having a 'cleanser'. Only in Australia could beer be described as a health food—a 'cleansing ale'! The first drink does the damage. As they say in AA, one is too many and a hundred is not enough. I was gradually becoming more and more detached from work and family, like a man living on a park bench in my own home.

Thank God I had wonderful staff at the gallery, because I was running the business from a distance. I was still very much drawn to Dom: she was attractive, she was powerfully capable, and I thought (selfishly, perhaps) that she could smoothly control my unmanageable life. Marriage, in my mind, was another form of custodial management. In the long term, this only made everything more damaging and more extreme.

Every day was a quiet rampage. It was a terrible burden for any partner to bear. At one stage Dom taped the bottle tops on the spirits so I would not jump up in the middle of the night and take another sip of brandy. She still had faith that one day I would stop.

When my drinking became an unmanageable crisis, I started having interventions—small stints in rehab—yet none were able to instil in me how powerless I was in the claws of addiction. So-called 'controlled' drinking was impossible. For an alcoholic, there is no such thing as a 'social drink'.

My early forties was a turning point. My business, in those great art-boom years, was expanding—and so was I. Drinking and eating far too much, I developed insulin resistance and pre-diabetes as the weight started to stack on. My face grew red, blotchy and bloated. I was literally fermenting. At 148 kilos I looked like the Michelin Man, my face melting into a circumference of fat, and I struggled to lift myself out of bed. At 42, I looked 30 years older. In summer, overweight and with a suntan, my mother would describe me as 'a map of self-indulgence'. Louise was terrified that I was going to have a heart attack. I was treating my body as an amusement park.

Alcohol, more than food, packed on the pounds. On a bad day, I could imbibe empty liquid calories from lunch to midnight, then beyond. When drunk, I was not openly offensive—more of a big noisy bear. It was not good for business, though: I looked indulged, undisciplined. Few can see their most negative manifestations gradually engulfing them. I would look in the mirror and not recognise myself. Obesity was a mask that I could not remove.

Everything that was spiralling in my inner life now hung in heavy folds off my frame. Most of my drinking was done at night as a cupboard drinker in a morbid state of self-pity. I lacked emotional proportion; in my mind, the smallest slight became a massive insult. Anything seemed like an insinuation, a threat or a source of constant blame. As the author John Burroughs put it so well: 'A man can fail many times, but he isn't a failure until he begins to blame somebody else.' This was the paradox. I did not see things as they were, rather as I was: toxic.

Once, terribly hungover and still drunk, I made a fool of myself at Andrew Upton's birthday party, held on the sprawling lawn overlooked by their elegant palatial sandstone home, an event stacked with Sydney's arts and media royalty. Instead of a string quartet, Andrew's and my favourite band, The Go-Betweens, was playing to the guests. Still intoxicated, I made the most silly, vulgar comment to Cate Blanchett, Andrew's wife. I was expressing how pleased Andrew must have been at having The Go-Betweens play for him, and my words were intended as a compliment, but they came out completely the wrong way. She was not amused, but to my relief she brushed it off and obviously has forgiven me. I also remember cornering Clive James, trying to converse about the state of the Australian art scene, but I was obviously so drunk and reeking of alcoholic hangover energy that he couldn't get away fast enough. Today it still stands as one of the most embarrassing days of my life, one that horrifies me. Whenever I think that perhaps I could enjoy a drink again,

I think of that day and am immediately reminded of what a fool alcohol makes of me.

At my lowest point, I found myself at The Gap, a dip in the sandstone cliffs adjacent to Watsons Bay at the head of Sydney Harbour, renowned as a suicide spot. Only the thought of James kept me from climbing over that fence to jump.

For a long time, I believed that I was born a natural escape artist and probably had a propensity for drinking. I saw alcoholism as a disease I had carried from birth, a silent addict's gene. Many people think that it's something you develop gradually or adopt desperately during a hard time, a character defect or lack of will-power. I'd held these thoughts in mind in part for many years until I met Elizabeth Cowley and became more educated about my health. I was gently advised that no, there was no single 'alcoholic' gene per se; I was not destined to become an alcoholic through no fault of my own, and I could not solely blame my DNA or make-up.

However, my DNA does possess a few indicators that mean my body is unable to break down toxins as easily as others via methylation in the liver. In other words, my body has an inability to break down alcohol efficiently, a trait common in alcoholics. Along with some other gene variations linked with a tendency to addiction, lower tolerance for stress and mood disorders such as anxiety and depression. Alcoholism is widely understood to be a disease of the mind, body and spirit.

Dad thought it was just a matter of willpower. He would sometimes open a nice bottle of champagne to get the day started; on calling him to touch base, I would hear the pop of a cork, the sound of bubbles and fizz. 'Dad, it's only 11 a.m.!' I would say.

'Well, it's better to have one at eleven than eleven at one,' he would reply. 'I do need my art starter!'

It was always only one glass that he needed to get him going—something I could never do. For me, once the bottle was open, it was gone in less than an hour. That is the difference between his drinking and mine. 'This is not a matter of willpower,' I told him. 'Was your father capable of only having one or two?'

'No,' he replied.

'Well, for me it is exactly the same,' I said.

Even if there was an inherited 'alcoholic' gene, though, it would not have necessarily manifested into a condition without the 'right' environment—nurture versus nature. There are many different genes underlying addiction and addictive tendencies that can then be 'expressed'. Early childhood trauma, chronic stress and lifestyle choices can all stimulate these genes into activity, which can then lead to a condition. Since I could tick each of those boxes (the car accident and my coma in France, sexual abuse, business and personal stress, my drinking habits and obesity), I was behind the eight ball. In rehab, they talk about 'crossing the thin red line' from controlled drinking to problem drinking. I believe that trauma was my line.

When I was little, we were staying in the old pub in Hill End that seemed haunted. One night, the late Paul Haefliger, artist and art critic, and his artist wife Jean Bellette came to dinner, and at the end of the night Paul read my palm. He was a very gothic man with an immaculate knowledge of art history. Paul told me that I would have an interesting life but at the age of 45 a terrible illness would strike me; however, if I survived, I would live to a good age. My whole childhood and young adulthood was haunted by the echo of Paul's prophecy.

When my drinking escalated, my mother, being the good

hippie sage that she was, consulted the I Ching, the Book of Changes. It talked about two armies marching towards each other, facing imminent tragedy. Unless one army changed direction there would be death, and that army could only change direction through spirituality. She literally prophesied my death.

I asked, 'How do I find spirituality?' as I was not religious then. She advised me to trust and to start praying.

When I first started going to AA meetings and saw the word 'God' on the wall I was terrified, but slowly came to realise that your own interpretation of God is up to you. You do not have to have a religious view of God: it could be a universal interpretation. That was how I started praying to something and, in turn, a higher power or an intangible force definitely helped me. I realised that I couldn't do it on my own: I had already tried that, and it had not worked.

When I finally hit my rock bottom, it dawned on me that perhaps the illness Paul was talking about was alcoholism. The addict is always the last to see what is painfully obvious to everyone else.

In 2007, the crunch came. Dom went away with some girlfriends. I was left with James for two hours and started drinking in the morning. I loved my time with him so much but after a certain number of drinks I experienced what is commonly described as an alcoholic blackout. The live-in nanny found me naked in the pool, oblivious and almost unconscious, with James in the shallow end. I was utterly unaware I was endangering him, and it wasn't the first time. There had been times I had left him strapped into his baby seat with a packet of chips and the windows open while I popped into the pub for a quick beer. There he would be, sitting outside and munching away, while I necked a schooner in order to be able to function. To my shame, I can still see his little blond head through that open window, gazing into the bar at me holding my 'medication'.

Alcoholism is an emotional abuse and dependency I have seen played out on both of my parents: in Dad's despair with his father, in Mum's hiding of her father's drinking problems. Remembering all of this, my greatest reason to stop was for James—to cease this cycle within the family permanently.

Looking back, I feel such a deep sense of shame and guilt. How could anyone put alcohol before the welfare of their child? You don't think it can get worse, but the true rock bottom was yet to come. One Christmas morning, after drinking all night, I found myself under the tree surrounded by empty bottles and yet-to-be-unwrapped Christmas presents. James was three, and he was sobbing, pleading, 'Daddy, Daddy, can you please help me open my presents?' Santa might have come and gone, but Dad was a mess on the floor.

In between Christmas lunch and the next morning, Dom booked me into the famous Betty Ford Center, and on Boxing Day I was on the first flight to Los Angeles.

I travelled from LA to Palm Springs by limousine, in the land of Bob Hope, the Rat Pack and Liberace, feeling like I would be in a safe haven where I could get well while flying under the radar, having been already written up in the Sydney social pages for being in rehab before. I was so full of grandiosity and self-importance about who I was. In truth, I needed to be somewhere where no one gave a damn about me and where being an 'art identity' and John Olsen's son meant nothing.

After being admitted, they gave me a complete medical check-up, and I was put into a pair of old men's pyjamas with drawstring pants before being led into an office for my initial assessment. The first thing I noticed was a shelf full of recovery books, and a man, sitting behind a desk, who resembled Keith Richards. He had obviously been to hell and back, and now he had assumed the calm mien of a wise sage of recovery.

'Sit back and relax, Tim,' he said. 'I am going to ask you one question and I want you to think about it. What is the worst thing that could happen to you if you left here and continued to drink?'

Almost mechanically, I said, 'I'm going to die.'

It must have been what he had heard every time a new patient arrived, because he immediately replied: 'Well, that might not be the worst thing. Because, according to your family, you are a pain in the arse. If you were to die, of course, they would be sad for a while but ultimately they would be better off without you.'

I felt like the room had received the aftershock of an explosion. The anticlimax of a truly wasted life was detonating inside my chain of memory and across three generations of drinkers. Because it was true. My life would be seen as a rise and fall that, in reality, had not amounted to much. If I died, my demise might be mentioned in a newspaper, a pathetic perpetuation of the lineage of alcoholism. A forgotten man dead well before his time.

I had worked hard all of my adult life, feeling the responsibility to support Mum and our broken family but, after establishing the gallery, I was now on the point of losing everything: my business, my family and ultimately my moral compass. The direct outcome of more drinking would be the squalid future of living in a boarding house where one day I would be found dead. But even the self-pity that vision inspired was riddled with my disease.

Betty Ford took an approach like no other rehab I had visited. Like a tattered tall ship, I had to have every sail of grandiosity, denial and delusion torn down and dismantled so I could be rebuilt as a stronger vessel. I had to forget everything I thought I knew. That afternoon I was led to my shared room where my roommate and I lay in the darkness, trying to talk ourselves to sleep between doses of valium, sweating it out and confessing our excesses. Teamed up with a complete stranger in the same struggle, we spoke openly: 'You think you have problems?' my new friend said, without a shred of irony. 'I am about to inherit a distillery.' It turned out that my roommate was one of the heirs to the Jim Beam empire.

The bitter humour in this initial exchange made me feel that the task was slightly more achievable. I was put on an ongoing diet of valium to prevent me from going into a seizure and choking on my own vomit. Meanwhile, Dom was proudly sending me photos of James on holiday at Lachlan and Sarah Murdoch's property. I felt like I had become one of the shamed untouchables, in contrast to Dom's uncrushable outlook, spirit and social charm.

Being American, my rehab experience had a slightly *Truman Show*-esque quality. An amplified gaiety and exaggerated sense of the positive were instilled into every moment. During the day we'd go off to sit in lectures, working our way through hardcore therapy that encompassed the twelve-step program. The first step is often the hardest one: accepting that you are completely powerless over alcohol. The second step was perhaps even more challenging: I had to learn to surrender and understand that I couldn't do this on my own. There before me was the concept of repenting to a greater power that could restore me to sanity. I had to believe in the prospect of a miracle in discovering a spiritual humility. I had to hand over my addiction to something that seemed invisible.

Although originally only intending to stay at Betty Ford for a month, this extended to three. The level of your sobriety runs parallel to your level of enlightenment, and in Rehab Deluxe there is a taxi meter ticking on your soul. It cost me a fortune to go to rehab in the United States, especially paying in US dollars. With Palm Springs being so full of retired actors, there were some real hardened John Waynes—elder sober gunslingers. I had had two months off the sauce when I went to a men's AA meeting in a Spanish-looking chapel where I shared my journey before an audience of 50 men, expressing what life was like when I drank and what life was like now. I was able to identify with my rock bottom in great depth, in a very honest way, and describe the despair I never wanted to go back to. Taking my seat, a long-term sober man got up. He would have been in his eighties, with over 40 years of sobriety, and he said, 'If that Australian guy that just got up before me gets this, he's got the potential to help a lot of people.' That was one thing that gave more hope than anything: someone could see that I still had potential to be a worthy and helpful member of society.

During those months at Betty Ford, we were given the occasional weekend off, and I would drive to Los Angeles and stay with friends—actor Rachel Griffiths and her artist husband Andrew Taylor. From rehab to Hollywood in a weekend. They lived in a beautiful Modernist home in the tradition of Frank Lloyd Wright that had been built by Wright's son, John. Andrew and Rachel are very dear to me; our children are also close, and Andrew has been one of my artists for many years. They treated me like family, making me feel completely at home and giving me a refuge, a contrast to being in rehab that was very intense and full of self-contemplation. Andy would take me to the Getty and we would wander around for hours, returning to the comfort of home-cooked meals with relaxed conversation. I would trundle back to rehab on Sunday evening, rested and revitalised.

A few years ago Rachel and Andrew moved back to Australia to be closer to family, settling back in their home town of Melbourne. Rachel always stays with Dom when she comes to Sydney, and Andrew exhibits with me almost annually. Rachel and Andy, and their kindness, were an integral part of my recovery.

When I came back from Betty Ford, everyone was still at lunch. I could hardly tell people I had been at Harvard, but in fact I was unashamed to admit to the odyssey that I had been through in the Californian desert. Overwhelmingly, I was so very happy to be back with James again. The relief at seeing my family was overwhelming, and my debt to them runs deep.

Then, about six months after rehab, I went to the most famous horserace in Australia, the Melbourne Cup. I had been invited to a glamorous marquee where the beautiful people mingled as trays of champagne and caviar canapés constantly passed by. With festivities on overdrive, drinking was almost mandatory. I was feeling a little awkward when a stunning woman said, 'Tim, you haven't even taken a sip.'

I took a sip. Unlike my father, I did not really like the taste of champagne. It was too effervescent and cut my tongue like acid, but the more I drank, the softer it became. Immediately, all the nerve endings and synapses in my brain surrendered. The next thing I knew, I was in a nightclub in Toorak sculling espresso martinis.

I ended up at a party in the penthouse of The Olsen hotel and remember telling a guy there how great it was to get sober. Such delusion. There I was pontificating on the virtues of being a non-drinker, holding a vodka in one hand, pretending it was water.

Even when I am not drinking, my alcoholism is in the background, doing push-ups, waiting for another Melbourne Cup moment. Each time you relapse, the consequences become worse. This one became a four-day bender. I crawled back into a meeting in Sydney. Luckily my head still fitted through the door; there are a lot of people who never make it back in. Everyone found out about my relapse, so I decided to go back to rehab, this time at The Sydney Clinic in Bronte.

Dom had washed her hands of me, so I arranged for a friend to collect me, went to the pub on the corner, lined up four double vodka tonics and two schooners of beer, and sculled the lot. The exhibitionism of the moment was grotesque. My friend came in and caught me on my last vodka tonic, put me in a headlock, dragged me out to his car and drove me straight to the clinic.

There have been other tiny relapses—mouthfuls—but this was the one that got me back to staying sober permanently. This rehab stint was the final turning point. It was a leaner, tougher rehab. No New Age bells and whistles. There I was, back in a dormitory, wearing those old men's pyjamas again. It was very confronting to see that whether you are an alcoholic or a junkie quivering from ice withdrawal, you are all in the same basket. An addiction is an addiction.

I then realised the pinnacle of sober living. You cannot think your way into a new way of living: you can only live your way into a new way of thinking. I could not *think* myself sober, only *live* myself into sobriety. It was not until I started putting days of avoiding alcohol together that abstinence became my lifestyle.

A successful path to a truly happy life in sobriety requires a huge deflation in ego. To become brutally honest with oneself. It is a constant challenge when people keep praising your success when there is always a part inside you that feels like you do not deserve it.

When I eventually found my credit card, I upgraded myself to what they call 'the Lindsay Lohan Suite', with my own room and bathroom. A very big part of sobering up is realising that you are not special, that you are no better than anyone else. When you develop some kind of humility and go to meetings with every kind of person, you realise that you are all reduced to being simply garden-variety alcoholics.

In the first weeks of going straight, I would use memory to trigger aversion. Memories of how squalid life had been with booze, waking up in the morning to reach into the freezer to take a swig of vodka, hanging out for the first pub to open—I had been an urbanised derelict. Memories of the death wish that got stronger and stronger in the justification that I wanted to be 'free' to drink myself to death, alone, left in peace, completely impoverished, with barely enough money to buy alcohol every day just to get drunk, like my grandfather Harry. Another fantasy was that I could move to Mexico like Albert Finney in *Under the Volcano*, or to Las Vegas like Nicolas Cage in *Leaving Las Vegas*, and just drink myself to death. The ability to drink had been more important to me than ever achieving anything or even being a father.

I had used my last get-out-of-jail-free card, ragged as it was. I was surrounded by so many gifts of life but I was overlooking them, too busy dealing with my anxieties. I had talked about burning out from my high-intensity lifestyle, acting as if nothing would get done unless I did it myself. I had become so engrossed with fighting with the frustrations of life that I had failed to see all the good things coming my way.

During my father's childhood in the 1930s, the Bondi Pavilion had a ballroom and a cabaret room where Dad's parents attended parties and Harry would drink to excess. Now I go there every morning to attend AA meetings. The irony is not lost on me.

When I got sober, the clarity was both enlightening and frightening. Finally facing the truth of my past mistakes and behaviour was highly confronting. The only way to dissipate the shame was to accept it as a learning experience, apologise and make amends where I could. Finally I was able to make sense of things and realise how interesting and great my life had actually been. Getting sober was the best way for me to stop being a self-saboteur, an obstacle to my own happiness. For me, it was simple: I can have alcohol, or I can have everything. In technicolour.

23

SOBER YET INTOXICATED

Going straight is full of hairpin curves. While it is tempting to depict sobriety as a Lazarus-like state, with the hero rising from the grave, renewed and potent, the road is rougher, slower and much more exposed than that. My commitment to battling alcoholism coincided with the spiky precipice that is turning 50 and the vulnerability to all that a midlife crisis implies. As I shed weight and bad memories, I felt like I had a lot to prove.

Subconsciously I had thought Dom could rescue me, but only I could do that. Our marriage ended not in addiction but in recovery as so many do. Dom believed that if I could get sober it would save our marriage; instead, it just illuminated our differences—and perhaps my shame. It is hard to change in the company of someone who has seen you constantly at your worst. Essentially, I paid the price in my next relationship.

When I moved out of the house and into the apartment above the gallery after being sober for one year, effectively it symbolised our separation. I was vulnerable and ripe for seduction. A sensuous woman, a Latin beauty, came to one of my openings and was enchanted with the art. With my lack of self-esteem, my early sobriety did not protect me from a predictable rescue scenario. She was getting no support from her ex-husband, for herself or her children. In 'rescuing' her I found a false sense of nobility that fed my ego when I should have been concentrating on saving myself.

After feeling emasculated by addiction, I found that she provided a goal for physical self-improvement, which I ultimately achieved; six months later she finally invited me into her bed and I rediscovered my mojo. At 120 kilos, I still had a lot to lose—on several levels. Sexuality is a great motivator and my new lover was the dream prize, the return of the violent kiss that I shared as a child with the girl who drove a compass deep into my thigh. Addiction so often starts and ends in pain.

In the end it became a co-dependent relationship and it was hard on my family, especially Dom.

Dom, after going through the worst of times with me, saw how vulnerable I was to exploitation. I am deeply sorry for how much I hurt her and how much I disappointed James in still not being a totally present father. It was of little consolation to become sober and then leave the pub for the bedroom, essentially closing another door. Sexual obsession is just addiction in another guise.

This was a confusing chapter of lust, self-loathing, grandiosity and drama, textbook behaviour for a midlife crisis. At least I didn't buy a red Ferrari! In some regards the toxic tango was a further exploration of the love affairs I saw as a child. Having grown up around flawed people trying to reinvent the moral compass, imperfections of a deep nature seemed normal. It was a little bit like history repeating itself.

Dom now tries not to look back on those dark times, thinking only, with her eternal optimism, of the good. While our marriage ended, I will never forget the support she gave me, and I appreciate greatly her understanding of how difficult I found it, especially in 'my' world when so much in a gallery is based around celebration and, in our culture, drinking. That she looks back on our courtship, marriage and ongoing life together as parents as she does is testament to her strength and personality, and it is so good for James. I know how much my parents' love mattered to me, so the fact that we have been able to retain a healthy and respectful relationship for James and ourselves is a highlight of my life.

When we were courting, Dom had been warned that I was a bit of a womaniser, which still makes me laugh. She said that I looked at her as if she was the only woman in the room, and when she talks about me as kind, generous, spontaneous and fun, I like the person she sees and will always be grateful that she helped me find myself again. Dom also helped me build up confidence, my self-esteem, pulling me up when I got down on myself. Her life is still studded with special events, and her phone is always ringing. But our priority, of course, is James. Whatever happened, he is the one thing we got right and still do.

We co-parent with ease. James spends most of his school week at his mother's house, staying at the gallery apartment when it suits him. Each year we have a family holiday in Europe and will continue this tradition as long as James wants to join us. I enjoy the love and friendship of the rest of Dom's family, in particular her brothers Mitchell and Brent and her sister, Sarah, who lives in Oxford.

Dom's mother, Antoinette, and I still share a deep affection. It is a relief that she recognises that I never meant to harm her daughter, or to embarrass or damage her family. Antoinette texts me the footy score before I have watched the game myself and jokingly says that she loves me as much as her own boys. Dom's family include me like nothing has changed, and it is reciprocal, as it is with my first wife Harriet and her parents.

The continuation of our family as a unit matters greatly to us all. We will always be in each other's lives, always connected because of James. To this we still, and always will, love each other, just now in a different way.

For his thirteenth birthday, James and I took a cooking class on Capri, taught to parcel ravioli and prepare other dishes under the shade of a fragrant lemon tree. Unfortunately, our visiting chef made a dish with such copious amounts of lemon rind that the creamy fettuccini was overwhelmed to the point of being inedible. We still laugh about it to this day. In Capri you can buy the most wonderful egg-shaped tomatoes called San Marzano, which come from the gardens of Amalfi in the volcanic soil around Mount Vesuvius. There is nothing quite like a Caprese salad made with local buffalo mozzarella and fresh basil.

We ate the day.

Swimming around Faraglioni, a rocky outcrop off Capri, is my daily routine that makes the island a place I like to be. When we are there I walk down to the coast, swim, then stroll back up to join the locals for coffee, chatting away in my broken Italian, the tourists still slumbering, delivery men passing through the square, stocking up the restaurants that all basically have the same menu. Truman Capote once said about Capri that 'it is a place billionaires like to go to eat like peasants'.

My morning swim is still everything to me. The lifesaver at the Alfresco Beach Club told me that I had 'a kick like an outboard motor'. Most ardent Mediterranean people cannot comprehend the Australians' lack of fear when it comes to swimming in the sea. We throw our kids off the back of a boat to sink or swim. (In fact, we just want to quickly get them on the rocks to have lunch at the restaurant.) Australians connect to swimming as much as Romans do to riding a Vespa. Swimming is the act of the nature lover, without even thinking that you are doing something to celebrate the earth.

Capri has also long been a haven for artists and writers. John Singer Sargent, Frank Hyde and John Wood Shortridge all stayed there, and writers Somerset Maugham and Graham Greene found inspiration in the lifestyle and the island's magical beauty. Despite stating that Capri 'isn't really my kind of place', Greene owned a house in the town of Anacapri with his lover, Catherine Walston, for over 40 years, visiting biannually until very late in his life. Made an honorary citizen of the town in 1978, he said that on the island 'in four weeks I do the work of six months elsewhere'.[1] It is a sentiment I can echo as I have written more, and far more succinctly, there than I have anywhere else.

Despite now attracting celebrities from around the world, movie and pop stars, and inhabited by the super-rich and famous, for me the island will always be a place to swim, relax and write, to enjoy the company of family and friends, and, of course, to relish the food.

La dolce vita.

24

ART DYNASTY

When Paloma Picasso, daughter of Pablo, came to Sydney to launch her new jewellery collection at Tiffany's in 2010, she especially wanted to view some contemporary Australian art. In conjunction with the AGNSW and Tiffany's publicist Nikki Andrews, we organised a meeting with Dad. Paloma had inherited a love of art from her father, and both she and her husband Eric were particularly passionate about contemporary art. Louise and I thought that it would be wonderful to meet her, and I suggested that we meet at the gallery to view some of John's works and then go on to lunch at Lucio's. We were all admirers of Picasso's work, so it was a serendipitous day.

Paloma and Eric were delightful. Dad presented some of his past and current work. The atmosphere was relaxed and convivial, the conversation flowing. It was inevitable that we would start to compare notes, especially Louise and Paloma. Looking at these two talented jewellery designers, both beautiful and stylish, each with an artist father, it was impossible not to see the similarities between them.

I could also relate on the father level. A driving force for all of us was to avoid the long shadow that can be cast and the attention you attract for your familial connections, and to be independently successful in a chosen field. Both Louise and Paloma had coincidentally chosen jewellery design, each achieving phenomenal success.

'I was talking to Louise and I was very much able to relate to what she was saying,' Paloma said. 'When you have a father who stands out so much you want to do your own thing because you know when you come out everyone will be watching.'[1]

Paloma also spoke about how much she loved her name, given to her by her father, meaning 'peace dove'. She was named in honour of the dove drawn by her father that became the symbol of the World Congress of Partisans for Peace, held in Paris in 1949, and a dove pendant has featured in one of her own collections. Coincidentally, when we were kids, 'Paloma' was my nickname for Louise; I would ask, 'Who do you think you are: Paloma Picasso?' (Louise means 'famous warrior'.)

At the end of lunch, Paloma expressed how much she had loved the day. She joked, 'Today it felt like a family event, but without the arguments.' We all received an open invitation to stay at her home in Marrakech, a city from which she draws inspiration for her work.

The young Paloma, too, was a victim of her father's complicated liaisons, and the negative impact of 'the stepmother'. When her mother, artist Françoise Gilot (the only woman to ever leave Picasso), wrote her 1964 book *Life with Picasso* a decade after she had left him, Pablo tried unsuccessfully to have the book banned. Incensed, and incited by his wife Jacqueline, he abruptly cut off relations with Paloma and her brother Claude. They barely saw him again.

There are photographs of Paloma as a child, drawing with Picasso on the beach, at play with him in his studio. Like ours, her childhood had a magical quality, with a larger-than-life parent who was enchanting, mesmerising. The sense of loss when such a vital force is removed from your orbit can be catastrophic and enduring.

While John has sometimes received criticism for prioritising his art over all else, we now understand and appreciate that the good well and truly outweighed the bad. While I have referred to Dad as being like the sun to me, Picasso literally forced his family to call him 'The Sun', as one of his granddaughters, Marina, revealed in her biography![2] While we have all put the hurt behind us, Marina sold Picasso's ceramics in an attempt at closure after her unhappy childhood; her family had had to beg for money from her grandfather, whom they rarely saw. When she first inherited her Cannes villa, she turned all the paintings to face the wall.[3]

I met Paloma's brother, the charming and hugely talented Claude, in 2016 at Art Basel Miami Beach. Claude and curator Sir Norman Rosenthal had collaborated with Zürich's Galerie Gmurzynska for an exhibition of Russian avant-garde works, and their booth was designed by Claude. We met during the exclusive Cocktail Dinatoire party, a Cirque du Soleil–style spectacular, which celebrated Claude's innovative booth design. With stunning decorations and elaborately costumed but scantily dressed women lounging around and serving drinks, it was like a scene from Kubrick's *Eyes Wide Shut*. It made me wonder if Claude had inherited his father's love of the erotic.

The whole Picasso family is involved in the arts. Another

granddaughter, Diana Widmaier Picasso, is an art historian and curator. Another Picasso who loves jewellery, Diana is the artistic director of Menē,[4] a luxury brand she founded with my close friend, designer Sunjoo Moon. Some years ago, we all arranged to meet in Paris at the chic restaurant in the Hôtel Costes. When Dom and I arrived at the opulent restaurant, our entrance was blocked by the maître d'hôtel, who looked us up and down with disdain. We thought that we were not going to be allowed in. Feeling strangely intimidated, I said, 'We have a reservation!'

'And what name would that be in?' he asked.

'Picasso!' The reaction was instantaneous—I've never experienced such a shift in attitude. It was the power of the Picasso name.

Diana's mother, Maya, was often a subject for Picasso's works during her childhood. Like us, Maya had had 'a papa who painted'. In 2017, Diana curated an exhibition of her grandfather's works at the Paris Gagosian Gallery, titled *Picasso and Maya: Father and Daughter*, featuring portraits of her grandmother, works created for her mother as a child, and a wall of intimate, personal photographs.[5] She has also written a book about her grandfather's erotic works (*Picasso: Art Can Only Be Erotic*) and has completed the catalogue raisonné of his sculptures.[6]

Diana was born after Picasso's death. When I asked about the 'long shadow' cast by her grandfather, she replied, 'I only see the light.'

Without comparing my father to Picasso, I must still enforce that we, the children of artists—whatever the art form—are linked. There are similarities in our unconventional upbringings, in the impact of mixed family relations with periods of estrangement, and in our artist parent's constant search for the muse that drives them. Our periods of estrangement from Dad only strengthened our resolve to forge our own paths in life, just as Paloma Picasso has done. However beneficial this was in the long term, we would all rather have had the continued presence of our father. We, too, will inevitably have to deal with the complexities of the legacy from an artist parent.

John has been meticulous in the recording of his prodigious output, and we will continue to protect Dad's legacy, preserving the integrity of his work for Australian art history. The public collections, numerous books on his work and extensive bibliography ensure verified references. The Picasso family, the art world's richest dynasty, have shared Picasso's collection, his legacy, with the world.

Works of art are meant to be seen, to educate and inspire, not be hidden away by gloating philistines. There are also the thieves of destruction, the grave robbers—the looting and decimation of cultural heritage and art history—with countries such as Iran, Syria, Afghanistan and Pakistan suffering irreparable damage. UNESCO considers intentional destruction of cultural heritage a crime.

At least Paris is still standing.

25

VALE VALERIE

By 2011, I had made strides in recovery from addiction. Little did I know the blow that was coming. The death of my mother was the loss of my greatest muse. It was a time of deep and unexpected sorrow.

Mum had been suffering from a loss of balance. I sensed that she knew something was wrong. She collapsed, was rushed to hospital and then diagnosed with a brain tumour. Mum ultimately ended up in the Sacred Heart Hospice, overlooking the National Art School where she had studied and had first met Dad all those years ago.

With Mum's birthday being on New Year's Day, my aim in sobriety had been to spend her birthday with her sober and not hungover. I am so pleased to have been able to attain that for her.

Shortly before she passed, she gave me the gift of self-discovery, saying: 'You never had to worry about becoming as famous and successful as your father. For you, to discover who you are is really what great success is all about.' She chose to speak plainly in those last days, telling me that she didn't care much for my gallery or my fashionable friends. My Range Rover didn't impress her either. I remarked that it was unlike her to speak that way, and she said that she had something far more powerful to tell me: 'I am so proud of you because you've learnt how to be yourself and to love yourself. That is all a mother ever wants for her child.'

I could have been anyone's son and still feel that I was living under the shadow of someone. It took those few words for me to finally realise that, and the true value of the gifts that both of my parents had given me. It was one of the crucial moments in my recovery, and I have never looked back. For that alone, I will be eternally grateful. Mum was always advising us to look at our lives through ordinary eyes, to see that the façade and fantasy about John Olsen and the family was just an illusion. We were not particularly special, nor were we the only ones to experience a different sort of life. We were not better than anyone else, and we should not measure things by ego.

When Mum was in the hospice, her partner Gil was by her side. Gil and friends would take turns reading to Mum, and one day, reading 'The Man from Snowy River', Gil thought to himself how hard it must have been on the horses, only for Mum to echo the same sentiments at the end of the poem: 'Those poor horses!' Mum's heart was immense.

Mum's eventual parting was beautiful in its way. She was surrounded by love right to the end. We had a mixed religious ceremony at the crematorium where a Buddhist nun carried out her last rites. A week later we held a memorial service on the top floor of the gallery. What a crystalline memory. With all its beaming natural light, the space felt more like a chapel. After hanging a plethora of her works, we had achieved a retrospective. People arrived, many of whom had never seen her work, and were amazed at how talented Valerie was, how sensitive, acute and dreamy her sonnets to the landscape were. We all took part in eulogies that honoured her quiet strength, her unassuming nature and humility, the poise and dignity that she maintained throughout her life. Her works were a by-product of her character, her personality, and stand as evidence of her sensitivity and spirituality. They offer an intimate insight into her soul.

At her memorial, I spoke of how important Mum had been to our lives, how Louise and I could not have chosen a better mother or better parents, how lucky we both have been to grow up in the environment our parents gave us, and the revealing, enduring perception of the world to which we were introduced. Valerie gave us a sacred vision of how life could be, through herself as a person and through her great empathy. Our parents offered us a unique and truthful perspective on life, on how wonderful the world could be if you wanted to make it that way. Through the pursuit of beauty, honesty and truth, there would always be a guiding light.

At the memorial service, it was extraordinary to see that almost every woman who had ever transgressed her relationship with John was there. It exemplified exactly the kind of woman Mum was, epitomising the depths of her forgiveness and wisdom. A woman full of leniency, she restored friendships with the people who had betrayed her—often the wives of other artists—in the very insular art world. One of those women at the service said to me: 'Your mother was a much better friend to me than your father was a lover.' It was the first time I had laughed out loud since Mum had passed.

Through trials and tribulations, Mum remained calm and stoic, a beacon of humility and integrity. She was not judgemental. If I was upset about anything, she would succinctly tell me to 'Think Eastern', to think of calm, space and peace. When

I was younger, she would dismiss my poor self-image and sense of intellectual inferiority, reassuring me that my super-sensitivity was a strength, one that could turn into a talent one day.

Today we are reluctant to sell her work. It has remained in storage for many years, both of us feeling that to break the chain would be sacrilege, but her art deserves better than to sit in the racks. My goal now is to catalogue all of her art, to have her work shown in a complete retrospective at the Newcastle Art Gallery and retained permanently if possible, hanging alongside Dad's and, more recently, Louise's works.

Thinking of Mum reminds me of the old mother angophora tree that grew by our house at Dural. Through the root system, the tree controlled the ecosystems of all the surrounding smaller, older trees. When the mother tree dies, the nitrogen released in the soil ensures the adjacent trees are nurtured, bursting with the strength to survive and grow even larger. This is exactly what my own mother's death was to me. Her loss signalled my own need to grow up and be responsible, to achieve my life's purpose. The sadness of her loss was the nitrogen hit that invigorated and inspired me to go on and do greater things. This is true for Louise as well, particularly now that, after all these years, she has returned to painting with Dad's support and blessing.

Grief is not nostalgia. Instead it is like a photo negative of falling in love. When we are infatuated we push our love into the future, but when we grieve, we seek out our love of the past. Nostalgia paints everything lilac. Grief is monochrome.

One of the hardest things anyone will ever do is to pack up the home of a loved one. It does not matter how long you have been aware of their imminent demise or how expected it has been.

The sadness of entering their shell of a home, sorting through their personal belongings, is gut wrenching. Mum's perpetual inner thoughts, externalised on tiny notepads, were littered around the house. Mum, to the end, was constantly seeking the deeper meaning of life. When she passed, Louise and I divided her beloved possessions between us—the innumerable books, her own paintings and other works of art, her jewellery, the life she had left behind. Her non-essential papers were put into storage, neither of us able nor willing to delve into them; it felt too intimate, intrusive. Going through the papers recently, I was struck again by her spirituality, her love of nature and her surroundings, her joy in the everyday.

Today, with the clarity to understand my life better, I realise that she is still with me. I have not lost her; our time together has an everlasting quality. Her life and the gift of her love give me a sense that death transcends mortality: I feel that Mum visits me regularly. She knocks on the door and on the cupboards, making quite a racket, especially if there is someone present who she does not approve of. For a ghost, this must take a lot of energy.

When a great love dies, it is both strange and difficult when you find what remnants you are left with. Mum's legacy clearly is both in her painting and a lifetime of kind acts, but for me there is also something else, something small, insignificant to anyone else: Valerie frequently wore a lovely blue scarf that I always admired. After she died, we found everything in its place in her quiet home. There, in the silence, was the beautiful silk scarf, coiled on the doorknob of her bedroom, a remnant from our time in Portugal, judging by its design. It really was as though she had left it out especially for me.

My next writing project, now well underway, is a book in tribute to the life and art of my mother. Louise and I have already started to photograph and catalogue her works in readiness. In talking to Dad, her friends and her students, we have gleaned new insights. These, coupled with her art, her notebooks and the research already completed on her family background and her life, have provided me with a deeper knowledge of her as a woman and as an artist.

There are discussions for the potential of a retrospective of Mum's work in a major institution—an exhibition of the works of a female artist who took a back seat to another artist, enabling him to pursue his own career, and putting aside her own exhibiting career for her family. With her longtime friends, colleagues and such a vast number of former students from her many years teaching at Hornsby TAFE and other institutions, we know that it will be well received.

26

AN ODD BUT FRUITFUL COUPLING

Rex Irwin became a partner in my gallery in February 2013. It was an odd yet strangely fertile coupling, and the Tim Olsen Gallery became Olsen Irwin. Rex and I went way back, to my first arts job in my student days, when I had worked for him for a pittance and been unceremoniously fired. We had moved on, becoming friends and colleagues. He gave me my first job in the art world, and I gave him his last.

Rex was a very proper Englishman whose father had been a captain in the British army. Raised in India, he had come to Australia to work for Frank McDonald, the very same dealer who, as we recuperated in Spain in the 1960s, had given John the run-around while we went hungry.

While we were in Europe, Frank McDonald had become a director at Terry Clune Galleries, later Clune Galleries. Frank joined forces with Violet Dulieu, director of South Yarra Gallery in Melbourne, crating up the works John had sent back from Europe and sending them down for exhibitions in 1965 and 1967. In both Sydney and Melbourne, the shows were hugely successful, marking significant milestones in John's career.

The 1965 show included the remarkable tapestry *Joie de Vivre* and two ceiling paintings, *Le Soleil* and *La Primavera*. Both the AGNSW and the NGV each acquired the tapestry, which was an edition of six. While we were struggling financially in Portugal, Frank McDonald told Violet to send all proceeds from the exhibitions to him, to 'drip-feed' to Dad, including an advance of £2000 from the 1965 exhibition, monies that would have drastically relieved our situation.[1] Dad is still ropeable at the distress it caused Mum. McDonald and Dulieu then conspired to reduce his artist's percentage, with McDonald writing in January 1968 about picking the right time to discuss 'cutting down the total amount of money he receives from us' with Dad. Rex always said that he had learned what NOT to do in the art world from Frank.[2]

It was Rex who proposed the merging of our galleries. 'Timothy,' he said, 'it is hard to get people upstairs these days and I don't want to close down completely. I'd love to find a way for us to work together so that I have some kind of exit strategy.' (Rex's Queen Street gallery space was on the first floor.) The merger enabled certain very important artists to exhibit in the gallery, and to realise the quality of my team, and the space and the energy of Woollahra as an art centre—an energy that had been felled by the increasing rents on Queen Street and the gradual replacement of fine arts and antique dealers with cafes and fashion boutiques. I had also respectfully invited him to bring his long-term gallery manager of 25 years, Brett Stone, to the gallery, despite already having Katrina as a manager. Rex assured me that Brett held certain intimate relationships with artists that in turn would aid the transition of Olsen Irwin.

It was a privilege to work with Rex. He has tremendous taste, a very good eye, a scholarship and sophistication then normally reserved for Northern Hemisphere galleries. In his career of 40 years as an art dealer, plus four with me, it should not be underestimated how much Rex contributed to the Australian art scene at large.

He taught me that the salon style of dealing could still work in Australia, and it did not have to be major paintings: quality work on paper could become very valuable pieces and a great entry point for a serious or novice collector—Freud etchings, drawings by Hockney or Frank Auerbach. My own collection includes a Max Beckmann, a Freud, an Auerbach and a Philip Guston as a result of our association. He relished new collectors, relating the acquisition of that 'first' work to losing one's virginity, and loved seeing younger generations taking their first plunge.

Working with Rex deepened my bravado in terms of buying and collecting slightly bigger names. He was fastidious and very old school, always dressing like a gentleman, and was known for his flashy cars—a Bentley and a Maserati—which were his main indulgence, along with his art and books. He did not care for the opinions of others, hence his habit of wearing a kilt in his family tartan at the Sydney Contemporary art fair each year: his anti–avant-garde stance. Yet anyone who understood modern art would always seek out his stand first because a multitude of avant-garde stands can start to fuse after a while.

Rex has very limited patience for experimental art or morbid images of a decayed sensibility. He showed Philip Guston but that was the line in the sand. Some of his artists have a black sense of humour, but that's a different sensibility—mordant, as opposed to morbid. A lot of modern art and postmodernism can be deliberately ugly, but people love and buy beautiful things. It can be hard to sell the more difficult pieces, when the darkness of the world has caught up with the tenebrosity of

273

art. I have shown Peter Booth but would struggle to sell those works today.

We also shared a respect for classical drawing. He came on board with some quality artists and his own list of those in my stable who were not in line with his aesthetic. We both endured a couple of exhibitions that were not to one of our tastes. I did not agree with all of his critiques but, collectively, we had too many artists when he joined the gallery and regrettably some artists had to go. In the years we worked together his favourite word was 'ghastly', a withering one-liner, and his cut-glass accent could be intimidating. Yet he was a kind, thoughtful and generous person, aware that the art world could be 'poisonous and arrogant', especially to a newcomer. Rex lamented the changes he saw in modern art selling, feeling it was becoming less personal; it's a sentiment I disagree with.

Rex has a real sense of quality, yet he could be acerbic and uncompromising with people he did not respect, struggling to deal with people if he felt that they lacked integrity or authenticity. The survival of the gallery was always paramount, and vast differences in our vision had developed. A frank discussion ensued and the next day Rex announced his departure, which was always the ultimate plan.

We naturally made a great effort to pave Rex's way to retirement and to give him a fitting farewell. While some artists did move on when he retired, others remained with the gallery and have continued to prosper. At the time, I said, 'No one else will emulate Rex's courage and astuteness, and the Australian art world will be poorer for his retirement.'

We maintain a good friendship, working together on the Fred Williams estate and with several other artists. Rex now lives an idyllic life in the NSW Southern Highlands with his dog, books, regular visits from friends and trips to the opera. He has said, 'I'm this new person who isn't who I was',[3] yet his sense of style and discipline are undiminished.

Rex is a very social being, mixing with Sydney's elite, and surrounds himself with the finer things in life. Among his large group of very good friends were Margaret and Gough Whitlam, whom he met at the opera.

In 1973, when Gough was prime minister, the decision of the NGA to buy Jackson Pollack's *Blue Poles* caused a public uproar at the purchase price (A$1.3 million). The work itself, painted in 1952, didn't fare much better: 'Barefoot drunk painted our $1m masterpiece', wrote *The Daily Mirror*. Gough had to personally approve the purchase, and did so on the advice of James Mollison, then director of the NGA. Rex suggested to Gough that he use *Blue Poles* on his official Christmas card that same year; his public endorsement of the work removed the picture from 'the criticism and ridicule to which it had been exposed', Rex said. The purchase was a world record at the time, sparking a debate over the value of abstract art and political extravagance.

Now worth about $350 million, a massive appreciation in anyone's eyes, Royal Academy of Arts curator Edith Devaney called it the 'wisest cultural investment ever made'.[4] Dad had his own reservations about abstract expressionism at the time, but now agrees that it was a very astute acquisition. *Blue Poles* is considered a seminal work and when on loan to London in 2016, was featured on the catalogue cover for the exhibition *Abstract Expressionism* at the Royal Academy of Arts. It was a painting that transfixed the nation.

One of the highlights of working with Rex was to have the opportunity to represent the works of Fred Williams, Dad's old friend and the favourite of Rudy Komon's stable.

Mum and Dad had a great Fred Williams, *Landscape with Water Ponds* (1964), a swap with Fred that Dad took with him when he left Dural. Although he had promised Mum never to sell it, he was persuaded to part with it by Rob and Carole Henty, our old Watsons Bay friends. Their daughters Paige and Rebecca inherited the painting. It is one of the few works I wish we could have retained, for the memory of Fred alone.

John was deeply fond of and inspired by Fred, saying that he was a true painter, 'our Corot'. Fred never pretended to be an intellectual, but he was anything but simple; his highly sophisticated marks suggested that he could cut to the chase of landscape. I sense that Dad learned so much from Fred's acute aesthetic, observations and abbreviations of the bush, which had a kind of Zen minimalist touch, like visual haikus that alluded to the sound of evening birds and a gentle breeze.

Only a year apart in age, John and Fred shared many experiences: they met up in Spain in the late 1950s; they lived and worked side by side at Dunmoochin; they shared a passion for the landscape, though each with a different sensibility in their view of Australian space, Fred obsessed with the horizon and Dad with the topography; and they shared a love of wine, food (John said Fred was 'good on the tooth') and companionship. There was an element of rivalry in their friendship, especially in the mid- to late 1970s when Dad's work was said to be influenced by Fred's; this, combined with the lavish praise for Whiteley at the time, was a little galling.

Their friendship endured. At the time of Fred's premature death in 1982, when the art world was in mourning, John wrote in his journal: 'Farewell, dear gentleman. Of all our painters he was the countryman of my sensibility.'

There is a small park on Halls Lane, adjacent to the main gallery. This little spot of greenery behind Queen Street is frequented by dog walkers, local residents and, sometimes, the overflow from exhibition openings. As part of the Woollahra Council Public Art Trust, when the gallery was Olsen Irwin, we donated, as a long-term loan, the sculpture *Horse at Water* by one of my international artists, Englishman Nic Fiddian-Green. The stunning bronze horse's head is the focal point of the reserve.

For Nic, sculpture has 'always been about the horse'. He was greatly inspired by the Elgin Marbles at the British Museum, fascinated by the 'fragmentation of sculptures from antiquity', much like Auguste Rodin had been over a century before, and parallels have been drawn between the two artists' work. As Nic put it, 'I've always been fascinated by fragments. Something from the past that's still present; something put back together.'[5] The horse was a fitting contribution considering the gallery's history as a tram shed, with stables behind it.

Jonathan Delafield Cook joined the gallery in the Olsen Irwin days, first exhibiting in 2014 with his beautifully executed life-size paintings of marine creatures and mammals 'conjured from charcoal onto gesso-primed linen . . . and mounted like so many trophies in a hunter's den'.[6] Jonathan will only work to the scale of the actual animal, whether a sperm whale, a bull or an ostrich; he will never compromise the fact of reality. Johnny and I have a brotherly relationship, him also being a 'son of the brush'. His parents, the late Bill Delafield Cook and his surviving wife, Sally, were family friends.

One of his works, the magnificent 12-metre-long painting *Sperm Whale II*, was purchased by fashion designer Collette Dinnigan for her Watsons Bay home, situated above the dining table: a site-specific picture, overlooking South Head.[7] During the annual whale migration, it was like one of the whales had been brought into the house. Collette and her husband now live in the south of Italy for most of the year. I am sure that they miss seeing the odd whale or two passing by—the Delafield Cook painting was included in the sale of the property when they relocated.

In late 2016, we rebranded to simply OLSEN Gallery, with a bold new logo and matching vision, for my artists and for the gallery's future. While being a gallerist means constantly reinventing and rebuilding to attract and retain the artists I want to show and represent, this change meant that it would now be on my terms only.

Using just the word 'OLSEN' and not reverting to my former self-named gallery was a letting go of my ego. It diffused the form of myself as an individual in the business, passing power to the artists that make up the gallery's identity. The OLSEN name is a powerful art brand in Australia. I learned early from art school that it does not always do you any favours.

A gallery is a function of many parts. As much as we try, we are not a Swiss watch. While clients and artists expect to see and feel my presence in the gallery, it is its myriad artists who make up the dialogue.

One thing I have learned that is vital in surviving the art business is being able to compartmentalise and separate my business life from my private, personal and emotional lives. It was difficult; I grew up immersed in art, seeing art as the total sum of one's existence. For decades I allowed so many unnecessary issues to inhabit my core. A word from someone, or a thought, could so easily disempower me. For so many years I was a self-saboteur in my behaviour and, as a result, in my health. In sobriety and getting healthy, I learned how to reverse this, detaching my professional life from my personal life and giving up the false perceptions that infected my mind with resentments. While not perfect, I now manage this part of my life much better. I live a happier life now that I know it is futile to blame others for how life deals out its successes and failures.

I have also come to realise how the most fortuitous things that have happened to me and to the gallery do not actually have my fingerprints on them. Things often happen through the power of being a centred person who can be trusted. How I felt about myself radiated outward and affected how people responded to me and the gallery. The beautiful energy of my staff and our special artists have all played major roles. Eliminating blame and resentment has cleared the path for so many good things to enter my life.

27

ANATOMY OF AN ART OPENING

There's a woman with hair the colour of flames putting her pale slender hand inside the cashmere jacket of a famously married doctor. A clump of bearded painters smoke like sulky school-boys on the pavement. A serious collector is trying to cross the floor to a painting that pulses like an open aorta and is being blocked by an amateur watercolourist who wants to talk about Lloyd Rees. Surveying the room, I see money, sex, ego, obscurity, fame, Botox, raw beauty and loneliness rubbing shoulders, and I am never sick of the spectacle. It is what I have been observing my entire life.

I went to my first art opening when still in utero, no doubt hearing the rumblings of tinkling glasses and shrieks of laughter. As the child of an artist and now an art dealer, I must have attended another thousand. After so many years for me, art open-ings are a necessary evil, a celebration, although there are some galleries that do not have openings at all anymore. I attended an Ian Fairweather exhibition in 1962 at Macquarie Galleries as a baby, carried around by Dad on his hip, dressed in my 'best woollies'. In *The Sydney Morning Herald*, it was reported that 'the youngest person to start his own collection of paintings is undoubtedly three-months-old Tim Olsen',[1] my future set from the very start. Dad said that by then there were already three works in my collection (one for each month) and that he had pressed my paint-covered palm into one of his works in progress, *6.30, The Rose and Crown*. When I recently audaciously asked where the works were now, he immediately responded that they had gone to pay for my education.

The new movement towards a Saturday afternoon vernissage is a more civilised alternative to the glorified pub crawl that was the weeknight opening, when patrons hopped from one gallery to another. The benefit of a smaller, more private view on a Saturday is that the friends and family are purely there for the artist. *Le vernissage* means 'the varnishing', where the works are hung and everything is ready to show. It is really a celebration of many years of hard work fused into one singular moment, so I raise my glass, toast the artists, thank them and enjoy watching the people regard the works, hopefully in awe. An exhibition reveals one's soul. A good show is a collection of themes, a compression and a culmination.

Openings are quixotic. No matter how familiar you think you are with your contacts, there are always people you have never seen before who turn up. There are the regular gallery visitors, the art lovers and enthusiasts, the collectors (established and fledgling), the friends and family of the artist, the students and, of course, the critics.

Then there are the other regulars such as the 'art sluts', a group of men and women who place themselves on every gallery mailing list and can be found on any day of the week having their night out for free, a splash of culture in their wine glasses: the wedding crashers of the art world.

Openings are also magnets for bores and energy vampires, sexual predators and blameless romantic optimists who come not for the art but the occasion. The number of marriages, divorces and white wine–marinated one-night stands that have transpired as a result of openings is unfathomable.

Men and women quickly realised that if you wanted a certain kind of partner with a cultural edge, an art gallery was a far preferable hunting ground than a club, bar or polo field. There is a dash of high/low seduction going on as well: the lawyer who fancies a mad young art student, or a young painter seducing a bored society wife. There is the inverted sexual snobbery of artists who will only sleep with other artists and hence must come to openings to find their own kind. An opening is a sea of faces and bodies compressed together, like a dance floor without music, and with bright gallery lighting, everyone is clearly visible. It is also a neat cultural façade for all sorts of desire, a playground for hedonism and debaucherous ambitions.

The worst opening I attended was when someone came in with a backpack, knocked over a half-a-million-dollar sculpture and ran off. Thankfully the work was completely repairable, but the silence when it fell was deafening.

We have had many an opening that has turned into a party, especially when music is involved. In a weird way, running a gallery is like owning a bar. I have a duty of care to patrons. Just because we are not charging them for drinks doesn't mean people can drink without impunity. Like any establishment, we have our 'do not serve' list, and known excessive tipplers are quickly dispatched.

These days, if half the show has not sold before the opening, you can generally ascertain that the show may be disappointing overall. Only 1 per cent of art is usually bought at openings now.

If the show is a success there will be reason to celebrate, to drink. If the show is anticlimactic, there will be a drowning of sorrows, which—fortunately, through careful planning and execution—has become less frequent.

Sydney art openings, and those elsewhere in the world, have never really been sedate affairs. It was common in the 1960s and '70s for artists to get critics in headlocks and for brawls to break out after the third round of drinks. There was something of the agora about the role of the gallery in those days. In my earlier days, there were punch-ups on the street, those inevitable boiling points when egos and rivalries erupted into a slanging match.

Usually there is someone who wants to take the stage once the speeches are over. I once had three art students strip off, pretending to be three Muses. It was beautiful but rather messy. Openings can be pretentious, full of all the affectations of society. They are also generally enjoyable, the culmination of sometimes years of work for the artist, celebratory social gatherings in a cultural setting. Some people have 'gallery friends', the ones they only catch up with at openings.

Speeches at art openings can be special if the speaker is appropriate. One particular gallery owner at every opening would talk before the guest speaker to the point that it became like a lecture. An art critic once described it as rather like listening to pennies being dropped into a tin bucket.

With all my years of experience and having worked with perfectionists such as Anders Ousback, I learned the formula of what makes people want to come back to a place. In most cases, it is very simple: employ people who are intelligent and approachable, and have beautiful light and tall ceilings, and you will create an ethereal space.

My main gallery manager, Katrina, is on duty at the openings, poised for the placement of the next red dot and keenly aware, with her encyclopaedic knowledge of everyone present, of who is a potential collector and what is needed to engage them. My staff may look as if they are simply standing there dressed beautifully, smiling and chatting, but their scan and vantage points have a microscopic precision. The momentum of the moment, the hot sellers, the coveted work in the window that night: it all matters.

A lot of contemporary galleries do not believe in or use red dots anymore. In the United States in particular, they have become an illustration of how the art market relies on different approaches depending upon the level of work. At art fairs, the availability of a work is visually evident, which is designed to create a sense of urgency. In the more high-end galleries where cultivating collector relationships is essential, the red dot is rarely seen, enticing the prospective client to engage, and perhaps to have their interest piqued with another still obtainable work of similar appeal. I find this practice manipulative and lacking transparency, almost putting the dealer in a position to choose who the buyer is and what the price will be.

Cultivating relationships is crucial, regardless of the size of gallery. For a coveted artist a waiting list is sometimes necessary, and is particularly important in Europe or New York where demand exceeds availability. It's a practice that is increasing here in Australia also, I am pleased to observe.

We have people reserve a work, and there is anticipation and excitement in that. Transparency is so important in the art world, and the opening is a place where the artist is revealed to the public. To buy art can be an emotional experience, but it should be smooth and direct, preferably immensely enjoyable. At least with a dot it is less of a roller-coaster for the collector. A red dot is a red dot. These days you may also see a blue or a green one, but all dots mean the same thing. 'Wall measles' are not unsightly. They offer a sense of satisfaction for the artist, the new owner and the gallerist alike.

Is there such a thing as a perfect opening? When it is a complete sell-out and only ten people turn up. Critics' coverage helps, but it is frequently the picture in the window that brings a person into the gallery. That picture is a portal. I love seeing people who have never been to a gallery or an opening before come in and be swept up in the experience. I believe in serving good wine because I think good wine is appreciated, enjoyable and makes people behave better, while bad wine sours the mood and the breath. Our bartender, Freddy Piper, has been working with me for over twenty years. He formerly worked for Sydney's elite, and knows who's who and what's what. If you want to see him smile, ask for a tall glass of mineral water.

One of the biggest jobs on an opening night is to calm the anxiety of the artist. Sometimes quiet time in my office with a pre-opening glass of champagne or a vodka tonic is necessary.

My main advice for them is to get a bit of perspective on success or failure, as all artists have to chip away at their careers. Instant gratification does not come with being an artist; an art career is a marathon, not a sprint. I have seen some artists fall into depression when almost every work has sold but just a few are left. 'What was wrong with the others?' they ask. Then the rest of them sell during the exhibition.

Success can bring out the worst in people. It is often worse to be ruined by praise than destroyed by criticism. Handling success can be as complex as accepting failure.

———+———

A gallery can witness frivolous banter or encounter serious moments of loss.

I was really saddened when artist and curator Bill Wright collapsed out the front of my gallery in 2014, dying two months later. What may have been perceived as an extra drink or a simple misstep in a noisy throng was actually the first symptom of advanced cancer. Wright was a scholarly member of our art world who was treasured and beloved by everyone and by every stripe of artist, making contributions as deputy director at the AGNSW and his inspiring position as a gallerist for William Wright Artists Projects in the heart of Darlinghurst. His worldly bonhomie and elegance were like a benediction at any opening. Not enough people realise or remember that his career was truly international: being Dean of New York Studio School brought him into contact with divergent art styles, from Philip Guston's raw expressionist angst to Carl Andre's cerebral installations.

Bill's Sydney Biennale of 1982, *Vision in Disbelief,* had tremendous reach and predicted most of the established art stars we have today.[2] To assemble an international show in less than eighteen months, Wright said that he used an alarm clock, a telephone and his long list of contacts, most of them personal friends. 'From the outset I had favoured the notion of an inclusive, of necessity large biennale,' Wright wrote eighteen years later, 'one that would meaningfully contextualise a plurality of diverse creative forms in a way that would engage the creative attention of Australian artists, students and public alike.' *Vision in Disbelief* was the first major museum show to put Indigenous art in a contemporary context and the first biennale to have a sound component, including Brian Eno and Laurie Anderson.

Other than Barry Humphries and my father, in my opinion there was no better storyteller than Bill, and if he told you his favourite anecdote about pissing on Yeats's grave it usually ended in the oration of a poem. His eye for the younger generation of talent helped me bring Sophie Cape into the stable.

In 2014, property developer Lang Walker approached me, asking if John was up to creating a new mural for his Collins Square building in Melbourne's Docklands. The brief was that the work had to have a 'wow' factor, something that would become an Australian icon like *Salute to Five Bells*, the Sydney Opera House mural. This became *King Sun*, a massive 6-by-8-metre show-stopper, a vibrant, glowing work that lifts the entire lobby of the building, transfixing visitors and regular commuters alike.[3]

We were concerned about the size of the work and the physical demands upon Dad, then aged 86, in creating such a monu-mental piece, second only in size to the Sydney Opera House mural that he had painted in his mid-forties. In the previous few years John had had a stroke, a double bypass operation and two knee replacements. Heart flutters and a series of blackouts were slowing him down. Being too large to fit onto one canvas, the work was to be painted directly onto marine ply panels on the floor of a friend's old garage, John's studio being too small. Not up to physically creating the work by himself—manoeuvring across such a vast space was too much—local artist Carlos Barrios was chosen to assist.

Carlos would hold the paint pot, 'trying not to be in the way', supporting John as he walked across the canvas in his red socks, his paintbrush attached to a pole. This was the same way Matisse had worked at the end of his life, when his eyesight was failing; John's eyesight is still amazing! He paints with his heart; even with the distance between the brush and the hand, there is still a connection. Some say that the longest journey you will ever make in your life is from your head to your heart.

John had long been inspired by remarkable photographs of a blazing red sun taken by NASA,[4] dynamic images of a molten energy with an incredible force, and had used them as inspiration for previous works. In *King Sun*, the sheer scale makes it mesmerising. 'I wanted to paint something that reminds people of the primary, of being back to nature, of how the sun finds its way into the darkest of places,' he said.[5]

Dad became obsessed, the work feeding him as he was feeding it, and he worked relentlessly for three months. It proved too much: he collapsed and was rushed to hospital. He had booked a bed at St Vincent's Hospital but decided that he wanted to swing past to sign the work on his way! Louise and I were beside ourselves. It gave us a huge fright.

In 'a kind of miracle', after being fitted with a pacemaker, he was back in the studio the next week and signed the mural shortly after. 'He reminds me of Picasso, with both that spiritual and physical strength [of an ox]. He still has the focus, that dexterity and an inner solace and wisdom you see in the later works of Monet or Lloyd Rees,' I said at the time.[6]

This brush with mortality (no pun intended) made him reflective and reminded him of Yeats's lines in 'Sailing to Byzantium':

Consume my heart away; sick with desire
And fastened to a dying animal
It knows not what it is; and gather me
Into the artifice of eternity.[7]

'Artists don't retire; they just gently or violently fade away,' he said. 'I'm just one aspect of the whole organic part of life, along with the trees and the plants and the lake that is so beautiful . . . All one hopes for is that the end is speedy.'[8] Still working nearly every day, 'like breathing', he is remarkable. His studio is his refuge, his 'iron lung'. It keeps me alive, he says.

The mural became a metaphor for continuing to live life, one of his best works ever. With the sun inside, the symbol of the soul, it is reminiscent of the iconic three-panelled *Sydney Sun*. Both have an exuberant vitality, with snaking tentacles of sunlight emanating from the central sun—'lines going out for a walk', I call them. In *King Sun*, he included his signature three little green frogs.

'It has got this kind of optimistic glow,' Dad said of the finished work. 'There's so much naysaying in the world . . . we're apt to forget that there is optimism. There is a spring after every winter and we've got to keep on this positive side of life. That's what I'm trying to do here with the sun.'[9]

Lang Walker and his wife Sue went down to the temporary studio with his art advisor, Gregg Cave. Lang loved it immediately, calling it 'magnificent'. We all sat in the Collins Square building foyer to watch it being hung, including James, who said, 'It's going to be the best mural in Australia.' He was too young then to know about *Salute to Five Bells* in the Sydney Opera House.

The El Salvador–born Carlos Barrios was the obvious choice as John's assistant, and he continued to work with him after *King Sun* was completed. Speaking in Spanish, they were able to navigate the painting together, discussing Spain, Spanish cooking and European women as the work evolved. While it is a sun, it is also a paella, with tentacles of saffron and crimson-red capsicums. Sprinkle in the black olives and you have all the colours and ingredients of the Spanish flag, as Dad has said.

Carlos, like Lucio Galletto from Lucio's Restaurant, calls Dad 'Maestro'. Carlos also sports a black beret; they look suitably arty side by side. Dad gave him the beret, saying, 'If we are going to do this together, you are going to need a beret, too.'

Like a hobbit, John is still as attracted to colour in his attire as he ever was: the red socks, mustard-coloured corduroy vests over white cashmere rollneck sweaters, velvet-brown corduroys, splashes of burnt orange or red. The original art dandy. His berets change colour depending upon his mood, often worn with a matching kerchief in his top pocket. He has long used a walking stick. Many are ornamental; a carved hare's head tops his current favourite.

I'm always having to find Dad replacement berets when in Europe as he is constantly giving them away to the butcher, the grocer, anyone who admires them. For John, his beret is an egalitarian symbol: in Europe you don't have to be an artist to wear a beret. Giving them away is his appreciation of the common man. One of the few artists to consistently derive a good income, he has always maintained that he is 'an artist of the people'.

In August 2011, as Dad underwent heart surgery, he and I were supposed to be on a flight over Lake Eyre with an ABC TV crew.

The lake was full for the second year in a row and, despite his many visits, for Dad it was still a sublime experience to observe the countless birds flocking to breed in the middle of the desert, to the 'unconscious plughole of Australia'.[10] Returning from a night flight, the helicopter went into a downward spiral, crashing on the shores of the lake and killing the three men inside, including Dad's friend, journalist Paul Lockyer. It was a five-seater helicopter, and we were meant to be in the two spare seats. Dad and Paul had struck up a conversation and a friendship based on the lake's incredible, freakish nature some years before. This was to be Lockyer's third program about the lake.

After his death, Dad wrote a poem and painted *Approaching Lake Eyre* (2015) as a tribute to his memory, unveiled at the posthumous launch of Paul's Lake Eyre book at the gallery. In the painting, just visible above the horizon, is a helicopter dipping slightly towards the ground. Dad has always thought that there should be a monument dedicated to them on the lake's shore, but no funding has ever been made available by the ABC. He thinks that this is a disgrace.

Dad's heart operation effectively saved his life twice and mine once. 'You've got to have the gods smiling down on you somewhere,' he said.

I was very fond of the wonderful Margaret Olley; she loved me dearly, having known me from birth. She understood the complexities of my childhood and stuck by me in the early days after rehab when I was still relapsing. After my mother died, she was the next voice telling me to believe in myself: 'Every time you drink, you know you are insulting yourself.' She would also say, 'When you are drinking, you are losing and your critics are winning.' Barry Humphries and I often reminisce about Margaret. I miss her still.

Margaret described herself as a 'non-practising alcoholic'. She didn't like going to AA meetings so would organise AA lunches at her home instead, with Barry and various other characters. At one of those lunches, Margaret said to me, 'You and your father—every opening when he makes a speech, he has to do a Spanish dance. I would have drunk out of embarrassment myself.'

At a garden party at Lady Marjorie Pagan's with the grandes dames of Bellevue Hill, there was Margaret Olley, obviously finding the other ladies rather pompous. Noticing I was not drinking, she leaned towards me and said, 'You know, Tim, I haven't had a drink now for 47 years and an orgasm for 50, and I don't know what I miss more.' I laughed so hard that I nearly choked on my cucumber sandwich.

Margaret painted beautiful still lifes but quite often she would put rather ordinary frames around them. Dad and I were driving through Paddington one day and spotted Margaret, on her walking frame, inching her way back home from Five Ways Shopping Centre. Her walking frame had so many plastic shopping bags tied to it, it looked like a Christmas tree. Dad said, 'That's the best frame I've ever seen on an Olley' as we drove past.

Flying from Melbourne to Sydney when Ansett Airlines still existed, Dad and I were waiting in the VIP lounge when John spotted an old friend, the great cricketer Keith Miller, and was shocked to see that he had one ear missing.

After warmly greeting one another, Dad queried, 'Keith, what happened to your ear?'

'Oh John, after all the years standing out in the middle of a cricket pitch, the sun got the better of me, and I ended up with a cancer on my ear, so they removed it,' Keith replied.

John's hilarious quickfire response was, 'Oh, thank God for that Keith, I thought for a minute there you were trying to be an artist!'

Dad said recently, 'Painting has become less and less respected in our culture. Art in general is more about multimedia. Art now is a young person's game. I am terribly flattered that people still enjoy my paintings.'

In many ways he is right. He wonders about the future carriers of the baton of the artistic world. Who will be the next Nolan or Boyd? He is the last of his generation. One has to wonder who will be the leaders of the next wave of Australian art?

28

ART AFFAIR

Critic Jerry Saltz has written about the inequality of international art fairs, how the upper-level galleries so often benefit at the expense of the smaller. Blue-chip galleries attend as drawcards, gratis or with special privileges, leaving the middle and lower tier galleries paying the full, sometimes exorbitant fees. They are often pressured to attend by their artists and, with no guarantee of sales, it can take them to financial breaking point. Some galleries simply are refused entry. With frequent overcrowding (of both booths and viewers), hard-to-navigate venues, and some galleries catering only to particular audiences—no risk or innovation—it can be a dispiriting experience, alienating and visually overwhelming, like art in a Woolworths or Walmart setting.

Art fairs can be 'adrenaline-addled spectacles', Saltz wrote in 2005 in *The Village Voice*, in a column titled 'Feeding Frenzy', where he compared art fairs to tent-city casinos.[1] Yet he, too, now admits that they are a 'necessary evil', places to make connections in a hurry, hopefully have some sales and, for the critics, to see galleries they might not visit and to experience new artists and their work. For Saltz, it is about assessing the environment, to get 'an overview of stylistic tendencies' rather than looking at individual works of art—you can't spend more than a few minutes looking at any one piece. Plus, there is free food and socialising.

With a massive increase in the number of art fairs in the last twenty years, popularity wanes from event to event, year to year. However, this can mean the opportunity to see new artists and to attract a new audience. From the gigantic Armory Show to the smaller international shows, demand and interest is keeping art fairs alive and flourishing, if not a monetary success for all those participating; many art dealers look to expand their reputations from the exposure.

The inequality still exists, with high-tier galleries usually benefiting most from the experience, with higher priced works and esteemed artists. For smaller galleries, if they are deemed worthy to attend, the entry and hire costs, transportation of works, staff and travel, and artist commissions if they do make a sale mean many treat art fairs as a loss-leader, banking on the exposure and future online sales to offset the cost.

For those curators and their directors who focus on the fairs, effectively ignoring their local galleries and instead viewing art en masse, they are missing out on the individual experience that an intimate viewing of art evokes.

If organisers continue to improve their location, design and selection processes, and start sharing the load financially between the upper- and lower-crust galleries to entice new blood, keeping costs to a minimum, they can become the ultimate display venue for which they were designed. Owner of Team Gallery in the United States, Jose Freire, has said that we are in 'the end game' phase of art fairs. Money, he says, 'can't corrupt the art world any more than it already has' and points to the lack of new blood: 'I feel like I haven't met a new person in Basel in at least ten years.'[2]

With a new gallery to promote and unknown artists outside Australia, we will have to attend more international art fairs in the future, for the ongoing success for all concerned. We have had tremendous success over the years and, when well organised, with hand-selected galleries showing in a stylishly designed environment, art fairs can be invigorating and rewarding—for the viewers, the galleries and the critics.

Perhaps I'll see you at the next Basel, Jose!

Eighteen years ago, we held an exhibition in Hong Kong for one of my former artists, renting a small gallery, and the exhibition was very successful. I was amazed at the number of expats who turned up to the opening. Many of them just wanted to drink, but others were looking for a new avenue, a new way to form new social circles in a city that was changing.

My immediate thought was that if there were more galleries there, a thriving art business would do very well. The expats were all earning substantial salaries, paying no tax and looking for new ways to spend their money.

Returning to Sydney, I participated in an art fair started by an English friend, Tim Etchells, who owned an international events company and ultimately established Sydney Contemporary. I said to him, 'Tim! You shouldn't be putting all your energy into doing an art fair here. You should be going straight to Hong Kong and registering the name Hong Kong Art Fair because I'm telling you, if you did one there, you'd find yourself with a goldmine.'

Tim detoured via Hong Kong on his way back to England, registered the name Hong Kong Art Fair and held the first fair the following year. From there it rose to such significance that, with everyone's knowledge of the booming Chinese economy, it became the most esteemed art fair in the world. The Basel Art Fair purchased half the rights and arranged with the head of Deutsche Bank at the time, Rob Rankin, to sponsor the fair.

The value of Etchells' half of the fair ran into the millions. On his next trip back to Australia, he took me to lunch to inform me that he had sold his half and thanked me for the idea.

We took three shows to Hong Kong before the fair swelled to the size of a corporate whale. The first was my father's, the second was Michael Johnson's and the third was a show by a much younger artist, Sophie Cape. Selling abstract art to the Chinese collectors was a struggle in the beginning, and I used a lot of landscape analogies to get paintings over the line: describing Michael's work as 'reflective lights on Hong Kong Harbour' was a stretch, but I made it work. Everything has become so much more sophisticated now because of the volume of collectors and the standard of galleries in Hong Kong itself. In a relatively short time, the level of the art fair has certainly risen and many galleries are no longer shoo-in participants.

It was a gem of an idea. Some gems are best kept to yourself—unless someone else can do something better with them. Well done Etchells!

Sydney Contemporary has now become the premier art show in Australia, with the art-world focus migrating from Melbourne to Sydney and our local artists now taken far more seriously. Sydney has becoming the contemporary art centre of Australia with the Biennale of Sydney, the MCA and Sydney Contemporary. If the Sydney Opera House was not enough to announce the city's cultural precedence in the 1970s, it is now following through in all of these other ways. Leo Schofield said to me once, 'You can compare Sydney and Melbourne by looking at their opera houses. On the outside, Melbourne Opera House is a disaster, but on the inside it is an absolute treasure, whereas Sydney Opera House is a delight on the outside, but lacking on the interior.' At least the John Olsen mural was something that they got right from the start!

Dad was my showcase in the 2011 Hong Kong Art Fair, with ten of the 'family jewels', his watercolour landscapes from Lake Eyre. We were described in the press as 'the most famous father and son team in the Australian art world'—Dad's prediction realised! It was gratifying to hear him joke about how Picasso's son was so useless that he could only use him as a chauffeur, and saying: 'Tim's very clever, he gets marks—it's good payback!' It was a sell-out.

A leading Dutch art critic who visited the stand said that it was the most sophisticated and sensitive exhibition of works on paper he had seen in years. Asian collectors, with their consummate and innate understanding of calligraphy and mark-making in reference to landscape, and the concepts of positive and negative space, have an established 'Zen' eye. Thinking of the negative reviews of the 2013 exhibition *Australia* at London's Royal Academy just two years later, this is in contrast to British observers who seem to struggle with the nature of our 'antique continent' in all its scruffy beauty.

Dad met Dr Paul Ettlinger and his partner, Raimund Berthold, on a European cruise with Katharine. I was at a dinner at Cipriani (now C London) restaurant in London hosted by the Massimo De Carlo gallery, full of formidable collectors and major world artists. De Carlo's reputation precedes him; with gallery spaces in Milan, London and Hong Kong, he has been included in *Artnet's* list of 'Europe's 10 most respected art dealers'.[3] Suddenly Paul popped up in his flowing black silk smoking jacket and said, 'Hi Tim, I hear you are John's son. I love your father. I spent two weeks with him on a Lucy cruise on the Mediterranean. He is one of my favourite men in the world.' Suddenly I was being introduced to every celebrity in the room, and Paul and I have been friends ever since.

Visiting Art Basel fair in Miami Beach in 2016, I was invited to a party, hosted by Paul, in Tracey Emin's honour. Emin's work, *The More of You the More I Love You*, was a large-scale neon installation, inspired by her childhood memories of illuminations, that lit up the Museum of Contemporary Art in North Miami.

The party was in a big studio apartment, packed with people, but the guest of honour was passed out in a bed in the centre of the room all night. People were milling around her with drinks as she lay prostrate. I found this ironic considering her infamous bed installation at the Tate Gallery in 1999. *My Bed*, short-listed for the Turner Prize, was a confessional work, complete with empty vodka bottles, used condoms, cigarette butts, stained sheets and discarded underwear, the result of a depressive, suicidal period when Emin remained in bed for several days. She recently revisited the 'bed' theme with a grid of self-portraits exhibited at the White Cube Bermondsey gallery, photos taken during periods of insomnia.

Tracey Emin, an enfant terrible of the Britarts or Young British Artists (YBA) movement in the late 1980s, has been battling her own demons of depression, sex, drugs and alcohol for decades. The entrepreneurial YBAs, including Damien Hirst, Angus Fairhurst, Sarah Lucas, Anya Gallaccio and Marc Quinn, became a visual arts subculture famous for their 'shock art', the new 'art celebrities'—the rock stars of the London art scene. Media-savvy, brash and confrontational, it was their perceived lack of artistic skill combined with often pornographic, violent imagery that caught the attention of the press (and the art world) as they deliberately pushed the limits of so-called public decency. The YBA label evolved into a hugely successful brand, with some becoming among the wealthiest artists in the world. Emin's *My Bed* was bought by Charles Saatchi for £150,000, was sold at auction in 2014 for just over £2.2 million and is now part of the Tate's permanent collection.

I do appreciate one of Emin's New Year's resolutions, though: 'To be nice to Jay Jopling, who's my art dealer, because I always take everything out on him.'[4] I am sure there are many dealers who would wish that one or two of their artists would do the same.

I met Jay Jopling—'JJ' to his friends—at Art Basel Miami Beach in his White Cube stand. Jay's gallery empire has achieved phenomenal success in England and Hong Kong since he first burst onto the London art scene nearly 25 years ago, and I have watched his progress with interest. Now he is a major player and showcasing his artists regularly at the international art fairs. Of note was his anniversary show in 2018, *Remembering Tomorrow: Artworks and Archive*, featuring many rarely displayed works and photography that he had collected throughout his career and preserved for 'posterity'. He is probably best known for the highly lucrative sales of the infamous Hirst shark *The Physical Impossibility of Death in the Mind of Someone Living* and Marc Quinn's sculpture *Self*, created from his own frozen blood. Both are rather gruesome but significant.

29

PHOTOGRAPHY AS ART

To view art is to be educated visually. Over time I became less painting-centric; in fact, all mediums excite me now. Especially photography.

The Year 2015 saw our first major photography exhibition with the survey show *Australian and International Contemporary Photography*, with works from 27 artists across four continents. Not having a reputation as a photography gallery, it was fantastic to see the response and hordes of visitors over the duration. One of the artists, Leila Jeffreys, had already been showing her iconic bird portraits with me since 2012. Another inclusion was newcomer George Byrne, whose career has skyrocketed since then.

Suddenly other photographers, appreciative that I would give newcomers a go, started knocking on the door, wanting to be discovered, to be exhibited and taken seriously as artists.

By seeing what Byrne, Jeffreys and Gary Heery have achieved, it is easy to think that this is a smooth transition. However, all those artists have worked relentlessly at their craft, and all have a point of difference and integrity in their work as highly talented, artistic professionals.

To achieve success today, a photographer has to be exceptional. Every person with a smartphone walks around with a camera and many consider themselves photographers, but this does not equate to having the talent to forge a career, having the essential 'eye', and simply being able to create something that no one else can.

Susan Sontag says: 'All photographs are *memento mori*. To take a photograph is to participate in another person's (or thing's) mortality, vulnerability, mutability. Precisely by slicing out this moment and freezing it, all photographs testify to time's relentless melt.'[1]

I am always looking for old or new talent, though.

The Perth-raised Leila Jeffreys began photographing birds in 2008, turning her obsession into a soaring career. Leila is truly the first of the ornithological portrait artists and has become one of Australia's most sought-after contemporary photographers and an advocate for birdlife conservation. Dedicated and patient, Leila spends hours with her many feathered friends to get her final evocative images. Her combination of technical skill and an eye for colour and composition produces large-scale works filled with character, wit and complexity.

To Leila, her portraits of birds are like self-reflections. John would describe them as her 'circus animals, which everyone loves'. Whether a commonplace wren or songbird, a native cockatoo or a magnificent bird of prey, each captures the essence, the personality of the subject, and the diversity of nature.

Travelling widely to source new subjects, Leila has experienced firsthand some of the most untouched and ecologically vulnerable parts of the world. Seeing wildlife in its natural habitats has stirred in her—and, subsequently, in the viewer—an urgent desire to protect our wildlife.

When we relocated our New York gallery to Orchard Street, Leila was the perfect choice to open the new space with her 2017 exhibition *Ornithurae Volume 1*. The opening was a star-studded evening, the exhibition officially opened by actor Brooke Shields, Leila's friend and a collector of her work. Local art aficionados, collectors, friends and supporters all attended.

Exhibiting in Sydney and New York in 2019, Leila now includes video art pieces, capturing the dynamics of flocks of birds rather than individuals. Her beautiful and mesmerising video art sequences offer a rare insight.

In 2016, I started showing photographer George Byrne, brother of actor Rose Byrne. George was introduced to me by Paul Davies, one of my long-term artists who I had discovered when he was at art school. Paul and George were both Australians based in Los Angeles, and when Paul saw George's work he introduced him to me, immediately seeing the appeal. Being a fan of the West Coast artist Richard Diebenkorn and his images of San Francisco, George created authentic portraits of the urban land-scape that reminded me immediately of the abstract, soft/hard edges of Diebenkorn's work, with elements of David Hockney and Jeffrey Smart. He names the New Topographics movement, along with photographers Stephen Shore and William Eggleston, as the 'first artists to really embrace photography as a fine art medium, pioneering the genre of very stark, empty urban land-scapes'.[2] Not to forget Mondrian.

His work homes in on tones and angles and the idea of colour and space; while they are photographs, they have an abstract, painterly feel. He uses objects to provide a figurative element in his work, pushing the boundaries of both painting and photography. 'I'm not really looking to tell a story,' George has said. 'I'm looking to create a feeling.'

George's work has universal appeal. Although decorative and winsome, his photographs have a true artistic-scholarship quality. I particularly like the way he creates his own partly fictional landscapes, ascetic collages of colour and geometric form. Also a talented musician, George is one of the few artists who has harnessed the power of social media without compromise, using it as a traditional visual diary and the perfect complement to his work. Aside from the fact that he is highly Instagrammable in himself—women and men alike are drawn to his natural charm—he is also a genuine, considerate human being and a pleasure to work with. Highly driven, he is the ultimate 'contemporary' artist, as industrious as he is creative, who will have long-term success. As such, he was one of the first artists I wanted to show in New York.

His sister Rose opened his latest sell-out Sydney exhibition in 2019, bringing another touch of Hollywood glamour to the arts. Her partner, actor Bobby Cannavale, has opened another. George himself is surprisingly modest and laidback for one who has achieved so much success at a relatively young age. I look forward to seeing how his work will progress.

When George was recently asked in an interview to name a quote that summed up how he lives his life, he quoted Camille Pissarro: 'Blessed are they who see beautiful things in humble places where other people see nothing.' I concur.

I have long admired Gary Heery's photography and was pleased to have him launch his book *Project X*, along with an archive exhibition, in 2019. From his images for prestigious international magazines and album covers, to his many celebrity (and non-celebrity) portraits, evocative horses, birds and flowers, his work is highly sought after. Over the decades, Gary has shot an enviable array of the international rich and famous—Andy Warhol, Madonna, Rod Stewart, Paul Simon—as well as our own homegrown talent, culminating in the self-publishing of books of his works as a career retrospective. Gary's partner Saskia Havekes, the celebrated Grandiflora florist, perfumer and author, is the daughter of one of my parents' best friends, so it seems like we have known each other forever.

In *Project X,* Gary gave his work another dimension: the collaboration between the photographer and the subject. After taking portraits of a variety of sitters—artists, actors, dancers, celebrities—the images were then given to the subjects to enhance in whatever way they wished, to represent their craft or to simply have free rein: 'To interrogate it. To paint it. To submerge it in the ocean or perhaps anoint it with a little human blood,' as my friend Anna Johnson described it. Then he rephotographed the image.

It was a fantastic concept. Many found it liberating to be able to edit or enhance themselves, to add graffiti, to have some fun. The images were pinned in a row down the walls of the gallery, the opening packed with everyone eager to see the results. Dad and Louise both did one. Cressida Campbell, Nicholas Harding, Alan Jones, Stephen Ormandy, Leo Schofield and Edmund Capon all contributed. As Edmund Capon wrote in the introduction to Gary's book *Selected Works 1976–2013,* 'It is that subjective, responsive faculty which has guided Heery to articulate and examine his subjects, to engage with them, sense their distinctive qualities and massage them into compositions that satisfy not only as visual experiences but also as revelations of the soul.'

Back in 2012, I put on a show called *1000 Years Beside Myself #1* for Ben Ali Ong, one of the first photographers I had in my stable. Ong's work had a growing profile; he had been in the finals of several leading prizes, his work gracing a range of publications. The show gained attention, but for all the wrong reasons.

Ong had included two bird portraits in the show, one of a bald eagle and another of a raven. The eagle was the hero image for the show; it featured on all publicity, on the invitations, in the gallery window. Ong had told me that he had photographed them at Taronga Zoo, which I naturally believed. When I called the zoo, they said that they didn't even have a bald eagle.

Within days of the show opening, it then transpired that Ong had used stock photographs to create his own montages, 're-creating' the images in his own style but without acknowledgement of the original creator. The meta-information stored in the images was intact, quoting the agency, copyright and photographer. The naiveté of this act exacerbated by the blatant lie incensed me. While appropriation is acknowledged as being part of making some art—Warhol was the master of it—an artist should never disguise the fact or falsify the origin of an image.

In his defence, Ong described himself not as a photographer but rather as a 'photo media artist', stating that he did not see a need to acknowledge the original images. The US photographer who took the original eagle image, Matt Hansen, disagreed, calling it 'extremely unethical'.

It was a sad, stupid situation. Ong had taken most of the images himself, yet the whole show, which was a good one, was derailed through youthful folly and deception. It was a deception that lost him his representation with me and another upcoming show, and that has cast a dubious shadow over his career.

For my part, I pulled the show, refunding the contentious purchases. As far as I was concerned, there are certain ways that appropriation can be passed, but this was just too close to the bone. Jerry Saltz is more damning: 'Appropriation is the idea that ate the art world,' he wrote. 'Go to any Chelsea gallery or international biennial and you'll find it. It's there in paintings of photographs, photographs of advertising, sculpture with ready-made objects, videos using already-existing film.'[3]

The integrity of the gallery has to be preserved. I would have supported Ong to the hilt if he had only been honest with me.

I met Elizabeth in a local Paddington bar. She was ordering a drink, and I noticed her immediately as a natural beauty. We started chatting when she saw that I was drinking Diet Coke, and the nutritionist in her was aghast. She said, 'the only thing worse than Diet Coke was drinking Draino', which made me laugh and we instantly connected.

Our relationship brought me love, happiness, companionship and inspired a massive change in my lifestyle and eating habits. Being around someone who works as a health professional is informative and enlightening. My diet and exercise regime changed remarkably. I lost a lot of weight and got off many of my medications. My cholesterol and blood markers all improved.

Not only did I receive emotional care, but also holistic care during our relationship. She has a very good mind and is extremely alert; she is left-brained and has a scientific leaning, while I am more creative and right-brained; our connection of opposites provided an environment in which we were both able to teach each other different perspectives. As a practising naturopath and healer, she views the world from an alternative vantage, so much so that I would often describe her as a huge 'nerve ending', which she found amusing. Art has taught me to experience and see the world more broadly than many perhaps, but Elizabeth gave me a different kind of awareness: with very different backgrounds and ideologies, we complemented one another nicely. Elizabeth and I had some very special holidays together, one in particular with James, and Elizabeth's daughter Charlotte.

At the suggestion of a friend, after Mum died in 2011 I went to see a clairvoyant. She immediately said: 'Your mother is here. She is giving me a headache. Did she die from a head injury?' I confirmed that Mum had died from brain cancer. This complete stranger, who could not have known anything about me, continued: 'Your mother is telling me to tell you to stop seeking your father's approval. Just believe in yourself.'

A few years later, I visited another clairvoyant out of interest. Asking how my relationship with my father would end, she replied that Dad, my sister and I would have some glorious times together. Curious, I mentioned our complex relationship with Katharine, and she predicted that Katharine would not live for much longer—that she had a brain tumour. Horrified, I told Dad, who told me not to be so ridiculous. Six months later, Katharine collapsed.

PART
FIVE

OL
SEN
GRUIN

30

SOTHEBY'S, SCANDAL AND
THE MOTHER

If the art world is an ecosystem then commercial galleries and auction houses inhabit the same ocean, but perhaps dwell at different depths.

In 2014, Sotheby's was selling a painting that had become something of a family enigma. *The Mother* was painted for Valerie in 1964 to commemorate Louise's birth. This large work is not at all literal. Abstract, organic, almost exploding, it probably holds the key to the secrets of just two people: John and Valerie.

In the 50 years in which it had 'disappeared', my mother had fretted over its whereabouts, the loss preoccupying her greatly in the last years of her life as she perhaps reprimanded herself for losing it during our storm of constant travel, or even in the painful reshuffle of divorce. At the age of 86, Dad could not recall the passage or the destiny of the painting. When we heard that Sotheby's was offering the work for private sale, we all naturally wanted to know who was selling it. After Mum's death, Louise and I had become the executors of her estate, and we felt that this work, possibly above all others, belonged to her. *The Mother* was so intensely personal and so treasured by Valerie that it was easy to assume it had been stolen rather than misplaced.

Dad simply felt that he had a right to know the provenance of the work and was more than happy to sign a confidentiality agreement with Sotheby's. However, the vendor preferred to remain anonymous and due to the general auction house protocol of priority of seller confidentiality, we decided to launch our own investigation to discover the truth. Our family enlisted the help of private investigator Guy Oatley, who unearthed the first lead. The path of provenance led back to the British art collectors Pat and Penny Allen, whom we had lived with in London. Immediately Dad called Pat and solved the mystery: the painting had been traded—or, as the term goes, 'gifted'—to Pat's cousin for accommodation in the cousin's Spanish house, where we recuperated from our near-fatal car accident in France. Ironically, the cousin who was given the work did not like it and for all these years had kept *The Mother* rolled up. The work had been exhibited in England, as lent by Mrs Valerie Olsen, so there was no dispute at the time.

Dad must have felt highly compromised to give away the painting in lieu of a shelter for us to convalesce, so did so without my mother's knowledge. At the time we had been homeless, on the other side of the world, virtually penniless. As soon as we discovered this important information we discontinued the court case, leaving the judge to rule on costs on the following Monday, 15 December 2014.

Just 100 metres down the road from the Supreme Court that very same day, Man Haron Monis took eighteen people, staff and patrons, hostage at the Lindt Cafe in Martin Place. The tragic deaths of two of the hostages—including my dear friend

Tori Johnson, who was the cafe manager—put our problems very much into perspective.

Tori, son of artist Ken Johnson, had come to a gallery opening shortly before he died. We hugged; we had known each other since he was a small boy and his family had rented our holiday home at Pearl Beach.

It was devastating when he was murdered in the siege. It continually echoes in my mind. I admire the courage that he must have shown as that terrible situation unfolded.

The Mother painting finally came up for auction at Sotheby's in April 2015. On principle Dad refused to buy it back, even though I wanted to.

For the future, I am interested in an innovation that will resolve issues of provenance for all artists, auction houses, buyers and sellers. While the right to privacy must be maintained, credible provenance is more and more important to the art market, and I would argue that respect for the artist who creates these much-loved works, prized by our community, is even more vital. Any artist has a right to know the origin of a work appearing on the market if they believe it may be stolen or even a forgery. How are we meant to protect any buyer in the art market from potentially buying stolen goods if auction houses have the right to refuse direct provenance under the artist's, or their estate's, clearance? The extremely personal nature of this work had made this situation all the more distressing for Dad, but the principle remains the same.

Only a few weeks before we were due in court, Justice John Sackar of the NSW Supreme Court had rebuked Sotheby's Australia for its refusal to reveal the identity of another painting's vendor or cooperate with the police. Justice Sackar echoed my own sentiments when he said that the emphasis on client confidentiality risked being 'against the public interest' as it 'could, perhaps unwittingly, prevent the exposure of a forgery or stolen property'.[1]

There have been other similar cases over the last few decades. Poor provenance can be brutal.

There was the fake Albert Tucker sold by Christie's to Sydney barrister Louise McBride in 2000 for $87,000. When she tried to sell the work a decade later, she discovered that it was worthless and no longer covered by Christie's guarantee, which only spans five years. Needless to say, she sued and—'after four years of legal torture'—won. Being a barrister herself no doubt helped. 'The case . . . revealed mismanagement at Christie's and a market still confused about how to deal properly with forgeries,' reported the *Australian Financial Review*.[2]

Christie's had had concerns about the authenticity of the painting shortly after the sale when advised by a panel of experts that it was likely a fake. However, no attempt was made to contact McBride and, within a month, Christie's proceeded to sell yet another fake Tucker to the Australia Club, now fully aware that it was not authentic. The Club was recompensed.

McBride said of the case, 'I didn't do this for me, I did it because the law in this area needs clarification. People have absolutely no recourse, no professional body they can complain to . . . there's just no rule of law to govern unconscionable conduct in the industry.'[3]

Being the most prolific and commercially successful living artist, my father is loved by auction houses. His paintings consistently attract attention for sales, return ever-increasing results and are therefore a good commission for them. Dad is certainly respected and valued by art collectors.

My father took the road less travelled. The life of a creator is not one that many seeking security, certainty and comfort might choose, especially in the aspirational society we live in today. Thankfully, his pure talent, prolific work ethic and deep love of the Australian landscape brought him prominence and sales, which have allowed him to continue to be a professional artist in a field that offers a slim chance of success. An artist comes as a totality, a lifetime achievement package, not just a signature on the bottom of the work. As he has said himself, 'The challenge for any artist is to find your way and own identity in what you create.'

In the 1950s, Australia was a cultural desert. Many who were creative or who sought a more colourful life left for Europe. My father's inner colour was confirmed and he brought it back with him, painting pictures that were more than avant-garde: they reflected an activism against a black-and-white country, sophisticated pictures that he knew few would like, apart from the visually educated. With his worldly vernacular, he was invited to the dinners of the elite. He was entertaining and charming, and even when the corporate movers and shakers or aficionados of the bohemian life were not exactly on board with his art, they still had to have him. He was his art, and his art was him. Like any new young celebrity, everybody wanted a piece of him.

My father is still the great interlocutor, the great social lubricant in all kinds of company. Whether he is teaching students or sitting on boards, or in his roles as a trustee at the AGNSW and the NGA, he can engage anyone to think more creatively, no matter what their background, and connect them with art that otherwise they had no affinity with. With his wisdom, wit and charm, he helps everyone to suddenly identify the artist within themselves.

Dad is one of the few masters whose art has never gone out of fashion as his work has constantly evolved. He made many mistakes and pissed off some people, but his glorious odyssey fascinated his critics and, like any lovable rogue, he was easily forgiven.

He has also made many compromises for love in his life. He has suffered betrayal at times, and paid the price for his impulsive and overly generous nature. My sisters and I have had to stand back at times; it has been hard to watch how some people have treated him. Ruthless and tough if you threaten his dream, he is nothing less than a constant giver, with the emotional capacity to give until there is nothing left. We always knew that his love was unconditional.

A lot of auction houses present themselves as institutions of integrity, representing centuries of honour and trust. But more and more we hear stories about them behaving like nothing more than shameless hustlers while presenting themselves as gentlemen in Savile Row suits. Joseph Duveen, Dede Brooks and Sir Anthony Tennant are names synonymous with some of the worst collusion and deception ever committed in corporate history—calculated crimes that go well beyond a few shady art deals. The British dealers Duveen and Berenson would be the most infamous wheeler-dealers of all time, handling great classical European art. Dad gave me a book that detailed their exploits, *Artful Partners*, saying, 'Don't turn out like these bastards.'

More recently friends of mine, siblings Mark, Victoria and Richard Coppleson, lost the entire revenue from their parents' art collection, the Malcolm and Patricia Coppleson Collection, as trusted auction house Mossgreen went into liquidation, having used the takings of the sale that normally go into the client account to pay off other debts. Not only did my friends grieve the loss of a family art collection and all of its emotional value, but they also suffered the loss of any windfall that may have softened the blow of having lost their parents. It was a collection that represented years of their parents' passion for things of beauty and interest, and it was evaporated in an act completely lacking in compassion.

'There are times when my stomach churns,' Mark Coppleson said. 'It's not about the money. It's the fact that this whole thing has tarnished Mum and Dad's memory. This was a collection they spent 50 years putting together and the proceeds of that were not supposed to go into a bottomless pit created by Mossgreen.'[4] I can only hope that every vendor who has trusted an auction house will be treated with more honesty and respect in the future.

Then there was the biggest art-fraud case in Australian history: the fake Brett Whiteleys involving respected art conservator Mohamed Aman Siddique and art dealer Peter Gant. In 2006, one of Siddique's employees, art conservator Guy Morel, became suspicious after hearing rumours about a mysterious painting being made in a partitioned-off room at the Collingwood workshop studio. Deciding to investigate further, he climbed on a chair and randomly shot images using his phone of the interior of the room, only to discover a painting in progress that strongly resembled a Brett Whiteley. In the corner of the room was an original Whiteley, seemingly to act as a guide. Siddique was considered one of the premier art conservators in Australia and had advised private and public galleries nationwide, restoring countless valuable works of art during his career. Having studied at London's Chelsea College of Arts, he had much artistic skill and discipline, but described his own work as 'meticulous but dull'.[5]

For Morel, the evidence was damning. There was no other explanation: he had witnessed a forgery in the making. Some months later, he realised that he had no alternative but to call the police, reaching Detective Sergeant James Macdonald on the fraud desk.

Art fraud is not a police priority. Police lack the resources, time and expertise to properly investigate. 'Art forgery is among the least despised of crimes, except by its victims,' *The New Yorker* art critic Peter Schjeldahl has written. 'The forger gratifies class resentment.'[6] It is art theft that gains more attention, mainly through media exposure.

Macdonald visited the workshop with another detective, posing as potential clients; however, at that stage no crime had been committed. It is not illegal to paint 'in the manner of', to copy works or—astoundingly—to even use another artist's signature. In Australia, I have found that Viscopy, now The Copyright Agency, which exists to protect artists' copyright, is not always willing to take a legal position or to fight to protect the artist when the artist's copyright has been breached. A crime is only really thought committed when a work is knowingly sold as a counterfeit.

In December 2007, Andrew Pridham, chairman of the Sydney Swans, purchased what he believed to be an authentic Whiteley, *Big Blue Lavender Bay*, from art consultant Anita Archer, who had acquired the work from dealer Peter Gant. Archer had emailed Pridham and offered him an exclusive opportunity to purchase the work, described as an excellent investment, at a cool $2.2 million. Archer provided provenance: the work had been privately commissioned by venture capitalist Robert Le Tet, and there was paperwork to prove it. (Le Tet would later deny all knowledge of the work.)

Wendy Whiteley, having heard about the painting, visited Pridham to inspect the work and raised concerns about its authenticity. Pridham's own suspicions grew, and in 2010 he asked Professor Robyn Sloggett from The University of Melbourne to examine the painting; she concluded that it was a fake. Pridham launched Supreme Court action against Archer for failing to exercise reasonable care, diligence and skill to verify the work and its provenance. They settled confidentially in 2013.

Steve Nasteski, a dealer himself, has been caught. In 2009, he bought a 'Whiteley' work that had originated from Gant, *Orange Lavender Bay*, for $1.1 million, purportedly bought directly from the artist in 1988 in a deal brokered through Christian Quintas (who was unaware of any wrongdoing). The work had already been offered unsuccessfully through auction house Bonhams & Goodman. Convinced it was authentic, Steve put the work with Deutscher and Hackett for auction. Chris Deutscher had his concerns and brought in three art experts: Brett Lichtenstein, Stuart Purves and, ironically, Mohamed Aman Siddique. Siddique said it was definitely a Whiteley; Lichtenstein, Whiteley's long-time framer, said it looked like one of his frames but not his screws. Only Stuart Purves denounced it immediately as a fake. Deutscher and Hackett pulled the work. Steve pursued a private art dealer in Melbourne relentlessly until he got his money back.

Forgeries are a constant in the art market and always have been. To forge a work is also to forge its provenance, the history of ownership, from the artist through galleries, the respective owners, auction and private sales, verified through gallery records, valuations or invoices. Experts, through various techniques, can ascertain a forgery: paints containing pigments that were only used decades later; various scanning techniques that pick up discrepancies in the work and underdrawings; and time variations in how a work would have aged, through splintered varnish, stains or the oxidisation of frames.

For the artist, viewing a forged version of their art can be sickening. John has disowned countless works over the years on immediate viewing. Fraudulent works also perpetuate the conception that some art dealers are 'dodgy', liars or cheats. In a recent disagreement over the price of one of Dad's works, a property developer asked how long it had taken Dad to paint a particular painting. I responded that if you considered the education, the trial and error, and all the life experience, the painting had taken a lifetime.

John still considers himself a Novocastrian—a native of Newcastle—and his home town will always have a special place in his heart. William 'Bill' Dobell, John Molvig, Ross Morrow and Bill Rose were also all born in Newcastle. Rose was one of the 'Victoria Street Group' of artists who, with Dad, John Passmore, Eric Smith and Robert Klippel mounted the infamous 1956 *Direction 1* exhibition at Macquarie Galleries.

The Newcastle Art Gallery has proudly repaid the compliment by showing John's 2016–17 exhibition, *John Olsen: The City's Son*. There are now more than 35 of his works in the gallery's collection through acquisitions and private donations, with Dad donating drawings and a sculpture from his own collection. Louise's work *Hidden Lake* was recently donated in the Les Renfrew Bequest and, now there is a work by Mum there, too, 'there is a nice family connection being formed', as the gallery's collection and exhibitions officer Lisa Kirkpatrick said.

Included in the collection is the 1964 ceiling painting *The Sea Sun of 5 Bells*, on permanent display on the gallery's ceiling, enabling viewers to see the work in its original context from both floors. Gifted to the gallery by Gallery A director Ann Lewis, the work was originally commissioned for her Sydney dining-room ceiling. John has said that he was driven to celebrate the 'life burst' of the harbour, the life-giver and life-taker: 'I wanted to show the Harbour as a movement, a sea suck, and the sound of the water as though I am part of the sea.'

31

KATHARINE

When John was married to Noela and Valerie, both artists, he came to recognise that artists are not natural householders. Mum's brother, Uncle Jim, always said that we lived in artistic squalor, but Mum always knew where everything was. What can look like a junkyard to one person can be a room full of treasure and exquisite ephemera to another.

My father believed that in Katharine he had found a stately woman. A natural chatelaine, Katharine had a perception of herself based on the ideals of Melbourne's old money. John was swept up in this elite world, taking on slightly more aristocratic values, all of which were the antitheses of those he had when he had been with my mother. Suddenly it was all about the upturned collar and the life of landed gentry, with stabled horses and grand dinners. Dad has said that he felt forever indebted to Katharine for taking him in after he left Noela. She did look after him: she ran the house impeccably and the farm ran like clockwork with its numerous staff, and this allowed him a daily routine and structure, giving him the freedom to work.

Katharine gave John a stability he craved but, for some reason, she seemed not to be fond of Jane, Louise and me. Although Katharine was loving to us at times, we became more excluded from Dad's day-to-day life. Slowly contact eroded, and days that should have been treasured milestones were just dates on the calendar. There were no Christmas dinners, and to see him on his birthday was also a struggle. Father's Day was a non-event. So we compromised: celebrating special events on another day, speaking regularly on the phone. Dad would stay with Louise or me when he was in town.

In those early years of Dad's relationship with Katharine, Louise and I both felt compromised, having to pretend all the time that we were one big happy family. In the end, everybody grew tired of the charade. John's relationships with his children and grandchildren were compromised in an attempt to keep his life 'simple' and free of confrontation.

Countless times I heard that John had driven up from the farm and was in our local eatery, Lucio's, but often he did not visit the gallery or try to catch up. If Louise and I were making great strides in our respective careers, it was rarely acknowledged, and the evasion cut deep.

One of the resonant and lingering wounds of this time was the difficulty in maintaining a father–son relationship. The fact that our conversation had to constantly skirt around the edges of our lives' deeper truths meant that we were both ill at ease in each other's company. It made our communication limited, stilted. It cramped my ability to open up to him honestly, and curtailed our freedom to exchange ideas, feelings and thoughts. We learned to never challenge Dad's integrity or paint him into a corner. It was a case of 'Don't mention the war'; if you did, he would simply withdraw.

These were the wilderness years of broken promises, punctuated with moments of material generosity. Dad never visited me in rehab. Maybe because of his own despair at having had an alcoholic father, he found it difficult to deal with. I was obsessed with the myth of John Olsen, not the vulnerable, fallible man I now know simply to be my father.

Dad, with his penchant for avoiding conflict at all costs ('happy wife, happy life'), buried himself in the sanctuary of his studio and his work. Fortunately for both Louise and me, it was also an opportunity for us to break free of his shadow and, out of necessity, forge our own unique paths. Ironically, it was Noela and Katharine who provided the greatest stimulus for both of us to do that.

It wasn't always harsh. There were times when Dad was distant and other times when he was as loving as we remembered him being when we were children. We would speak on the phone frequently, but Louise and I always knew when Katharine had walked into the room—the tone of his voice would change. In keeping my opinions to myself, my tongue still bears the scars from constant biting.

It was as if my father was made up of two people: one person with Katharine, and another kinder, more integrated person with us. If angered, John sometimes wrote critical letters that temporarily dislocated his bond with us. We started to know our place. He may not have been a present father at all times, but because of his subtle and sometimes overt ways of expressing his love for us, never did we feel any sense of fatherlessness.

Dad had always put his art and his women first, but this time around the order of importance was art, Katharine, the horses and then us. Extravagance was never a quality that our mother taught us; she had inspired Louise to look beautiful in a simple cotton dress and a few Indian bracelets. For Katharine, clothes

324

were a passion and horses an obsession. John found himself spending a fortune on the horses. Two horses that Katharine imported ended up in quarantine and, after a pile of vet bills, they arrived having by then cost a king's ransom. And then one died! At one point there were over 120 horses on the property, many of them the progeny of the horses originally imported from Brazil, Spain or Portugal. The combination of tax bills and the horses—which were in Dad's words an 'absolutely ridiculous' extravagance—forced him to sometimes agree to unwise financial decisions. He always refused to let me advance him money, whether out of pride or embarrassment. Perhaps not wanting to appear inadequate in my eyes or feel obliged to me.

Katharine was rather an enigma, hard to be close to, very aloof. It was onerous to have a conversation with her. Louise and I would ask about the horses, her obvious passion, but that proved unproductive. 'It was even impossible to talk about art with her,' says Louise.

In her will, Katharine had left an old horse to us, the proceeds to be split between Louise, Georgia, Gus and me. The elderly horse sold for just a few thousand dollars, which we never saw. None of us had ever expected anything from Katharine, so in a way, to be given a poor old horse, way past its prime, that none of us would enjoy, was laughable.

It did not concern us overly, though, as Katharine had never really made any effort to get to know any of us. She was simply not interested. Louise remembers that when she turned forty, Katharine asked her what she could give her, and Louise replied, 'Don't give me anything. Why don't we go for a coffee or a lovely lunch somewhere?', but it never eventuated.

Dad feels now that Katharine betrayed his trust and that, blinded by love, he let her go far beyond what he should have.

After Mum and Dad separated, Mum had given him back seminal works that he had requested in their divorce settlement on the proviso that he would ultimately leave them to Louise and me in his will. He had pleaded that he needed them back as they were important to him both sentimentally, as milestones in his career, and as references for future paintings. Katharine, knowing full well that these paintings were to be bequeathed to Louise and me, insisted that they be sold as quickly as possible. This, coupled with the sale of works such as *Love in the Kitchen* (1969) and *Two Eyes of the Dam* (1970), made it feel like our family and the memories of our past were being sold off.

The one good thing was that she never tried to distract him from his work, or compete with it.

Dad and Katharine had rooms at either end of their house, Dad next to the studio to be close to his work, and Katharine, still completely obsessed with her horses, at the other end. When Katharine became ill, Dad did everything possible to ease her suffering. He employed staff around the clock to care for her every need but, like so many men, found it difficult to cope and would retreat to his studio to work—his therapy and solace.[1] As the cancer took hold, Katharine became increasingly confused, paranoid and uncharacteristically aggressive, her whole personality changing dramatically. It was the sanctuary of the studio that saved him, the place where he could work and only feel sadness and compassion for what she was going through as her brain slowly deteriorated.

I often wonder how Dad himself has ended up living into his nineties when he has lived so hard at times: alcohol, his difficult relationships and their associated stress, and his high-fat diet should have worked against him, yet his attitude and his long-living genes have prevailed. His art, the escape of the creative process, perhaps even his subject of the timeless landscape, have given him longevity. He has understood and accepted change as much as the endlessness of the ancient dry continent that has perpetually provided him with creative ideas.

In his nineties he still professed, and many have agreed, that his work was getting better. It may have lost its slickness but it has become more uncompromising, a better work with less effort and a rawer touch. I would ask him at the end of the day, 'Did you have a good day in the studio?'

And he would reply as usual, 'I went in there and took the line for a walk.' His mind, and his fascination for making art, gave him unquenchable enjoyment.

On the day Katharine died in December 2016, we felt John's loss. We had lost our mother and now a stepmother to a brain tumour, and both had fought passionately to the last day for their survival. For the months before she died, Katharine had come home to the Southern Highlands to rest in the place she loved. Cancer is a cruel and arbitrary disease. It is both random and ravaging. Anyone who attributes it to 'karma' has not lost someone they love to a brain tumour, or any other type of cancer.

In those tender months after she died, everyone around John stepped back to allow him to grieve, and those closest to him encircled him with love. With fierce tenacity Dad threw himself into the studio, working hard on his retrospective *John Olsen: The You Beaut Country* with co-curator Deborah Edwards at the AGNSW, and painting through the pain and loss for his upcoming exhibition with me. In every difficult time Dad experiences, he reverts to the studio. For him, art is the highest form of hope.

His exhibition *John Olsen: New Paintings 2017* opened the following March, just three months after Katharine's passing. In the catalogue essay, I wrote of how this had been a particularly difficult and emotional time for John. One would normally assume that after such an experience, an artist would 'entertain a lugubrious theme encompassing dark palettes and reflective metaphors of mortality', but paradoxically Dad had taken refuge in the joyous genes of his life's work. 'Adversity often centres us to work from our core,' I wrote, and death brings new life. The exhibition was dedicated to Katharine, a celebration of both their lives, of human life and nature. For Dad, through the melancholy, there was a subsequent rebirth.

Loneliness is human, but artists always have the comfort of their first love. Still grieving but still very much alive and kicking, John has said, 'For me, work is like breathing. I'm an artist like a dog is a dog.'[2]

If life forces us to face our greatest fears, it was not going to let my father escape his. He dreaded the idea of ultimately ending up alone, divorced or abandoned. Katharine's death presented him with what he ultimately feared. Maintaining our relationship has been difficult at times, but we have always forgiven one another and always will.

32

NEW YORK, NEW YORK

Olsen Gruin started as a pop-up gallery in a storefront that my sister's company, Dinosaur Designs, had vacated on Elizabeth Street in Manhattan's Nolita district ('North of Little Italy'). These narrow artisan streets still feature lots of small owner-occupied design shops, a smattering of vintage, and something of the atmosphere that SoHo and Little Italy had in the early 1970s. 'Everyone ought to have a Lower East Side in their life,' said Irving Berlin.[1]

Emerald Gruin and I thought that introducing both young Australian and New York/American artists in a small gallery setting would be a winning combination. She had acquainted herself with some interesting New York artists, and giving it a whirl felt natural and without pressure. Both Emerald and her husband Adrian came on board as partners.

Emerald and I by then had had a long and fruitful friendship. She had gone to New York on an art scholarship and interned at various art organisations before working for Mary Boone at her self-named gallery in SoHo. We met up on one of my trips to New York and spent the afternoon wandering the streets of

Chelsea, both thinking how great it would be to have a New York gallery one day. Emerald says that she doesn't recall many of the exhibitions we saw that day but does remember seeing some graffiti that said, 'Addicted to being medicated', and thinking how we were both addicted to art.

Emerald returned to Sydney briefly to work with me, and had curated a couple of shows at OLSEN Gallery—Jan Frank, and a contemporary photography exhibition—that both had done well. However, the lure of the Big Apple and an opportunity saw her return to New York to become director of a gallery on the Lower East Side, only a few doors down from what would become the Olsen Gruin space. When Emerald met Adrian Gruin, they began to curate various hotels and spaces in New York for a year, but she said that her missing link was a physical space and the desire for longstanding establishment in the art world.

Just as we began to discuss the possibility of a gallery, Louise's space on Elizabeth Street became available and we decided to give Olsen Gruin a trial run, opening on 4 March 2017. Emerald and Adrian had a six-month-old baby girl, so they had two new babies to contend with, but in the first few months we did surprisingly well. The artists we were exhibiting were selling, and we very quickly outgrew Elizabeth Street and started looking for a larger space more in keeping with the Sydney gallery feel.

When Emerald came across 30 Orchard Street, we immediately knew that this was 'it'. The striking building, designed by Ogawa/Depardon Architects, stands out on the Manhattan skyline, sleek and modern, with a smooth glass façade and steel-sheathed sides. The ground floor has more than 200 square metres of concrete flooring and 7-metre-high ceilings, making it the perfect exhibition space. Emerald had visited the space in its previous gallery incarnation called Untitled, run by Jay Jopling, when looking for a position in her early days in New York and had immediately admired this particular location.

I flew to New York a few weeks later and we did not even look at another space. For three weeks we 'lost' Orchard Street when our lease offer was rejected, and we were both devastated. Just when we were considering signing another lease in a space next door to Perrotin, also on Orchard Street, which would require an expensive and time-consuming renovation, Orchard became available again. We jumped on it. Some things are meant to be; you just have to follow your instincts.

The popular 'Lower East Gallery Walk' ensured that we had a lot of foot traffic both from serious collectors and gallery hoppers, especially at weekends. Packed with cafes, bars and restaurants, several of which are owned by Australians, it is like 'Little Australia meets Chinatown', and it is nice to hear an Australian accent occasionally. With a massage and tattoo parlour opposite and the nearby chic boutiques, Emerald describes the area as 'an interesting mix of real New York grit and grime on Delancey Street and a cool young fashion crowd on Canal'. With celebrities such as actor Gabriel Byrne and musicians Moby, the late David Bowie and John Mayer as notable residents, the area has a people-watching appeal—although the locals are far too cool to notice.

Within a year, the gallery became a serious going concern and a place where I felt that I could show slightly more experimental and challenging artists. A small review in *Artforum* of the Wesley Martin Berg and Warlimpirrnga Tjapaltjarri show was a critical detail of presence. Emerald's eye for young and experimental work and my background in blue-chip artists struck a balance that had been missing in the area.

The day after Jerry Saltz reviewed the Aboriginal women's exhibition *Beyond the Veil* in May 2018 in *Vulture* magazine[2] we found queues of the curious on the street before we opened the doors. A review in *The New York Times* followed. To top it off, we were then listed in the *New York* magazine matrix as a high-brow/highlight exhibition.

Running a gallery always brings some interesting aspects, and all the planning possible could not cover the unexpected demands of stressed-out artists, the new challenge of New York weather and other unforeseen dramas. An exhibition by Australian, New York–based artist TV Moore proved too experimental for even New Yorkers when his 'cardboard' sculptures were seen exactly as that—cut-outs from cardboard boxes. Dale Frank freaked out over light coming through the windows and melting his epoxy-resin artworks (it was autumn and freezing), so we had to cover the stunning windows with an unsightly tarp; we only realised that the new gallery door was too small when crates of artwork arrived in the middle of a blizzard and we had to dismantle them on the sidewalk.

Openings are increasingly popular as we have become more well-known and attract an interesting mix of collectors, press, our loyal expat friends, and other gallerists and dealers from uptown and abroad. The ultimate compliment to the gallery was the arrival of Larry Gagosian in his beanie at the opening night of our first exhibition of 2019, *Penumbra*.

Another huge early highlight, as already mentioned, was the opening of Leila Jeffreys' *Ornithurae Volume 1* exhibition in 2017, with Brooke Shields and influential fashion editor Laura Brown in attendance. (Leila's works were later featured in the *Feathers Pair with Fashion* display in the windows of the Bergdorf Goodman department store.)

Entertaining is part and parcel of the art scene, and our gallery's Gala Dinner is proving a popular annual event. The gala of 2019 was our fanciest yet, centred around a photograph of a horse with a giant erect penis by Nick Samartis.

As proud Australians, we promote our culture as well as our art. Having the Central Australian Aboriginal Women's Choir (CAAWC) perform at the opening of one of the Aboriginal exhibitions was incredibly moving.

Emerald is now a US citizen and entrenched in her New York life. It helps that New Yorkers love Australians and are so welcoming, and there are numerous expats around. She says that she is slowly starting to feel more 'New Yorker' than Australian but will always be a Sydney/Brisbane girl at heart. Growing up among such stunning beaches has made her a beach snob when she compares the beaches of Long Island and the Hamptons.

My joy in this space is that it is not a specifically Australian gallery. It is an empty canvas, a big experiment and a place where I am completely unknown—a small fish in a big pond. New York is a hard city but an open one. Lots of things are difficult. Happily, though, nothing is impossible.

Pierre Matisse, the youngest child of Henri Matisse, came to New York in 1924, opening his own gallery at 41 East 57th Street. The Pierre Matisse Gallery became an influential part of the modern art movement, remaining operational until his death in 1989. In his rich career he exhibited many European artists, often their first showing in New York, including his own father. I can only hope to emulate his success with my own artists. Matisse's philosophy of living with imperfection resonates with me even more now. Like Dad and me, the relationship between Henri and Pierre was professional as well as personal: the artist and the art dealer. I once remarked on the similarities to Dad—that we were an artist and a dealer, too, just not as famous or grand as Henri and Pierre—and he responded, 'Son, just wait!'[3]

Jan Frank, the Amsterdam-born, New-York based artist and curator, was introduced to me by my friend (and later gallery partner) Emerald Gruin. Jan is entrenched in the downtown New York art scene. His stories encompassing the superlative artists of the twentieth century are engrossing: from getting stoned with Louise Bourgeois, drinking with Willem de Kooning and sculptor Richard Chamberlain, and fighting in the street with Jeff Koons, to the domesticity of sharing a studio with Chuck Close. He has always had a reputation as a hard-drinking, hard-living playboy.

Jan is still living in the famous artists' loft building on Bond Street where Mary Boone, Chuck Close, sculptor Carl Andre and artist Ana Mendieta used to all live and work. Split into multiple studios, the loft became a hothouse for contemporary artists and had a notorious reputation to match: it is remembered as the building where Carl Andre allegedly pushed his wife Ana Mendieta out of the window to her death from the 33rd floor (he was acquitted of her murder). Jan told me that he still can remember her agonised scream as she fell, more than 30 years ago. He talked constantly about the mythology of the New York art world, stories shocking and fascinating in equal measure.

Emerald had been a successful model so when struggling as an intern in her early days in New York, she was told that Jan Frank was looking for a new life model. She jumped at the opportunity.

As well as entertaining Emerald with his sometimes audacious tales of the art scene, Jan would talk about his paintings and his practice while she sat for him, and she knew immediately that I would be interested to meet him. This was Jan's 'nude' period; his paintings started from the minimalistic studies of live models such as Emerald. Jan says that the idea for using the figure like this came to him at Willem de Kooning's funeral, while he sat alongside gallerists Larry Gagosian and Matthew Marks. 'I use the figure to get the paint on the canvas,' he says. He would frequently paint with a long brush, more than 2 metres in length, which reminds me of John working on his much larger works: he would attach a brush to a long pole to cover the vast expanse of canvas.

Jan and I quickly decided that he should have an exhibition with me, and over a period of six months he created the series of works that became his 2012 exhibition *Minimalism to Modernism: Painting for Australia*. Emerald had to carry the paintings back to Sydney in ski bags for them to arrive in time. Jan arrived in Australia with the works still untitled, so he looked at the racing form guide and chose names from the racehorses of the time—one work in the exhibition was called *Black Caviar*. It's something he still does. The show was amazing, a sell-out, even though Jan was a completely unknown name in Australia then.

Jan ended up being signed up by Nahmad Contemporary, a blue-chip gallery in the same building as Gagosian in uptown New York. I have to accept that his works are now out of the reach of most Australians, though at least I had the opportunity to socialise with him and show him when I did.

I saw him again recently. He was a 'dry drunk'—he'd stopped drinking but did not go to AA meetings or have that support. For a year or so, my conversations with him indicated that he felt things were not going right for him, which I thought was contradictory as, looking around the studio, I saw so many beautiful paintings. Yet Jan could not see how much there was to celebrate and to do. The last time I saw him, he was very shaken up and talked about his struggle with prescription drugs. He was having neurological issues and went on to have a nervous breakdown, his lifestyle catching up with him. Like so many other artists, he found success was hard to bear, part of him feeling that he did not deserve it.

I met his old friend Chuck Close at a party in Miami during Art Basel; he was aware of me and my gallery through Jan's exhibition. 'I have much love for Jan,' he told me. 'But the only thing that gets in the way of Jan is Jan himself.' I agree with that, and note that it is true for many people, especially artists. The highly publicised benders, street brawls and general excessive behaviour had made Jan a bit of a liability. He had a reputation for changing his gallery as frequently as his underpants. One thing I had learned quickly after getting sober was to get out of my own way.

Despite continually exhibiting worldwide and still showing in New York with Nahmad, Jan has not achieved the renown of many of his peers in his home town. He now refers to himself as being 'not politically correct', saying, 'I'm probably the most famous unfamous artist.'

Perhaps when I started dealing I was a purist, but I soon realised that the worlds of film, music and art are not separate realms. Plenty of stars dabble at the easel; however, while many an actor has a garage band, very few can really create visual art.

When Australian actor Claudia Karvan—the step-daughter of my former boss, Arthur Karvan, of Arthur's in Darlinghurst—introduced me to her longtime friend and fellow thespian

Noah Taylor in 2012, she suggested that I look at his work. A week later Noah turned up at the gallery, nervous and modest. He expressed his love of other creative pursuits outside acting— his music, writing and, most relevantly, his passion for creating art—and his keen desire to exhibit. When I looked at his work, there was an autobiographical drama about it, a satirical directness and brutal honesty that grabbed me immediately.

He was living in Brighton, England, dividing his time between there and New Orleans to be close to work, with intermittent trips back to Australia. He was by then an international film star, having featured in major movies and television series, but has always painted and drawn, and been involved in the visual arts. He says that acting is his job, but making things, whether music or art, is his passion. It was his standout performance playing the pianist David Helfgott as an adolescent in the 1996 film *Shine* that gained him international recognition, and many feel that Geoffrey Rush's Oscar win for playing the adult Helfgott should have been Noah's. I see the same raw emotion in his work that I saw then in the film.

I was pleased that Noah came to me when he felt confident enough to exhibit. Previously he had simply discarded, destroyed or given away works. To see Noah now engage with so much confidence in his art touches me. Facilitating others, whoever they are, to realise their creative powers helps me validate what the gallery does.

Noah has mass appeal. There is a certain uncertainty about him, not only as an artist but as a person, and he never behaves like a famous actor. He articulates like a good draughtsman; it's just Noah being his real satirical self, in a sense expressing his cynical view of the world, which is twisted, and full of satire and black humour. 'Sex and violence are staples of the arts,' he says.

'They are classical.' People love his works, and they love him. He draws the best characters that he plays. Noah has exhibited with me almost annually since 2013, his shows selling out almost immediately.

Noah has become a close friend. I visit him when I'm in England, catching the train to Brighton for the day. His wife Dee is gorgeous and complements him perfectly—she looks like a 1950s rockabilly star in a contemporary style. In return, when he is in Sydney he stays above my Annexe gallery in Woollahra, known as the Artist Residency. He sets himself up a table in front of the French doors, facing the laneway, painting away shirtless, a cigarette constantly hanging out of his mouth as he works. He paints frenetically in black ink on paper recording his subconscious thoughts, producing an exhibition in a matter of days.

While there may be a star factor at work, primarily he is successful because he has something very relevant to say. The fame factor rubs off at his openings as his friends and other local celebrities come to support him—even if the man himself is absent, once missing his own opening due to one of his films premiering on the other side of the world.

Unimpressed by fame alone, I have turned down showing works by other celebrities, from Martina Navratilova (she had hit tennis balls soaked in paint against a canvas) to Sir Paul McCartney and Dire Straits' John Illsley. But, as for Noah, I think he's an honest, good artist.

Deborra-Lee Furness and Hugh Jackman have approached me to hold an event in the gallery to thank the loyal supporters of their charity, Adopt Change. The charity seeks to overhaul the anti-adoption culture and raise awareness worldwide of the global orphan crisis. Having adopted two children themselves, this is a very personal cause for Deborra-Lee and Hugh. Unfortunately, COVID-19 has postponed the event indefinitely.

We first met when I was invited to a weekend opening of a new spa at the Gwinganna health retreat that Hugh partly owns in the Gold Coast hinterland in Queensland. I liked them both immensely.

They are both very egalitarian and I admire Deborra for her work, so I was delighted to offer the gallery for the event and proud to see her honoured as 2015 NSW Australian of the Year; she is so down to earth and unpretentious. We have a few friends in common and, funnily enough, decades ago a mutual friend wanted to introduce us as a potential match. It never happened, and now the idea seems absurd—she married Wolverine, for God's sake!

During a recent email exchange with Deborra, I mentioned writing this memoir and how I felt that I was channelling my great-uncle James Vance Marshall, author. I wrote how Vance wanted to humanise and break down the perception of Aboriginal people in white Australian and British culture. Perhaps representing Indigenous artists in New York is my way of helping to do my bit. Her response was immediate: 'Writing our story is also the greatest therapy and is the road map to self-realization.'

There is a long journey ahead with the New York gallery to ensure our longevity in the notoriously fickle art scene. It is difficult to represent artists who are unknown in the Northern Hemisphere unless their work is in the collections of cultural institutions or recognised in the global art world. With the artists who are neither American nor European, it has been challenging to attract as many visitors to exhibitions as I would like and therefore for some of my artists to receive the appreciation they deserve. With over 1500 galleries operating in New York alone, it is hugely competitive and even local artists, galleries, curators and institutions struggle in a city known for its capacious appetite for the latest 'new thing'. With the prevailing attitude towards Australian art still being rather unappreciative, simply through lack of exposure, it can be a hard nut to crack. However, having a show in New York is most Antipodean artists' dream, and I have been pleased to be able to fulfil that. Having a gallery in the 'City of Dreams' was certainly mine.

We still budget from month to month, sometimes stretching to stay on top financially. There have been some small windfalls, but we are understandably light-years away from the success of the longstanding New York galleries in reputation and, sadly, in financial returns.

We will persevere, doing our time as we did in my first minuscule gallery in Sydney—in comparison, the New York gallery is colossal. I have faith in my colleagues, the belief that together we will have the patience and tenacity to build the gallery as one of great vision, integrity and innovation, nurturing Australian and international contemporary artists. Our plans, however, were abruptly put on hold with the emergence of COVID-19 and its devastating worldwide effect.

I need to steer the ships with both the galleries. Katrina is, as always, amazing in Sydney and I trust her completely. Emerald is a dedicated professional and is steadily building her own network of art lovers, press and industry contacts. Whatever eventuates, we have achieved our goals and have both benefited from the experience, professionally and personally.

With the best intentions to expose good Australian art to the mix in the New York art scene, it is a sad reality that the freight bills to and from the gallery, on top of the return of unsold works eventually coming back to Australia, mean that representing Australian art in the Northern Hemisphere can become almost a philanthropic act. As an outsider, it can take ten years and a lot of parties and art fairs to establish yourself.

I always knew that integrating Australian art in such a competitive market was going to be a lengthy process. Going forward, we will be focusing on increasing awareness of the gallery and our artists through art fair presence, presenting the pre-eminent artists of our stable—and schmoozing more curators and collectors.

Travelling to the States so regularly, I now have it down pat: a couple of melatonin and a *Vanity Fair*, wake up and you're there.

33

BEYOND THE VEIL

Authenticity is an issue for every dealer, whether it involves the literal provenance of a work or the basic idea of theft, of which there has been plenty even among artists I have admired. Picasso said that 'Good artists copy, great artists steal', but almost everything he did was a bold reinvention.

So, when Damien Hirst presented his dot paintings in his show *The Veil Paintings* at the Gagosian in Los Angeles in March 2018, it felt like a good time to play Bob Dylan's *Love and Theft* (loudly) and take a long, fresh look at the masters of desert 'dot paintings'.

Hirst contends that the large-scale dot paintings in soft, splotchy pastel colours he made for *The Veil Paintings* were influenced by the post-impressionist paintings of Bonnard, Seurat's innovative pointillism techniques and his own dot works of the 1990s: Hirst's series *Visual Candy* featured one dot painting, *Super Happy Happy Dabby*, as galling a title as one could summon if looking at desert art.[1]

Artnet, the popular art blog, begged to differ and illustrated the striking resemblance between Hirst's painting *Veil of Love*

John working in his Clarendon studio on *Golden Summer, Clarendon* in 1983, with *Fleurieu Peninsula* in the background. (Photo: Jan Dalman)

Art student Tim in front of his paintings, 1983.

Tim, Louise and John at Louise's 21st birthday, 1985.

Tim's graduation from the University of New South Wales in 1989, with John fighting over his degree, saying 'This is mine! I paid for it!'

John, his daughter Jane, Tim and Jane's son Gus at Chapel House Farm, Rydal, early 1990.

The 1991 wedding day of Tim Olsen and Harriet France, Sydney.

Tim and Harriet with Heathcliff (the horse), 1992.

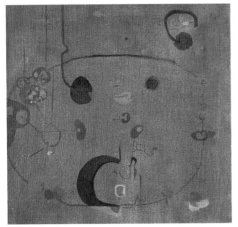

Valerie Strong, *Untitled (Abstract)*, c. early 1970s, a painting of the dam at Dunmoochin. Collection of Louise Olsen.

Tim hanging an exhibition at Tim Olsen Gallery, Paddington, 1992. (Photo by Andrew Taylor/ *Sydney Morning Herald*)

Valerie, 1985, captured by Louise for an art-school project.

John and Tim modelling for Ermenegildo Zegna, 1989. (Photo: Monty Coles/Courtesy *Vogue Entertaining + Travel*)

Arthur Boyd (left) with John and Tim at the Paddington gallery, Sydney, 1997.

Valerie Strong, *Still Life with Flowers*, 1985. Collection of Louise Olsen.

John and Tim with Jeffrey Smart (right), 2006.

12 January 2000: Dominique Ogilvie and Tim on their wedding day in Aspen, Colorado, United States.

Tim and Dom's son James as a baby, 2004. (Photo: Nicole Bonython)

Tim Olsen Gallery, Paddington (Tim's second gallery), 2005.

Dom, James and Tim at the Tim Olsen Gallery, 2005. (Courtesy *Vogue Australia*)

Valerie, Tim, James (aged two) and John, 2006.

Tim, James, John and Margaret Olley outside
Lucio's restaurant, Paddington, 2007.

There are lovers...
...and there are others.

Cartoon by Michael Lodge featuring Tim
and John with James, 2009.

John with James and Tim in front of *Popping Blue
Bottles*, 2007, at John's exhibition *A Salute to Sydney* at
Tim Olsen Gallery. It was the first exhibition held at the
new gallery on Jersey Road, Woollahra.

Jane with her daughter Georgia Blake, in 2008. (Photo: Eryca Green)

Jamie Oliver cooking paella for John, 2010.
(Photo: David Loftus)

Rocky the dog with James, 2009. (Photo: Eryca Green)

Lunch with Paloma Picasso at Lucio's, Paddington,
2010. Left to right: Tim, Paloma, John.

Valerie in August 2011, not long before she died, with Louise's daughter Camille. (Photo: Eryca Green)

Tim with Sophie Cape at the Hong Kong International Art Fair, May 2012.

Tim with Jan Frank, at Jan's exhibition at Tim Olsen Gallery, 2012. (Courtesy BlouinArtinfo)

Tim with artist Paul Davies. (Photo: Gary Heery)

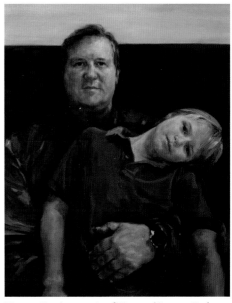

Yvonne East's portrait of Tim and James, *Father and Son, After Janus*, 2012.

Noah Taylor with Tim before his first exhibition at Tim Olsen Gallery, early 2013.

James after his rugby match at Cranbrook, 2016, with John.

Tim with Claude Picasso at Art Basel Miami Beach in 2016.

Tim with Stephen Ormandy, artist and Louise's partner, in a London black cab, 2015.

Tim and Guy Maestri, artist and friend, in Guy's studio, Sydney, 2016.

Tim, Sophie Cape and Rex Irwin at the opening of Sophie's 2016 exhibition at Olsen Irwin.

John and Tim at the launch of John's book *My Salute to Five Bells* at the Sydney Opera House, 2015.

James learning to make pasta on his thirteenth birthday, Capri, 2017.

Tim at Olsen Irwin Gallery with works by John, 2015. (Photo: Steven Siewert/ *The Sydney Morning Herald*)

Tim at OLSEN Gallery, 2017.
(Photo: Greg Weight)

James and Tim in Aspen, 2017.

Emerald Gruin (left) and Tim with actors
Elizabeth Debicki and Rachel Griffiths at the
G'Day USA Gala in Los Angeles, 2018.

Tim and James in Capri, 2017.

John and Tim at the retrospective *John Olsen: The You Beaut Country*, National Gallery of Victoria, 2017. (Courtesy National Gallery of Victoria)

Nicholas Harding exhibition at OLSEN Gallery, Woollahra, August 2020. (Photo: Brett East)

Leila Jeffreys exhibition at Olsen Gruin Gallery, Orchard Street, New York, 2017.

Upstairs stockroom at OLSEN Gallery, Sydney, 2017. Left wall: Brett Whiteley, *Beach Polyptych*, 1984, 1991–92. Centre, on table: Robert Klippel, *Opus 363 Ninety-three constructions of coloured paper*, 1980, courtesy the estate of Robert Klippel. (Photo: Brett East)

OLSEN Gallery at Sydney Contemporary, September 2019. Left: John Olsen, *Holiday by the Sea*, 1993. Right: Jonathan Delafield Cook, *Bull*, 2019. Works by Julian Meagher, Laura Jones, Philjames, Jacqui Stockdale, Vipoo Srivilasa, Alan Jones, Luke Storrier and Stephen Ormandy were also included. (Photo: Brett East)

Antumbra: A Summer Group Exhibition in the OLSEN Gallery main gallery space, Woollahra, December 2017 – January 2018. Works included John's *Parrots in Paradise*, 2014 (left) and *Wattle Pond, Bathurst*, 1977–78 (right, front). (Photo: Brett East)

The *Nganampa Ngura Kurunjara* exhibition of APY Lands artists at Olsen Gruin Gallery, New York, 31 October–18 November 2018.

Dad with his 90th birthday cake at OLSEN Gallery in January 2018; cake by SweetArt. (Photo: Brett East)

Tim, John and Louise celebrating John's 90th birthday at The Olsen hotel, Melbourne, February 2018.

Barry Humphries and Tim at John's 90th birthday lunch at OLSEN Gallery, Sydney, January 2018. (Photo: Brett East)

Katrina Arent, OLSEN Gallery Director, at the artists' lunch in February 2020. (Photo: Kitty Callaghan/Courtesy RUSSH magazine)

The 2017 Olsen family Christmas. Clockwise from back left: Tim, Louise, Stephen, Aditi with Georgia, Camille, John and James. (Photo: Eryca Green)

Actor Brooke Shields, Tim and Emerald Gruin at the opening of the Leila Jeffreys exhibition at Olsen Gruin, New York, in 2017.

Celebrating John's 91st birthday, January 2019, at Catalina, Rose Bay: John, Louise, Tim and Barry Humphries.

Tim at the artists' lunch at OLSEN Gallery, February 2020, in front of Louise's painting *Changing Sea*, 2019. (Photo: Kitty Callaghan/ Courtesy *RUSSH* magazine)

Louise and John in a group drawing lesson via Zoom during COVID-19 isolation, in John's studio at Hidden Lake, 2020, with Ken Redpath.

Everlasting and *Anwekety* by Polly Ngale. Other very experienced dealers of Aboriginal art in Australia raged hard in *The Guardian* and elsewhere, demanding that the artist whose work Hirst's most resembled—the late and great Emily Kame Kngwarreye—be named as his primary influence.

Interest in the work of Kngwarreye is not new to the international art market. Her work found a new audience after the Queensland Art Gallery staged a major retrospective of her work in 1997, and she represented Australia (posthumously) at the Venice Biennale the same year. *Utopia: The Genius of Emily Kame Kngwarreye* was shown in Osaka and Tokyo in 2008 before coming back to the National Museum of Australia, cementing appreciation of her short but brilliant career. It is more than likely that Hirst may have stumbled across her incredibly unique and physically imposing paintings.

After the dust settled and the outcry died down, Hirst had actually done something great for Aboriginal artists and Emily's work in particular. His dots, either knowingly or unwittingly, shone a bright international spotlight on a group of artists who deserve more international attention. The combination of Hirst's popular appeal, the Gagosian name, Kngwarreye standing and the subsequent press did just that. It did not hurt that Gagosian had scheduled the exhibition as their 2018 Oscars show, aligned with one of the most popular and anticipated events of the Los Angeles cultural calendar, ensuring maximum exposure.

Emerald and I had been already planning a show featuring the work of Aboriginal artists Kathy Maringka, Polly Ngale and Gabriella Possum Nungurrayi. It was purely serendipitous that we opened this long-scheduled show a month after Hirst's show closed. The exhibition title, however, was opportunistic: *Beyond the Veil.*

The most gifted artists are attuned to both the song of the earth and the universe. Working with Indigenous art made this more evident to me. I was raised to revere Aboriginal art and have always seen it as a powerful entity unto itself. Aboriginal art is physically contemporary and conceptually ancient, but it is not abstract—despite the many critical and commercial associations made between it and Western abstraction, and it being often hung in the context of very modern interiors. In Indigenous consciousness, the 'land' and the 'sky' are as much a part of each other, which gives you an insight into the interpretation that Indigenous people have about living on Earth. Yaritji Young's work, in particular, where the cosmos collides with the land, is a good example. The mythology and the stories within that, known as the 'Dreamtime', present themselves as stables of creation; however, many stories have already been lost.

These works are telling stories and writing maps; they are making history. Aboriginal art is a highly sophisticated form of expression. It has an enormous inner power that stands up against all of the great ancient or contemporary art forms. Like all great cultural objects, it comes from a place of commercial innocence.

Knowing all of this, I was not flustered by the storm Damien Hirst's *Veil* paintings raised in the Aboriginal art community among the curators, experts, artists, Elders and supporters. The conversation going on between contemporary artists from different cultures did not offend me as an Australian or a dealer; instead, it interested Emerald and me even more. When *Artnet* contacted Emerald for her comments, she said plainly that the show was in no way a critique of Hirst, and I agree.

Emerald succinctly said the show was about 'a conversation we are trying to foster within the community . . . [about] the spectrum of inspiration versus appropriation versus stealing, of which, of course, there are many examples within art history'.

Our show reopened the door to the cosmology and the meaning of the marks known as 'dots'. There is so much more to Central Desert painting than technical similarities. It is not, in fact, a style of painting; rather, it is a way of seeing. I have to concur with Robert Hughes when he said that Aboriginal art was the last great art movement of the twentieth century that was in fact 40,000 years old.

Aboriginal art is a very potent celebration of country. You keep coming back to it because a good work does not reveal its layers and complexity in one view. These works are mutable and compelling but many of the conventions we take for granted in Western art, such as light source and perspective, do not apply here. There is no light in Indigenous art. The artists use pigments. It is not trying to capture light; it is trying to capture the content of country.

The conceptions of time and space in Aboriginal art do not follow night and day or any hour of the clock. You cannot say something is a morning, twilight or nocturnal picture, for example. Their colour is not seasonal. All of these departures from a Eurocentric perception are what draws me to these works. It is work for people who are spiritually demanding or perhaps a salve for those who are spiritually bereft, but it is certainly much more than the sum of its parts. That was the core idea of a show such as *Beyond the Veil*.

We ran this show long, deliberately long, so New Yorkers would 'get it'. The slow pace of summer echoed beautifully with the subtle explosions of colour on the walls. Thankfully the art critic from *New York* magazine also got it. God bless Jerry Saltz who, the day after accepting his Pulitzer, published the following review that I am proud to reproduce in full.[2]

Beyond the Veil
Curated by Adam Knight
OLSEN GRUIN

No doubt many of the bigwigs in town for all the art stars, megagalleries and super-auctions, missed maybe the best secret show in New York at the moment, this six-artist exhibition of Australian Aboriginal women painters curated by the president of the Aboriginal Art Association of Australia—a show that gives us a breathtaking small survey of what critic Robert Hughes (who in almost every case except this I disagreed with) called 'the last great art movement of the twentieth century'. Start with the tremendous late Emily Kame Kngwarreye, who started painting in her 70s, but whose strangely structured, still amorphous compositions of smears, dots, daubs, and squiggles create rippling worlds, undergrowth, river scenes, and complex cosmic interior space; and contrast her Rothko-like ruminations to the more detailed, pictorial, and symbolic images created by Gabriella Possum Nungurrayi, and then to a mind-blowing group effort made by a collective of women that looks like a magic-carpet quilt for the spirit. It's time for these artists and many others to be shown in and collected by museums, placed in context, installed for good in permanent collections along with other such 'outsider' and 'self-taught' artists, and to finally scrap our sick, desolated, apartheid-like systematic exclusion of any but 'insider' artists.

Amen.

In 2017, in an indication of the enduring value of exceptional art, Emily Kame Kngwarreye's work continued to increase in both value and appeal. As an example of the perseverance of blue-chip art investment, Elton John sold one of her paintings, the 1.34 by 3.7-metre *My Country* (1993), for almost A$500,000, ten times what the 'melodic genius' (as he was described by French President Emmanuel Macron in 2019) had paid for it two decades earlier at Sotheby's Melbourne. Like Dad's *Love in the Kitchen*, the work sold for over double the auction-house expectations.

Later that year, I bought Kngwarreye's revolutionary work *Earth's Creation I* (1994) for A$2.1 million at auction on behalf of a client, proudly setting a record price for an Australian female artist. The work had been previously bought by Mbantua Fine Art Gallery and Cultural Museum in Alice Springs for A$1.1 million in 2007 and was shown at the 2015 Venice Biennale.

Astoundingly, Emily did not start painting until she was nearly 80, finding her true medium only in 1988 when she started painting on canvas. In a mere eight years, the body of work she produced was astounding.

Katrina is responsible for liaising with artists and specifically with the Anangu Pitjantjatjara Yankunytjatjara (APY) communities in the remote north-west of South Australia. Our focus with the APY Art Centre Collective is on building a respectful and sensitive relationship with the ten Indigenous-owned enterprises that make up the collective. Katrina feels privileged to be working with them, to have the opportunity to visit, meet with the artists and view their incredible works. The Art Centre Collective brings a lot of support and income to the communities and to the artists individually, elevating the entire community. They are incredibly isolated, so the art income stream means greater access to education, plus improvements in the local infrastructure and their society as a whole. It has been a wonderful opportunity for the gallery, and we are doing our best to honour that privilege of representing the work and the artists we are fortunate enough to be associated with. Personally, I left APY lands feeling changed, spiritually enlightened and honoured to be associated with the artists' beautiful, spiritual artwork.

In 2018, Lang Walker came to me again to consult for the art for his new four-tower development at Parramatta Square. With Lang being a longtime art collector, the Walker Corporation offices in Sydney are a private collector's dream. Thrilled with the impact of *King Sun*, the commission John created for the Docklands building, Lang wanted a work with similar 'wow' factor and size for one of his Parramatta Square towers, now considered the hub of Parramatta.

With *King Sun* having taken its toll, John regretfully declined, instead suggesting APY Lands artist Yaritji Young, whose work does bear a similarity to John's in line and composition, although using a completely different palette. The work was completed in mid-2020 and continues Young's narration of the *tjala tjukurpa* (honey ant story). I once asked Yaritji about the similarities between her work and Dad's, and she replied, 'Same dream, different country.'

A lot of what an artist does can be channelled from some-where else. The artist is often just the vehicle. Indigenous people, many of whom traditionally did not live under roofs, often see the night sky as solid, as walking upon the earth. Hence many of the Dreaming stories are about the interaction of spirits between the stars and the earth. The early works of my father also resembled these kind of vortexes, like images beamed back from deep space. For Yaritji, her works are a means of conveying her love and knowledge of her country and culture to younger generations of Indigenous and non-Indigenous people.

We were hoping that Lang would fly John back to Lake Eyre, and we planned to stop in at APY Lands to inspect Yaritji's 6-by-4-metre work. John has said that he would like to grab a brush and put his own touch in there as well, so it would become a sort of collaboration, but they declined, saying it would be bad juju.

During our APY Lands exhibition in New York in 2019, we held a special cocktail reception at the gallery for UNSW graduates living and working in New York. As a UNSW alumnus and UNSW Foundation Board member, it was a pleasure for me to celebrate their connection through the university and its values around diversity and inclusivity. I spoke of how life-changing my time as an art-education student had been, and about art being a window into another person's life. 'My mother once told me that one of the greatest acts of humility is to be interested in what other people think,' I said to them. 'Art really is an adventure into how other people feel, see and experience their time here on Earth.'[3]

What inspired me most when studying at UNSW was the insight I gained from the diversity of my fellow students who had come from around the world, and the resultant cross-pollination of ideas in our creative world was inspirational to us all. Looking around the gallery, that diversity was even more evident. My role on the UNSW Foundation Board has been important to me in giving back, helping to raise money for scholarships, to improve buildings and to make a university education more accessible.

However, I still feel that art schools have no place in universities because universities are more to do with academic rather than practical education. Art is to do with intuition, not reason. Practical experience in making art, in trying and failing, is what facilitates that intuition. Academics are in a sense sending students in completely the wrong direction. As my father has said, 'How can any great painting by Picasso or another seminal artist be a masterpiece if only inspired by reason?' He says that the best education comes from the 'atelier system', where every student is allocated a studio space.

In early 2018, I received a phone call from one of my artists. He was so intoxicated I could barely make out his words. 'Mate,' he said between choking sobs and gasps, 'it's bad, mate. I'm losing everything. It's been bad before but this . . . this isn't . . .' He did not have to say any more. His weeping echoed through the empty studio. His vulnerability was total. This was a conversation he probably would not remember in a few hours; this was rock bottom. Making the call is everything, but so few do make that call. There are a handful of friends and artists close to me that I wish could be that open, to ask for help, yet few can. Either life is not bad enough (yet) or they are so deep inside their crisis that it seems like their own brand of normal.

Within 48 hours of the call, the artist was in rehab. Three weeks later, he was back in his studio. Clean. Painting. I am sure the bright, sober daylight made everything look shabby and harsh, but he persisted. He has now gone years without relapsing. We are planning a major show for him but it's fragile. It could all be obliterated by one drink: that razor's edge for anyone who reaches the point where they think they've got the monkey by the tail. No matter how many glasses of fancy Italian mineral water you drink, you can never say 'I've got this', because basically it is never over. Every day is a commitment. It is that basic and profound.

Being sober in the art world is like being fully dressed at an orgy. Bohemian boozers are devout and practise every day. When I returned from Betty Ford, there seemed to be a sign on every corner tempting me with invitations to imbibe: 'Double Wild Turkey and Coke!' It is actually amazing that I did not die of diabetes, a stroke or a heart attack. The key, for me, to staying sober in that environment of complacent seduction, with frosty bottles open at every lunch and a chorus of champagne corks popping at every opening, was to simply avoid that first drink and go to meetings. Any AA meeting, anywhere.

Barry Humphries always reminds me that 'there are very few of us who make it', and I tell myself that every day. It is still one day at a time. More than thirteen years into recovery, nine years unbroken, I have no desire, not even a twinge, for a drink, because I know that I am not bigger than the craving. I may not be participating, but the disease is constantly doing push-ups in the background. My memories of damage and oblivion serve as a constant reminder. It is hard for non-addicts to understand the most fundamental point about alcoholism: there is no proportion. There is no 'social drink'. The line is drawn. It may seem strange, but I am grateful for my addiction as it led to my awakening. All the suffering led to my ability to transcend my repetitive and addictive behaviour. I realised that I had more than a drinking problem—I also had a thinking one.

Leaving the restaurant, Le Club 55, on the beach in

Saint-Tropez one day, I saw Sir Elton John. He had been a huge inspiration to me in my recovery, so I approached him to thank him. I said, 'Knowing your previous lifestyle, for you to be able to recover, it certainly minimised my issues and made me think I could do it, too.'

He put his hand on my face. 'Congratulations and thank you,' he said. 'You're a beautiful man.' As a result of me supporting his AIDS foundation, I was invited to his 70th birthday party in Los Angeles in 2017, where I gave him a copy of Dad's book. He wrote me a lovely card to say thank you, which I still have.

Elton spent some time in Australia in the summer of 2019–20, staying at the home of a friend of mine. Tempting as it was to knock on the door, I resisted, out of respect for his privacy.

34

LOST IN THE LANDSCAPE

My stand for Sydney Contemporary in September 2017 was almost purely monochromatic and abstract. The show was curated to be all about colour, in contradiction to the tonal and impasto work that had dominated the gallery walls the decade before. It was a bold move; we had become known as the go-to gallery for contemporary landscape paintings. One artist friend commented on how far the gallery had come, because my earlier reputation had been as the gallery of 'lumpy landscapes'. Many of these were painted with palette knives, not brushes, and of the plethora of artists working this way, eventually only Nicholas Harding remained with me. He, in turn, was inspired by Leon Kossoff and Frank Auerbach, not to mention Lucian Freud. My father would also testify to having no fear of a 'lumpy landscape' as he, too, has been known to apply paint straight from the tube, impasto.

Over time, the landscape synthesises into an experience that you do not have to engage with literally. It distils into pure colour and concentrated energy. I've never drawn the line between abstract art and representation because there are many very brilliant artists who have engaged with both within their canon.

That said, Australian art has always had to fight its way out of the box of the landscape genre, and that is a reality riven with irony. The collectors and the major museums dwell on the urban and suburban coastline, and only a handful of our best artists depict the city: Bill Henson, Paul Davies, Howard Arkley, Jeffrey Smart and John Brack. Looking at architecture is a way of gauging civilisation, and a tremendous number of Australian painters and filmmakers now obsess over suburbia.

The heroics of our national identity are played out in terrains that few inhabit. Landscape is not a welcoming pastoral in our art. Essentially, the struggle of the pioneer is about the landscape rejecting the white man. Tim Storrier's *Burning Rope* is interesting because it is almost like Storrier is a pioneer trying to compete with the sunset and nature, trying to control something far more powerful than we will ever be. Australia is an obliterating landscape. The *Burning Rope* is a 'fuck you' to the forces of the earth, which is probably why it is so popular.

Our architecture has a similarly defensive, almost oblivious relationship with the landscape. In my boyhood, the architectural visionaries—Glenn Murcutt, Neville Guzman, Richard Leplastrier—developed a highly tuned response to the landscape, and the difference was that their houses were designed to be lived in, not built to sell. If you build a house to sell it is often a dead object but if you design a house to live in, it will live forever. It is very similar with painting. The best paintings of the Australian landscape really inhabit it. It is more than a view.

People paint landscapes because the landscape is omnipresent. This in turn helps us realise how infinitesimal we really are, especially in regard to the vastness of the Australian landscape. To emulate nature is one of the greatest tasks for any artist.

We are part of nature. We are organic objects, not just observers.

Léger saw the essential qualities of nature in the cone, cube and sphere. It is the same with life drawing: through making our own individual marks and lines, we navigate our own self-discovery, encountering our own idiosyncrasies. The value of learning to draw is the process of finding identity; how a student draws reflects how they do things. To me, that is the great sadness of the computer keyboard. Children are not really learning about their own creativity because they are not learning about their own marks. When I started school at Cranbrook, I learned to write with an ink pen; there was an inkwell at the end of my desk. The nib teaches you the quality of the thick and the thin, something a ballpoint pen lacks. Looking at a screen is a totally different aesthetic to gazing into nature. Technology is taking us away from that healing immersion. I question how we can save nature when we've lost our feel for it, and our physical sense of custodial responsibility.

My main obsession at art school was landscape. As time has passed, and definitely in the last five years, the number of landscape artists in the gallery's stable has been shrinking. With an overload of landscapers, it had become congested. Nicholas Harding, who we retained, had come with Rex; he seems to embody the best of the genre in contemporary terms. Nicholas is a very urbane, intelligent and dedicated artist. His work may be conventional in certain ways, but there is a skill and an internal edge to his work that does touch on the avant-garde.

I take my hat off to the painters who make a committed annual pilgrimage to Wilcannia, the Central Desert, the Kimberley coast and the wilder reaches of our land. The brilliant colourist Elisabeth Cummings exploded the intimacy of still life into the broad expanses of the communities and desert places in which she painted. Her sense of place reflects a lifelong devotion to ecology, light and colour. I have reverence for the Indigenous artists who live 'in the landscape' and whose lives are lived seamlessly between art and existence. But for all my appreciation of the landscape, it is not the sum total of our art.

Is that a heresy, given my upbringing and my father's contribution to expanding and even exploding the genre of Australian landscape? In a word, no.

At UNSW, I was one of the first male students to enrol in a feminist subject, inspired by what I had learned from my mother. In the Art and Feminism class, one of the assignments was comparing feminine and masculine landscapes. Male artists frequently put themselves on top of the landscape, below the horizon, as if to say 'this is my land' when all they are doing is looking at it; women are more likely to place themselves within the landscape, looking at it more intimately, as Margaret Preston and my mother did. A lot of white male landscapers have approached the landscape like conquerors rather than as artists, taming and capturing the landscape with a desire to possess. My presence raised a few eyebrows back then; I was the progeny of what they were fighting against.

My enrolment in the course was not an attempt to be reactionary or politically correct. Growing up in a male-dominated art scene, I saw that it was subordination and oversight that prevented so much talent and great art from achieving respect and the place in art history it deserved. I was proud to realise that, without any deliberate curation, more women than men are represented in my gallery.

In his 2019 Wynne Prize entry *A Terrible Burden*, artist Abdul Abdullah transposed the words of its title—'a terrible burden'— over his landscape. It was a reference to my father's response when asked what it felt like to be 'Australia's greatest living artist': 'A terrible burden,' John had replied.

In his artist's statement, Abdullah referred to Australian landscape painters—including Dad, though not mentioning him by name—as seeking to own the landscape that they depicted. 'Like the settlers before them,' Abdullah wrote, 'the moral obligation to claim the Australian landscape is the cross they feel the need to bear.'

Rumour has it that the painting made it to the Wynne Prize's final three, but the AGNSW trustees could not select a picture that was derogatory towards a former longstanding donor, trustee and seminal artist. Considering Dad's deferential approach to the landscape he loves so much, Abdullah probably targeted the least appropriate artist.

Sitting in his studio recently, Dad and I were discussing how some art dealers get a bad rap because of the behaviour of a few. Some of Dad's favourite mottos are:

> When you ultimately leave this world, be remembered as someone who gave more than they took. Be remembered for your kindness and compassion. Use your ego to lift others, not to make other lives feel less.
>
> Let your authentic happiness be infectious, especially when people feel they can't find it in themselves.
>
> We are all creative in some form.
>
> Learn to recognise that the creative act is a process of self-discovery, not a competition. Make art for the enjoyment of it, not to prove something to others.
>
> Just make things without caring about what others might think. Be selfless and allow the spirits to work through you.

35

THE DANDY OF THE ART WORLD

Ray Hughes died in December 2017 at the age of 72. In his 45 years as an art dealer, he was painted for the Archibald almost annually. These paintings show the rake's progress, from a dandyish young man in pop-art ties and braces, to a crumpled body in a wheelchair topped by a reddened face with cloudy eyes and barely recognisable features. When someone's persona is that of a drinker, there will rarely be a portrait of them without a glass in their hand; in so many of Ray's portraits, the goblet of red was his griff.

Ray ran his Surry Hills gallery like an exclusive club. An old-school bon vivant like John, he held regular Thursday lunches that were a meeting of like minds, with animated conversation among the platters of gourmet food. I was never invited to one of Ray's lunches but heard and read about them: artists, writers, politicians and actors graced his table, and anyone whom he found interesting (but not pretentious) was invited and expected to contribute. The lavishly catered lunches were leisurely, and the discussions on art and politics were sometimes heated, always intelligent and frequently inspiring. Like Rudy Komon, Ray built lasting relationships with his artists, friends and clients over the dining table. Food and art, and the accompanying travel to source art, were his nourishment.

Ray and his son Evan were the perfect hosts, and the lunches rapidly became legendary. Journalist Steve Meacham from *The Sydney Morning Herald* attended one in 2012 and was surprised to see Tim Storrier in attendance; Ray and Storrier had had a momentous public falling out nearly two decades earlier. At the lunch, Meacham noted the guests' discussion about who should be included in a book about the most important people in the Sydney art scene. 'You'd have to have one of the Olsens,' someone said.

'But which one?' asked Tim Storrier.

Ray answered, 'Louise Olsen.' Which the table, of course, found hilarious, and the story appeared in the *Herald* the following weekend.[1]

On reading this, Dad shrugged it off immediately as the nonsense that it was. Tim Storrier was a longtime close friend of Dad's and the family. Unfortunately, at the time I was just out of rehab, still fragile, and I found it galling. It was a puerile comment meant as a witticism, but no one likes to be the very public butt of a joke. It is all water under the bridge now; Evan later wrote to me to apologise.

Ray had a sick liver. An angry liver makes an angry person. As he aged, and his health deteriorated, his tongue had become more and more acerbic, his behaviour erratic, often abusive and aggressive. The wit for which he was renowned was reduced to spite and eventually paranoia. He fought with artists, clients, anyone who frustrated or irritated him. Eventually he alienated his wife and, for a short time, his beloved son.

Yet I will always say that Ray had the best aesthetic and the most eclectic eye of any art dealer I have ever known. He was not bound by parochial taste. Ray was only 21 when he opened his first gallery but hit the jackpot when he bought the balance of Rudy Komon's stockroom after Rudy's death. The hundreds of works by Boyd, Blackman, Williams and Dobell raised his reputation and standing as an art dealer, attracting a new clientele, enabling him to cast his eye far and wide.

Aside from being an intimidating figure, Ray Hughes was also misunderstood by some. He was a pioneer in taste and vision, yet is possibly known more for his ties and his persona. It was Ray who introduced Judith Neilson, of White Rabbit Gallery, to the rising new wave of post-revolutionary contemporary Chinese artists at least a decade before it was in vogue with art critic John McDonald and museum curators; who filled his gallery with massive, gaudy, hand-carved and handpainted coffins shaped like shoes and chilli peppers from Ghana; and who championed art that was expressive, awkward and raw long after the wave of German neo-expressionism had soared and crashed in the mid-1980s.

Ray had a taste for folk, but he also had a taste for things that had an inner spirit. It wasn't just about pop art and derivative tribal objects. Some of the works had a real inner poetry; some were very selfless artworks. It really reflected that Ray was a gregarious person in lots of ways, but also that he was an isolator with an inner depth.

Whatever reservations he had about other dealers (and he had plenty), he truly loved art and his artists, inspiring loyalty and nurturing careers over decades. Like Rudy, if he didn't like you, he wouldn't sell works to you. He cared about where things ended up. It was a passion of process. He fostered the extreme originality of William Robinson, Joe Furlonger, Lucy Culliton and Davida Allen. He had a big belly, yes, but more importantly, when it came to showing what he liked, he had guts. He was often referred to as 'larger than life', a depiction his son Evan says he loathed. Size is irrelevant. Having had my own big belly, I could relate.

At his last Archibald in 2017, I encountered Ray, sitting in his wheelchair in front of his last portrait, which had been painted by one of his favourite artists, Jun Chen. Ray was having his photograph taken just as John was being photographed in front of his portrait by Nicholas Harding. Pointing to me, Ray exclaimed, 'There's Dorian Gray!'

Softly I replied, 'Hello, Oscar.' One of my favourite passages from *The Picture of Dorian Gray* by Oscar Wilde is the brutally frank assertion that posits whether it is possible to be a nice person and be an artist:

> The only artists I have ever known who are personally delightful are bad artists. Good artists exist simply in what they make, and consequently are perfectly uninteresting in what they are. A great poet, a really great poet, is the most unpoetical of all creatures. But the inferior poets are absolutely fascinating. The worse their rhymes are, the more picturesque they look. The mere fact of having published a book of second-rate sonnets makes a man quite irresistible. He lives the poetry that he cannot write. The others write the poetry that they dare not realise.[2]

The same rationale might be used for the art dealer. Usually when you encounter a sacred monster in the art world, their bark really is worse than their bite.

I always felt that Ray thought of me as a bit of an entitled upstart and, in my youth, he was partly right. There was a professional rivalry between us, and he was often put out when artists chose to exhibit elsewhere rather than be part of his stable. But perhaps in recompense for his habitual bagging (he used to refer to me as 'Little Timmy Olsen'), Ray invited me to his 70th birthday party. It was a rare gesture and an acknowledgement of finally being part of Ray's extended family.

Evan, too, knew all about living under the 'long shadow'. He had lived like I had lived, surrounded by crazy talismanic objects, falling asleep under noisy tables. From the age of about ten, when Ray had him fitted for handmade suits on their flamboyant trips to China, Evan was being trained to go into the art trade— braces, big ties and all. Presiding over an incredible building in Surry Hills and educated from knee-high to maturity in inter-national painting and sculpture, Evan had all the makings of a great dealer. That is a lot easier when dealing (and not making) art is in your line. Yet I understand why this sensitive and deeply intelligent young man chose to not follow in the footsteps of a famous and infamous patriarch. Dealing is rarely dynastic. You either live for it, or you run from it.

The Ray Hughes Gallery eventually became The Hughes Gallery, with Evan taking over. In 2015 he closed the doors, devoting himself to politics and running against Malcolm Turnbull. It was a courageous act to run for a left-wing party in a blue-ribbon Liberal electorate. He realised that his campaign had the potential to be swatted like a fly. Like a brother, I am proud of him for attempting it.

Being his father's travelling companion to exotic, some-times hazardous places was his education. Through Africa (searching for the art of voodoo), Europe, Asia and particularly China, their annual travels remain a highlight of his memo-ries. He frequently travelled with the artists from his father's stable, helping them forge relationships with artists from other cultures, widening their life experience, a supportive, nurturing figure. For Evan, his father's love of art will always be instilled in him. He has passed that on to his own son, saying, 'The fact that my little boy loves going to the AGNSW is the greatest gift Dad gave me.'

In autumn 2018, Shapiro held a two-day auction of Ray's treasures, *Ray Hughes—A Life with Art*.[3] When I went to the auction, it was like buying my own house back as there were so many pieces I remembered from growing up. There was neither rhyme nor reason in the way Ray collected. He was eclectic and anti-thematic. An art collection that has many parts always ends up in the same place—a place of diversity, representing the cross-pollination of civilisation. That is the essence of an interesting collection. A good art collection mirrors the world, and that's what Ray Hughes's did.

His philosophy on collecting and being an art dealer was well known:

> Being an art dealer is not about selling things. It's about somehow acquiring a bunch of things that are worth considering . . . Why can this stuff keep you involved for 40 years? Because it means something. Being chic or just making money, it's not enough. In a way it's about the poetic thoughts, the notion that you were there as something quite wonderful was flowering and you happened to be holding the hose. What price on that?[4]

One quality that Ray always extolled was abundance, and that virtue (among the sins) stood out at the auction. The variety and quality was incredible: you could buy a Bonnard, a Roger

Hilton, a Howard Hodgkin, a Fred Williams; there was a tapestry of John's, *Dunk Island*, that took two months to weave and that relates to *Five Bells* and the Sydney Opera House mural. All of this magical, pertinent stuff—you could not curate a show like that! It was a treasure trove.

Nearing the end of his life, Ray had worked with Evan to gift parts of his substantial collection: his favourite drawings to the AGNSW, a selection of prized works to the Queensland Art Gallery. Even after the donations and the auction, the remaining pieces are still posing a storage problem.

I felt Ray's ghost patting me on the back, telling me to go for it. It was almost sad, in a way, that after all the many meetings, journeys, experiences, and spontaneous and serendipitous events that had brought this collection together, it was all sold within a few hours under the hammer. You don't need to be friends, or even rivals, to learn something important from someone you respect. I look back on Ray now as a mentor. It was like Ray was still reaching out to provoke and question accepted ideas about taste. I draw no judgement on his life, but his gallery had bite: it was a thinking man's circus.

Each of us has memories that stick with us through time. I bumped into Ray and Evan in Paris one year on their travels. Evan, then only fourteen, was dressed up as Ray's doppelgänger in a wide-lapelled suit and tie, a smaller version of his father. We dined together, polishing off trays of oysters followed by boeuf bourguignon, then left to move on to a bar. Walking down the street, I could hear the sound of clinking and rattling from Evan's pockets. 'What's that noise?' I asked, and Evan, like a magician pulling scarves out of his hat, withdrew an ashtray, salt and pepper shakers, a plate—anything he had been able to fit into his pockets as a souvenir.

The next day we went to the quintessential symbol of Montparnasse's artistic history, La Coupole, for lunch. This heritage-listed art deco masterpiece is the most famous Parisian brasserie, a mecca for artists, writers and performers of the mid-twentieth century: Derain, Léger, Soutine, Man Ray, Picasso, Matisse, Hemingway, Henry Miller, James Joyce, Sartre, Chagall. The pillars and pilasters were all decorated in 1927 by 27 artists, each hand-selected by a committee, including Auffray, Grünewald, Latapie, Rij-Rousseau, Seifert and Friesz. It is a must-see experience.

Two famous French primitive art dealer friends of Ray's were at the next table. They were so drunk they passed out, asleep, virtually crashing into their plates, something I had never seen before. In hindsight, it certainly minimised Ray's and my own drinking problems. Evan left again with his usual restaurant souvenirs jingling in his pockets. I was shocked, but Ray was spurring him on!

Much later, I recounted to Evan the story of his delinquent days, and we laughed. When I was in Europe in 2019 with Dom and James, he sent me one of the plates that he had appropriated. God knows how he had managed that one: it must have looked like a codpiece, or have been tucked under his jacket at the back.

36

PATERNITY

In the seven years I struggled to get sober, there was one crucial thing on my mind: to redeem myself in the eyes of my son. If the first half of my life was spent trying to connect to my own father, trying to resonate with him in so many subtle and obvious ways, then the second act is definitely about being a better father to my own boy.

There is a photograph on my wall at home of James on his first day at Cranbrook School; it sits next to one of myself at the same age. Our eyes are both shadowed by the Cranbrook School cap, squinting into the sun. We have the same Scandinavian blue eyes and blond hair, but my boy is not me; he is perhaps a subtler branch of the Olsen/Ogilvie tree.

When I think of how much I love James, it feels so whole and total. I feel responsible for how he sees and feels the world. Although it does feel like I let him down in the same way we felt when our parents divorced: the breakdown of the love between a mother and a father, as children of divorce often feel. Separating from Dom felt like an echo of my past and

366

a perpetuation of three generations of paternal failing. I had simply become a different person, it was no fault of hers.

As a young child, James was the most beautiful little boy—angelic, like a child in a Raphael, sweet natured with a happy disposition. As a small child he was a hugger and you could not give him enough affection, though these days hugs and kisses aren't cool.

After rehab, I was walking on eggshells as a parent, trying to earn his trust again. It was a measure of Dom's belief in my recovery that she trusted me enough to take him on holiday. I took James to Port Douglas when he was about six. We stayed at a lovely resort and went out fishing daily on the reef. As we had our own kitchen, we cooked the fish that we caught and made hand-cut chips, then sat out by the pool, looking at the view, to eat our catch of the day. He loved it, and it helped me come full circle to my memories of Dad when I had been his age.

Dom was fulfilled as a mother; it became her everything. I have always struggled with trying not to repeat history, that frequent and subtle sense I had that everything else was always more important to Dad than me. I never want to do this to James. I want to keep him elevated, so he can become who he was born to be. There is still the constant fear that he may suffer addiction and my hope is that he will remember where I was, and where I am now—still flawed but trying my best.

Children are born to surprise you, to occasionally shock you, and James has always had a bit of a pious streak. His favourite song as a four-year-old was James Blunt's 'Here We Go Again'. In the car he would want us to play it over and over again; the first thing he would say on being strapped in his car seat was 'Daddy put on "Here We Go Again"!' On another day when he was a few years older, before I drove the car into the garage, he demanded, 'Daddy, stop, stop.' He let himself out of the car and looked up to the sun as it headed down over the buildings towards the west, then raised his open hand to the sky and exclaimed, 'God, I repent, I repent!' I struggled to work out how he could know of such a righteous act; he was still so young and had spent barely any time in church or religious study except a couple of Christmas services.

Since then, James has enhanced my understanding and the possible belief in reincarnation, certainly in spirituality. Always an intuitive and deep thinker for a young child, he has an innate inner goodness and impulse to be kind that comes instinctively. It brought back my own religious leanings as a child. Dad had those leanings, too, so it must go back to our Presbyterian roots on both sides. He remembers standing outside his house in Newcastle on a wheelbarrow at around six years of age, yelling at the passers-by: 'Jesus Christ will get you bastards!'

I have been guilty of smoothing the yellow brick road for James to compensate for the lost early years, and am not alone in that as a parent. A lot of modern parents use money to compensate for their absences or distractions, to steamroll the path and make the magic happen. We romanticise the simplicity of our own childhoods and ramp up the materialism for our offspring. But deep down we know the real luxury is time. These days I am there with James for the day-to-day and the milestone moments.

As a young boy, James was not really aware of what the gallery openings were about but knew that something important was happening. He always attended openings, even as a baby, and by the time he was around six or seven, Dom would dress him up in a hat and scarf, a debonair mini-me. He would position himself as close as possible when he knew I was about to speak, and if the crowd did not quieten down immediately he would stand on the nearest chair and demand loudly, 'Everyone be quiet as Daddy wants to say something.'

I have never broached the subject of James taking over the gallery, and have never assumed that he will be anything other than his own person. He probably will not work out what he wants to do with his life until he is around 30 anyway, as I did. I am proud to have raised such a confident, outgoing young man, secure in his own self.

Like most others of his age, he has not yet worked out his true strengths but applies himself fully to everything he tackles; knowing my rugby history, he has played continually from an early age, and Dad and I have enjoyed watching him play, taking us both back to my own games at King's. These days he is obsessed with American 1990s West Coast grunge music and has taken to playing the guitar.

James is aware now of his privileged position, the legacy he has inherited, and does not take anything for granted. Growing up in a gallery environment seemed perfectly normal to him, just as growing up surrounded by artists seemed normal to me. I wish I had had his confidence but take comfort when I see him striding through life, comfortable in any social situation. Older people love him! Never intimated, he enjoys meeting new people in whatever capacity, especially when it entails receiving hugs from the likes of Naomi Campbell or Elle Macpherson.

He was always obsessed with animals and their welfare, running out to visit the horses and especially the miniature Shetland pony, Benson, at John's farm, and playing with the family dogs. When he was little he would cry if he saw an animal suffering on television or elsewhere, and would hold burials in the park next door to the gallery whenever a goldfish in the gallery pool died. A year ago we had a tragedy when the pump in the pool stopped working; there are several goldfish waiting for James in the gallery freezer still.

Dropping him off to Geelong Grammar's Timbertop outreach boarding school last year, we witnessed his advanced maturity and inner strength. It is known as the school of tough love, a place that removes any attitudes of entitlement, without computer screens, mobile phones or the direct ability to cry for help to the outside world. There is no way of calling your mum if you are homesick, with letters the only form of communication allowed for any expression toward your loved ones. Still, James was excited by the notion of a solitary year of hardly seeing his family. He accepted this experience as an opportunity. After a privileged childhood being smothered and spoilt by daily love, it was time for him to learn about his deeper self and develop his independence. To enhance his ability to think for himself—and give him an insight into living alongside the opposite sex, as the school is co-ed. As we were leaving the bush institution that first day, with parents and children alike emotional and scared by this loving form of deliberate abandonment, James was only exhilarated. I was proud to see him console another boy who was clearly upset at being left behind. He had automatically taken it upon himself to nurture and care for others. He is able to express his feelings so openly now, and has grown in confidence in his validation of self, having learned how to live with others and to share.

We are blessed to have such a fine and honest son, who possesses emotional intellect and sensitivity, and who thinks of others before himself. He gave me the courage to value my own life. Instead of drinking myself to death, he gave me the inspiration to be a better man, beyond just being a better father. In a sense, he saved my life. Like most parents, we were never given a handbook on how to be parents; Dad, in turn, had been abandoned by his own father in his own way, and his father by *his* father (or so he always thought). It has taken a long time for us to move on, and my father is still pained by memories of his own upbringing.

With James being an only child, he has had to work at building relationships with people his own age, but unlike me he is not afraid to ask for help if he needs it. I try very much to have patience, especially when I see James struggling a little as all of us do as we go through adolescence. With this in mind, I try to be accepting and understanding, and offer support and advice.

My father, because of my sobriety, found a pride in me that brought him joy. Today we finally have a semblance of a healthy father–son relationship, possibly through the blessing of having James. Suffering can be passed down through generations, through the sins of the father, but I believe that the parental troubles for this line of Olsen men are finally over. Philip Larkin sheds light on the precariousness of parenting in his poem 'This Be the Verse':

They fuck you up, your mum and dad.
They may not mean to, but they do.
They fill you with the faults they had
And add some extra, just for you.

But they were fucked up in their turn
By fools in old-style hats and coats,
Who half the time were soppy-stern
And half at one another's throats.

Man hands on misery to man.
It deepens like a coastal shelf.
Get out as early as you can,
And don't have any kids yourself.[1]

Both Louise and I were becoming increasingly concerned about Dad's health, and at one point we did not think he would make it to his 90th birthday. So we were relieved when he arrived two days early to the big lunch at the gallery. On the eve of his actual birthday, on 21 January, we went out to dinner, arriving home at 10.30 p.m. Thinking he would need to rest, I suggested that we should retire, having the big celebration day the following day, but he insisted on another glass of wine and we sat up chatting about life, gossiping like two old women. One glass turned into two, two into three, and time had suddenly slipped away. Normally he is not one for what he refers to as the 'late, late show', but this time he was determined. The clock struck midnight and I was exhausted, but his eyes were keen and glittering. 'Dad, can we please go to bed now?' I implored.

He replied, 'Yes, we can now. I just wanted to make sure I reached 90!' He can be a tricky bugger, but there's always a method behind his wiliness.

The lunch was a huge success. Barry Humphries gave a great speech; my friend Warren Fahey, a folk-music expert, brought his accordion along and sang bush ballads and drovers' songs, to the delight of Dad and the crowd. Dad has always loved bush poetry and folklore. His love of literature and poetry has fuelled his endless capacity for metaphor and looking at life.

Dad makes his artistic plans as if he is going to live forever. The picture finished the day before is a precursor to the one to be started on the following day. Exhibitions are segments of a body of work. No singular work defines the beginning of a show, and none define the end. The body is a vehicle, not an engine. Artists are conduits. When they claim their art with their ego, they shut down the muse.

The day I turned 56 was a bittersweet day for me. It was the age at which Jane, my elder half-sister, had died. I had lunch with Dad at the farm, and he gave me a beautiful book on the Papunya Tula desert painters. I realised that I have been fortunate in my life. When a family name attracts kudos, as the name Olsen does, the second or third generation sometimes has to work twice as hard to prove themselves. There is a perception of entitlement.

Yet life has given me my fair share of lumps and bruises, and learning to overcome obstacles has been character building, personally and professionally. My exterior life may have looked fantastic, but my interior life was miserable. Now, having worked through all this, I have nothing but gratitude for all the good and bad things. The mistakes have been the greatest lessons.

37

MOVING ON

While somewhat irritating, you have to take it as a compliment when other galleries try to poach staff and artists. There is a natural progression with staff: the younger ones tend to leave to travel or return to study, so as one goes another appears. The standing of the gallery means that we are approached by students wanting to intern or work, and we essentially always find staff by word of mouth. It is gratifying that people want to work at the gallery and enjoy the whole working experience; the inclusion of the gallery name on their résumé can be extremely beneficial. Additionally, it gives them the opportunity to work with and learn from talented and experienced longtime staff such as Katrina. It is gratifying to have staff move on to senior positions with other institutions in the knowledge that their time with the gallery has been advantageous in securing their position.

The poaching of artists is another issue and something that all gallerists can be accused of to varying degrees. To be a commercially viable, curatorial, interesting, diverse and inclusive gallery without your stable looking like a dog's breakfast can be, at times, a real juggling act. Getting the right mix of artists is like putting together an intelligent menu in a restaurant: you want variation without losing your visual identity.

New galleries opening creates a larger art market and, in turn, more awareness of the idea of living with art. It is an ever-evolving, widening circle of venues that in turn can stimulate more people to become collectors. To embrace even just one piece of art places you in the category of collector. As the gallery owner, my responsibility is to consistently elevate the visual and intellectual substance of my existing and future artists. To stimulate collectors, the artists and staff alike. To experience and work with extraordinary art and artists is a privilege.

Artists are capricious, clannish and susceptible, and form definite cliques in their social circles. Some years ago, some artists left me in quick succession to go to other galleries. When one left, another followed, and this led me first to disillusion and, in time, to an inevitable curatorial shift in the gallery's prevailing aesthetic. Although disappointing at the time, from a curatorial perspective, the shift was ultimately highly fruitful and remunerative.

When an artist is discovered by and joins a gallery, they are nurtured, and much investment goes into their promotion, their shows and catalogues, and encouraging awareness of their body of work with collectors and the press. For gallery owners such as Rudy Komon and myself, an investment in an artist is emotional as well as material. You literally have to anticipate their potential—their future—before they can. My intuition is one thing, but not everyone will always agree. It can be hit or miss. Fortunately, so far, it has been more hit than miss.

When you believe in an artist, it's all encompassing. You need to know they have somewhere to work and live and a good place for their kids to go to school. That they are happy, secure and productive. Their success is the gallery's success.

The boozy lack of boundaries when I socialised with my artists in the early years has evolved into a slightly warier but more respectful professional relationship, still sometimes a little volatile and often emotional. We are not selling tyres but showing shards of the human soul. Nothing makes me feel better than seeing the lives of artists I have known and shown for nearly 30 years blossom.

I asked Dad recently what qualities he thought I had as a dealer, from his perspective as an artist in my stable, not just as my father. He said:

> First of all, you know what you are talking about, the benefit of listening to endless conversations . . . You have been listening to the vernacular, the engine room of what artists think your entire life. On top of that you had a developing eye, now a good eye and are able to articulate it. Plus you have the proper business sense. There are many, many galleries, it is something like opening a restaurant, but you must have a good business sense to be able to handle money and be responsible with the money that belongs to the artist. So, it comes in a parcel, and I would have to add ambition, and from then on, it's bon voyage.

While so many people focus on the hardships of the artist's path, I believe the focus should be on the opposite. This compulsion is a rarity, not a cross to bear! Feel the joy of making art. Feel lucky and grateful you have been given the life to be an artist. This is no activity for the faint-hearted. If the thought of creating art does not continuously excite you, then you are not fulfilling your part of the creative process. If you do not love art or the idea of being an artist completely, forget it. This is a club for the passionate and courageous. This is a mindset, not a dream.

The best mathematics you can do is to calculate the future cost of your current decisions. The gallery has backed some winners and losers over its lifetime, has turned strugglers into winners, with some winners regressing over time. Owning any business is a constant gamble. Galleries have come and gone, while we have prevailed. Yet every day I still wake up exhilarated, feeling like we have only just begun.

Once upon a time everyone had a horse and only the rich had a car. Now everyone has a car and usually only the rich have horses. Judging by the plethora of biennales and art fairs, art has never been so widely appreciated or so bankable. Many galleries were once owned by people just madly passionate about art, without consideration for the monetary returns. Now certain collectors have become art dealers, and there are galleries now owned or backed by entrepreneurs and private billionaire patrons. Art philanthropy means that people can give to institutions out of the generosity of their heart, sharing their collections with the people (and get a tax deduction). Many of the collections in our public galleries have been built upon the generosity of these patrons. The evolution of privately owned art foundations is changing the cultural landscape, with some rivalling public museums with their exhibits, collections and influence. Art, in some countries, has become the latest sport of kings.

The rudest correspondence I have ever received was a vitriolic fax from an artist whom I did not wish to show. I retained the printed message to remind myself that some of my decisions in politely declining certain artists were sound ones—and to remind myself to never, ever send an email or communication when angry. When artists vent their frustration at rejection, it has to be taken as an inverted compliment.

The sweetest letter ever written to me was from artist Sophie Cape, a dear friend. Her handwritten letter is framed and hangs on my apartment wall. The abusive rant from the other artist is pasted on the back as its true obverse.

I had 'discovered' Sophie with the guidance of Bill Wright, who led me to her studio at the National Art School and said, simply, 'This one's got it.' Obviously, my father agreed as he awarded her the National Art School Drawing Prize the same day, completely without my knowledge.

Sophie is an original working artist with a haptic and visceral relationship to nature. Her work is raw and immersive, with an art performative aspect. In the sense that the way it is made is something of a St Vitus dance as she drags charred wood across vast pieces of art paper, paints with raw pigments dug from a riverbed, and weathers the surface of her monumental works in wind, rain and the baking sun.[1]

Dad and I fell on Sophie's work, loving it. Between us we awarded her a drawing prize every year that she was at the National Art School. When we saw her work, we were astonished by the sophistication of it, the drive, and I offered her an exhibition as soon as she graduated. Sophie looks and has the charisma of a rock star. She just has what it takes. A former elite athlete, before multiple injuries and overtraining blocked her path to the Olympic Games, Sophie has a drive and an intense focus that are both evident in her work.[2]

She comes from an artistic family. Her grandmother Gwenna Welch and her mother Ann Cape were both artists, and have been shown in the Archibald and won many awards. Like me with Dad, Sophie felt that she was being constantly compared to her mother at art school until she created her own style and bold approach. Loving working en plein air, she throws paint around, hauling her canvases through the bush, attracted by the chaos and uncertainty of nature. In 2014, she climbed to Mount Everest base camp, carrying her canvas on her back, through rivers and over the ice. Everybody at base camp signed the back of the canvas.

When it comes to Sophie's creative trajectory, the best of her work is still ahead.

An established auctioneer, Chris Deutsche, said to me once, 'Don't blow all the money you make out of your father by investing in too many young emerging artists.' Representing young artists is a gamble, but we are continually proud to see good ones come of age under the gallery's flag.

Having listened to my father complaining about his dealers—not being paid, not providing enough in return for the commissions levied, pressuring artists to produce work with complete disregard for their circumstances, neglecting one artist for another, and more—I know both sides of the coin all too well. This makes me in one sense not your average dealer, as I have empathy for the challenges an artist can face, for both male and female artists—and yes, there are still differences.

My goal now is to nurture more emerging artists and to ensure the longevity and ongoing success of the more established ones. I have no wish to radically change the commercial art-gallery system, but will continue to improve our presentation, service and knowledge to the benefit of our artists, clients and staff. My own experiences as a dealer, and those vicariously with Dad, have presented almost every possible variation in working in the art world. My aim is to impart my unique experience—for the love of art, and the respect of my artists. This book may give an insight into my life and who I am, but it is the artists who create the magic and draw the crowd.

The biggest issue that galleries and artists are currently facing is not dealers short-changing artists but the artists themselves becoming the dealers. With websites and social media, many collectors are now going directly to artists. The artists see the opportunity to make a sale on the side, 'back-dooring', avoiding paying the gallery their commission. For them, it seems like a win–win but instead can be a catastrophic career move, affecting their long-term livelihood, reputation and, ultimately, their legacy. Word gets out, and the artist's market price becomes affected as their collectors lose trust. This creates a platform of distrust that can rot the symbiotic artist–dealer relationship. Quick, dirty money in the long run is not good karma.

This is not just a financial issue, but one about the quality of the work and mutual trust. When an artist is selling their best work privately, they cannot reasonably expect the dealer to still hold regular exhibitions when it suits the artist. As in any relationship, loyalty, transparency and honesty are paramount.

The dealer is not the devil. I want to be able to look my artists in the eye, knowing that they have always been paid promptly and that they have total faith in my supporting the financial side of their career. Trust is the foundation of all relationships, creative, romantic or otherwise.

While it is true that their gallery, collectors, critics, museums and the public play invaluable roles in an artist's success, many artists today have risen to a standard of repute (and maintained their position there) by virtue of their own capacity to market themselves like the YBAs. 'Public recognition' is no longer the final frontier to be crossed before an artist achieves success; rather, instant public recognition appears to be a major requirement for any highly ambitious, competitive and impatient artist.

Contemporary art institutions and poor funding are often linked to commercial sponsorship, and this link is too often ignored. For instance, institutional shows are not given to artists solely based on merit, but on what fiscal objectives need to be met. The argument that commerciality and fame are interrelated forces is not a new one—as vulgar as it may be considered by the purists—but it is more patent and transparent now in our digital economy, and the ethical standards of public institutions deserve more thorough interrogation. Certain collectors have been known to contribute financially to sponsor a retrospective or survey show to ensure that their personal works are included, thus strengthening the provenance and subsequent commercial value of those works. In contrast, so many collectors are willing to lend works on the basis that they would never sell them.

The gallery's reputation has grown through us consistently exhibiting good artists with a proven track record of originality, quality and longevity. As art advisors, clients look to us to guide them in building their own collections, whether a single purchase or multiple works, without the limitations of stable or locality. Good art is ageless and crosses all genres. Limiting oneself to a particular approach—to purely postmodernism or conceptual art, for example—can adversely distract the client from works that may be the better fit.

Every exhibition, every piece of art, is a milestone in the midst of endlessness, in a continuous story of how artists and humans experience life, how they feel and what they see. The ways of looking at the figure, still life and landscape continually evolve. When I look at a lot of new abstract art, I see derivations of what artists were creating in the last century. In this aspect, the more we change the more we stay the same.

When teaching, I used to say that nobody can really fail at art unless they refuse to participate. Unless working in realism, you cannot make mistakes, if you have no observer. The act of making art should be applauded in itself. However, there is good and bad art, according to the artist's skill, their aesthetic, and their spiritual and emotional intellect. Art is a physical representation of human and world history. Humanity tends to want to separate what is right and wrong, good and evil. Art is the material mask of eternity that can reveal the contradictory morals we see throughout the history of the human condition. The polarities of art and its inner thinking can reflect both virtue and sin.

Many curators and critics often dismissively write off much interesting and skilful art as decorative. However, decorative art can take you to a place of deeper consciousness, where one may feel peace and self-reflection, unlike some conceptual art. Not all art has to possess an underlying metaphor. It is how it is able to transport you to a place that provokes deeper thoughts and emotions that determines its intrinsic value. The attitude of decorative art being a lesser form of creativity, by many conceptualists, is snobbery. The art experience cannot be prejudiced as being banal because it is pleasurable to view.

Pleasure seeking in art is not lacking in intellect; it can be a very pertinent experience, but it doesn't necessarily need to address the axioms of culture, politics or global issues. Some conceptual art is undoubtedly decorative. Cy Twombly is recognised as a great draughtsman, but is a scribbler to others. Bridget Riley's work can be viewed as an exercise in intellectual geometry and colour field, while some have described her work as wallpaper.

These modern artists now have a place in contemporary conceptual art and passed the test of time despite the decorative undertones. The important aspect of such art is that it still provides a sense of hope for drawing and colour, while facilitating a connection to believing and recognising the artist's deeper thoughts and feelings.

All art can be considered decorative according to the individual viewer. What one may find an aesthetic experience is ugly to someone else. Hence why we desire to live with it daily and intimately. It provides a kind of visual and physiological sustenance. Much like beauty is in the eye of the beholder. Developing an eye and passion for art is also a process of exploring and expanding your own consciousness. My father always said, 'There is nothing wrong with what people like, no matter what any critic says.'

My philosophy is simple: buy work that speaks to you personally. Look at everything, listen to sound advice, but know that ultimately the decision is yours. Buy what you love.

From the very first day, I have been integral in how the gallery is curated. Early on, we made good commercial decisions with regard to what was shown, with some more decorative works mixed in with some more cutting-edge artists. While some of those artists may have envisaged being with a more pointy-headed, curatorial-orientated gallery, there were financial rewards in being in my stable as I ran the gallery as a business, never an indulgence. This meant continually investing back into the gallery, buying stock, until the gallery became an asset, a branded business.

A gallery is based upon your stable, the stockroom, and the prospect of new, quality works from artists. My artists' works are often acquired by institutions and serious collectors and, most importantly, they are bought by passionate people who truly love the work, with little regard for art investment. Often the best art investments come out of buying for love. The hardest thing is often selling.

My education turned me into a capable artist, but my temperament was not that of a true artist. Then I wanted to be a teacher and, in a way, being an art gallerist *is* being a teacher: through selling people art, referential knowledge and knowing how to make it. My success is aligned with both recognising talent, and convincing and educating collectors how to appreciate it. Without ever picking up a brush, I have found a niche in the art world that involves a different kind creativity. Dad says that I may not have got the temperament of an artist and that I am blessed not to have the gambling gene from his father: Pop would bet on two flies crawling up a wall. But I certainly inherited his appreciation of women and the penchant for a tipple.

Not all art is to everyone's taste, and sometimes you have to hold exhibitions that are not a commercial venture to showcase a particular artist's groundbreaking work. Knowing these shows are not going to be financially successful is frustrating but a necessary part of a contemporary art gallery's modus operandi. To run a successful gallery is also to understand the need for constant reinvention.

A gallery has to have depth, engaging in a larger dialogue that addresses art history to a point. To only show older or younger artists will limit a gallery's relevance in the broader art world.

I have an intergenerational gallery; there are few who can say that they represent important post-war moderns. So many of the people who come in to buy an Olsen or Williams ask who is up and coming, and often end up walking away with the work of one of my younger artists. This is the same model that Gagosian, White Cube and David Zwirner employ.

All art success is a team effort, the alchemy of triumph created in conjunction with the effort of employees and the historical reputation of a gallery. Staff are paramount; for me, Katrina is very much part of the mechanism in how the business is run, the vital cog—or perhaps even the axle. A dealer might blame failures on the artist and proclaim, 'Oh, their work went off'; an artist might say, 'Oh, the gallery did nothing'. Both accusations can have their basis in truth, but often it is the collector who determines the success of sales, and frequently collectors have their own conditions to consider—a financial crisis, a viral pandemic—beyond whether they like a work or not.

Watching Dad work quietly away, with only the sound of a brush caressing the canvas, it seems sometimes that there was a kind of channelling occurring, a dealing with the intangible to make it real.

For me, the function of art is to reveal, through the work, the underlying radiance that is experienced in sacred objects, painted or otherwise. Art should possess an integral construct that reveals an order to life, so that when you see it, you consciously or subconsciously recognise something that gives you that 'Aha!' moment.

Watching artists create works has always fascinated me, and generally it all happens in silence. Dad sometimes works with music, but Mum used to say, 'Your father has never really been a musical man. He likes to party to music, but not to work to music.' He finds that music can be a distraction. The mind of a genius often operates, and masterpieces can be created, in tranquillity. When watching art documentaries with classical music playing in the background, John has often said that it belies the fact that nearly everything we were looking at was made in an environment of peace and silence. This stanza from W.B. Yeats's poem 'Long-Legged Fly' is one of John's favourites, and exemplifies this:

That girls at puberty may find
The first Adam in their thought,
Shut the door of the Pope's chapel,
Keep those children out.
There on that scaffolding reclines
Michael Angelo.
With no more sound than the mice make
His hand moves to and fro.
Like a long-legged fly upon the stream
His mind moves upon silence.[3]

38

LOUISE

I think that my sister might be the most famous unfamous person in the world. Her designs have been worn by Venus Williams, Jennifer Lopez, Jessica Alba, Kylie Minogue and Alicia Keys, but stop someone on a Manhattan street corner with a *Vogue* magazine in your hand and they would say, 'Louise who?' That doesn't bother her. She is like a silent bee in the centre of a hive, as happy in the collective hum as in a glamorous magazine. Her existence seems to pivot on making. There has not been a day in my life when she has not had something in her slender, frenetic hands: a stubby crayon, a beaded necklace, a ball of mutable clay. She wears success lightly, and she gives back quietly. Her most touching achievements are the causes she cares about—design development and ecology—and how the Dinosaur Design studios never miss an Earth Day.

The success of her business can be attributed to two factors, one very plain and the other rather more unpredictable. The bare-bones essence of building an international design house—as Grayson Perry says of success in the art world—is 'staying on the bus'. In other words, it is about persisting with your own aesthetic mission no matter what the climate or what the season is like. Despite our haphazard upbringing, Louise is very good at staying the course. Her other very public 'secret' is a relentless, never-ending and churning cauldron of ideas. She is a perpetual creative, restless in the urge to make something, forever foraging, drawing and kneading a form until it transmutes into art. Louise thinks like a sculptor. A pebble in her hands becomes a monolith.

I am proud of Louise because she is a silent achiever, and she is proud of me because I stopped drinking. It had caused her so much concern: 'Oh Timmy, you were naughty,' she says, with characteristic understatement. When reading this to Louise, she immediately replied that stopping drinking was not the only thing—she was proud of my 'natural talent of putting the most beautiful gallery together and as an artist'. She said I have 'incredible insight and see the funny in all things' and that I have 'a great imagination'. Hearing this made me quite emotional. I love my sister!

Sometimes over the years we have had our moments, but it has always been real. We both know how to press one another's buttons. I used to feel we had a competitive relationship growing up, possibly more so because, to me, Dad seemed sometimes to play us off one another. He was at times aloof, so we would both continually seek his approval. Trying to be Daddy's favourite does not pollute our friendship anymore, since we have both reached a point of forgiveness and wholeness in our own lives and in our work, as parents and as creative thinkers.

Louise saw more of Mum than I did, which meant they were probably closer, and I never knew where to fit into the dynamic between mother and daughter. Subtle rifts developed when I was at boarding school and Louise was the full-time daughter, with all of the emotional demands that implies, but as children we never seriously fought. We have been comrades in life's ups and downs, and we are now so close that we sometimes dispense with the niceties: if Louise calls me or I call her, there is rarely a 'hello'. She is much more direct with me than anyone else, and knows how to cut me down to size if she has to.

We have both been lucky enough to have been allotted creative gifts from our parents; Louise is the more visual one—she is more creative with her hands and very artistic, especially now that she is painting again. I, too, inherited artistic skill (without the temperament to be an artist) and am the more articulate one. Mum and I had some very real and intimate conversations, though at times I would avoid Mum because she would only tell me the brutal truths that I did not want to hear, particularly when it came to my alcoholism and obesity.

One thing we both did inherit, with the mixed blessing of our background, is a complete faith in the nobility of a creative life. Money, power and politics do not mean much to either of us. To be an artist is to be more real.

Louise has incredible tenacity. In the early days, Louise, Stephen Ormandy and Liane Rossler took a small stand at Paddington Markets selling jewellery—brooches made of Fimo, a type of polymer oven-baked clay—and textiles.[1] Later, they formed Dinosaur Designs. They stuck at and honed it, and it grew into a multimillion-dollar international design and homewares brand. Dinosaur Designs is an Australian original that translates easily to SoHo New York or Soho London, and the success of the label is all seeded in art. Mum and Dad took something of a risk sending Louise to a Steiner school as they did not adhere to a standard curriculum, but the school advocated creative expression, and the primal shapes, delicate earthy colours and sensuality of her sculptural aesthetic form the entire basis of her success.

Louise and Steve went from strength to strength. They were invited to exhibit at the 9 Australia and the Contemporary Art of Dress show at the Victoria & Albert Museum in London in 1989 and created a sculpture commission for GoMA in Brisbane.

Louise's imagination and creative fire amaze me. She is always making something, whether those first creations in clay at Dunmoochin or something she mocked up in her studio yesterday. The walls of her office are jam-packed with images of contemporary art and the beauty of raw nature: she can roll a gum leaf around her wrist and cast it in gold, and suddenly it evolves into an exquisite piece of jewellery. There are stones, crystals, pebbles and feathers all over her desk; it looks more like the office of a nineteenth-century naturalist and explorer than a 21st-century CEO and designer. She is a natural artist.

On opening up a new Dinosaur Designs catalogue, I am always pleasantly surprised that there are so many new ideas. Louise keeps coming up with more and more haptic visions that are linear, fluid and quietly iconic.

As an Aquarius, Louise thrives beautifully in the abstract stream of ideas. As a Taurus, I am much more pragmatic, sorting things out on a practical plane, slowly and steadily. Louise was like a Botticelli Venus as a child and young woman, ethereal, floating inside her shell. She wasn't aware of her beauty and, like Mum, she has very little vanity. She has innate style and has always dressed well, even when she has had a very limited wardrobe.

Her first serious relationship was with photographer Jon Lewis. He was a little older than Louise, and it probably filled a void after Dad had left; we were both seeking mentors. There is a beautiful portrait that he took of Louise and Dad in front of his studio at Clarendon, South Australia, during Dad's marriage to Noela.

Louise and Stephen Ormandy had been longtime friends, meeting at art school where the students were grouped alphabetically by surname. It now seems inevitable that they would have ended up together, their friendship blossoming into so much more. Stephen is her creative and life partner, and the father of their beautiful daughter Camille. Louise has had a tremendously successful and remarkably long relationship with a man who believes that she is the most beautiful woman on Earth. Louise and Stephen recently published a book of their work, their ideas and philosophy, *The Art of Dinosaur Designs*.[2] The book is a chronicle of decades of work that shows the progression of their ideas, illuminating their ability to keep evolving. Their story is about passion, about the love of creating. The depth of who they are as people is something that permeates their work. There is a celebration of life that goes beyond design.

Dinosaur Designs has stores in London, New York and Tokyo. When she opened her store in London, a place of great wealth (for some), Louise was astonished to see rich women enter the stores, spending thousands buying literally whole cabinets of colourful jewellery. She loves the idea that these women are celebrating her work, adding colour to enhance their lives.

Louise adapted to convention the hard way. After travelling around Europe, then back to Vaucluse Public School when we lived in Watsons Bay, Dunmoochin and lastly the Steiner primary school, for senior school she was sent to Tara Anglican Girls' School. After having had such an alternative education, she found herself among girls better versed in English, maths and the sciences, and, like me at the same age, she was behind academically. As a result, she was singled out, assumed to be unintelligent and teased endlessly, in and out of the classroom. The world-famous actor Rebel Wilson was also an alumnus of Tara, a while after Louise. She, too, has expressed how she felt like a black sheep at the school, preferring to spend most of her time in the school library.

Louise knows me too well. She calls me 'Timmy' like a haughty older sister even though she is two years younger than me! I might be a bit more hardened than Louise by virtue of going to school with country boys whose opinions were black and white. While I am artistic, Louise is completely arty. It is a huge and sometimes amusing difference between us. Louise still lives in a lovely dreamland, which is a great contradiction: she is so commercially successful, yet she lives in an ethereal utopia. Some part of her keeps the best parts of our childhood alive: the mystical afternoons in Dural, sculpting clay; the affectionate secret coven she shared with Mum, making things in silence; that concentrated stillness we were both shown, but that Louise perfected and still emanates.

Louise is better at holding and building her assets than I am. Her nature is patient, with an eye to the long game; like Mum, she sees the light in the room before the objects. She treasures details and translates them with subtlety into many mediums. I notice in her styling, photography and campaigns that there are always long, slender, beautiful hands. It is as if the secret message is pointing to the self-sufficiency of all that can be made and held in a human hand. For an artist, your hand is really just an extension between the mind, the heart and the soul.

In many ways, Louise is very similar to Mum. She understands the power of simplicity. As children, our parents worried so much about us: what is going to become of these children who constantly travel? How will they make their way in the world after such an unconventional childhood? How will they fit into society? Her drive answered that question in a way that did not, until recently, involve a paintbrush. Essentially, as siblings, we are very lucky because both of our parents were great artists. I think that the underlying belief in creativity gave Louise her quiet strength and the idea that the future is in your own hands. Literally.

Louise has always considered herself as an artist, and she is. Art was a natural pursuit; we thought everyone did it. 'For me it was never a choice; it totally seeped into me since the day I was born,' she says. Louise made woodcuts with Mum, and her schoolbooks were full of colourful illustrations. It seemed predestined that she would eventually return to painting at some point.

Louise had the same reticence with her art that I had had: the reluctance to be compared to Dad, the desire to create her own unique style and to follow her own creative endeavours and vision. She was also rather shy of showing her paintings, even though her designs were being displayed internationally.

Louise and John had already collaborated together in her primary art form—resin sculpture—creating a frog (of course) and a fish, individually cast and handpainted by them both. They had been invited to create the limited-edition pieces for the NGV in celebration of John's 2016–17 retrospective. He calls them his 'feelies' and strokes them absentmindedly while talking. 'Dad's an explorer: it was wonderful to grow up with someone like that,' Louise said at the time. 'The resin's a new material for him—he also did an owl and a beautiful long fish—and he loved it.'[3]

Louise started attending John's life-drawing groups at his

farm on Saturday mornings and quickly progressed to painting. Louise and Stephen had presented a touring exhibition of their design work, so when the Newcastle Art Gallery invited them both to hold a celebratory exhibition of their work, Louise decided that this would be the perfect way to present her art. Seeing her enthusiasm, John turned Katharine's old study into one for her and she began to completely focus, almost obsessively, on painting. John was fascinated by her progress and would go into the studio to watch her work, sharing her passion. Sometimes he had to be told, 'Dad! Back off!'

Just a year later, Louise exhibited her work for the first time alongside Stephen's in the retrospective at Newcastle Art Gallery called *OLSEN ORMANDY: a creative force*. The exhibition was a celebration of their partnership: individual paintings, resin sculptures, large-scale installations, colourful discs suspended from the ceiling—some solo works, others collaborations. They drew from their extensive archives as well as creating new pieces. This exhibition did not just take a year: it had taken a lifetime.

Louise is an abstract landscape artist. Remembering her working side by side with Mum, and their love of nature, it touched me that she feels inspired by Mum's work as well as John's. Like her designs, her work is filled with colour and abstract forms, rather than John's more figurative, symbolic approach.

The transition from design professional to artist can sometimes be under appreciated. Louise sells her designs through Bergdorf Goodman, Stephen has created windows for Hermès in the Sydney city centre, *and* they are both serious artists, just like the great artists in history who have created wine labels or theatre backdrops. Steve is also represented in galleries in Paris and London.

The Newcastle exhibition ran for three months, attracting record numbers of visitors to the gallery. It was a massive exhibition in terms of scale, with over 50 works of art and sculpture: hanging from the walls and ceiling, displayed on the floor, in rows or in random sequence. There were paintings, tapestries and sculptures in marble, aluminium, wood and resin. The gallery has some of their works in their collection and, with so many of John's works already included and their recent acquisition of a drawing and a painting of Mum's (painted under her maiden name of 'Strong'), the Olsen extended family is taking over!

The Sea Sun of 5 Bells, the large ceiling painting of John's that is permanently displayed on Newcastle Art Gallery's ceiling, was one of the works that I 'helped' with as a toddler; my two-year-old handprint is still clearly visible, really making it a family affair. Louise said that being in the gallery felt like 'all our works were all talking to one another—Mum's, Dad's and mine'.

Louise and Stephen showed in Olsen Gruin in New York in a group exhibition shortly after, and Louise showed in the Sydney gallery in early 2020, both with great success.

Steve's third favourite hobby—after art, design and surfing— is music and DJ'ing, and he will do it at any opportunity. At the Newcastle Art Gallery opening, they had a band playing but when they stopped playing, people started to leave. Concerned about the exodus of the audience, Steve leaped onto the stage and started DJ'ing with equipment he has set up earlier. There were 200 people standing around, with Steve, a lone figure, pumping out tunes on the stage. He turned to me and said, 'Tim, can you get up and get everyone moving?' I jumped up and suddenly the whole street was dancing with me, the stage covered in swirling children. Like a frog in a sock, suddenly everyone was going off. It turned into a big street party.

We knew the Sydney opening was going to be the same so Steve set up a sound system again, and the party began, lasting until the early hours of the morning. The gallery was at bursting point, with people spilling out onto the street. When I told Louise that all of her work had sold, she excitedly replied, 'Don't worry, I'm never going to stop painting.'

When Louise met Steve at art school, he was already determined to be a working artist and saw himself making a comfortable living. My very practical sister, who had seen it all before, suggested they start with something smaller and so they set up the stall at Paddington Markets. They have the perfect collaboration: in art, work, love and life.

Steve's skill and knowledge of resin, his artistry and his business skills, combined with Louise's creative talent and business acumen was a recipe for success. For most people, being partners in work and love could be problematic, but Steve and Louise make it look easy.

At art school Steve had got to know artist John Coburn, through family picnics at Pearl Beach, and Coburn allowed him to share his studio. There Steve learned about colour and shape. He uses photo montages of paper shapes as the foundation for his paintings and totem resin sculptures. His work is inspired by Matisse, Miró and his hero, Victor Passmore. Stephen continued to paint after art school, but only started exhibiting with me in 2008 after I saw his latest work one Christmas Day, and said, 'Yes, you're ready.' Steve has been showing with me biennially since then, along with two solo exhibitions in New York.

My sister helped me refine and expand so many of my perceptions. She also gave me my beautiful niece, Camille Olsen-Ormandy.

Proving yet again that art is in the blood and the desire for gum turpentine flows into the next generation, Camille has embarked on her own artistic career as a portrait artist.[4] On leaving school, she followed the Olsen path by enrolling in art school and then started producing the most extraordinary portraits, full of colour. Camille is a contemporary primitive, painting portraits in the pre-Renaissance style, like the Roman-style portraits of Pompeii. They are surreal. When I ask her who they represent, she says, 'Some are portraits of friends. Others, no one in particular—they just come to me.' She has the 'passion of the brush'. John says her work is 'outstanding'.

Camille grew up on design, immersed in visual imagery. Art and the creative process for her are as natural as breathing, a way of life. She was constantly visiting galleries with her parents, so her art knowledge and appreciation are remarkable, enabling her to develop her own unique style at a very young age. In a recent *Vogue* article, she talked about how creativity has enriched her family life, with everyone 'focusing on the art and celebrating it', a highly stimulating environment.[5]

Camille, while still studying, is inundated with commissions to paint portraits. I had offered her a show, but Louise wanted me to wait, saying that she wasn't ready. 'Leave her alone,' she said. 'Always the art dealer!'—although in the end it was Camille's own decision to wait. I've got my eye on her, and I'll leave it up to the rest of the family as to when I am allowed to show her work.

She has a social-media following that puts me to shame, and her Instagram posts are inspirational. Literally growing up in the Dinosaur Designs studio, Camille is already a canny budding businesswoman and consummate professional. A muse for design house Marimekko, she takes after her chic mother with an amazing personal style, dressing incredibly in vibrant prints, glitter and pearls.[6] While clearly genetically blessed with her mother's genes, it has been wonderful to see her become a lovely person, kind and generous.

Camille and James have grown up together; they are like brother and sister. Both are highly empathetic individuals and are very supportive of one another, with a wonderful bond. While we don't know yet what career path James may take, I can only imagine it will also be inspirational. Most importantly, it will be his alone.

Like Mum and me, Louise exhibited at Galaxy Gallery in Balmain as a student, accompanied by John Coburn's daughter Kristin and Charles Blackman's daughter Christabel. This next generation of artists all remember sitting up into the early hours of the morning, listening to long hours of theoretical debate between their parents and their friends, with art a constant presence. At the time, Louise spoke of how Dad was 'never very encouraging as he was always so wrapped up in his own work' and that it was 'hard for him to see me as an artist'.[7]

In contrast, on the cusp of Louise's first solo exhibition, *Pollination*, in 2020 at the Sydney gallery, Dad wrote in tribute to her unique approach, an accolade to her talent as an artist:

> Am I prejudiced? Yes, I'm prejudiced—but my eye cannot lie . . . Her decisions are electric—breathtaking in their vitality. Nature blooming.
>
> It is a vision, running parallel to nature.
>
> This is her first exhibition, she is independent and carries no family style.
>
> Bon voyage, my darling Louise.[8]

39

THE SHARED TABLE

Food! It is something of a family fixation. My earliest culinary memory is my grandmother realising that we were out of cereal and heating up a traditional country breakfast: warm milk, cut-up white bread and sugar. At the time it was delicious, hitting the spot when the Coco Pops had run out. Maybe I just liked it because it did not contain garlic in any form!

Dad put crushed garlic into everything with gay abandon. His key ingredients were sacred: there were always pots of herbes de Provence and, no matter how poor we were, saffron. Garlic lolled on the table like bleached bouquets, bruised with purple veins. There used to be the smelliest Portuguese deli on Oxford Street, and I will never forget its delightfully pungent atmosphere. These were the days before the health departments of the world infringed and clamped down on salamis and cheeses hanging in the open. Exposed punnets of olives had a fetid yet compelling stench. I remember that Dad liked to make a Spanish tortilla—in actual fact more of a frittata, but my friends at school called it a failed omelette. Often my lunchbox stank like a connoisseur's napkin.

Having an educated and curious palate opens your mind. This was the time of meat and three veg, the stodgy food of the British. Immigration had lifted the bar, but Anglo Australia mostly grazed on uninspired plates of pale grey food in those days. Meanwhile, at the Olsens' every meal was like an exhibition, and we were brought up to eat everything. I remember having a friend stay once, and Dad had made a simple omelette with chopped parsley. My poor carnivorous mate was almost in tears as he pulled out every bit of green from the egg. At boarding school, I ended up back on stodge.

Here's the rub about crap, basic food: some of the great chefs of the world secretly love comfort food. I know I do, too. I have seen a seriously famous chef on the way home after a late shift stopping in at McDonald's, just hours after serving a seafood boudin blanc covered in a scallop froth!

There are essentially five colours, with mutations beyond what can be seen. Likewise, there are only five flavours, but their alchemy can flow beyond everything that can ever be tasted. A great painter knows about colour, but a great chef knows about colour *and* flavour. Once it was all about supermodels; now it's all about superchefs, but they are not untouchable, and you can actually enjoy the fruits of their labour.

Mum cooked macrobiotic food. In rural Dural she would shop at Warrah, an organic farm tended by people with special needs. I was consciously eating organic food from the age of twelve. When Dad was around, a pork knuckle would always find its way into a lentil stew, and one of the most profound ways I felt his absence was when that knuckle went missing. It seems unfair that Mum, who was so health conscious, never used a mobile phone and swam every morning, died at only 78 from brain cancer, while my father still lives on, having broken every food and wellness rule in the book.

Louise cooks food that is more wholesome, like Mum's. I cook more like my father; we virtually dance while we are doing it. We still cook together to this day, but I'm careful not to drop anything in. For good reason . . . one memorable occasion, as we were feasting on an incredible spinach lasagne with a beefy ragout sauce prepared by John (my mouth had watered at the sight of it emerging from the oven), we found that a certain part of it was very scratchy, chewy and fibrous. It turned out that a Scotch-Brite sponge had fallen into the dish, disguising itself as a spinach-green lasagne strip! A cheese toastie was quickly served up to stop us all going to bed hungry. On another evening, a watch ended up in a beef stew that he had cooked.

'It is the best life,' Dad once said, 'painting and drawing all day, with the crackling sound of a wood fire, and cooking things together—beans, tongue, garlic, chicken, parsley, wine. Then add spirited conversation. Is there anything better in life?'[1] In the busyness of our days, mealtimes were the only time we were a collective and able to communicate. It was a time for happy discourse and sometimes the opportunity for a few home truths. All discussion and any disputes were resolved at the table.

Just as a chef needs a restaurant, an artist needs a gallery or a studio. Both restaurants and galleries are, in a sense, their cultural venues. In 2010, Dad had his exhibition *Culinaria— The Cuisine of the Sun*, featuring works inspired by all of his most-loved recipes.[2] He said at the time, 'These pictures are to do with longstanding memories. Art is also memory.' Evocative of smells and flavours, experiences of laughter and tears, these works conjured up memories of dishes that keep us coming back for more.

The exhibition was a visual feast. Dish after dish adorned the walls, all of the favourite dishes he had learned to cook from Elizabeth David's *A Book of Mediterranean Food* after settling in Deià de Mallorca as a young man. Dad had become fascinated by how the elements of ingredients—onions, tomatoes, olive oil, parsley, chicken and chorizo—melded together, becoming a family. He imparted that passion to Louise and me: sharing a paella will always be remembered as a family tradition, our time spent together. The older you become, the more you realise how precious sharing a family meal is. In its colour and exuberance, his cooking is not dissimilar to his painting. Once you've eaten one of Dad's paellas, he owns your soul.

For the exhibition Dad created a cookbook, illustrating each of his treasured recipes. The book was edited by my friend Andy Harris, a food editor who has worked closely with one of my favourite chefs, the famously idealistic Jamie Oliver. It so happened that Jamie was launching his restaurant chain in Australia and the *Jamie* magazine at the same time.

The opportunity for Jamie to host his launch at the gallery was a natural and joyous one. We put a huge poster of the magazine cover in the main window of the gallery, with my beloved red Vespa parked out the front for the promotional shoot.

Jamie made a paella for 60 guests. He was loving and embracing to everyone. If you think all his hugging is an affectation, you're wrong. He's a hugger. In those days I was huge, and he said to me, 'Thanks, big fella'—but kindly.

For such a special launch, I did not mind turning the gallery into a trattoria for the day. Other painters and John were there, so we laid a roll of butcher's paper all the way down the table as a cloth. One of the artists sketched a series of his signature squid and other sea creatures, a veritable plateau de fruits de mer. At the end of the meal, sections of the work were torn off, isolating squid and fish, and everyone took one. Jamie still has his squid framed and hung in his London office, touched by the spontaneity and the detail.

That's the great thing about having a celebrity at a gallery event. When Barry Humphries, Cate Blanchett or Brooke Shields turns up, it adds energy to the environment. Actors love a gallery: in some ways it is a bit like a stage, but so many of them are also collectors. To share a crowded room with a celebrity elevates the atmosphere, like truffle shavings on an omelette. As long as famous people are not bombarded by fans, their presence adds great spice to any opening. People feel special when there are celebrities there. They lift the whole room.

I've shared a few meals with Rick Stein and his wife Sarah, and we all agree on nouvelle cuisine, which Rick describes as 'tweezer food'. (Dad goes even further and refers to it as 'doll's house' cuisine; Barry Humphries says that there is nothing worse than going out to dine and being served a plate of froth.) It is the antithesis of what I have always understood the great cooks and artists to be about: the best ones all share an overwhelming sense of generosity and the spirit of giving. I am sure that many of these fashionable chefs who cook as though they are looking through a microscope are capable of going home at the end of a shift to dance on a pin's head. It often does not surprise me that so many sublime restaurants in the world, despite their success, operate on such small margins.

Recently, I asked my father: 'What do you fear about death?'

He replied, coolly, 'I don't fear death at all. My only concern is . . . when I presumably enter heaven (or hell), what am I going to eat?' Like wine and women, food has always played a crucial role in his art and his life, and for me, too.

John always took chefs as seriously as painters, and he taught me to revere them. He once said that he had never met a good artist who couldn't cook, and vice versa. It's not just the end product but the attitude of these people that we like. There is generosity, selflessness and humility in the acts of cooking and making art. These artists and chefs truly run on honed instinct and on rules so internalised that they appear to be abandoned. That's the secret.

If I was sentenced to death, my last meal would be prepared by Armando Percuoco or Lucio Galletto. With Armando it would be his fettuccine al tartufovo, a carbonara without pancetta that uses eggs infused with fresh truffles, probably one of the richest dishes. With Lucio it would be his tagliolini alla granseola, blue swimmer crab tagliolini. I will never forget Armando complaining that a table of ladies had all ordered his calorie-laden dish and then collectively ordered skim-milk cappuccinos. One was not going to offset the other. What an incredibly rich and contradictory mouthgasm!

Restaurants are a conduit for conversation, which is why some chefs are the most interesting people on Earth (bar other artists, of course): they mix with everyone. The idea of the raconteur is shared by artists and chefs. The celebrity chef today behaves as histrionically as any neurotic artist. We live in an era when chefs are now glorified like screen heroes or rock stars.

In my early twenties, I worked with Gay Bilson and Janni Kyritsis at the Berowra Waters Inn a few times. Andrew Burleigh, my good friend from art school, was the sous-chef, and I started as the dishwasher, then ended up doing a few stints as a waiter—this was as close as I got to a Michelin-starred restaurant at that age. As with Anders Ousback, what the experience reinforced to me is that the ambience matters as much as the plate. You don't want a sterile experience.

Janni was the head chef at the Berowra Waters Inn with Gay from 1983 until Gay retired, having worked previously for Stephanie Alexander in Melbourne. MG Garage in Surry Hills was his first solo restaurant, complete with a row of shiny new cars on the boardwalk.

Every great chef sets the mood. Lucio, before every sitting, would fry off garlic in hot oil and parade the pan through the restaurant, saying, 'This stimulates the appetite and makes them hungry!' My memories of Lucio's have fused into one glowing, fragrant continuum.

Lucio's knowledge of food—and art—is impeccable. His restaurant has every available wall space crammed with paintings; some are magnificent, some more ordinary, but, like the food, all are made with the best intentions. Artists would almost hijack Lucio with work, some turning up unsolicited, gifting Lucio their art, and Lucio reciprocating with food. He was ultimately advised by his accountant that over the decades his accumulated art collection was probably worth as much as the restaurant. As the artists' reputations grew over the years, so did the value of some of the works. Lucio's version of art patronage continues to be a win–win today, even for the punters' enjoyment of the art alone. The collection on Lucio's walls does not represent currency, but his love of art.

Chefs and artists play in different creative paddocks, each having their own kind of madness. Both are prone to alcoholism. Given the choice, I'd rather be threatened with a brush than a knife, and chefs are definitely more violent. A restaurant under pressure at least has money coming in, but a bad opening night in a gallery, with no red dots, has none.

I count Damien Pignolet as a precious friend. He ran and owned Claude's, celebrated as one of the all-time great Sydney restaurants, for almost twelve years, the first six years with his talented late wife, chef Josephine. You would once have to book months ahead to get into the tiny converted terrace on Oxford Street. Only accommodating 36 covers, it was always a lottery to get in.

At the high point of Claude's success in the late 1980s, Damien was returning to Sydney from the countryside with Josephine and two other chefs asleep in the back seat when he fell asleep for a split second, colliding with another car. The driver of the oncoming car and Josephine were both killed. Damien and the two other chefs were seriously injured. Damien's face still bears the scars from the accident, but the scars of his heart have never healed. He has never recovered from losing Josephine. Claude's was never the same without them, both cooking in symbiosis.

In tribute to her memory, Damien established the Josephine Pignolet Young Chef of the Year Award, the most coveted award for young chefs; the winner is sent overseas for further training in the profession Josephine loved so much. A beautiful man, Damien went on to establish my favourite Woollahra eatery, Bistro Moncur. His authentic passion for true French bistro cooking is second to none. His Provençal fish soup served with a saffron rouille and croutons is one of his signature specials. It is the most refined bouillabaisse reduction, without the fuss of shells, bones and fish flesh—a culinary transportation to Nice or Marseilles, while saving on an airfare.

Damien is an institution. When it comes to French cooking in Australia, if you are not eating at Bistro Moncur in Sydney, you're at France-Soir in South Yarra. When my old boss and mentor Anders Ousback would go to Claude's, Damien has said that they would both bow to the ground to one another in respect. He recalls serving Anders suckling lamb, and Anders demanding their hottest English mustard. That was our mentor's wickedness and deliberate barbarism, and we bow to it.

In 2015, I filmed a pilot for a TV show that combined art, artists' studios and lunch. Lunch, a subject I am highly versed in and once a daily ritual for me as an art dealer, was to be the cornerstone of each episode. A friend of mine, Tim Goodman, was a great barbecue master with a colourful past, and he had probably been watching *The Hairy Bikers* and *Two Fat Ladies*. So he approached Fremantle Productions and we filmed a pilot. The format was visiting collectors, artists and aesthetes, and cooking with them.

At the time, I thought that lunch was the axis of the art world. I hadn't yet cleaned up my act, and nicknames such as 'Sir Lunch-A-Lot', or 'Lunchy' for short, were commonplace. Of course, those people had to be out to lunch, too, to know that I was—we all have to eat. Thanks to the proximity of Lucio's, often the waft of onions, garlic, duck breasts or stuffed pig's trotters being fried off before the restaurants filled found its way through my window into my office. My sad cheese and ham sandwich, supposed to be sustaining me for the day, was soon in the bin or passed on as the delicious scents came into the gallery. Over the years, all of those lunches and my dietary issues ultimately took their toll. Today, I diligently try to make my own niçoise or caesar salads, but dressings with anchovy aioli or lashings of parmigiana and pancetta find their way into the bowl. I'm hardly eating healthier or with lower calorie counts, but the intention is there, and there have been results.

In the pilot footage, I was three times my current size—maybe good for a connoisseur, but not for business. The show did not fly, and my career as a bon vivant in the Jamie Oliver/Rick Stein vein was short-lived, shot down like a flambéed prawn. Maybe a cookbook? John burps them out beautifully. I'm amazed that Louise hasn't been tempted yet.

Louise travels annually to visit her stores in New York, Tokyo and London, the latter in the Ham Yard Hotel complex. One particular year, she held a party on the roof of the hotel when I just happened to be in London. Among the milling guests I noticed the colourful Italian chef, restaurateur, writer, food expert and much-loved character Antonio Carluccio. He was sitting quietly at a table, bashing away with a mortar and pestle, making pesto, having called down to the kitchen for basil, pine nuts and garlic. The chefs were so in awe to have *the* Antonio Carluccio on the rooftop that they had sent him up a mountain of ingredients and the largest mortar and pestle I had ever seen.

This was a typical move for him at gatherings; to be cooking, preparing or giving something culinary was his way. He did not normally stay too long at parties, but this time he was quite happy sitting there. Antonio, despite his celebrity status, cookery books and appearances on television, was still at heart a provincial village man, living for foraging and the simplicity of preparing food. He would rather listen in to conversations than be at their centre, but when he did join in, there would be a wonderful story of his childhood growing up in Italy with his railway-master father. He laughed when I told him that my son James used to call me 'The Fat Controller' when bigger and looking pickled myself. (My staff probably still call me 'The Controller'!) Despite his reputation as a gastronomic raconteur, he was a shy, sometimes socially awkward man. He told me once that he did not think of himself as being particularly clever: 'Tim, cooking is really a simple thing in communicating. It is easier, and more honest, than trying to tell some interesting story.'

I bumped into Antonio again when staying with close friend Andy Harris in London another year. Antonio had been out in the country, picking mushrooms all day. While Andy was making woodfired pizzas outside in the garden, we sat chatting as he delicately removed debris from the pile of porcini mushrooms using tweezers, with the concentration of a surgeon. Fascinated, he told me that he was preparing them for pickling, and that every foreign particle must be removed to avoid introducing bacteria.

If Antonio wasn't doing something involved with food, he would love to gather branches in the forest, carving and whittling them into walking sticks. He made one for my father, who reciprocated by sending him back one of his food-inspired artworks. They had a mutual respect, were kindred spirits, even though they never met in person.

When Antonio sadly died in 2017, the tributes poured in. He had been a close friend of Jamie Oliver, and Jamie credited Antonio with starting his own long love affair with Italian cooking and all things culinary. He will be remembered as the 'godfather of Italian gastronomy in the United Kingdom',[3] an inspirational man who changed the face of English cooking, full of a zest for life and a great sense of humour. His motto was 'mof mof': 'minimum of fuss, maximum of flavour'. If Anna Del Conte was the doyenne of Italian food who changed the way that the British ate at home, Antonio was a leader in transforming the culinary landscape in England. He inspired great chefs and those that just liked to cook.

Another great chef who invited me to lunch one day is Gennaro Contaldo, another of Jamie Oliver's mentors who was the inspiration for Jamie's Fifteen, a non-profit restaurant chain to train apprentice chefs from disadvantaged backgrounds, regrettably now defunct. Jamie has said that he learned everything from Gennaro—'heart, soul, romance, fantasy'—and used to call him his 'London Dad'. For Jamie, he took him past the sterility of learning about food in college to show him the love and sensitivity in creating nourishment. A mentor in the truest sense of the word.

Although I no longer drink, I am intoxicated by food. Being a sober chef and gourmand is not hard. Smoking destroys a palate even more than alcohol. The drunker you are, the duller your palate becomes. I was always advised to drink the great wines first because in the end, if you are drinking too much, it would be like drinking flagon wine at five in the morning. Alcohol burns off when cooking food. The tannins that come from wine are an important element for certain dishes, like the humble bolognese. Verjuice is my substitute for wine; you cannot use cheap wine to make great food. Using wine in cooking has not led to me relapsing; it is just that tiramisu with amaretto or chocolate mousse with cognac are off the menu. It can be difficult navigating restaurants, particularly with menus that offer matching wines. It was intriguing to learn that Rothschild himself, of Château Mouton Rothschild fame, was unable to drink his own product, having crossed that thin red line.

I have no hesitation in saying that sometimes something you eat can only be described as nothing less than a 'palate fuck'. To eat slowly, ingest and masticate is like a sexual process. To allow oil to dribble down your chin to suck an oyster out of its shell are provocative activities, like sharing a mango naked in the bath, or in bed.

European food is deliberately erotic. Latin cooking is spontaneous and sexy; Mediterranean food will always be my favourite, harking back to my childhood in Southern Europe. The further north you go, the more flour, beer and sausage you find. However, the Scandinavians are now into foraging cuisine. Visiting Noma in Copenhagen in 2015, relishing the degustation of foraged and homegrown morsels with matching juices, is an experience that I will never forget.

The older I get, the less complicated my cooking becomes. When I want to indulge, my specialty is stuffed spatchcock with potatoes roasted in duck fat. My son James likes fish and salad, and Dad's specialty is still his paella. We all cook together, three generations of Olsen men in the kitchen. We recently cooked Rick Stein's Moroccan chicken, working in unison with Dad as the conductor, him slicing preserved lemons as James and I steeped the saffron and chopped the almonds, following his every direction.

Dining in Italy is a bit underwhelming for me. Australia's abundance of fresh produce and exemplary chefs offer a wealth of sensational eating. Remarkably, Italian restaurants in Australia can actually be better than those in Italy! It is well known that the Italians initially taught the French how to cook, Catherine de' Medici changed the course of culinary history when she brought her entourage of Florentine chefs to the French court.

My father's favourite food poem is 'Oysters' by Seamus Heaney. It is so evocative that it always reminds him of living by the sea on the Mediterranean coast and the flavour of the ocean.

Oysters

Our shells clacked on the plates.
My tongue was a filling estuary,
My palate hung with starlight:
As I tasted the salty Pleiades
Orion dipped his foot into the water.
Alive and violated,
They lay on their bed of ice:
Bivalves: the split bulb
And philandering sigh of ocean
Millions of them ripped and shucked and scattered.
We had driven to that coast
Through flowers and limestone
And there we were, toasting friendship,
Laying down a perfect memory
In the cool of thatch and crockery.
Over the Alps, packed deep in hay and snow,
The Romans hauled their oysters south to Rome:
I saw damp panniers disgorge
The frond-lipped, brine-stung
Glut of privilege
And was angry that my trust could not repose
In the clear light, like poetry or freedom
Leaning in from sea. I ate the day
Deliberately, that its tang
Might quicken me all into verb, pure verb.[4]

As a student, all I ate was Thai food or spaghetti bolognese.
Now my favourite restaurants are Chez Allard's in Paris's Saint-
Germain quarter, whose signature dish is roast duck with green

olives, and Bocca di Lupo in London. Simply going to restaurants such as Le Coucou on Lafayette Street in New York is an amazing experience, but I've also simply enjoyed a burger in a diner or a milk bar—as long as there is plenty of beetroot. I intend to experiment more with dining in New York. Having been more adventurous with art, my dining experience should match.

'A little bad taste is like a nice splash of paprika,' Diana Vreeland once said. 'We all need a splash of bad taste—it's hearty, it's healthy, it's physical. I think we could use more of it. NO taste is what I'm against.'

As long as it is made with love and soul, I'll eat it.

40

THE ART SCENE AT THE BOTTOM OF THE WORLD

I read a quote recently by playwright Sir Peter Shaffer that struck a chord: 'If London is a watercolour, New York is an oil painting.' Would not that make Australia an etching?

Australian art is not an anachronism. It's not (always) exotic or covered in red dust and raw pigment. It is, largely, contemporary. It is diverse, subtle, energised and sometimes raw. But most of all it is often misunderstood. Commercially and curatorially, it has also been underrated by international critics, museum directors, private collectors and gallerists. To paraphrase Dr Seuss: 'An art scene is an art scene, no matter how small!' We are here, even if the central media focus and pumped up economy of art are somewhere over *there*.

When our art is showcased overseas in museum shows or commercial exhibitions, the curatorial fit is often bizarre, with no thematic cohesion. A still-life painter, a super-realist portraitist and a hard-edged abstractionist will be hung in an uneasy trio (perhaps to hedge all bets, or save on shipping), leading sophisticated eyes to question the awareness of art trends in this country.

It is astonishing that until relatively recently the Royal Academy in London had not exhibited anything from the Antipodes since 1923—and, when they did, British art critics were lost in a colonial time warp. *Australia*, the greatest hits show mounted at the Royal Academy in 2013, crammed so many names into one timeline that many of our best painters were reduced to a single offering, each under the loose theme of 'landscape'. Abstract art had almost no presence. One serious omission was the London generation of the 1960s put into their own context. Michael Johnson was making extraordinary shaped canvases in London as early as 1965, and was a close friend to both Francis Bacon and David Hockney yet painted nothing like them, adhering to a strict and brilliant aesthetic of minimal geometric abstraction. Entire movements such as colour field germinated in London yet there was no allusion to support this dynamic chapter. On top of that, almost 200 years of sculpture were ignored in favour of a selection that looked like both a cacophony and an apology.

My father's iconic ceiling work, *Sydney Sun* (1965), now in the NGA's collection, was included in that same exhibition. In the cavernous Royal Academy, the work looked like wallpaper hung in the wrong place. It was stripped of all context by hanging alone, in a sea of discordant single offerings by equally important artists.

It still amazes me that the British arts press continue to be culturally condescending towards Australia. The stain of colonial chauvinism is almost indelible, and nowhere was it more evident than in reviews of this show. Waldemar Januszczak compared *Sydney Sun* to shit. Literally. He spouted: '[it] successfully evokes the sensation of standing under a cascade of diarrhoea'.[1] Dad was dignified in reply, qualifying that the work was actually based on a cosmic rather parochial vision, inspired by NASA's photographs of the sun's surface. Anyone who knows John knows that he is heliocentric, a pantheist energised by solar power, an artist whose centrifugal source and muse has always been the sun. His rebuke was almost one of weary defence to the same old dated anti-contemporary jibe that he has been copping for the entire length of his career. 'You can call it diarrhoea or energy,' he replied. 'It just depends on what you ate last night!'

It was a relief to see the work properly exhibited during his 2016–17 retrospective at both the NGV and the AGNSW, where special viewing chairs were installed, and patrons could enjoy the experience in immersive repose.

Another critic from *The Guardian*, Adrian Searle, said blandly, 'I am not interested in what might constitute some sort of Australian artistic identity, because I doubt there is one.'[2] I agree with his curational comment, like the bland annual summer show at the British Royal Academy, it turns into an incongruent conversation; to cover a span of Australian art history like this was a ridiculous notion. This is the colonial condescension that we continue to endure despite the exhaustive wealth of Antipodean talent: the extraordinary music of Peter Sculthorpe; the poetry of Peter Porter; our astounding acting pool including the legendary Cate Blanchett, Geoffrey Rush and Hugh Jackman; Barry Humphries's wit; and the films by Peter Cox and George Miller. The list goes on.

Cultural cringe cuts both ways, too. We continue to grovel to visiting monarchy and art media 'royalty' with obsequious humility, literally rolling out the red carpet for Prince Philip, or figuratively doing the same for Grayson Perry when he exhibited at the MCA in Sydney.

For some strange reason, the massive history books on Australian art written by our most esteemed experts—Robert

Hughes, John McDonald, Edmund Capon and Barry Pearce—once favoured male artists and faltered anywhere near the avant-garde. Huge gusts of hot air were expended on our great post-impressionist landscape painters with their Naples-yellow valleys and scudding clouds, or the raw proto-naive kitsch of Sidney Nolan, then each one of these authors seemed to run out of steam, cramming important movements such as abstraction; non-objective, feminist and abject art; and video and performance into a cursory paragraph.

Some people used to think that any art created in Australia that was not landscape was a derivative of international art. Australian artists are credited as innovators, capable of irony, quotation, pastiche and raw invention the equal of anywhere in the world. We stopped being an import-orientated culture a long time ago. The only Australian culture that truly stands out in world history is Indigenous art, however the modern post-war period of Australian art that includes Nolan, Boyd, Drysdale and Williams is probably one of the most underrated art movements anywhere. I stand for the integrity of our best work when viewing the tremendous uniformity of art at the international fairs I visit up to four times a year.

Art fairs, as they grow vaster and more homogeneous, feel a lot like luxury shopping malls, as many galleries brand themselves with the faceless gilded authority of Gucci or Prada. In that context, a small independent Australian gallery can drown. Art reflects economies. So, in Europe and America, art is studied, marketed and collected on an industrial scale. The young fashion designers who broke into couture in Paris and the Marc Newsons who took Milan and then continued on into the stratosphere have few equivalents in our art world. It is just that hard a market.

417

Frankly, it has been perplexing to watch my father paint for 70 years and not truly 'crack' America or Europe. Unfortunately, he probably will not live to see the shift in global art collecting. It is inevitable that Australian art will gain prominence beyond Indigenous painters and biennale showcases. In the meantime, Australian collectors still have the privilege of being able to afford their country's best artists. They also get to galvanise their own faith in painters, photographers and sculptors whose names are not global brands.

Being a true believer, I would be deeply disappointed to see another generation of great Australian artists remain relevant in only this hemisphere. We have tried art fairs to promote Australian creativity, but the difference with a stand-alone gallery is its perpetual presence. It was this stimulus that prompted me to open the gallery space in New York to showcase Australian and international art and to exhibit Indigenous Australian art recently in Los Angeles.

Back home, our art scene is only going to be strengthened by people putting a value on art beyond fiscal investment. Somehow the concept that art is like a luxury car needs to shift. The tide needs to change, but in the last decade the currency of art as an Australian export has gradually been demoted. The crippling of arts funding in successive budgets, the inability of artists to afford studios (with almost zero state-run initiatives), and the general cultural focus on sport, renovation and food have not helped. Art seems sometimes to have left the conversation.

In the 1960s, Sydney had at least six regular newspaper art critics (Paul Haefliger, James Gleeson, Gavin Souter, Wallace Thornton and, from London, John Olsen were writing for *The Sydney Morning Herald* alone). The best way to get an Australian art writer to cover a show now is to put them on a plane, preferably business class, to China or Venice. We are famous for not taking our own artists seriously, for seeking out intellectual credibility in the exotic and the offshore.

I once spoke to an editor of a major newspaper, complaining about how critics no longer have the gravitas that they once had. A critic could once make or break an artist. He replied, 'Tim, when you consider the shit pay and that nearly everybody hates you, who would really want the job?'

Art criticism is surely an honourable, passionate vocation in the interests of cultural commentary, even without the gravitas and remuneration of previous eras.

The impact of commercial galleries lacking objective comment and critical support is that young collectors feel more apprehensive. As culture becomes less versed in art and more informed about lifestyle, visual art becomes an afterthought. People buy an unsigned print or a floating neon sign that looks a bit 'artish' at a design store. It is not the same. Furniture is decor. Art transcends and outstrips its context.

Yet again we return to the idea that art is seen as a luxury, or an extra, that few can afford. It is not actually about the money or what art costs; it is more a matter of value. Quality Australian art can be expensive but it holds prestige, even in the secondary market. The cachet of label culture is failing art, and it is probably eclipsing what could be a whole new generation of new collectors—those who confidently spend thousands on a dress or a suit but cannot name any young painters whose work they covet.

It is saddening to compare the prices of a work in a New York, Berlin or London gallery to a similar work in a leading Australian gallery. With the exception of a handful of artists of John's calibre, the comparison reveals a huge discrepancy. Status, prestige and glamour, not critical acclaim, so often drive sales in the upper echelons of the elite contemporary art market.

Some dealers are still reluctant to encourage artists to make it overseas, worried that they will lose their right to representation if their artist performs on an international level. The bitter fruit of this fear-driven logic is that several generations of very talented artists who could have gone and lived abroad and made it didn't, because we still believe that we are the art scene at the bottom of the world.

To state the obvious: collecting Australian art matters. Everything is interconnected. Thirty years ago I bought an etching, then, slowly but surely, I bought drawings and then a painting. When we understand and engage with a work of art, we learn as much about ourselves as we do about the artist.

To contribute to our culture, buy your first piece, be it big or small, crazy or conservative. Buy it because you love it.

Steve Nasteski was essentially a prestige car dealer, an entrepreneur and a wheeler-dealer when he started visiting Sydney galleries. He instantly became hooked on art and the idea of selling not only luxury cars but also artworks to his various clients. A very clever operator, he has worked his way up, amassing his own covetable collection and developing those of his clients. He has hustled himself into the art world, both locally and internationally—including with Wendy Whiteley, as Brett is his favourite artist—and Whiteley's *Bondi Beach* is the pride of his collection.

I have watched Steve's progress with a sense of bemused admiration. Somehow this suburban boy without any background in art has become, in the words of John McDonald, 'Australia's leading dealer in international contemporary art'. In the rarefied art world that only deals with the very wealthy elite, he is now dealing with the top tier of international art.

Steve purchased many works from Contemporary Fine Arts (CFA) gallery in Berlin and, with a 'crazy idea', suggested an exhibition of works by Australian artists to test the waters. The 2017 exhibition featured blue-chip artists Tim Storrier and Cressida Campbell, and Steve took along critic John McDonald as a 'kind of diplomatic observer'. CFA was unfamiliar with Australian art at the time so it was something of a gamble, although the works looked sensational in the museum-like setting of the gallery.

The show was a success for Campbell but not so much for Storrier. What it did do, though, was shine a spotlight on Steve as a member of the international inner circle of elite collectors, on the discrepancy in prices and perceived value of Australian art compared to international art in the global market, and on the continual gap between the leading and aspiring galleries. In that exclusive club created by the uber-galleries, you have to be one of the chosen few to be allowed to even buy something, to be recommended and have your credentials confirmed—irrespective of your personal wealth.

Unfortunately, Campbell and Storrier did not end up being represented by CFA, but for Australian artists to be shown in one of the uber-galleries is an achievement in itself—even a show held in the middle of a European winter.

Seeing how Steve operates makes me realise how good he is as a deal maker. He is not infallible, though. He bought a Jonathan Horowitz sculpture of Hillary Clinton as Queen of America, *Hillary Clinton is a Person Too* (2008). He was convinced that Clinton was going to be the next US president, saying, 'I can't possibly fail with that sculpture—as if Donald Trump is going to win that election.' Much of the world was shocked and horrified when Trump won.

Steve and I are still friends. We go to Miami every year and have a lot of fun. He is the 'captain flipper' of the art world, with a raw instinct for what sells. While keeping a low profile, he is very good at dealing at an exceptional level. He is a lovable rogue who has upset a few people along the way through back-door dealing, buying up exhibitions and then reselling them through auction—a dangerous approach in the tenuous international art world.

One year at Art Basel Miami Beach, we had walked around for several days with Steve trying to broker a deal with a top gallery for a great artist. At the time, none of the dealers were willing to offer him anything, so he flew back to Los Angeles to where the other galleries were more negotiable. His ability to think outside the box and be in the best place to broker the deal is part of his talent and instinct. Every year we attend the White Cube Soho house party on the beach, rubbing shoulders with the cream of the artists, whether George Condo, Chuck Close, Damien Hirst or Tracey Emin. It is such an amicable scene to experience; everyone is welcoming and drops their guard. It takes me back to the days when I could saunter up to the likes of Sidney Nolan at a drinks party, as normal as walking up to anyone else at any soirée.

Steve and I once visited every major gallery in Berkeley Square, Mayfair. Every front-of-house person at each esteemed art space would immediately recognise Steve and buzz the director to say that he was in the gallery. We would be fast-tracked up to the private exhibiting space to meet with the boss, the likes of Sadie Coles, Simon Lee and Tim Jefferies. Steve got the red-carpet treatment from all of them. Steve's ocker accent, an accent so unlike that of any other art aficionado or art-collecting sophisticate, was never scrutinised when it came to be known that he was capable of dropping a seven-figure amount on an Ed Ruscha.

He is an anomaly, a contradiction. I love just watching his unorthodox methods as he outsmarts some of the shrewdest dealers in the world. He can speculate in a smart art deal as well as any Cork Street spruiker in the business.

Another artist whom Steve saw potential in is painter and filmmaker Del Kathryn Barton, buying up most of her 2017 New York exhibition. Barton's auction results have seen her become the first woman to make the list of Australia's top 10-selling living artists, on which John is currently at number one. The excitement being generated by Barton's work has been compared to that of a young emerging Brett Whiteley. It is good to see works by female artists increasing in value as collectors realise their worth.

Coincidentally, Larry Gagosian and Stuart Purves also began their careers selling prestige cars.

The art market today is driven by so many aspects. Supply, curators, biennale inclusions and auction-house results are some of the myriad influences that shape an artist's career. Very few critics have the power to spike the value of an artist's work like they used to; the aesthetic or intellectual opinion of one person is no longer the biggest deciding factor.

If an artist is not in fashion, or does not seem to be working with the right curators, institutions and collectors, their career can be limited. Some artists employ publicists in an attempt to become a 'brand'. Being a successful artist these days can be a complex trapeze act, giving a whole new meaning to the term 'stunt artist'. In this brave new art world, it has never been tougher to manoeuvre yourself into the right position.

41

SECRETS OF A NATIONAL TREASURE

The long shadow of the famous father does not just loom over a small child. When Dad staged his major retrospective in 2016–17, I heard the echoing strains of 'How do you live with a genius in the family?' It was not a new gambit; this is a dinner-party question I have fielded for 30 years. When Dad was asked how he felt about being referred to as 'Australia's greatest living artist', he explained that the 'terrible burden' was one of expectation. 'If only it helped you paint better pictures, but it doesn't,' he said. 'People expect you to print a Rembrandt masterpiece every day, which is nonsense; no one can do that. Right now, I'm painting a raw prawn. It's such fun; I love its interrogating feelers. I'm not going to be Rembrandt today.'[1]

Even the most ambitious painter sees the comic hubris in that. Sometimes John is impossible; he can be slippery and salty and wise. He is great because he is so original and so broad, a forger's nightmare. The mantle is upheld by a rambling and prolific recent retrospective (first at the NGV in Melbourne, then at the AGNSW) and a body of work that embraces almost every medium. It has been a rare privilege to grow from infancy to maturity within the vast canon of his work. To Louise and me, the experience of walking through museum interiors hung with all of Dad's major works is intensely personal because there it all is: our life in pictures. To be there when iconic future legends were unfolding, and they were simply puzzles being assembled in long silent sessions in the studio; to hear my parents discussing the intricacies; to hear the quiet but definite creak of a studio door closing. We never wondered what kept him so long. Always painting. Always the next show. He was an artist, continually painting, eternally in the studio. If we weren't having family time, he was working.

At about age twelve my appreciation for his works grew when I discovered his drawings and painting of birds and animals. Without any idea of space or abstraction or what made a work avant-garde, I immediately related to the *You Beaut Country* pictures. They connected to children's art—not really abstract, more haptic. I believed the whole world thought in that way: spontaneously, directly, intensely. And I've never recovered.

Louise and I have lived with our father's pictures longer than many marriages. If you live with art from birth, there will be a moment when one day an image comes alive for you, when it stops being an inanimate object and starts telling a story. We have watched him work firsthand and seen the iconic fluidity of his line, his seamless pleasure (and success) in life. What seemed like a rolling cavalcade of great and major works took tremendous drive and concentration.

In many ways, John's paintings have the ability to distort and play with time. The joyful immediacy of his mark conceals the gravitas that forms the bedrock of seven decades of painting. As his famously dark self-portrait, *Self-Portrait Janus-Faced*, attests, my father has two very distinct personas. Two faces. The first is the public identity: the gregarious host, the bon vivant flinging saffron, bon mots and rare pigment into the void, the Zen calligrapher inventing his own frenetic lexicon of line. It is probably that deceptively direct approach that has been interpreted in some art-history circles as capturing the essence of a child.

The lesser known face is that of the introvert: the darker palette, the minimal and existential moments. The man working in complete cloistered silence, standing deep in doubt before an unfinished painting. Reflecting the day in his rambling art journal. Alone in the bush or with a private thought. We were taught from an early age that it was the things that could not be seen that manifested most powerfully: 'If you haven't got the feeling right,' John admonished, 'just forget it.'

My idea about why his work matters equates to quality, quantity and dogged perseverance. His lineage as a painter shoots an arrow through half a century of Modernism, and his compositional experimentation literally turned Australian landscape upside down. Within his vast body of work he mastered many mediums: oils, watercolours, etchings, ceramics, even his own calligraphy. He challenges himself despite his success and not because of it. 'When you are the Sydney darling you are in big, big trouble,' he said. 'They use you up as if you are blotting paper for their own entertainment, and someone else comes along and then they throw you away like a rag. That's when you get on with being a person.'

This is another critical gift of having lived so closely within the orbit of an art star: good artists always leave room for doubt. The fallow moment. The dark night. 'The billabong period', as my father has called it many times, his 'midlife crisis'.

Yet he has had his detractors. Many times during his career his work has passed in and out of fashion. When he was out with the conceptualists, by God was he out. Old hat. Scrapped. Thoughtlessly diminished. With honour and acknowledgement came the changing and fickle tastes of new generations. It baffles me that some conceptual or 'post-postmodern' artists are not more generous to him. There is more raw experimentation in his process than in entire museum wings, and his work has a strong (if little known) performative streak. These are intensely physical paintings full of unmapped gestures and unplanned outbursts. Intensity is something he has sustained over time. Simply staying a painter in the stream of contemporary whims and honing his language outside of trends, to my eye, is rare in itself. He carved the path, but he also stayed the course. While many young artists do the same thing over and over again, a true master—Boyd, Nolan, Picasso—has many dimensions, working in so many mediums to articulate so many ideas.

On a recent wintry morning, Dad sent me a photo: beret on, brush in hand, frenetic energised lines leaping onto the canvas. It was probably taken while the world was still sleeping, long before breakfast. They say Cézanne died painting, but he probably would not have seen it like that. He *lived* painting, and the line between art and life was not drawn. Age is not a barrier to creating art. Picasso worked on his last self-portrait, the aptly named *Self-Portrait Facing Death*, confronting his own mortality, before he passed away at 91.

The gifts an artist leaves his children are always measured in frames. People look at the heirs of Henri Matisse or Lucian Freud as living with priceless artefacts. As a gallerist, there is the strange duality of knowing the market value of a work of art and the spiritual value of living with something rare and original.

My advice to young collectors is to look at their motivation in investing in a work of art. It has to be emotional, not real estate or decoration. It was horrific to once hear a millionaire say, 'Art to me is like wallpaper, but it just sticks out a bit.'

I walk past the major work *Lake Hindmarsh* (1970) every day, breathing in the dormant majesty and emotional solemnity of this immense, moody brown canvas. The painting owns its place in art history as a major work, a mysterious, pivotal piece that moved John's understanding of the landscape towards topography, and just as strongly glowers with memory. It is a precursor to his *Edge of the Void* series, depicting where life is drawn towards water. The lake itself from above is a sensuous object, like a breast, symbolic in understanding the methodology of our planet being described as 'Mother Earth'. Just as some tribes live with ancestral talismans, for me, the power of family is evoked through art.

Dad has said that the bush has the scattered rhythms of a dog's hind leg. Like Goya, who Dad believes was the master of turning ugliness into beauty, he sees beauty in the unremarkable dark-patterned birds and ugly insects, in the crows' astonished response to the white man's manipulation of the landscape and land clearing, their calls sounding like 'fuck, fuck'.

It is John's imagination and interpretation of the landscape that captures the viewer. He draws upon memory, the derivative of where he has been and where he is. They are not invented landscapes but are the combined influence of creative depth and power, a curiosity and passion for his surroundings and astounding power of recall. 'Memory is the powerful thing,' he says.

Walking down the street in the local village, or down leafy Queen Street, Woollahra, Dad and I are always stopped every 20 metres or so by people he knows, or by complete strangers wanting a hug or a selfie, desiring to tell him they love his work or just to share a quick story or an anecdote. They see this colourful man with a huge smile, in his beret, clutching a bag from the butcher or from the bookshop, and are stopped in their tracks. To friends, he will proclaim, 'Amigo'. People want to connect to his charm; to some he is almost like an art deity. Everyone walks away from Dad feeling as though they have experienced a rare moment. He has charisma in spades.

People are always telling me he is a bona fide sartorialist, an Orson Welles or Quentin Crisp, looking like a Marlon Brando. Invariably attired like a Mediterranean poet or thespian, Dad believes that fashion is for people who do not have any style. He often comments about other poorly dressed artists: 'Why do they have to dress like they have no talent?' Another of Dad's favourite stories is about when Degas and Whistler were in Paris. Whistler walked into a cafe dressed in a refined tailored suit, with a cane and polished top hat. Degas commented that he was over-dressed and not authentically attired as an artist should be—that he was trying to be too aristocratic. While sometimes artists are so absorbed in their art to not care about their appearance, Dad finds it hilarious that some young artists go out of their way to deliberately drip paint over themselves to announce to the world their vocation. He thinks they are trying too hard to look like creatives instead of just being artists.

Dad's bohemian get-up earned him the nickname Johnny Bojangles. His school buddies called him 'Lolly Legs' for his bow-legged running style. Another popular sobriquet is 'Olly Paint', or 'Moon Face' because of his idiosyncratic chin and profile. Dad often puts himself in his paintings, like a Hitchcock cameo, or latter-day selfie. That chin and profile is his silhouette, appearing in many paintings, often more than once, which does suggest that he gets around. In the 1960s he was called 'The Emperor', a tribute to his particular leadership as the 'monarch of Sydney's avant-garde', but also owing something to his passing resemblance to Napoleon Bonaparte.[2]

It was a poignant if a little melancholy trip for Dad back to Europe in 2019, revisiting places from his youth. It was the first time he had returned to Deià, that place so formative to his work and life. There he discovered that the grave of poet Robert Graves, his old friend, had been recently disinterred from the cemetery, perhaps to rest in Poets' Corner, Westminster Abbey. Graves is already commemorated there, his name among sixteen Great War poets on a slate stone, with the inscription written by Wilfred Owen: 'My subject is War, and the pity of War. The Poetry is in the pity.'

Mum told me that Dad had said he had met Ava Gardner at a party at Graves's home and that they had shared a night of passion. (Dad says he can't remember! I think I would.) He also visited Cézanne's studio, which was the highlight of the trip. He felt so at home that he wanted to pick up a brush and start to paint himself.

Having two John Olsen retrospectives within a year was a great enlightenment for the many people in Australia who still were not familiar with John's work and, judging by the numbers at both retrospectives, undoubtedly John can pull a crowd. The total number of visitors exceeded the attendance at the AFL grand final at the Melbourne Cricket Ground.

The reviews of the 'brilliant' retrospectives were full of praise: for such a vast body of work, for their ongoing contribution to Australian contemporary art history and for the man himself. Every time I opened a newspaper at the time, there was Dad. The retrospective was an emotional experience for us all. Dad said, 'I'm seeing these works afresh . . . like it's a family enjoined . . . and I think they're shaking hands.'[3] There was one detractor, a critic, who wrote, 'The more John Olsens that you put into a room, the uglier it becomes' and said the works looked 'messy and dull'.[4] Fortunately, the thousands who visited disagreed. Dad's response was: 'The artist's opinion of the critic is rather like what a lamp-post thinks of a dog.'[5]

Ultimately, many people underestimate how much Dad and Fred Williams have changed the way people look at the Australian landscape. Indigenous art may have a topographical quality, but it's a different type of Dreaming. It is like looking at the maps and tracks of a psychological landscape, where the earth collides with the universe into a simultaneous image: psychological landscape meets the physical. John's work is more literal, or so many people say to me: after flying back from Europe across the Simpson Desert, across South Australia, Lake Eyre or the Murray delta, you realise that John Olsen is not an abstract artist after all. From up above, the Australian landscape can look like one continuous Olsen.

It is a memory of the landscape that Dad is interested in, not its actuality. He is looking at the landscape from the point of view of an all-encompassing vision—side on, above and within—hence his axiom: 'I am in the landscape and the land-scape is in me.' That line, over time, has become indivisible from his artistic identity, and in the process he has changed the face of how we see the terrain, altering the very essence of what modern landscape painting is by shrinking the sky, turning his back on conventional geometry, speaking his own language and always returning to the magnetic egg-yolk energy of the sun.

There have been people—like the late Edmund Capon, when director of the AGNSW—who have said that John Olsen and the late Fred Williams are the most evocative Australian painters of the twentieth century. It is to do with empathy. He is not trying to paint an en plein air work that transports people into an impressionist or a surreal space; he is taking you into the sentiment of the bush, the vastness. Australia is a flat country, and it's only from above that you get an idea of its space. The Western interpretation of foreground, mid-ground and background is unable to capture it.

When Dad talks about his art, he talks more about nature, poetry and life than about painting. He is never wanting to exclude anyone in his audience. His work constantly has a positive message, and his view of the world is that of a life-changing, passivist kind of activist. Like a poet–painter, he is always fascinated by the lyricism of the landscape. Beyond the song and the written word, art is the universal language of the soul.

His link to poetry is his other great strength. He has been gifted an ability to understand beauty and yet still praise the ugly, the uneven, the difficult. People see pain as profound and pleasure as mildly suspicious, yet both are present in equal measure in his work. You just have to delve a little deeper.

Everything my father touches is full of passion, intensity, truth and curiosity. The child is always alive. All my life he has been watching, absorbing and doing much more than just taking notes: he has been reliving everything like a new experience.

A few months after Dad's 90th birthday, I bought him a Bonnard lithograph called *Woman in the Bath*, knowing that he would appreciate the message within the image. The function of a bath is the space; in Australia's emptiness we discover its fullness. It is the space that humbles us and puts us in awe of where we live. Even though, essentially, we are saucer-dwellers, with most of the population living on the edge, when we talk about the soul of Australia, we always seem to end up in the desert.

While Dad's work is still undervalued compared to that of his deceased peers, sadly it will only be posthumously, in the memory of him, that Australia will realise what they had: a true national treasure. When Brett Whiteley died, I felt a sadness not only for the loss of a friend, but also for the world: we had all lost a rare and beautiful way of looking at things. It will be the same for Dad. The whole world will sit up one day and discover the extraordinary talent that evaded the attention of his time.

Dad is frequently referred to as a 'national living treasure', but remarkably this has never been made official. The status of 'National Living Treasure' is awarded by the National Trust of Australia's NSW branch, with recipients 'selected by popular vote for having made outstanding contributions to Australian society in any field or endeavour'. Started in 1997, the list originally was intended to include up to 100 living people, but with a high mortality rate and a couple of scandalous expulsions (Rolf Harris was one of those de-listed), it remains consistently smaller than that. Only occasionally updated, it was last refreshed in 2014, a memorable year when mining magnate Clive Palmer allegedly influenced his employees to vote for him.[6]

It is a sad indictment on the appreciation of the visual arts in Australia that only two painters, Arthur Boyd and Margaret Olley, have ever made the list. The current rollcall is primarily an assortment of sportspeople, politicians, singers, actors, writers and social activists. While agreeing with many of the inclusions and acknowledging that this is a popular vote, I find the omission of the visual arts both astounding and incredibly disappointing. This is not about the exclusion of my father from the list, rather the continued lack of appreciation of all Australian artists, of any medium, who have enriched our everyday lives, providing beauty and evoking emotion through their work. At the list's next review, we can only hope that the visual arts may at long last be given the recognition they deserve. If painting is dead, as some art critics say, nobody told John Olsen. 'I'd like to know the time of death,' he says with the brightest of glints in his eye. 'I'm alive. So painting isn't dead.'

Dad was fascinated by the landscapes of the Pilbara region. In 1982 he went on a two-week, 30,000-kilometre journey in Australia's north-west, sponsored by the Christensen Fund and conceived by art dealer and collector Alex Bortignon. They covered approximately 18,500 kilometres by land and 11,500 in helicopters or fixed-wing aircraft. It was Dad's first time painting in Western Australia and his inaugural visit to the north-west. They were a talented group—writer Dame Mary Durack, poet and writer Geoffrey Dutton, Vincent Serventy from the old Pearl Beach days as naturalist and conservationist, and Bortignon as photographer—and their aim was to use their art to distil the essence of the region in paintings and writings. The epic adventure took them from Geraldton up the coast, circumnavigating the Pilbara and Broome, then up to Beagle Bay, the King Leopold Ranges, Kalumburu, Lake Gregory and south-east through the Camballin. It was a privilege and an amazing experience for them all, in 'a territory with a fearful fascination and an unforgettable charisma which have no relationship to any human experience', as Dad wrote in his preface to the expedition book, *The Land Beyond Time*.

The original agreement with the Christensen Fund's founder, Allen D. Christensen, had been that the works created by Dad—100 oils and drawings—would be donated to the Art Gallery of Western Australia, but this did not eventuate. After extensively touring the country, the works were eventually sold on the open market, much to Dad's distress.[7] At the time of the trip Dad was married to Noela, who was overseeing the renovation of their home and the construction of his new studio in Clarendon. He would write to her from around the campfire, much as he had written to Mum and us when he had visited the Northern Territory in the early 1970s.

So in 2017, when Western Australian mining magnate Andrew Forrest AO and his wife Nicola invited Dad to his family property, Minderoo, in the Pilbara, Dad was keen to go. He met the Forrests when they were seated next to him at a lunch hosted by a local friend, a former politician. The Forrests were so enthralled by Dad's passion for the landscape that they came up with the idea of asking John to capture their landscape, the Pilbara, halfway through the lunch.

Soon after, Andrew sent their private jet to Sydney and, joined by Nicola, we made our way from the eastern coastline to the western—to Perth, then on to Minderoo, landing on the Forrests' private airstrip and taxiing into an enormous hangar. It was a green oasis amid a red landscape of iron ore, which Dad describes as the colour of cinnamon.

One evening over dinner, after a bottle of Grange Hermitage, Andrew and Nicola commissioned a collection of works from the visit. They knew all the works would be superb, alluding to them being a part of their personal art collection and mentioning that, at some stage, certain works may be publicly gifted. That same night, Dad and Andrew's elegant mother Judith sang old songs like 'Along the Road to Gundagai', a charming duet that transported us to another era before our time.

We were both a little overwhelmed. It was a commission on the scale of winning the Archibald Prize. 'This is serious stuff, this is a big responsibility,' I said on our return trip.

Dad leaned across the aeroplane with a glass of champagne in his hand and said, with a wry smile, 'Not if you know what you're doing.'

From then on we traversed the vast landscape by helicopter and four-wheel drive, with me as Dad's photographer to document the experience. No one but Dad works on his journals; my role was for reference. It was a familiar one for me, having been with Dad on previous trips to Kalgoorlie in the mid-1980s for a similar project, with the resulting works exhibited in *John Olsen: Gold* at the AGNSW. Those trips were for Pancontinental Mining Limited to mark the opening of its new Paddington goldmine, and we had both felt compromised when we saw the landscape. There were so many craters—it looked like a dog had been digging everywhere, as if it had forgotten where it had buried its bone.

John painted for a year from that Pilbara trip and, true to their word, the Forrests bought every one of the works. They were wonderful hosts, providing whatever Dad needed, with 'lively dinners—much jollity' he wrote in his journal after a barbecue for the station hands. Daily we explored the different aspects of the landscape in this ancient land; its sheer size and scale made me feel small and insignificant, with Minderoo alone occupying more than 2400 square kilometres. We went 'bush-bashing', bumping down tracks, through red dust, flanked by white gum trees, towards an endless horizon. There was a helicopter journey to savour the oysters on the edge of the Exmouth Gulf, downing 'oyster catchers': Andrew's favourite Minderoo cocktail of oysters immersed in vodka. Dad was fascinated by the omnipresent birdlife, the zebra finches, kingfishers, kookaburras, the raucous sounds of the cockatoos, the ducks on the green–yellow-ochre river. At night we would hear the roaring of the desert frogs and the squeaks of guinea fowl, which the Forrests kept like free-range chickens. On these expeditions we would feast beside the river on Minderoo-raised beef and sausages, smoked over the campfire.

Andrew and Nicola flew us to parts of the property where there were some of the oldest rock formations on Earth, geology that made the ancient Chinese terracotta warriors look fresh.

The Forrest family secured the leasehold for Minderoo in 1878 for 120 years until it was sold due to drought and debt. Andrew had spent his early years as a jackaroo on the property and bought it back into the family in 2009. This enormous property is not a gift; it requires expensive infrastructure to meet its needs, and a loyal and dedicated staff. Andrew has installed a weir to guarantee water supply and regeneration of the river, and established centre-pivot irrigation to produce vegetables and cattle feed that look like emerald-green and yellow crop circles. The Forrest family has a deep respect for their unique property, and a commitment to a sustainable future for the environment.

The focus of Andrew and Nicola is now on their philanthropic pursuits. In 2008, Andrew was the richest man in Australia, having made his massive fortune selling iron ore to the

Chinese for steel production. In 2013, he and Nicola were the first Australians to pledge the majority of their wealth to charities in their lifetimes through the Minderoo Foundation, committing A$1.5 billion to a range of global initiatives. During the recent devastating bushfires, Andrew and Nicola donated $70 million alone. More recently, they have donated an enormous amount to chosen charities to assist the aged, disabled and homeless during the pandemic. I admire them immensely.

Creativity feeds the soul. Mum wrote beautifully about the creative process, how it changes a person when they have a creative outlet, how it changes 'one's blood', a passionate means of being able to find 'a vision to follow and see the world'. This gentle woman spoke with such integrity and insight into how art had changed her life: 'The thing is to be absolutely fearless, fearless of one's incongruity, not wanting gifts only, just going along, appreciating the incidentals, the trivia, the banalities. I think one of the greatest things that art has taught me is this: things that I thought were commonplace and not worth noticing are perhaps the richest things around us.'

My father once had a Malaysian studio artist assistant who was an atheist. After months of working together, he convinced John that there was no God or life force, that we are all just matter risen from the earth and we will finally return to the earth as dust. John tells how all the magic in his art disappeared: the work became lifeless, deadpan. He soon found himself depressed and lost in the studio, not knowing where to go next with his work, with his art. The earth had turned grey.

He was by no means a Christian, despite his Catholic education, but he always believed in the intangible power of the planet, and his depictions of landscape and nature were the core of his work. So he had to find his way out of it. On a daily basis he prayed in his mind for the muse of creativity to return. Sure enough, it did, and again 'the life force', the positive light of life, reappeared.

I always felt that John, with his work being so evocative and semiotic in its vision, was a vehicle for past creative spirits to work through him. I believe that his perspective of the topographic landscape, his universal understanding of the sun, and the Western forces in his use of colour, his palette and figurative sensibility are all results of a kind of subconscious channelling of these forces. Beyond DNA and instinct, where does someone who grew up in a house with no art or books find this passion, talent and aesthetic ability? Without question, the intangible forces of the universe work through him.

My father's metaphor for a successful idea or image was a 'circus animal'. If he thought that an artist had exhausted an idea or was producing nothing but ubiquitous potboilers, he would proclaim, 'That artist needs a new circus animal.' He said it about Sidney Nolan's highly prolific final works made with paint out of a spray can.

That circus animal reared its head one day at lunch with John and Tim Storrier, in a Chinese restaurant in Bathurst. Tim is famous for his distinctive paintings of burning ropes, a kind of homage to Turner's works depicting the Great Fire of London. Each has a very accomplished painted sunset set in contrast to, and in competition with, a long, floating, burning rope across the canvas. They were and still are very sought after.

The flamboyant art dealer Barry Stern once said that 'the best thing about Tim Storrier's work is that it goes so well with leather furniture'. It is not uncommon to find a burning rope in a corporate foyer, in an airport lounge or on a mega-yacht.

Over lunch, John was complaining about Katharine's spending on her Lusitano horses at the farm, and Tim suggested that he paint more of his famous frogs. John, a little insulted, responded, 'With your burning ropes, you're the one who needs to invent a new circus animal.'

Tim shot back, 'Well, with Katharine's horses, your paddocks are full of them.'

Sparring artists have provided some of the funniest moments in my life, and sometimes the most insulting verbal and physical confrontations. A fragile ego is a no-go zone.

I had to leave the restaurant I was laughing so hard.

John has always had studio cats, saying that they bring mystical energy into the space. As he has aged, though, he has also needed human help in the studio, for small jobs or even just to keep him company. Louise and I both try to spend as much time as we can with him, and it does frustrate me that I have not been able to fulfil this role more. Interestingly, the mischievousness of his assistants, and the gossip that John finds so entertaining, play into the dance.

Yet many a sycophant has found their way into his life by promising to make it easier, moonlighting as a studio assistant while actually supplying the secondary art market or having the sole focus of redirecting works to non-representing galleries. Ben Quilty aptly describes these art charlatans as 'bottom-feeders'.

One 'assistant' was stealing what John calls 'studio droppings'—unfinished or discarded works—and then 'embellishing' them. John became suspicious after seeing works appear on the secondary market; a dealer challenged them, and they ended up in court. The embellisher presented photographs of John with a glass of wine in his hand, visibly the worse for wear, saying, 'What would John know? He was always drunk.' It was a terrible betrayal after a very long friendship. John made an etching called *The Forger* about it. The gallery and John ended up settling on the steps of the court in Melbourne. The Forger has been banished.

After a recent visit by another 'assistant', it was noticed that an oil painting was missing. 'For restoration', the assistant said when challenged. Unconvinced, John reviewed the work and asked why he had not been consulted about it needing conservation and where the conservation was needed, only to be told that 'preventative work' was required. This was a defining moment for John when he finally realised that his long-term friend could not be trusted and, likewise, he was summarily told never to return.

Going into business with family is not always recommended; mixing money and relationships doesn't always work. But when Dad said to me, when I was a small boy, 'You and I will do great things together', I believed that was what we would always ultimately do, having no concept back then of how challenging it would be. Looking back, we have achieved that much, if not more, in the end.

42

THE ARTIST, THE COOK, HIS WIFE AND HER DAUGHTER

For Dad, the loss of Katharine in December 2016 was heart-breaking. To then discover the duplicity and deceit of Katharine's daughter, Karen, sent him into a deep melancholy that was hard for Louise and me to see. The thought that Katharine had been duplicitous, whether knowingly or not, in the transference of funds devastated him. The monetary loss was one thing, but the idea of that ultimate betrayal compounded his pain.

Karen and her siblings had been part of Dad's life. With characteristic generosity, he had paid for their education and that of their children, lavish weddings, cars and first-class trips around the world, and provided them with continual financial assistance. Karen's own relationship with her mother 'fluctuated', Dad has said: 'It was tidal.' For Dad, though, we were all still one family, however fractured.

In the last two months of Katharine's life, Karen moved into a cottage at the farm to be close to her mother while her kitchen was being renovated. Not long before her death, Karen persuaded her mother to write a new will, changing Karen's inheritance, effectively more than doubling the amount. The next day, without Dad's knowledge, Katharine transferred $2.73 million from her account to her daughter. A further $30,000 was transferred to pay off Karen's credit card debt. After Katharine's surgery, her doctor said that she was mentally incapacitated as a result, and that nothing she did or said during this period could be considered valid.

Just before Katharine died, she had tried to warn Dad, saying: 'Karen is after money and the properties.' Astoundingly, at Katharine's funeral, in her eulogy to her mother Karen even described Dad as 'The Bank'. It was unforgivable, even to a man who is known for his generosity, compassion and tolerance.

Karen's behaviour became increasingly intolerable. She presented Dad with a list of items that she would like; these included not just Katharine's personal possessions but valuable paintings belonging to Dad, even his own works. With some works and items, Dad relented to appease her, and with others he refused. Soon after, she arrived, unannounced again, with George, this time to confront Dad. They were aggressive and intimidating. Fortunately, Louise was there and filmed everything.[1] Hurt beyond belief at Karen's actions, Dad could only naturally feel differently about her. A few weeks later she turned up with a tow truck but the gardener, Peter, intervened. John would later give evidence in court that paintings, prints and treasured objects suddenly disappeared.

To add insult to injury, Karen then proceeded to ask Dad for more, even after everything she had already received. In this I actually feel compassion for Karen, that she had never been pushed to be emotionally and financially independent like Louise and I were. In reality, Katharine only facilitated Karen's dependency and sense of entitlement. Karen's behaviour was symptomatic of what we recognise as entitlement, of losing a comfortable existence and the privileged lifestyle she so prized.

This left Dad in a legal quagmire. Despite trying to resolve the situation amicably and through mediation, Dad ended up in the NSW Supreme Court in July 2019 to retrieve the sums transferred.[2] We tried to excuse it through grief or ignorance, but the simple truth is that the courts would later determine that Karen had taken advantage of an elderly, trusting man and, in hindsight, her own mother.

Louise and I were not involved in Dad's decision to launch legal action against Karen. For Dad, it was not the money but the principle. He had given Katharine everything. Karen inherited her mother's estate. All Dad wanted was his paintings back.

The court case was splashed across all the papers, accompanied by the video footage Louise had taken that had been submitted as evidence. The witness statements and supporting documentation tendered in evidence at the hearing were damning: the gardener testified that very valuable paintings, including a couple of Brett Whiteleys and a Ben Quilty, 'seemed to disappear'. As the days went on, Karen's evidence became more and more outlandish. The judge had to intervene after several excruciating exchanges in cross-examination, culminating in Karen's ultimate reply—'I do have some morality'—when she was accused of bullying her mother into 'giving' her money without Dad's knowledge and consent.

We did not think Karen could stoop any lower until the last days of her evidence when she claimed that her mother's 'gift' of the money transferred was motivated by Dad flirting with their close friend Nicky McKay—in essence, an act of revenge.[3]

Dad just said that he flirts with everyone and always has. Nicky and Dad have developed a 'companionship' since Katharine died, but this is a friendship and not a sexual relationship, nor a cohabitation.[4] Considering Dad's age, I find it hilarious that his sex life is a matter of public scrutiny, and I hope that I'm still flirting at his age. The emotional toll this has taken on Dad is inconceivable, yet he has maintained his stoicism.

On 27 September 2019, the judgment by Justice John Sackar was announced and Karen was found to have procured the monies through 'unconscionable conduct or undue influence'. Justice Sackar said, '[It] shows a degree of selfishness and utter self-indulgence. She was in my view plainly ignoring her mother's vulnerability and instead was focused on her own material gain.'[5] It was damning on every count. Dad, who always avoids conflict, was victorious. He felt that he had won the war, with the terms and repayments still to be decided. Whatever the result, to have Karen's actions exposed has been a relief; we just regret that Dad had to go through this to clear his name and Katharine's. The court papers revealed the lengths that Dad and Katharine had gone to in order be fair to all the children involved in the eventual distribution of their estate. Karen's actions have now excluded her from our family forever.

To our amazement, in February 2020, Karen appealed the decision. Despite Dad's advanced age and health, and the impact of the stress involved in any legal battle, her appeal went ahead. We could only hope it would be fully resolved expediently.

The appeal took six months to be resolved. Dad has said of the duration of the trial, nearly a four-year period, that his 'life was not his own', a tragic situation for a man of any age. The verdict on the appeal was read to an empty court room at 11 am on Friday 21 August, just two weeks before this book went to print. John rang me at 11.30 expressing his absolute relief that the ordeal was finally over. It was resolved, the appeal was dismissed. We are now in the position to truly enjoy these remaining years with John, with no outsider's actions hanging over our heads.

Dad's stunning work *Holiday by the Sea* (1993) came up for resale in 2019. This stunning painting is an amalgamation of the memories of long, sun-drenched summer days of Dad growing up at Bondi Beach, the early experiences living at Deià and, most poignantly, the halcyon days at Watsons Bay and Pearl Beach. It draws upon his recollections of the multifaceted holiday activities around the ocean and joyous children playing on the beach, culminating in the pleasure of cooking and sharing relaxed Mediterranean-inspired meals by the water. The home depicted resembles the house at Pearl Beach. The warm, vibrant palette is quintessentially Olsen: the life-giving energy of the sun's rays like yellow-orange saffron tentacles in a paella, the blue pylons of the wharf at Camp Cove. It is an exuberant interpretation of an ideal place and time. Dad had painted it while he was living at Rydal. He had a holiday house at Broome at the time—a different landscape to the harbour, yet still a cottage by the sea.

The work, as an example of a great Olsen, was the showpiece of the gallery at the Sydney Contemporary art fair. Having just sold another large work of Dad's, *Spring at Rydal*, as a family, we decided to buy back *Holiday by the Sea* on the opening day of the fair, loath to miss out on obtaining a work that epitomised such an idyllic time. For Louise and me, it really is our own special holiday by the sea.

Immediately after, we received an offer for the work, but we all rejected it on the basis of the painting being such a treasured part of our family history. Perhaps, by ensuring that this work remains in the family, we have offset some of the grief of losing *The Mother*.

43

THE FULL CIRCLE

As a preview to the 2020 season at the Sydney gallery, we held an artists' lunch. It was a few days after a ferocious storm had hit the east coast of Australia; the power had been out at the gallery for four days, miraculously returning that morning to our collective relief. Called a 'Summer Feast', it was a celebration of our upcoming program and the group show featuring over 50 works from the stable. Many of the artists attended; McLean Edwards, Sophie Cape, Anna-Wili Highfield, Dani McKenzie, Nicholas Harding and Marisa Purcell were there to toast the coming year—and, of course, so were Louise and Stephen, along with friends and staff. A long table adorned with flowers ran the length of the gallery, the food served on brightly hued Dinosaur Designs platters and bowls as we feasted, surrounded by paintings, sculptures and other works of art: a showcase of the talented artists I am so fortunate to work with.

In my welcoming speech, I said that we were 'changing the dialogue'. We had kept on some very important artists and gained some new ones, and I said that we wanted to 'create a dialogue that more people find interesting', and for people to find in us a gallery active in representing contemporary art practice. To close, I recited a Gerard Manley Hopkins poem that John would often say at dinner, one that has stuck with me in regard to the idea of what is beautiful.

Pied Beauty

Glory be to God for dappled things—
    For skies of couple-colour as a brinded cow;
      For rose-moles all in stipple upon trout that swim;
Fresh-firecoal chestnut-falls; finches' wings;
    Landscape plotted and pieced—fold, fallow, and plough;
      And áll trádes, their gear and tackle and trim.

All things counter, original, spare, strange;
    Whatever is fickle, freckled (who knows how?)
      With swift, slow; sweet, sour; adazzle, dim;
He fathers-forth whose beauty is past change:
          Praise him.[1]

Looking around the room, at all the artists, family and friends, I was filled with contentment and satisfaction, looking forward to the years to come.

It had always seemed possible for me to walk endlessly everywhere, if there was the time. But as I crept into my fifties, I ended up with osteoarthritis and, like Dad, faced the fate of a double knee replacement. Throughout the pain of the operation and recovery, the thoughts that kept me going were being able to dance again, playing tennis with James and moving around freely like I used to.

Although warned about the operation, nothing prepared me for the weeks of agonising pain, despite the medication. Weaning myself off the strong opiates was like going cold turkey, and it was terrifying to think that I may have to go through rehab all over again. The excruciatingly familiar pangs of withdrawal were another endurance test and made me realise, once more, how susceptible I was to addiction and the black dog of depression. Thanks to my health practitioner, I was prescribed medicinal cannabis, which took the edge off the withdrawal. Medicinal cannabis is certainly the panacea of the future.

Just as the world was shattered by COVID-19, the lease on our New York gallery was up. Emerald, with Adrian's support, had done all she could and had worked so hard, but we were losing traction. The hardest reality about having the gallery in New York was that, when Dad most needed support, I was never really able to be there. Being a present father for James was another consideration. Torn between my responsibilities in Australia and the effort and time of the constant travel, I had not had the opportunity to effectively meld into New York society and the art world.

And something grave was in the air. It was not widely reported by China, and Trump was more concerned about his economy than human lives, but everything had started to stall. No one could have known that a deadly black spider had started to creep its way around the globe from Wuhan, spinning its web across the world. The threat of this new virus was subdued and played down, with Trump announcing that it was just a tiny flu that would go away.

An emergency whistle-stop return trip to New York was a necessity. The government had insisted that all art galleries close.

Everything had to be placed in storage, and the gallery door closed until further notice. Travel bans around the world were being implemented, and although realising the danger, the stubborn Taurus in me still took the risk, and I arrived feeling safe, even invincible. No one suggested that I would be entering what would rapidly become a pandemic hot spot. I was both relieved and optimistic that we had a temporary 'out' of the Big Apple. We had dodged a bullet, but another one was on its way.

In the early days of the New York gallery, a friend had metaphorically proclaimed, 'Opening a gallery in America could kill you.' How those words resonate today.

I contracted COVID-19 on my way back from New York, on flight QF11, the second-last plane back to Sydney via Los Angeles before the borders shut down. It was chilling to discover later that on that flight were sixteen other infected people. One man, three rows back, had a disturbing persistent cough throughout the overnight flight.

Arriving home without any symptoms and seemingly well, I was placed into isolation following the government order. After two weeks, still feeling well and wanting to visit Dad, something inside me prompted me to get tested. It was devastating to discover, after the intrusive nasal test, that I had actually caught the virus. Although afraid, not knowing how it was going navigate my middle-aged disposition, I was more scared for anyone else I might have infected than for myself. Before my positive result, while keeping my distance, I had had a brief encounter with my son, Dom and Ya Ya ('Grandma' in Greek), my beautiful 80-year-old housekeeper of 25 years, who all met me on arrival off the plane.

Terrified that I could have unintentionally risked their safety, every day that I woke with no reports of them displaying symptoms was a relief, a reward beyond any lottery. I lay awake every night worrying about them, filled with remorse that I could have endangered the lives of my loved ones.

One night, a week later, I was suddenly gasping for air, as if someone large was sitting on my chest, and alternating between chills and sweats. Alone and afflicted, my only hope was to revert to prayer and attempt to reinvigorate my belief in the divine. With no vaccine or cure in sight, or any real medical advice, how to tackle the virus was my immediate dilemma. Having dealt with addiction ten years earlier, I wondered anew if this could be the mortal challenge that Paul Haefliger had spoken of back in Hill End when I was just a boy.

When I gave up alcohol, I had accepted and applied a silent surrender, knowing I was happy and had been gifted a wonderful life, and content with all of my achievements. Now, I decided to gently, not aggressively, engage my immune system in dealing with the virus, not to handle it by panicking as I have so often done in the past, but instead staying calm and not overreacting.

Remembering Gandhi's advice, I felt that only peaceful resistance and inner strength would prevail. Ultimately, I truly hoped that God was bigger than this. Eventually, it gently arrested itself and my body slowly return to wellness. Unlike many, I was very lucky not to pay the ultimate price. Most importantly, the family members I had crossed paths with remained free of the virus; their test results were clear. I would never have been able to forgive myself if it had been otherwise.

I am well aware that the manifestations of my infection were relatively mild and brief compared to so many. Yet it was the fear it instilled, rather than the depth of the illness, that brought my mortality into such sharp focus. If I had still been alcoholic and obese, and not had wellbeing health advice from Elizabeth through diet and supplements, it could have been so much worse.

My fear is that our society could become one of 'BC' and 'AC': Before COVID and After COVID. We can only hope a vaccine or cure will be developed swiftly. I am grateful to be here but desolate for the worldwide loss of life.

In the life of my family, nothing was ever ordinary. There was so much uncertainty about where the family was going, which line we would follow next. Yet perhaps to more free spirits we were seen as conservative; to the avant-garde, more bourgeois than bohemian. We were an unconventional family attuned to a conventional existence. We never went out of our way to be different; we just were.

My parents always believed in the artistic spirit, and embraced the way that its force interacted with and inhabited nature. Children inhale their parents' attitudes and their environment.

Somehow, with all of our different paths throughout our lives, we have stuck together. Even Mum and Dad, right to the end, still communicated in ideas, sharing a bond through family, books and poetry, many years after their marriage had ended. They remained friends with an enduring mutual respect. The family love between us never faltered.

The shadow of my father has evaporated. I now feel that I have earned my success and have found my place at the table.

My life now is one of serendipity; it is fluid, manageable. I am constantly surprised by what comes out of a day, and the oddities and opportunities that present themselves. When I began to write this book, it was a story about how I saw my life as a struggle against circumstances. Now it is a recognition of the gifts that have presented themselves to me in many forms. At first I blamed the people, places and things that orbited me, or I blamed life itself, for all of the things that had happened to me or that were wrong. Now I see the part I played in everything, good and bad, and moving forward I have the power to decide how things affect me. It is said that 'how people treat you is their karma, and how you respond is yours'. I know this to be truer now than ever before.

No matter how much money was spent on infrastructure, advertising and sourcing exemplary staff, the gallery was never going to be where I wanted it to be until I became more discerning and accepted that, actually, it was not the gallery that was wrong: it was my attitude and approach, and the necessity to take a personal inventory. In my early days, I felt that my education and artistic background gave me an advantage and with that came a sense of entitlement. Now I know that any success is simply down to me.

Deep within me was an authentic person who could engage with integrity and honesty to convey my vision and true passion for art—the visual, the intangible and the existential. Determination alone was not going to get me there; I needed humility, and to navigate the art world by seeing art as an essential service for the awakening it brings to people.

I realise now that so much of my life has been spent being angry, and one of my ongoing goals is to better manage my emotions. Dad always reminds me of Seneca's philosophy that the best way to deal with anger is with delay. I still struggle to take that advice. I had told myself a story about my life and my father that ultimately turned out to be untrue.

As an adult, my anger was often born of frustration with my own shortcomings—and, sometimes, my powerlessness— particularly when learning how to run a gallery. My exasperation with others was really an exasperation with myself; I unfairly expect perfection from everyone else when I am far from faultless myself. I have had to find my own metaphorical set of paints and brushes, to find some kind of outlet to calm my creative urge. Running a gallery, and now writing, has filled that art-shaped hole.

My mindfulness, meditation, exercise, diet and abstinence have helped me make huge inroads. I strive to lead a happier, more positive life. Today I hope that I am a better person to be around, with more empathy for others and a better recognition of the great things that are happening around me. The word 'God' is rarely mentioned in this book, but it is because of faith that I was able to become sober and have everything I have in my life today. This life was not designed to necessarily make you happy, it was gifted to you to challenge you. Abstinence is really a process of being pulled apart and re-sculptured.

My parents may have paid for my education, but life experience has taught me my greatest lessons. My experience continues to enrich my wisdom. Art is long, and life is short. My parents being art teachers was a lesson in the importance of handing it on. You succeed, then you help other people achieve their own success.'

With James, and with Dad becoming increasingly frail, my personal life and priorities revolve around home. Dad is living alone in Bowral, in the NSW Southern Highlands, the equivalent to the Cotswolds or the Hamptons. He loves his studio and the property. Both Louise and I spend as much time as possible at the farm with him, and it is one of my greatest joys. Typically, Dad sketches, Louise paints and I write, reading finished chapters to Dad and Louise as we relax later in the day. These times infuse me with a contentment similar to those memorable times growing up—the only omission being Mum. These are wonderful, golden years that we are having with Dad: cooking, conversing, reading or reciting poems, a little bit of travelling (before COVID), all making up for lost time. The things that were still unsaid have now been aired and are now forgiven.

When John told me that he had been taking the final draft of my book to bed with him to read I was thrilled, even though it was because he'd already finished the paper! For Dad, such an eloquent wordsmith, to say that he thought it was 'beautifully written' was immensely gratifying. He told me that he knew I had it in me, but was concerned that I might not ever finish it (at times I had my own doubts; it has been a long gestation).

'Well, you've finished your book, now you've got to face the music,' he said.

'Rather like you did after completing the Opera House mural?' I asked.

'Yes, but I was dealing with the music the whole time,' he said, referring to the constant heckling and criticism he received from the onsite tradesmen.

When my illusions about my father subsided, I awoke to so many greater things about him. The paradox is that it is the flaws in his art that are the essence of what makes it real. His haptic dexterity makes his art so profoundly skilled and authentic. The idea that his art is more about memory than reality allows him the lucidity of remembering time. His intellect, wit and wisdom all underlie a vulnerability to life and to the truth of the human condition. 'My greatest failures often turned into my greatest successes,' he often says.

Just to live each day and not care what my life may mean in the future is highly liberating. I am sticking to my own path now and am mindful not to define myself by others. As novelist Matt Haig so succinctly put it: 'Never be cool. Never try and be cool. Never worry what the cool people think. Head for the warm people. Life is warmth. You'll be cool when you're dead.'[2]

Dad has always been philosophical about dying—apart from his concern with what he is going to eat! 'My final wish would be to go like Renoir,' he has said. 'On the last day of his life, he painted his final picture, put down his brushes, sighed and said, "I think I'm beginning to learn something now."'

When the bushfires raged across New South Wales in the summer of 2019–20, Louise and I were deeply concerned for Dad at the farm. I spent some terrifying days with him, monitoring the outbreaks, walking around the property, checking the hoses. We suggested evacuating him and putting his art in storage but he refused, even as the looming bushfires crept closer to the house from either side. John has to be surrounded by his art even at the risk of losing it. Dad is a climate change sceptic, despite living through the worst drought in Australian history. He believes it is something that happens naturally every few thousand years. Louise and I have given up arguing with him. The paradox is that the landscape that provided him with so much inspiration could have ended up being the source of his ultimate loss. Of course, Dad (and his art) prevailed.

James, after a year at Timbertop, is happier and thriving, growing into the wonderful young adult we knew he would become. We can see the man emerging and cannot wait to meet him. While always feeling torn when away for business, it is perpetually a pleasure and a relief to return home, where my heart is. James joked the other day that after a lifetime of 'Where's Tim?' the epitaph on my tombstone should read: 'Tim's here!'

What makes me happiest now is my daily routine: my morning AA meetings with sober friends, the gym, the ocean swims and the coffee afterwards, then work. I still feel invigorated and excited by the future. With a greater trust, my eye, discernment and decision-making have become easier. Today, it is increasingly difficult living next to the gallery: my home and work life are blurred. This, too, will evolve.

I always planned to add a third storey to the gallery, creating an educational space and private viewing area for students and clients. From the roof, there is a view across Paddington to the harbour, a view too good not to be enjoyed. We were finally granted council approval to proceed in mid-2020. Once the world economy improves, this will be a welcome addition to the building. For many collectors, discretion is everything.

Now, more than ever, I think more about family, the talented people and artists whom I work with and believe in, and continuing my work as an AA sponsor. For the galleries to maintain their trajectory, taking Australian art to a greater world market while hardly ever having to use the words 'Australia' is my ambition. Even if this does not eventuate in the near future, I will never be ashamed of saying, 'At least I tried.'

I have conquered many personal defects and, thank God, my only addiction left is an addiction to art, a chronic and incurable condition I am blessed with.

At the expense of exhausting a cliché (or worse, a pun, given my ultimate trajectory!) my life begun as a blank canvas, in every sense. Over the ensuing years, that canvas has endured everything from nervous, tentative scribbles to arrogant, overly ambitious brushstrokes, but throughout the adventure I've benefited from a solid frame provided by the generous embrace and patience of a family I will always be grateful for. This little book is dedicated to them, and all those, like me, for whom the paint will never be quite dry.

But fuck art, let's dance!

ACKNOWLEDGEMENTS

Thank you to Allen & Unwin for their patience, in particular Sue Hind and Tom Gilliat. With everything that has happened in the last years since I started this book, I hope that it was worth the wait. To Victoria Mills, my life coach, who put me up to this in the first place, and Melanie Cain who introduced me to Allen & Unwin.

I would like to thank Anna Johnson for the first draft of this book and then the assistance of Gudrun Willcocks. To Gretel Killeen, for her critical eye over the first draft and her advice. And to Kylie Norton, for putting this whole jigsaw together, from a draft to a book. Her contribution, research and advice have been invaluable.

Thank you to all the people who gave me an opportunity—Stuart and Anne Purves, and Caroline Purves of the Australian Galleries Archive for allowing access to the John Olsen records for the purpose of the John Olsen catalogue raisonné also referenced in this book. Thank you also to Ros Oxley, Rex Irwin and, most importantly, to all the wonderfully talented artists who have been with me from the beginning and who have joined me since: Paul Davies, Leila Jeffreys, George Byrne, Sophie Cape, Jacqui Stockdale and Sally Anderson, to name just a few. I am particularly grateful to still be working with Nicholas Harding, Lynne Watkins, Chris Langlois and with Lyn Williams (regarding the estate of her husband Fred Williams), along with Amanda Marburg and Stephen Bird. Great gratitude to Lyn Williams for maintaining her belief in me. Often in the art world it is not easy for people to stick by you, and I am so grateful to those people who have.

A special thanks to all the art lovers, especially Lee Seng Hui and his wife Elaine for their long-term support and trust in the gallery. To Sue and Lang Walker, Laurence Freedman and so many others.

There have been many mentors in my life. Rudy Komon was the first, along with my father, both men of great character. In my latter years, I have contributed to various boards: the City Art Institute, now UNSW Art & Design, and I thank Ian Howard for choosing me as an alumnus; and the board of the University of New South Wales, invited by David Gonski. Attending meetings with some of Australia's captains of industry has given me a different perspective.

There are other mentors, too: author and filmmaker Robert Raymond; Pat Corrigan, the great philanthropist and art collector; and Dr Peter Elliott, an old friend of Rudy and Dad's, who in my early days introduced important collectors to my gallery and spoke generously of my younger artists. All of these men to me represent mentorship in one way or another but most of all they epitomise 'true character', their tenacity, honesty and integrity making them people of real value.

To my dear friends who made me accountable to prevent me stepping back into a pub and spent much time with me as sponsors: Roger Joyce, Rick Grossman and Chris Mordue, and Professor Ross Fitzgerald. And to Margaret Olley and Barry Humphries, who never judged me and who, in caring, reached out and facilitated my sobriety. I appreciate that they could see in me what I could not see in myself.

I thank Katrina Arent in Sydney, and Emerald and Adrian Gruin in New York, for helping to keep everything afloat in recent times. My gratitude to Dom Ogilvie, for our time together, for our ongoing friendship and for James. And to Mitchell and Samantha, and Dom's sister Sarah and her partner Jane Shaw, who provided profound spiritual advice, not just to me but the family during the toughest time of my recovery. And, of course, my family, especially the continuing love and support from my father, Louise, Stephen, Camille and James.

NOTES

Where my father, John, my mother, Valerie, or other close members of the family are quoted and no reference is provided, the sources are the many, many discussions I've had with my parents and other family members over the years, about our early lives in particular. Some stories have been previously published and differ slightly to those told by my father; where known, these have been noted.

Chapter 2: Daddy's Boy
1   Hart, Deborah. *John Olsen*. Second edition. Sydney: Craftsman House, 2000.

Chapter 3: Spanish Encounter
1   Pierse, Simon. *Australian Art and Artists in London, 1950–1965: An Antipodean Summer*. Farnham, UK: Ashgate, 2012.
2   Pringle, John Douglas. *Australian Painting Today*. London: Thames & Hudson, 1963, p. 88.
3   This collection was sold in 2000. See Luck, Ross K. *The Australian Painters, 1964–1966: Contemporary Australian Painting from the Mertz Collection*. Washington, D.C.: Corcoran Gallery of Art, c. 1966.
4   Olsen, John. Journal entry, 21 May 1966.
5   Nicklin, Lenore. 'Our island weavers: Australians are making tapestry'. *The Sydney Morning Herald*, 12 January 1971.
6   Olsen, John. Journal entry, 18 December 1966.
7   Schlunke, Juliet. *Buns in the Oven: John Olsen's Bakery Art School*. Melbourne: Thames & Hudson, 2016.
8   Art Gallery of NSW Collection. *Spanish Encounter* by John Olsen. <www.artgallery.nsw.gov.au/collection/works/OA29.1960.a-c/>.
9   Olsen, John. *Drawn from Life*. Sydney: Duffy & Snellgrove, 1997, p. 193.

Chapter 4: Utopia Does Not Exist

1   Olsen, John. Journal entry, 27 January 1970.
2   *The Australian*, 15 January 1970.
3   Olsen, John. Journal entry, 15 March 1970.
4   Olsen, John. *My Complete Graphics, 1957–1979*. Melbourne: Gryphon Books & Australian Galleries, 1980, p. 23.

Chapter 5: Bohemian Royalty

1   Nicklin, Lenore. '$35,000 mural by Olsen'. *The Sydney Morning Herald*, 29 August 1972.
2   Olsen, John. *Drawn from Life*. Sydney: Duffy & Snellgrove, 1997, p. 105.
3   Quoted in McInerney, Jackson. '"My Salute to Five Bells": John Olsen explains his beguiling masterpiece'. *Books & Arts*, ABC, 26 August 2015.
4   McRae, Toni. 'Opening scene thrills the Queen', *The Sun-Herald*, Special Opera House Souvenir Issue, 21 October 1973.
5   Olsen, John. Journal entry, 21 August 1970.
6   Wilson, Ashleigh. 'John Olsen retrospective salutes living treasure from September 16'. *The Australian*, 10 September 2016.
7   Pitt, Helen. 'The "crazy and epic" story of John Coburn's Opera House curtain call'. *The Sydney Morning Herald*, Arts, 20 April 2019.

Chapter 6: Into the Valley

1   Farrelly, Kate. 'The former Watsons Bay home of legendary artist John Olsen has hit the market'. *The Sydney Morning Herald*, Domain, 23 March 2018.

Chapter 7: Of Cabbages and Kings

1   The King's School. 'King's 2020 Art Prize & Exhibition', 2020. <www.king sartshow.com.au/artprize.php>.
2   Olsen, John. Journal entry, January 1986: 'My divorce to Valerie came through.' He married Noela on 31 May 1986.

Chapter 8: Pearly: Almost Paradise

1   Pearl Beach Aboriginal History Group. <www.pearlbeachprogress.org.au/aboriginal-history-group>.
2   Stephens, Tony. 'Green before it was fashionable'. *The Sydney Morning Herald*, 12 September 2007.
3   Serventy, Vincent. *Dryandra: The Story of an Australian Forest*. Sydney: A.H. & A.W. Reed, 1970.
4   McDonald, John. 'Art of the clear, precise and joyful'. *The Sydney Morning Herald*, 6 November 2006.

Chapter 9: Valerie

1   *The Australian Women's Weekly* (1933–1982), 25 July 1951, front cover. <http://nla.gov.au/nla.news-article44794004>, accessed 24 August 2020.

2 All quotes from Valerie Strong are from Strong, Valerie & de Berg, Hazel. *Valerie Strong Interviewed by Hazel de Berg in the Hazel de Berg Collection* (sound recording) 1965, TRC 1/119. National Library of Australia.

3 Strong & de Berg, *Valerie Strong Interviewed by Hazel de Berg*.

4 Olsen, John & Norton, Kylie. Interview with John Olsen at OLSEN Gallery, Sydney, 2019.

5 Wright, Judith. 'The Cicadas'. *The Gateway*. Sydney: Angus & Robertson, 1953.

6 'Five Women in Same Art Show.' *The Sydney Morning Herald*, 26 June 1963.

7 Davies, Linda. 'Gypsy life led Gil Docking into feted arts administration career'. *The Sydney Morning Herald*, 22 January 2016.

8 Newcastle Art Gallery Foundation. '*Black Totem II*'. 2020, <www.nag foundation.org.au/artwork/black-totem-11>.

9 Diaz, Tina. 'Fighting for poetic justice in Iraq'. *The Sydney Morning Herald*, 17 January 1992.

10 Dr Kübler-Ross, Elizabeth. *Death: The Final Stage of Growth*. Prentice Hall, 1975.

Chapter 10: The Roots of the Tree

1 McCubbin Family History Association. <https://mccubbinfamily.info>.

2 Gibson, James. *Inscriptions on the Tombstones and Monuments Erected in Memory of the Covenanters*. Glasgow: Dunn & Wright, c. 1881.

3 Swedish Household Examination Books, 1880–1930.

4 'Rev. James Marshall'. *The Sydney Morning Herald*, 24 April 1930.

5 Cameron, James & Walker, John. *Centenary History of the Presbyterian Church in New South Wales*. Sydney: Angus & Robertson, 1905.

6 'Vance Marshall's father, death at Ravensworth, pioneer Presbyterian'. *Windsor and Richmond Gazette*, 2 May 1930.

7 Eikos. 'How the Hunter region "fits" into the economic and social story of NSW'. 18 March 2016. <www.eikos.com.au/how-the-hunter-region-fits-into-the-economic-and-social-story-of-nsw/>.

8 Nichols, Louise. 'Historic homestead finds itself atop a valuable coal reserve'. *Singleton Arms*, 28 August 2018.

9 Kevans, Denis. 'Vance Marshall trod the path to Socialism'. *The Tribune*, 19 February 1964.

10 Marshall, James Vance. *World of the Living Dead*. Sydney: Anderson, 1919; Pankhurst Walsh, Adela. 'Adela Pankhurst Walsh on Vance Marshall's book: "The World of the Living Dead"'. *Socialist*, 16 January 1920.

Chapter 11: If You Can Remember Art School

1 Jones, Jonathan. 'The Show Is Over: Has painting really had its day?'. *The Guardian*, 11 October 2013.

Chapter 13: Mentors

1 Ousback, Anders. 'On the care, preparation and consumption of humble pie'. Conference report, *Celebrating the Maker: 7th National Ceramics Conference*, Adelaide, 1993.

2 Newton, John. 'A man born with good taste'. *The Sydney Morning Herald*, 3 June 2004.

3 Newton, 'A man born with good taste'.

4 'Lonely death of restaurateur with perfect taste'. *The Sydney Morning Herald*, 31 May 2004.

5 'Lonely death of restaurateur with perfect taste'.

6 Newton, 'A man born with good taste'.

7 Hemingway, Ernest. *For Whom the Bell Tolls*. New York, NY: Scribner Paperback Fiction, 1995.

8 Nicklin, Lenore. 'Komon, Rudolph John (Rudy) (1908–1982)'. *Australian Dictionary of Biography*. Canberra: National Centre of Biography, Australian National University.

9 Rudy Komon Art Gallery. *The First Gallery in Paddington: The Artists and their Work Tell the Story of the Rudy Komon Art Gallery*. Sydney: Edwards & Shaw, 1981.

10 Komon, Rudy & Gleeson, James. *Rudy Komon Interview with James Gleeson* (sound recording). The James Gleeson Oral History Collection. Canberra: National Library of Australia, 6 March 1979.

11 Brack, John. 'Death of the artists' friend'. *The Age*, Arts, 28 October 1982.

12 Art Gallery of New South Wales & Raymond, Robert (ed.). *52 Views of Rudy Komon*. Sydney: The Beagle Press & Rudy Komon Memorial Fund, 1999.

13 Woollahra Municipal Council. 'Rudy Komon MBE: Plaque location'. <www.woollahra.nsw.gov.au/library/local_history/woollahra_plaque_scheme/plaques/rudy_komon_mbe>.

Chapter 14: Lunch with Donald Friend

1 Wilson, Ashleigh. 'Friend's dark past comes into the frame'. *Australian*, Arts, 18 June 2019.

2 Hughes, Robert. *Donald Friend*. Sydney: Edwards & Shaw, 1965.

3 Pearce, Barry, et al. *Donald Friend, 1915–1989: Retrospective* (2nd ed.). Sydney: Art Gallery of New South Wales, 1990.

4 Boland, Michaela. 'Donald Friend sexual abuse victim seeks compensation from National Library'. *ABC News*, 25 January 2018.

5 Wilson, Ashleigh. 'Back in the frame? Jailed artist finds the bar's set high'. *The Australian*, 4 May 2019; Byrne, Elizabeth. 'Indigenous artist Dennis Nona sentenced to five years jail after getting 12yo girl pregnant'. *ABC News*, 22 April 2015.

6 Klepac, Lou. *The Genius of Donald Friend: Drawings from the Diaries 1942–1989*. Canberra: National Library of Australia, 2006.

7 Uriah Moses. Uriah Moses, one of 301 convicts transported on the *Royal*

Admiral, March 1800. The 18-year-old Uriah was sentenced to death at the Old Bailey, later commuted to life, for breaking and entering and stealing, arriving in Australia on 22 November 1800. He received a Conditional Pardon aged 48 and became very prosperous, living at Windsor on the Hawkesbury, shortly after marrying Ann Daley (daughter of convicts) aged 21. They had a family of nine. <https://convictrecords.com.au/convicts/moses/uriah/79053>, accessed 24 October 2019.

Chapter 15: The Godfather

1 Hughes, Robert. 'The Artist as Entrepreneur'. *The New Republic*, 14 December 1987. <https://newrepublic.com/article/105864/the-artist-entrepreneur>, accessed 12 June 2020.

2 Quoted in Kaplan, James. 'Big'. *New York Magazine*, 12 August 1996, pp. 35–6.

3 McCaughey, Patrick. 'The rancor of Robert Hughes'. *Meanjin*, Spring 2016.

4 The Pulitzer Prizes. 'The 2011 Pulitzer Prize Winner in Criticism: Sebastian Smee of *The Boston Globe*'. <www.pulitzer.org/winners/sebastian-smee>.

5 Smee, Sebastian. 'Robert Hughes: The genuine article in *The Spectacle of Skill*'. *The Australian*, 9 January 2016.

6 Smee, Sebastian. *The Art of Rivalry: Four Friendships, Betrayals, and Breakthroughs in Modern Art*. Melbourne: Text Publishing, 2016.

7 *Agnes Martin: Homage to [a] Life: Paintings 1990–2004*. Dia Beacon, Beacon, New York, NY, 6 April – 26 November 2007.

8 Hazel de Berg's series of interviews included one with Ian Fairweather. I strongly recommend listening to the recording of him rather than merely reading the transcripts. Fairweather, Ian & de Berg, Hazel. *Ian Fairweather Interviewed by Hazel de Berg in the Hazel de Berg Collection* (sound recording). Canberra: National Library of Australia, 1963.

9 Sutherland, Kathie. *Brett Whiteley: Catalogue Raisonné: 1955–1992*. Melbourne: Schwartz City, 2019; Coslovich, Gabriella. 'Whiteley painting bought for $1.5 million is bathed in doubt'. *The Sydney Morning Herald*, 13 May 2019.

10 Meacham, Steve. 'Kind of blue'. *The Sydney Morning Herald*, 12 November 2011.

11 Power, Liza. 'A brush with rebellion'. *The Sydney Morning Herald*, 12 November 2011.

12 Angel, Anita. 'Looking at Art—March: Mike Brown'. Charles Darwin University Art Collection and Art Gallery, 5 March 2014. <www.cdu.edu.au/artcollection-gallery/looking-at-art/mike-brown>.

13 Brown, Mike. *Kite*. 1964. Heide Museum of Modern Art, Melbourne. <https://collection.heide.com.au/objects/1815>.

14 Hetherington, John. 'Ian Fairweather: Gentle nomad who lives a lonely life'. *The Age*, 9 June 1962.

Chapter 17: First Love and Artistic Rivalry

1   'Now it's argy-bargy over Arkie's millions'. *The Sydney Morning Herald*, 14 December 2002.
2   Hawley, Janet. 'Whiteley, Arkie (1964–2001)'. *The Sydney Morning Herald*, 22 December 2001.
3   'The will to win'. *The Sydney Morning Herald*, 14 December 2002.
4   Hawley, 'Whiteley, Arkie'.

Chapter 19: Early Instincts

1   Buggins, Anne & Guest, Debbie. 'Gordon Stephenson, Guy Grey-Smith, Eric Edgar Cooke'. *The West Australian*, 9 November 2006.
2   From *AGNSW Handbook*, 1999. Quoted in Art Gallery of New South Wales Collection. '*Cosimo I de' Medici in Armour* by Agnolo Bronzino'. <www.artgallery.nsw.gov.au/collection/works/78.1996/>.
3   McIlroy, Tom. 'Malcolm and Lucy Turnbull's art selection showcases Indigenous and female artists'. *The Sydney Morning Herald*, 3 September 2016.
4   Domjen, Briana. 'Malcolm Turnbull gives funny speech at Catalina'. *The Sunday Telegraph*, 1 July 2018.

Chapter 20: Going It Alone

1   Hughes, Robert. Speech delivered to Royal Academy of Art, Burlington House, London, 2 June 2004.
2   Strickland, Katrina. 'Artwork tops $1m'. *Australian Financial Review*, Saleroom, 19 October 2006.
3   Ross, Peter. *Let's Face It: The History of the Archibald Prize* (6th ed.). Sydney: Art Gallery of New South Wales, 2017.
4   McDonald, John. 'Arch rivals racing for brush with fame'. *The Sydney Morning Herald*, 14 December 1989.

Chapter 21: Art Temple

1   Olsen, John. *A Salute to Sydney* (exhibition catalogue). Tim Olsen Gallery, Sydney, 2007.
2   Kaldor Public Art Projects. 'Project 10—Jeff Koons: Project summary'. 1995. <kaldorartprojects.org.au/projects/project-10-jeff-koons>.
3   Morris, Linda. 'Puppy love: How Jeff Koons' famous sculpture could have been ours'. *The Sydney Morning Herald*, 7 September 2019.
4   'The Olsens.' *Family Fortunes* (television series), episode 3. ABC TV, 29 July 2008.

Chapter 23: Sober Yet Intoxicated

1   Begley, Adam. 'In search of Graham Greene's Capri'. *The New York Times*, 27 May 2007.

Chapter 24: Art Dynasty

1 'Blood ties: Artists prove that talent transcends family'. *Sydney Morning Herald*, 15 February 2010.

2 Delistraty, Cody. 'How Picasso bled the women in his life for art'. *Paris Review*, 9 November 2017.

3 Chrisafis, Angelique & Brown, Mark. 'Marina Picasso: Selling my grandfather's art is a way of helping me heal'. *The Guardian*, 24 May 2015.

4 Govani, Shinan. 'Picasso's granddaughter is a woman rarely seated'. *Star*, Visual Arts, 9 November 2018.

5 Gagosian Gallery. *Picasso and Maya: Father and Daughter* (press release). Gagosian Gallery, 15 December 2017. <https://gagosian.com/exhibitions/2017/picasso-and-maya-father-and-daughter-curated-by-diana-widmaier-picasso/>.

6 Widmaier-Picasso, Diana & Coliva, Anna. *Picasso: The Sculpture*. Rome: Galleria Borghese, 2019.

Chapter 26: An Odd but Fruitful Coupling

1 Olsen, John. *Drawn from Life*. Sydney: Duffy & Snellgrove, 1997, p. 248.

2 McDonald, Frank. Letter to Mrs R. Dulieu (South Yarra Gallery), 3 May 1965; Dulieu, R. Letter to 'Barbara' (Terry Clune Galleries), 12 July 1965. South Yarra Gallery, Australian Gallery file, State Library of Victoria.

3 Irwin, Rex. 'Rex Irwin: Why I swapped Sydney for the Southern Highlands after 40 years as an art dealer'. *The Sydney Morning Herald*, 14 May 2017.

4 Bourke, Latika. '*Blue Poles*, Australia's most controversial art acquisition, on display in London'. *The Sydney Morning Herald*, 21 September 2016.

5 Merrick, Jay. 'Nic Fiddian-Green: A Greek colossus'. *Goodwood*, 2010, p. 89.

6 Anderson, Patricia. 'New drawings by Jonathan Delafield Cook review (Olsen Irwin Gallery, Sydney)'. *Daily Review*, 13 January 2014.

7 McCarthy, Fiona. 'A grandeur plan: Fashion designer Collette Dinnigan's beautiful home overlooking Sydney Harbour'. *Daily Mail*, 18 September 2016.

Chapter 27: Anatomy of an Art Opening

1 Robertson, Constance. 'Getting around'. *The Sydney Morning Herald*, 23 August 1962.

2 Biennale of Sydney, Art Gallery of New South Wales & Wright, William. *Vision in Disbelief: The 4th Biennale of Sydney*. Sydney: Biennale Committee, 1982.

3 Cooke, Dewi. 'Olsen's salute to the sun'. *The Sydney Morning Herald*, 11 May 2013.

4 Walker Corporation. 'Olsen's salute to the sun rises at Docklands' (press release). 18 July 2013. <www.walkercorp.com.au/news/olsens-salute-to-the-sun-rises-at-dock-lands/>.

5 Cooke, Dewi. 'Olsen's King Sun rises'. *The Sydney Morning Herald*, 30 July 2013.

6   Gripper, Ali. 'Salute the Sun'. *The Sydney Morning Herald*, 22 June 2013.

7   Yeats, W.B. *Sailing to Byzantium*. London: Phoenix Books, 1995.

8   Gripper, 'Salute the Sun'.

9   Cooke, 'Olsen's King Sun rises'.

10   Hart, Deborah. *John Olsen*. Second edition. Sydney: Craftsman House, 2000, p. 133.

Chapter 28: Art Affair

1   Saltz, Jerry. 'Feeding frenzy'. *The Village Voice*, 25 January 2005.

2   Goldstein, Andrew. 'Team Gallery's Jose Freire on the new zero-sum art market'. *Artnet*, 6 March 2018.

3   Neuendorf, Henri. 'Europe's 10 most respected art dealers'. *Artnet*, 18 July 2016.

4   Blasberg, Derek. 'Tracey Emin on being "bombarded" by 2017, and her year of honesty ahead'. *Vanity Fair*, 11 December 2017.

Chapter 29: Photography as Art

1   Sontag, Susan. 'In Plato's cave', in *On Photography*. London: Penguin, 1977.

2   Xidias, Angelica. 'The LA-based Australian artist bringing Palm Springs to Sydney'. *Vogue* (Australia), 1 June 2017.

3   Saltz, Jerry. 'Great artists steal'. *New York Magazine*, 7 May 2009.

Chapter 30: Sotheby's, Scandal and *The Mother*

1   Snow, Deborah. 'The mystery of the "missing" John Olsen painting *The Mother* and a row with Sotheby's'. *The Sydney Morning Herald*, 3 January 2015. <www.smh.com.au/national/the-mystery-of-the-missing-john-olsen-painting-the-mother-and-a-row-with-sothebys-20150102-12gwrg.html>.

2   Papadakis, Marianna & Hutchinson, Samantha. 'Tucker fake shines light on Christie's and art world mismanagement'. *Australian Financial Review*, 12 January 2015. <www.afr.com/life-and-luxury/arts-and-culture/tucker-fake-shines-light-on-christie-s-and-art-world-mismanagement-20150112-12mjh9>.

3   Papadakis & Hutchinson, 'Tucker fake shines light on Christie's and art world mismanagement'.

4   Drummond, Matthew. 'Inside the collapse of art auction house Mossgreen'. *Australian Financial Review*, 22 February 2018.

5   McKenzie-Murray, Martin. 'Inside the Brett Whiteley Lavender Bay fakes trial'. *Saturday Paper*, no. 109, 21–27 May 2016.

6   Schjeldhal, Peter. 'Dutch master'. *The New Yorker*, 20 October 2008.

Chapter 31: Katharine

1   Fortescue, Elizabeth. 'How art helped John Olsen through heartbreak'. *The Daily Telegraph*, 9 March 2017.

2   Fortescue, 'How art helped John Olsen through heartbreak'.

Chapter 32: New York, New York

1   Berlin, Irving. Interviewed by Allene Talmey. *Vogue Magazine*, 1 November 1962. <https://archive.vogue.com/article/1962/11/01/irving-berlin>.
2   Saltz, Jerry. '*Beyond the Veil*: Curated by Adam Knight: Olsen Gruin'. *Vulture*, 31 May 2018.
3   Olsen, John & Olsen, Tim. 'The two of us'. Interviewed by Janet Hawley. *The Age*, 8 January 2000.

Chapter 33: Beyond the Veil

1   Cascone, Sarah. 'Is Damien Hirst's latest series a ripoff of an Aboriginal Australian artist? See the works side-by-side'. *Artnet News*, 30 March 2018.
2   Saltz, Jerry. '*Beyond the Veil*: Curated by Adam Knight: Olsen Gruin'. *Vulture*, 31 May 2018.
3   Olsen, Tim. 'Celebrate diversity, with Olsen Gruin Gallery'. UNSW News & Events, 11 April 2019. <www.alumni.giving.unsw.edu.au/news-events/news/celebrate-diversity-olsen-gruin-gallery>.

Chapter 35: The Dandy of the Art World

1   Meacham, Steve. 'The ties that bind'. *The Sydney Morning Herald*, 14 July 2012.
2   Wilde, Oscar. *The Picture of Dorian Gray*. New York, NY: Penguin Random House, 2004.
3   Hughes, Evan & Shapiro Auctioneers. *Ray Hughes: A Life with Art* (auction catalogue). Sydney: Shapiro Auctioneers, 2018.
4   Strickland, Katrina. 'Vale Ray Hughes, legendary art dealer'. *The Sydney Morning Herald*, 8 December 2017.

Chapter 36: Paternity

1   Larkin, Philip. 'This Be the Verse'. *Collected Poems*. London: Faber & Faber, 1988.

Chapter 37: Moving On

1   'Adrenaline brush: Sophie Cape'. *Australian Story* (television series). ABC TV, 6 February 2017.
2   Roberts, Harry. 'Into the wild'. *Belle*, 6 February 2015.
3   Jeffares, A. Norman (ed.). *W.B. Yeats: Selected Poetry*. London: Macmillan, 1968, pp. 181–2.

Chapter 38: Louise

1   University of New South Wales. 'UNSW alumni Olsen and Ormandy stepping forward as the artists they are'. *UNSW Art and Design*, 9 January 2019.
2   Olsen, Louise & Ormandy, Stephen. *The Art of Dinosaur Designs*. Melbourne: Lantern, 2016.
3   Hooton, Amanda. 'John Olsen: At home with the Australian artist'. *The Sydney Morning Herald*, Good Weekend, 30 August 2016.

4   Rout, Milanda. 'Olsen's creative legacy crosses generations'. *The Australian*, WISH Magazine, 3 May 2019.

5   Wong, Zara. 'How artist Camille Olsen-Ormandy is carving out her own niche, one paint stroke and splash of colour at a time'. *Vogue* (Australia), 25 December 2018.

6   Wong, 'How artist Camille Olsen-Ormandy is carving out her own niche'.

7   Steinhauer, Yvette. 'Face to face'. *The Sydney Morning Herald*, 27 February 1988.

8   Olsen, John. Poem written for the catalogue for *Pollination*, Louise Olsen's first solo exhibition. OLSEN Gallery, Sydney, March 2020.

Chapter 39: The Shared Table

1   Quoted in Zimmer, Jenny & McGregor, Ken. *John Olsen: Journeys into the 'You Beaut Country'*. Melbourne: Thames & Hudson, 2016, p. 6.

2   Strickland, Katrina. 'A taste of Spain—Olsen mixes memory and desire'. *Australian Financial Review*, March 2010.

3   Khomami, Nadia. 'Italian chef Antonio Carluccio dies aged 80'. *The Guardian*, 9 November 2017.

4   Heaney, Seamus. *Field Work*. London: Faber & Faber, 1979.

Chapter 40: The Art Scene at the Bottom of the World

1   Januszczak, Waldemar. 'A desert of new ideas'. *The Times*, 22 September 2013.

2   Searle, Adrian. 'Australia at the Royal Academy: Ned Kelly to the rescue'. *The Guardian*, 17 September 2013.

Chapter 41: Secrets of a National Treasure

1   Olsen, John. 'The getting of wisdom: John Olsen'. Interviewed by Janet Hawley. *The Sydney Morning Herald*, Good Weekend, 11 December 2010.

2   Hetherington, John. 'John Olsen: A wanderer in the You Beaut Country'. *The Age*, 15 September 1962.

3   Ferrier, Stephanie. 'John Olsen retrospective: More than 100 artworks capture Australian landscape'. *ABC News*, 15 September 2016.

4   Nelson, Robert. 'John Olsen retrospective: Mildly entertaining at best'. *The Sydney Morning Herald*, 20 September 2016.

5   Paraphrasing John Osborne, 'Asking a working writer what he thinks about critics is like asking a lamp-post what it feels about dogs.' *Time Magazine*, October 31, 1977.

6   Elks, Sarah. 'Sacked workers told "vote for Clive Palmer" as national treasure'. *The Australian*, 19 September 2016. <www.theaustralian.com.au/news/investigations/clive-palmer/sacked-workers-told-vote-for-clive-palmer-as-national-treasure/news-story/1404646445de320c0f8218ff4981ff47>, accessed 7 July 2019.

7   Olsen, John. Journal entry, 9 September 1994. John wrote: 'Struggling with the fact that the Christensen Fund is about to sell its Australian art

collection. They have 100 works of mine, which if suddenly placed on the market en bloc, say with Christie's or Sotheby's, would be a disaster for me. It's very depressing. The collection is the *Land Beyond Time* work, from the Kimberleys. Christensen has told us that these works, with his comprehensive Asian collection, were to be given to a public gallery. At his death this never happened, and the fund is now divesting and going to operate from America.'

Chapter 42: The Artist, the Cook, His Wife and Her Daughter

1   'Artist John Olsen confronted by step daughter (20 November 2017)'. *The Australian*, 29 July 2019.
2   Drewitt-Smith, Ainslie. 'Artist John Olsen sues stepdaughter, saying she influenced dying mother to withdraw $2m'. *ABC News*, 30 July 2019.
3   Alexander, Harriet. 'Olsen's wife motivated by vengeance in making secret gift, court hears'. *The Sydney Morning Herald*, 4 September 2019.
4   Cornwall, Deborah. 'Artist and the artless: Stepdaughter exploited dying mum for $2.2m'. *The Australian*, 28 September 2019.
5   *Olsen v. Mentink* (2019). Supreme Court New South Wales, NSWSC 1299. <www.caselaw.nsw.gov.au/decision/5d8c2887e4b0c3247d71204a>.

Chapter 43: The Full Circle

1   Hopkins, Gerard Manley. *Pied Beauty: A Selection of Poems*. London: Simon King Press, 1994.
2   Haig, Matt (@matthaig1). 'Never be cool. Never try and be cool . . .' (tweet). 2 October 2018, 8.49 a.m.

SELECT BIBLIOGRAPHY

Beck, Deborah. *Hope in Hell: A History of Darlinghurst Gaol and the National Art School.* Sydney: Allen & Unwin, 2005.

Bungey, Darleen. *John Olsen: An Artist's Life.* Sydney: HarperCollins, 2014.

Friend, Donald & Hetherington, Paul (ed.). *The Diaries of Donald Friend*, vol. 4. Canberra: National Library of Australia, 2006.

Gleeson, James. *Modern Painters 1931–1970.* Sydney: Lansdowne Press, 1971.

Haese, Richard. *Permanent Revolution: Mike Brown and the Australian Avant-Garde 1953–1997.* Melbourne: The Miegunyah Press, 2011.

Hart, Deborah. *John Olsen: Encounters with Drawing.* Melbourne: Australian Galleries, 1988.

Hart, Deborah. *John Olsen.* Second edition. Sydney: Craftsman House, 2000.

Hawley, Janet. *Australian Painters: Forty Profiles.* Melbourne: F.W. Cheshire, 1963.

Hughes, Robert. *The Art of Australia.* Melbourne: Penguin, 1981.

Lockyer, Paul. *Lake Eyre: A Journey through the Heart of the Continent.* Sydney: ABC Books, 2012.

McGrath, Sandra & Olsen, John. *The Artist and the Desert.* Sydney: Bay Books, 1981.

McGregor, Ken & Crawford, Ashley. *William Creek & Beyond: Australian Artists Explore the Outback*. Sydney: Craftsman House, 2002.

Olsen, John. *My Complete Graphics, 1957–1979*. Melbourne: Gryphon Books & Australian Galleries, 1980.

Olsen, John. *My Salute to Five Bells*. Canberra: NLA Publishing, 2015.

Olsen, John, Durack, Mary, Dutton, Geoffrey, Serventy, Vincent & Bortignon, Alex. *The Land Beyond Time: A Modern Exploration of Australia's North-West Frontiers*. Melbourne: Macmillan, 1984.

Olsen, John & Gray, Robert (ed.). *Drawn from Life: The Journals of John Olsen*. Sydney: Duffy & Snellgrove, 1997.

Olsen, John, Hurlston, David (ed.) & Edwards, Deborah (ed.). *John Olsen: The You Beaut Country*. Melbourne: National Gallery of Victoria, 2016.

Pierse, Simon. *Australian Art and Artists in London, 1950–1965: An Antipodean Summer*. Farnham, United Kingdom: Ashgate, 2012.

Serventy, Vincent. *The Desert Sea: The Miracle of Lake Eyre in Flood*. Melbourne: Macmillan, 1985.

Spate, Virginia. *John Olsen*. Melbourne: Georgian House, 1963.

Zimmer, Jenny & McGregor, Ken. *John Olsen: Journeys into the 'You Beaut Country'*. Melbourne: Thames & Hudson, 2016.

INDEX

476